P9-CMT-390

Narrowing the Achievement Gap

Narrowing the Achievement Gap

———

Perspectives and Strategies for Challenging Times

Edited by

THOMAS B. TIMAR

JULIE MAXWELL-JOLLY

Harvard Education Press
Cambridge, Massachusetts

Copyright © 2012 by the President and Fellows of Harvard College

All rights reserved. No part of this publication may be reproduced or transmitted in any form or by any means, electronic or mechanical, including photocopy, recording, or any information storage and retrieval systems, without permission in writing from the publisher.

Library of Congress Control Number 2011941946

Paperback ISBN 978-1-61250-123-9
Library Edition ISBN 978-1-61250-124-6

Published by Harvard Education Press,
an imprint of the Harvard Education Publishing Group

Harvard Education Press
8 Story Street
Cambridge, MA 02138

Cover Design: Sarah Henderson

The typefaces used in this book are Adobe Garamond and ITC Stome Sans.

Contents

1   Introduction
      Thomas B. Timar

CHAPTER ONE
11   Slow and Uneven Progress in Narrowing Achievement Gaps on
      State Tests
         Nancy Kober, Victor Chudowsky, and Naomi Chudowsky

CHAPTER TWO
35   Reframing the Ecology of Opportunity and Achievement Gaps
      Why "No Excuses" Reforms Have Failed to Narrow Student Group
      Differences in Educational Outcomes
         Robert K. Ream, Sarah M. Ryan, and Jose A. Espinoza

CHAPTER THREE
57   Narrowing the Multiple Achievement Gaps in the United States
      Eight Goals for the Long Haul
         W. Norton Grubb

CHAPTER FOUR
77   The Achievement Gap in California and Beyond
      Context, Status, and Approaches for Improvement
         Eva L. Baker, Noelle C. Griffin, and Kilchan Choi

CHAPTER FIVE
95   Accessing High-Quality Instructional Strategies
         Edmund T. Hamann and Jenelle Reeves

CHAPTER SIX

111 Organizational Strategies for Addressing the Educational
     Achievement Gap
        *Douglas E. Mitchell, Robert K. Ream, Sarah M. Ryan, and Jose A.
        Espinoza*

CHAPTER SEVEN

141 Improving High Schools as a Strategy for Closing the Achievement
     Gap
        Russell W. Rumberger

CHAPTER EIGHT

163 Teaching All Our Children Well
     Teachers and Teaching to Close the Achievement Gap
        Julie Maxwell-Jolly and Patricia Gándara

CHAPTER NINE

187 Narrowing Achievement Gaps in Tough Times
     Rethinking the Roles of Money and School Resources
        W. Norton Grubb

CHAPTER TEN

205 Partnering with Families and Communities to Address Academic
     Disparities
        Nancy Erbstein and Elizabeth Miller

CHAPTER ELEVEN

227 Reframing Policy and Practice to Close the Achievement Gap
        Thomas B. Timar

251 Notes

299 Acknowledgments

301 About the Editors

303 About the Contributors

307 Index

Introduction

THOMAS B. TIMAR

Among the most ambitious policy goals of the Great Society reforms of the 1960s was the equalization of educational opportunity and outcomes for ethnic and racial minority students. It was a central goal of the American civil rights movement, which turned to schools to provide the solution to many of the larger and glaring problems of social inequality. By equalizing educational outcomes, policy makers looked to create a society more closely aligned with the founders' vision of freedom and justice for all. To that end, school and social reformers marshaled a panoply of legal, regulatory, and programmatic strategies to improve educational outcomes for mainly black and Latino children, most of whom lagged far behind white students by all measures of academic achievement. However, it was not until Congress enacted No Child Left Behind (NCLB) in 2002 that closing the achievement gap became the centerpiece of federal and state education reform. No Child Left Behind and its cousins like Race to the Top have pushed education policy and practice in directions that would have been difficult to imagine thirty years earlier. The idea that federal policy could trump local decision making by invoking a list of ever-intrusive sanctions against districts that did not meet federal student achievement standards was unprecedented in American education history. What the federal government signaled by this massive shift in policy was a commitment to close the achievement gap in education through increased federal intervention. It would do so by focusing explicitly on differences in academic achievement among racial and ethnic minorities, handicapped and learning-disabled students, and poor students. NCLB held schools accountable for the academic progress of all students.

The commitment to close existing achievement gaps in education poses an unprecedented challenge to policy makers. It does so for three main reasons. First, there is no proven policy prescription for closing existing achievement gaps. Some states have made some progress in closing gaps, but no state offers an unambiguous example of consistent, sustained success. All states continue to wrestle with the challenge of improving the performance of disadvantaged groups of students.

Second, the diverse and idiosyncratic mix of policies adopted in each state makes it virtually impossible to identify the specific contribution of any single strategy or set of policies to closing the gaps at the state level. Third, there exist multiple achievement gaps. They include the gap measured by SAT and NAEP scores, but they also include huge differences in dropout rates as well as college attendance and completion rates.

Because the problem is complex and its sources multiple, solutions will also be complex and will require multiple strategies. The goal of narrowing achievement gaps is further complicated by the fact that it cannot be successfully accomplished at the federal, state, or local level in isolation. Neither a set of policy prescriptions nor a combination of educational practices—no matter how well crafted and carefully managed—is likely to be successful unless the players, politics, policies, and practices are mutually reinforcing and aligned. Perhaps most frustrating to both policy makers and practitioners is the fact that there are no quick fixes. The ubiquitous "ten things that every school can do to close the achievement gap" is likely to produce more frustration and failure than genuine improvement.

While there are no ready road maps for policy makers, the press for solutions is nonetheless acute. Standards-based accountability, particularly as it is embodied in No Child Left Behind, places tremendous pressure on states and schools to bring the academic achievement of racial and ethnic minority studies on par with white and Asian students. While some elements of the No Child Left Behind Act may change with the eventual reauthorization of the Elementary and Secondary Education Act (ESEA), there is little doubt that the law's underlying principles will remain unchanged. As of this writing, there are no visible signals from the Obama administration that it wishes to change the course laid out by the Bush administration. The policy drivers the administration has chosen—value-added teacher evaluation, charter schools, "turnaround" schools, teacher-proof curriculum—hew closely to the Bush administration playbook.

The purpose of this book is to take a fresh look at the achievement gap through a variety of lenses. The chapters provide a contextual framework for understanding both the achievement gap and the in- and out-of-school factors that cause and define it. The intent of the book is to provide multiple perspectives on closing the achievement gap. The various chapters examine the conditions—both in school and out of school—that research has shown to be highly correlated with the achievement gap. Further, the chapters point to multiple reasons for the achievement gap and why it has been so resistant to narrowing. Students in low-performing, low-SES (socioeconomic status) schools, for instance, may not have access to high-quality instruction—certainly not comparable to what students in high-performing, high-SES schools receive. The obvious question is why not.

What are the barriers to high-quality teaching and learning in low-performing schools? What would it take to provide the same quality of instruction to poor, low-achieving students that we provide to high-SES, high-achieving students? And, does being an English language learner (ELL) increase the likelihood of low achievement?

The chapters address the following related questions:

- How has the achievement gap narrowed over the past twenty years? If past and present trends continue, what are the prospects of closing the achievement gap and how long will it take?
- What are the multiple sources of the achievement gap and how are they reflected in current strategies to eliminate the achievement gap?
- What long-term goals should inform policies to narrow existing achievement gaps?
- Since current assessment policies have had have had minimal impact on closing the achievement gap, how should assessment policies be reframed?
- How can poor and ethnic and racial minority students be provided greater access to quality instruction?
- What is the relationship between schools' organizational characteristics and the achievement gap?
- What role can high schools play in closing the achievement gap?
- How can schools serve non-English-speaking students more effectively?
- How can money and school resources be used differently to improve the quality of education to poor and minority children?
- What is the role of community partnerships in closing the achievement gap?
- How does the relationship between policy, politics, and practice need to be reframed in order to close the achievement gap?

The chapters in this volume were originally prepared in 2008 as papers for California's P-16 Council, a council created by then superintendent of public instruction, Jack O'Connell. The UC Davis Center for Applied Policy in Education was asked to develop a set of research and policy papers on various dimensions of the achievement gap. The purpose of the papers was to provide the council with the necessary background information, research findings, and policy recommendations so that the council, in turn, could develop a set of policy initiatives for the superintendent. Although the papers were written initially with a California focus, the authors have since broadened their papers in order to speak to a national audience. It should be noted also that California exemplifies all of the difficulties associated with closing the achievement gap. Conditions in California education can readily be generalized to other states.

CHAPTER OVERVIEW

Each chapter of this book addresses different dimensions of the achievement gap, answering one of the questions posed above. Each chapter examines both the research and the policies as they relate to different facets of education policy and practice. For example, the chapter on partnering with communities examines research on partnerships that engage families and a broad variety of community organizations and makes policy recommendations that, according to research evidence, would narrow the achievement gap. The chapter on finance argues that the long-standing policy debate over the question, "does money matter," will not lead to fruitful answers. Instead, Grubb posits that what is important is not how resources are allocated, but how they are used to build effective instructional regimes. Together, the chapters of the book conclude that there is no simple solution, no "magic bullet" that policy makers have failed to find that will turn around five thousand low-performing schools and close the achievement gap.

In chapter 1, "Slow and Uneven Progress in Narrowing Achievement Gaps on State Tests," Kober, Chudowsky, and Chudowsky frame the context by examining what progress has been made in closing the achievement gap. What do results from the state tests used for federal and state accountability reveal about trends in the achievement gap and overall performance for major racial and ethnic and income groups? Their analysis is based on a study they conducted for the Center on Education Policy (CEP), which analyzed trends on state tests from 2002 to 2009 for African American, Latino, Native American, Asian, and white students and for students from low-income families. The study looks at trends in the performance of each of these groups, as well as changes in gaps between groups. Authors conclude that there have been gains and some slight narrowing of the achievement gap. However, those gains have been quite modest, and if present trends continue, it will take several decades to make significant progress in closing the achievement gap.

In chapter 2, "Reframing the Ecology of Opportunity and Achievement Gaps," Ream, Ryan, and Espinoza argue that the current agenda for the reform of primary and secondary education in the United States needs to be altered from the present path, which almost exclusively offers school-centered formulations of the problems and possible solutions. They discuss the multiple causes of the gaps in educational performance, offer an account of how these gaps affect the lives of disenfranchised minority and poor students, as well as society at large, and note how the standards and accountability reforms of the past twenty years have failed to narrow—and may have helped perpetuate—differences in educational outcomes persisting at the group level. They conclude that our ability to repair educational inequity will depend on an honest reckoning of what schools can and cannot do and suggest a thoroughgoing effort to mobilize the social institutions outside of school that play such a large—but still to this day often unacknowledged—role in students' educational experiences.

In chapter 3, "Narrowing the Multiple Achievement Gaps in the United States: Eight Goals for the Long Haul," Grubb outlines eight goals that could guide policy over the long run, and that if followed consistently would narrow (though not eliminate) many existing achievement gaps, in both learning and progress through formal schooling. The goals include enhancing the capacity and the effectiveness of resources in schools with low-performing students; recognizing different types of gaps, and multiple strategies for reducing them; reducing the inequality among students that now increases over time; improving the quality of interventions that schools now use for low-performing students; addressing racial and ethnic differences head on, especially in a state with a large and increasing Latino population; addressing the special issues of immigrant students; providing a greater variety of support services; and reforming the existing school finance system, both to increase funding and to distribute it in different ways. Each of these goals is a substantial undertaking, but it is crucial for educators and policy makers to confront the entire landscape of policies necessary to narrow achievement gaps.

In chapter 4, "The Achievement Gap in California and Beyond: Context, Status, and Approaches for Improvement," Baker, Griffin, and Choi examine the achievement gap from international and national perspectives. They compare student academic performance by various subgroups, and conclude that the gap is not closing, nor is it likely to close soon.

The authors recommend changes in measures and assessments that include trading breadth of knowledge and cognition for depth. They further recommend adding transfer tasks to support the adaptability needed for twenty-first century proficiencies. Finally, the chapter suggests that focusing on the individual student, rather than on groups or subgroups, is the desired way to make rapid changes that will have significant meaning as opposed to simply raising test scores. At the middle school and secondary level, where gaps are most resilient, the authors recommend course-level tests, a wide range of options for students that include both practical and academic certifications, and the need to allow the community and business world to help as partners in providing real experiences and certifying competence.

In chapter 5, "Accessing High-Quality Instructional Strategies," Hamann and Reeves argue that an important explanation for K–12 academic achievement gaps is differential access to high-quality instruction. In this chapter, the authors consider this topic in three complementary ways: first, by considering variations in student access to veteran, well-trained, high-performing teachers; second, by considering whether trained teachers work in contexts where they can exercise their professional expertise and discretion to their most effective extent; and third, by depicting what highly effective instruction looks like in terms of the three-part relationship between teachers, students, and the academic content to be mastered. This third component acknowledges that the elements of high-quality instruction will vary according to the content area to be taught, the physical and social context of the learning environment, and the use of constructivist strategies that help learners connect their new knowledge and skills to that which is already familiar.

In chapter 6, "Organizational Strategies for Addressing the Educational Achievement Gap," Mitchell, Ream, Ryan, and Espinoza examine the relationship between school organization and the achievement gap. The authors review the research on organizational strategies, resources, and opportunities that promise to have a substantial impact on improving student learning and closing achievement gaps. They focus on the organizational and operational characteristics of schools and classrooms. A framework for addressing policy issues is grounded in three preliminary ideas: (1) many different factors in children's social and cultural backgrounds influence student achievement as much or more than their school experiences; (2) the achievement gaps separating rich and poor, English speakers and English language learners, and majority and minority children are deep and persistent, and require changes that reorganize achievement within as well as between classrooms; and (3) there are no "silver bullet" policies, and no universal answers—schools have to respond to very local conditions and do so in myriad complex and subtle ways. Thus, the authors propose that the organizational and policy reforms needed must emphasize deregulation, local initiative, leadership, and continuous program and policy improvements.

In chapter 7, "Improving High Schools as a Strategy for Closing the Achievement Gap," Rumberger assesses the special role of high schools in closing the achievement gap. High schools play a critical role in preparing students for careers, college, and citizenship. Thus, disparities in outcomes from high school may contribute to long-term disparities in economic and social outcomes throughout adulthood. At the same time, reducing these inequities in high school outcomes may play a critical role in reducing disparities in adult outcomes and improving the lives of the state's most disadvantaged student populations. Rumberger also examines the nature of the achievement gap in California high school outcomes. Finally, the author reviews the research on which features of high schools have been found to contribute to student achievement.

In chapter 8, "Teaching All Our Children Well: Teachers and Teaching to Close the Achievement Gap," Maxwell-Jolly and Gándara examine some of the critically important questions about the recruitment, preparation, assignment, and retention of teachers that remain unanswered, especially with regard to the role of teachers in the education of diverse students. They argue that meeting the needs of diverse students is a major challenge for teachers, and understanding the ways that diversity affects classroom learning and students' adaptation to school are key aspects of this challenge. They also argue that simply being aware of the broad range of diversity in the classroom is insufficient to meet individual students' needs: that it is also important to know about the *specific* ways in which being an ELL, an African American, or an immigrant student, for example, are likely to affect students' learning. They then address strategies that may help teachers to meet this considerable challenge.

In chapter 9, "Narrowing Achievement Gaps in Tough Times: Rethinking the Roles of Money and School Resources," Grubb presents a new approach, one that—unlike conventional school finance, which emphasizes spending and revenue per student—focuses instead on a variety of different resources. The chapter also shows why spending and outcomes are so weakly related to one another. Finally, Grubb outlines various strategies to continue narrowing achievement gaps, even when schools cannot count on additional funding.

In chapter 10, "Partnering with Families and Communities to Address Academic Disparities," Erbstein and Miller argue that "community partnerships," in one form or another, have long been a persistent, albeit sometimes vaguely and variously defined, element of school reform efforts. Echoing the proverb "it takes a village to raise a child," for example, the 2008 P-16 Council report, *Closing the Achievement Gap: Report of Superintendent Jack O'Connell's California P-16 Council*, also encourages fostering partnerships to close the achievement gap. In particular, the report calls for a "high-quality and inclusive educational program" and a "comprehensive student support system" that will involve nurturing community collaboration and family involvement. This chapter provides an overview of what we know about the role of school-community partnerships in addressing disparities in school outcomes by (1) highlighting the mutually constitutive nature of persistent educational challenges and other local and regional conditions; (2) providing background on the variety of ways that education practitioners in successful schools conceptualize and implement community-school collaborations; and (3) reviewing research on two common approaches to partnerships to examine their effects on academic outcomes and the qualities of promising practices. Based on this review of research, the authors identify key conditions required for powerful partnerships and highlight steps that policy makers can take to foster them.

In chapter 11, "Reframing Policy and Practice to Close the Achievement Gap," Timar argues that narrowing or closing existing achievement gaps is unlikely to occur without reframing current education policy and practice. The chapter proposes that reform policies over the past forty years have focused predominantly on the symptoms of problems without addressing their underlying causes. Out-of school factors such as poverty, urban decay, crime, and violence and the impact they have on children's lives are given short shrift. Instead, policy makers have focused almost exclusively on school factors such as funding, professional development, teacher and administrator preparation, and governance. According to Timar, however, policy can't touch the critical factors that shape teaching and learning in schools. Researchers are finding that social capital—trust, relationships between professionals and the communities they serve—is critical to building effective instructional systems. But policy can't regulate relationships, require teachers to collaborate with one another, or make teachers care about their students. Finally, the author proposes that policy makers must focus on support for collaboration and professional networks to create a policy system centered on instructional improvement.

CONCEPTUAL FRAMEWORK

While each chapter in this volume provides a different analytic perspective on the achievement gap, collectively they cohere around several overarching ideas. First among these themes is that schools can't do it alone. As is so often the case in the history of American education, schools are made responsible for fixing whatever problems ail the country. So, too, the achievement gap—the result of social inequality among racial and ethnic groups—has become a problem for schools to solve. And while schools do play an important role in eliminating the achievement gap, in many respects this gap, as it manifests in schooling, is symptomatic of more encompassing social, economic, political, and cultural problems that, as a society, we are not willing to face.

The counterargument is that taking nonschool factors into account excuses schools from accountability for high-quality instruction. Proponents of this view argue that value-added models of teacher evaluation, high expectations for students, good data systems for tracking student progress, merit pay for teachers based on student progress, eliminating teacher tenure, and closing down persistently low-performing schools and creating charter schools are the solutions to the achievement gap. The documentary *Waiting for Superman*, for instance, paints a bleak picture of public schools as "failure factories," and attributes their inability to provide quality education for students to indifference, incompetence, malfeasance, and union intransigence. Incompetent teachers can't be fired and good teachers can't be rewarded. According to the filmmaker, charter schools such as Green Dot, KIPP, and the Harlem Children's Zone provide families with credible alternatives to low-performing public schools.

There are schools that provide high-quality instruction to poor and minority students. But the success of Harlem Children's Zone, for instance, is attributable not only to what occurs in the classroom, but also to the array of social and medical services that schools provide to students and their families. Integral to the Harlem Children's Zone model are community development efforts and the school-community relationships that connect school, children, and their families in a common cause of educational achievement. The idea that schools can—and, moreover, should—"do it alone" is unrealistic and evades dealing with the context of many children's lives, especially poor and minority children who attend low-performing schools.

Another of the book's central themes is that closing the achievement gaps in education will require a different policy paradigm from that of the past forty years. The top-down policy instruments described by McDonnell and Elmore have not been effective in producing predictable, consistent results.[1] As Cohen and Moffitt argue, none of the variations on ESEA's Title I have had a meaningful, sustained impact on teaching and learning in low-performing schools.[2] Further exacerbating the lack of instructional improvement is the racial isolation and concentration of students in many urban schools. It is testimony to the marginal success of school integration efforts.

California has invested billions of dollars in an ongoing effort to improve teaching and learning: the state has over sixty categorical programs that regulate, among many other things, class size, the frequency of textbook purchases, professional development for teachers and administrators, school libraries, afterschool programs, programs for gifted students, programs for English language learners, and art and music programs. Until the recent economic meltdown, over 30 percent of funding to schools was tied up in restricted, special-purpose programs. California's reform model is essentially a top-down model that relies on a combination of marginal resources, regulations, new programs, and new institutional structures to drive school improvement. Yet, none of these strategies either singly or in combination have been found to have any predictable, systematic impact on student achievement.

We need a very different policy paradigm, one that fundamentally reframes relations among federal, state, and local levels. The model that this book proposes is one in which policy flows from the bottom up. After forty years of policy tinkering, what we have learned is that school improvement policies can be effective only if conditions at the local level allow them to be effective. The central concern of all the chapters in this volume is not what kinds of new programs, resources, or mandates are needed to close the achievement gap, but rather what is the capacity of schools to convert resources and mandates into high-quality teaching and learning. What does it take for schools to create effective instructional regimes? And what can federal and state policy makers do to help schools develop and sustain high-quality instructional programs?

The prevailing top-down policy model grows out of central policy makers' mistrust of local communities. Reformers generally assumed that local school officials, bowing to local pressure, would not provide adequate education services to handicapped or English language learner students. Nor would they provide the equivalent education opportunities to females that they do to males. Local school officials could simply not be trusted to treat poor, disadvantaged children who had no political voice in the community fairly. In California, and presumably in other states as well, it appeared that policy makers did not believe that schools would purchase textbooks, provide professional development for teachers, or provide supplementary services to either gifted or struggling students unless they were forced to do so by the state. However, the logic of having the same people who are thought to be the cause of the problem also be the solutions to the problem is unjustifiably optimistic at best.

Absent the organizational and institutional capacity to convert programs and policies into effective instructional regimes, current school improvement efforts will make little progress. The alternative to current practice is to begin at the grass-roots level—to build out from schools, districts, and the communities they serve. As the final chapter in this volume proposes, this is the direction of new reform efforts that are based on building collaborative professional networks of teachers, administrators, and parents from the bottom up. Professional networks focused on sustained instructional improvement provide a better chance for closing the achievement gap than the grab-bag of policy strategies currently deployed.

## CHAPTER ONE

Slow and Uneven Progress in Narrowing Achievement Gaps on State Tests

NANCY KOBER, VICTOR CHUDOWSKY,
AND NAOMI CHUDOWSKY

For the past few decades, states, school districts, and schools have devoted considerable attention and resources to closing gaps in student achievement based on race, ethnicity, and income. Pressure to close these gaps intensified in 2002 with the No Child Left Behind Act, which required states and districts not only to track test results for major racial/ethnic groups and other student subgroups, but also to demonstrate progress in ensuring that all groups reach their state's definition of proficient performance.

After many years of effort, how much progress has been made in narrowing achievement gaps? What do results from the state tests used for federal and state accountability reveal about trends in achievement gaps and overall performance for major racial/ethnic and income groups? To help answer these questions, we conducted a study for the Center on Education Policy (CEP), which analyzed trends on state tests from 2002 (or a more recent year in some states) through 2009 for African American, Asian American, Latino, Native American, and white students and for students from low-income families. The study looked at trends in the performance of each of these groups, as well as changes in gaps between groups, at grades 4, 8, and the high school grade tested for No Child Left Behind (usually grade 10 or 11).

Data for the study were drawn from an extensive database assembled by CEP of test results for all fifty states and the District of Columbia. Not all states had the data needed for every analysis. States were excluded from an analysis if they lacked three or more years of comparable test data through 2009 or if the number of students in a particular subgroup was too small to yield reliable trends.

We analyzed trends on state tests using two indicators of achievement. The first, the percentage proficient, is the percentage of students who have met or exceeded the cut score for proficient performance on a state's test; this is the indicator for which schools are held accountable under No Child Left Behind. The second, the mean score, is the average of a group of test scores expressed on the scoring scale for a particular state's test. Mean scores are independent of cut scores and show changes across the achievement spectrum, including changes well above or below the proficiency cut score, and are generally considered a better indicator of gap trends than percentages proficient.

In addition, we analyzed state-level trends between 2005 and 2009 for subgroups on the main National Assessment of Educational Progress (NAEP) at grades 4 and 8. The goal was to see whether trends on NAEP have moved in the same direction as trends on state tests within the same state.

Additional information about study methods can be found at the end of this chapter.

MAIN FINDINGS

Although minority and low-income students have made achievement gains in recent years and although gaps have narrowed to some extent, progress has been inconsistent and relatively slow, our study concluded. Achievement gaps are a long way from closing. Four main findings support this conclusion:

1. *Each major student subgroup has made gains since 2002 on state reading and math tests in a large majority of the states with sufficient data for the study.*

   This pattern was evident for African American, Asian American, Latino, Native American, and white students, as well as low-income students, using both the percentages of students scoring proficient on state tests and mean scores. Trends on the state-level NAEP corroborated the rising trends for subgroups on state tests to a moderate degree, although the correspondence was greater in math than in reading. But even though achievement has increased for all groups, gaps have not always narrowed.

2. *State test score gaps between racial/ethnic groups have narrowed in many cases since 2002, but this has occurred less often for some subgroups than for others and less often using mean scores than percentages proficient.*

   In general, gaps in percentages proficient between Latino and white students and between African American and white students have narrowed more often than Native American–white gaps or gaps between low-income and more advantaged students. Mean test scores give a somewhat less positive picture of shrinking gaps. And while gaps for some groups narrowed on both state tests and NAEP in a majority of the states with sufficient data, there were many instances of gaps that narrowed on one assessment but widened on the other or widened on both.

Progress in reducing gaps has not come at the expense of higher-performing groups. When gaps narrowed, it was usually because both groups improved, but the lower-performing group improved at a faster rate; only rarely was it due to a decline in achievement for the higher-performing group.

3. *Achievement gaps remain large and persistent.*

Despite some progress in raising achievement for all groups and in narrowing gaps, the percentage of African American students scoring proficient on state tests remained 20 to 30 points lower in 2009 than the percentage proficient for white students in many states. Gaps between Native American and white students were similarly wide. Gaps between Latino and white students often amounted to 15 to 20 percentage points. Many states had gaps in percentages proficient of 25 points or more between students from low-income families and those who were not low income.

4. *Closing achievement gaps will take many years, sometimes decades, if current rates of progress continue unchanged.*

In general, Latino-white gaps and African American–white gaps have narrowed at a faster rate than gaps for Native American or low-income students, as gauged by the median rates of change in the gaps across the states with sufficient data for the study. (The median is the midpoint; half of the states with sufficient data had annual rates of change above the median and half had rates below it.) In grade 8 math, for example, the Latino-white gap has narrowed since 2002 at a median rate of 1.3 percentage points per year across the states with sufficient data; this compares with median rates of 1.1 for African Americans, 0.7 for Native Americans, and 0.6 for low-income students.

If gaps were to continue to narrow steadily at these rates and if other critical factors were to remain unchanged, it would take one or more decades for these gaps to close in most states. Together, these four main findings indicate a need for more intensive, different, and far-reaching strategies at all levels of government to close achievement gaps. The remainder of this chapter discusses these findings in more detail, provides tables with key supporting data, and describes the methodology for the CEP study.

EVERY MAJOR SUBGROUP HAS MADE GAINS ON STATE TESTS

State tests vary greatly in difficulty, content, scoring scales, cut scores for proficiency, and other aspects. Within two different states, the same percentage proficient may signify quite different degrees of achievement and learning. To arrive at broad findings about achievement based on a diverse array of state test results that cannot and should not be directly compared, we calculated the number and percentage of trend lines that showed a gain, decline, or no net change in performance for a particular subgroup. (A trend line is a record of change in performance over a period of years for a specific subgroup or a specific gap in one state, subject, and grade level; for example, the change from 2002 to 2009 in the percentage proficient in math for Asian American eighth graders in Colorado constitutes one trend line.) The analyses included only those states with three or more years of comparable test data through 2009. The starting year of the trends varied from 2002 to 2007, depending on whether a state had made changes in its testing program after 2002 that affected the year-to-year comparability of test data.

For every subgroup, states with gains on state tests far outnumbered those with declines or flat trends in both reading and math at grades 4, 8, and the tested high school grade. African American, Asian American, Latino, Native American, and white students, as well as low-income students, have made gains since 2002 in two-thirds or more of the states with sufficient data. Table 1.1 (reading) and table 1.2 (math) show the percentages of these states that posted gains, declines, or flat trends on state reading and math tests for each subgroup.

Progress was especially noteworthy for Latino and African American students in grade 8 math; all or nearly all states made gains for these two groups in this grade and subject.

As tables 1.1 and 1.2 make clear, the pattern of states with gains for subgroups outnumbering those with declines was evident in both percentages proficient and mean test scores. This pattern becomes especially apparent if one combines all of the trend lines analyzed across all three grade levels in both reading and math, as displayed in table 1.3. Whether one looks at percentages proficient or mean scores, the proportion of trend lines that showed gains was at least 80 percent—and sometimes more than 90 percent—for every major racial/ethnic subgroup and for low-income students.

We also examined whether trends in subgroup achievement on the main state-level NAEP assessments for grades 4 and 8 had moved in the same upward or downward direction as trends on state tests.[1] States were included in the state and NAEP comparisons if they had sufficient data on both assessments for 2005 through 2009; twenty-five states had sufficient data for at least some of the state and NAEP comparisons. Trends in mean scores were analyzed for both state tests and NAEP, and trends in the percentages of students reaching the *basic* level on NAEP were compared with trends in the percentages reaching the *proficient* level on state tests. Increases or decreases of any size on either NAEP or state tests were

TABLE 1.1
Reading: Percentage of states with sufficient data showing various trends for subgroups on state tests, 2002–2009

	African American	Asian American	Latino	Native American	White	Low-income
Grade 4 PP						
% of states with gain	88%	84%	89%	81%	88%	90%
% of states with decline	12%	13%	11%	19%	2%	5%
No change	0%	3%	0%	0%	10%	5%
# of states with data	*34*	*31*	*37*	*16*	*42*	*42*
Grade 4 MS						
% of states with gain	79%	85%	84%	67%	92%	91%
% of states with decline	10%	12%	16%	20%	6%	6%
No change	10%	4%	0%	13%	3%	3%
# of states with data	*29*	*26*	*31*	*15*	*36*	*34*
Grade 8 PP						
% of states with gain	94%	83%	92%	89%	93%	93%
% of states with decline	6%	13%	8%	11%	7%	7%
No change	0%	3%	0%	0%	0%	0%
# of states with data	*34*	*30*	*36*	*18*	*42*	*42*
Grade 8 MS						
% of states with gain	90%	84%	87%	82%	92%	97%
% of states with decline	7%	16%	13%	12%	8%	0%
No change	3%	0%	0%	6%	0%	3%
# of states with data	*29*	*25*	*30*	*17*	*36*	*34*
High school PP						
% of states with gain	83%	82%	91%	82%	92%	92%
% of states with decline	10%	14%	6%	12%	8%	8%
No change	7%	4%	3%	6%	0%	0%
# of states with data	*30*	*28*	*33*	*17*	*37*	*38*
High school MS						
% of states with gain	88%	87%	85%	86%	77%	84%
% of states with decline	12%	13%	11%	14%	16%	13%
No change	0%	0%	4%	0%	6%	3%
# of states with data	*25*	*23*	*27*	*14*	*31*	*31*

Table reads: On state grade 4 reading tests, 88% of the 34 states with sufficient data showed gains since 2002 in the percentage of African American students scoring proficient, and 12% showed declines. Of the 29 states with sufficient mean score data in grade 4 reading, 79% showed gains in average scores for African American students, 10% showed declines, and 10% had no net change.

PP = percentage proficient; MS = mean score

Source: Center on Education Policy.

TABLE 1.2
Mathematics: Percentage of states with sufficient data showing various trends for subgroups on state tests, 2002–2009

	African American	Asian American	Latino	Native American	White	Low-income
Grade 4 PP						
% of states with gain	94%	87%	92%	82%	98%	91%
% of states with decline	6%	7%	3%	12%	2%	7%
No change	0%	7%	5%	6%	0%	2%
# of states with data	*33*	*30*	*37*	*17*	*42*	*43*
Grade 4 MS						
% of states with gain	86%	92%	90%	81%	97%	89%
% of states with decline	14%	8%	10%	19%	3%	9%
No change	0%	0%	0%	0%	0%	3%
# of states with data	*28*	*25*	*31*	*16*	*36*	*35*
Grade 8 PP						
% of states with gain	97%	93%	100%	95%	98%	98%
% of states with decline	3%	3%	0%	5%	2%	2%
No change	0%	3%	0%	0%	0%	0%
# of states with data	*33*	*29*	*35*	*19*	*42*	*43*
Grade 8 MS						
% of states with gain	100%	100%	100%	89%	94%	94%
% of states with decline	0%	0%	0%	11%	3%	3%
No change	0%	0%	0%	0%	3%	3%
# of states with data	*28*	*24*	*29*	*18*	*36*	*35*
High school PP						
% of states with gain	77%	83%	97%	83%	77%	92%
% of states with decline	23%	14%	3%	11%	18%	8%
No change	0%	3%	0%	6%	5%	0%
# of states with data	*31*	*29*	*34*	*18*	*39*	*39*
High school MS						
% of states with gain	88%	91%	93%	71%	75%	84%
% of states with decline	12%	9%	7%	29%	13%	13%
No change	0%	0%	0%	0%	13%	3%
# of states with data	*25*	*23*	*27*	*14*	*32*	*31*

Table reads: On state grade 4 math tests, 94% of the 33 states with sufficient data showed gains since 2002 in the percentage of African American students scoring proficient, and 6% showed declines. Of the 28 states with sufficient mean score data in grade 4 math, 86% showed gains in average scores for African American students, and 14% showed declines.

PP = percentage proficient; MS = mean score

Source: Center on Education Policy.

TABLE 1.3

Percentage of trend lines across two subjects and three grade levels that showed gains on state tests for subgroups, 2002–2009

	African American	Asian American	Latino	Native American	White	Low-income
% with gains in PP	89%	85%	93%	86%	91%	93%
% with gains in MS	88%	90%	90%	80%	88%	90%

Table reads: Across both reading and math and grades 4, 8, and high school, 89% of the trend lines analyzed showed gains in percentages proficient for African American students, and 88% showed gains in average test scores.

PP = percentage proficient; MS = mean score

Source: Center on Education Policy.

counted as gains or declines. (The additional information on study methods at the end of this chapter explains these decisions and provides other details about the state and NAEP comparisons.)

In math, NAEP results tended to confirm the direction of trends in state test results. In most of the states studied, all subgroups except Asian American students, as explained below, made gains in math on both state tests and NAEP, and according to mean scores as well as percentages proficient/basic. Within the same state, trends on NAEP in math often moved in the same upward direction as trends on state tests. Trends were especially positive for most subgroups in grade 8 math. In reading, trends in subgroup achievement on NAEP confirmed the gains on state tests to a moderate extent, but there were more contradictions between the two assessments than in math.

Trends for Asian American students were an exception to the general pattern of rising math scores on both state tests and NAEP. (Only a small number of states, between seven and eleven depending on the grade/subject, had sufficient data or large enough subgroups on both types of assessments to compare Asian American trends.) Although the majority of the states analyzed showed gains in mean scores for Asian American students on both types of assessments, trends for this subgroup often moved in conflicting directions on state tests and NAEP when percentages proficient/basic were used. This may be because the Asian American subgroup is the highest-performing in math, and the vast majority of Asian American students already score above the state proficient/NAEP basic levels.

Rising achievement for all groups does not necessarily mean gaps will narrow. For gaps to narrow and eventually close, not only must achievement for lower-scoring subgroups increase, but it must do so at a faster rate than for the higher-scoring comparison group.

STATE TEST SCORE GAPS HAVE NARROWED
IN MANY CASES BUT TRENDS VARY BY SUBGROUP
AND ACHIEVEMENT INDICATOR

To determine trends in achievement gaps, we calculated the number and percentage of trend lines that showed a narrowing, widening, or no net change in a particular achievement gap.

Gap Trends on State Tests

For most student groups, achievement gaps on state tests have narrowed more often than they have widened since 2002 in a majority of the states with sufficient data. But this pattern is not consistent for all subgroups and all grade levels, especially when gaps are measured in terms of mean scores rather than percentages proficient. In addition, state tests and NAEP showed little agreement about whether achievement gaps at grades 4 and 8 have narrowed since 2005.

Table 1.4 (reading) and table 1.5 (math) show the percentages of states with sufficient data in which achievement gaps have narrowed, widened, or stayed the same at grades 4, 8, and high school.

Differences Among Subgroups

As tables 1.4 and 1.5 indicate, gaps on state tests have shrunk more consistently for African American and Latino students than for Native American or low-income students. In both reading and math, black-white and Latino-white gaps have narrowed in the majority of states with sufficient data—a pattern that holds across all three grade levels, according to both percentages proficient and mean scores. In grade 8 math, for example, the African American–white gap narrowed in about three-fourths of the states with sufficient data; this was also the case for the Latino-white gap. Even so, gaps for African Americans and Latinos widened or stayed the same in some grades and subjects in a sizable minority of states. In grade 4 reading and math, for example, the black-white gap in mean scores widened in roughly 40 percent of the states with sufficient data. In grade 4 reading, the Latino-white gap increased in about one-third of the states with sufficient data.

Progress in narrowing gaps has been more erratic for Native American and low-income students. In most grade/subject combinations, gaps for these groups narrowed in a majority of the states with sufficient data. But in grade 4 reading and math, gaps in mean scores for Native Americans and low-income students widened or stayed the same in a majority of the states with sufficient data. And in high school reading and math, the Native American–white gap in mean scores

TABLE 1.4
Reading: Percentage of states with sufficient data showing various trends in achievement gaps on state tests, 2002–2009

	African American/ white	Latino/ white	Native American/ white	Low-income/ not low- income
Grade 4 PP				
% of states where gaps narrowed	82%	78%	56%	74%
% of states where gaps widened	18%	19%	38%	24%
No change	0%	3%	6%	3%
# of states with data	*33*	*37*	*16*	*38*
Grade 4 MS				
% of states where gaps narrowed	54%	58%	27%	44%
% of states where gaps widened	43%	32%	73%	38%
No change	4%	10%	0%	19%
# of states with data	*28*	*31*	*15*	*32*
Grade 8 PP				
% of states where gaps narrowed	82%	89%	67%	66%
% of states where gaps widened	12%	8%	22%	26%
No change	6%	3%	11%	8%
# of states with data	*33*	*36*	*18*	*38*
Grade 8 MS				
% of states where gaps narrowed	57%	67%	53%	72%
% of states where gaps widened	29%	27%	41%	19%
No change	14%	7%	6%	9%
# of states with data	*27*	*30*	*17*	*32*
High school PP				
% of states where gaps narrowed	69%	85%	71%	65%
% of states where gaps widened	31%	15%	24%	18%
No change	0%	0%	6%	18%
# of states with data	*29*	*33*	*17*	*34*
High school MS				
% of states where gaps narrowed	67%	85%	50%	66%
% of states where gaps widened	21%	15%	43%	17%
No change	13%	0%	7%	17%
# of states with data	*24*	*27*	*14*	*29*

Table reads: In grade 4 reading, the gap between African American and white students in percentages proficient on state tests narrowed in 82% of the 33 states with sufficient data and widened in 18% of states. The African American–white gap in mean scores for grade 4 reading narrowed in 54% of the 28 states with sufficient data, widened in 43% of states, and showed no net change in 4% of states.

PP = percentage proficient; MS = mean score

Source: Center on Education Policy.

TABLE 1.5
Mathematics: Percentage of states with sufficient data showing various trends in achievement gaps on state tests, 2002–2009

	African American/ white	Latino/ white	Native American/ white	Low-income/ not low-income
Grade 4 PP				
% of states where gaps narrowed	88%	83%	65%	79%
% of states where gaps widened	13%	14%	29%	18%
No change	0%	3%	6%	3%
# of states with data	*32*	*36*	*17*	*38*
Grade 4 MS				
% of states where gaps narrowed	56%	63%	31%	42%
% of states where gaps widened	37%	33%	69%	39%
No change	7%	3%	0%	18%
# of states with data	*27*	*30*	*16*	*33*
Grade 8 PP				
% of states where gaps narrowed	78%	86%	58%	74%
% of states where gaps widened	19%	9%	37%	24%
No change	3%	6%	5%	3%
# of states with data	*32*	*35*	*19*	*38*
Grade 8 MS				
% of states where gaps narrowed	74%	76%	61%	64%
% of states where gaps widened	15%	17%	33%	27%
No change	11%	7%	6%	9%
# of states with data	*27*	*29*	*18*	*33*
High school PP				
% of states where gaps narrowed	70%	91%	56%	76%
% of states where gaps widened	23%	6%	28%	15%
No change	7%	3%	17%	9%
# of states with data	*30*	*34*	*18*	*34*
High school MS				
% of states where gaps narrowed	63%	85%	50%	55%
% of states where gaps widened	33%	15%	50%	34%
No change	4%	0%	0%	10%
# of states with data	*24*	*27*	*14*	*29*

Table reads: In grade 4 math, the gap between African American and white students in percentages proficient on state tests narrowed in 88% of the 32 states with sufficient data and widened in 13% of states. The African American–white gap in mean scores in grade 4 math narrowed in 56% of the 27 states with sufficient data, widened in 37% of states, and showed no net change in 7% of states.

PP = percentage proficient; MS = mean score

Source: Center on Education Policy.

narrowed in half the states with adequate data but widened or stayed the same in the other half.

Although gaps can shrink even if achievement goes down for one or both of the groups being compared, in our study this was not typical. Usually when gaps narrowed, it was because both the lower- and the higher-achieving subgroups improved, but the lower-performing group improved at a greater rate. When gaps widened, it was often because both subgroups made gains, but the higher-achieving group improved more rapidly than the lower-achieving one. In other cases, gaps increased because the higher-achieving group made gains while the lower-achieving group had declining or flat performance. Occasionally, both groups posted declines, but the lower-performing group declined at a greater rate, thus widening the gap.

Differences Between Percentages Proficient and Mean Scores

As shown in tables 1.4 and 1.5, mean scores tended to give a somewhat less positive picture of gaps narrowing. This finding warrants attention because mean scores avoid a limitation inherent in percentages proficient—namely, that achievement gaps may appear smaller or larger depending on where a state has set its proficiency cut score. If the cut score is so low that nearly all students exceed it, or so high that few students reach it, achievement gaps will appear smaller than if the cut score is set closer to the middle of the scoring scale, where most students' scores cluster. In addition, if mean scores for two subgroups of students improve, the percentage proficient will go up faster for the group of students whose scores are clustered closer to the proficient cut score, as discussed further below.

The differences between percentage proficient and mean score trends that are evident in tables 1.4 and 1.5 become especially clear if one looks at the share of trend lines across both subjects and all three grade levels that show a narrowing, widening, or no net change in a particular gap. As displayed in table 1.6, the proportion of trend lines with narrowing gaps was smaller for all subgroups according to mean scores than according to percentages proficient. The gap between low-income students and those who are not low income, for instance, narrowed in 57 percent of the trend lines using mean scores, compared with 72 percent of the trend lines using percentages proficient. The Native American–white gap narrowed in just 46 percent of the trend lines using mean scores but 62 percent of the trend lines using percentages proficient.

The less positive findings for mean scores appear to be unrelated to the fact that fewer states (and a somewhat different group of states) provided mean score data than provided percentages proficient. Rather, this pattern seems to be a result of mean scores picking up different kinds of changes in achievement. In some cases, a lower-achieving subgroup made larger gains than a higher-achieving

TABLE 1.6

Percentage of trend lines across two subjects and three grades levels that show achievement gaps narrowing on state tests, 2002–2009

	African American/ white	Latino/ whIte	Native American/ whiLe	Low-income/ not low- income
% of MS trend lines narrowed	61%	72%	46%	57%
% of PP trend lines narrowed	78%	85%	62%	72%

Table reads: Across both reading and math and grades 4, 8, and high school, achievement gaps narrowed between the African American and white subgroups 61% of the time using the mean score indicator and 78% of the time using the percentage proficient indicator.

PP = percentage proficient; MS = mean score

Source: Center on Education Policy.

subgroup in percentages proficient but smaller gains in mean scores. In grade 4 math, for example, African American students made greater gains than white students in percentages proficient but smaller gains in mean scores. This could occur if large numbers of African American students improved their performance enough to move from just below the proficiency cut score to just above it or higher. If, during the same period, many students in the white subgroup were already scoring above the proficient level, then improvements in these students' scores would not affect the white percentage proficient to the same extent. Thus the black-white gap in percentages proficient could narrow while the mean score gap could stay the same or widen.

Little Agreement on Gap Trends Between State Tests and NAEP

If real progress were being made on achievement gaps, one would expect to see this progress on multiple assessments of the same subject area, most notably on both state tests and NAEP. We found little agreement, however, on gap trends between these two types of assessments. Progress in narrowing achievement gaps on the NAEP assessments was mixed between 2005 and 2009 in the states with sufficient data on both state tests and NAEP. Within the same state, NAEP results often contradicted state test results. In many instances, a gap narrowed on the state test but widened on NAEP, or vice versa.

Table 1.7 shows the percentage of states in which NAEP gap trends moved in the same direction, either narrowing or widening, as gap trends on state tests. The table also includes data on the percentages of states in which gaps *narrowed* on both assessments. In a number of instances, fewer than half the states with sufficient data could show that achievement gaps were narrowing on both assessments according to the percentage proficient/basic indicator; this was true for the

TABLE 1.7
Extent of agreement in gap trends between state tests and NAEP, 2005–2009

Percentage of states in which gap trends on state tests and NAEP moved in the same direction	African American/ white	Latino/ white	Low-income/ not low-income
Grade 4 reading, percentages proficient/basic			
% of states same direction on both	77%[a]	59%[a]	69%[a]
% of states gaps narrowed on both	65%[a]	47%[a]	50%[a]
Grade 4 reading, mean scores			
% of states same direction on both	36%[a]	46%[a]	46%[a]
% of states gaps narrowed on both	27%[a]	36%[a]	36%[a]
Grade 8 reading, percentages proficient/basic			
% of states same direction on both	69%[a]	50%[a]	52%
% of states gaps narrowed on both	56%[a]	50%[a]	48%
Grade 8 reading, mean scores			
% of states same direction on both	58%[a]	62%[a]	56%[a]
% of states gaps narrowed on both	33%[a]	38%[a]	31%[a]
Grade 4 math, percentages proficient/basic			
% of states same direction on both	75%[a]	67%	69%[a]
% of states gaps narrowed on both	69%[a]	67%	62%[a]
Grade 4 math, mean scores			
% of states same direction on both	55%[a]	20%	55%[a]
% of states gaps narrowed on both	27%[a]	20%	18%[a]
Grade 8 math, percentages proficient/basic			
% of states same direction on both	83%	63%[a]	43%[a]
% of states gaps narrowed on both	83%	56%[a]	29%
Grade 8 math, mean scores			
% of states same direction on both	64%	58%[a]	73%[a]
% of states gaps narrowed on both	64%	50%[a]	47%[a]

Table reads: In 77% of states with sufficient data, trends in the African American–white achievement gap on state tests and NAEP were in agreement—both assessments showed this gap narrowing (or both showed it widening) within a state according to the percentage proficient on state tests and the percentage basic on NAEP. In 65% of these states, the African American–white achievement gap *narrowed* according to both state tests and NAEP.

[a]This level of agreement is greater than what would have been expected by chance.

Source: Center on Education Policy.

Latino-white gap in grade 4 reading and for the gaps between low-income and more advantaged students in grade 8 reading and math. Even less convergence of state and NAEP trends was apparent in mean score results. For example, mean scores in grade 4 math showed gaps narrowing on both assessments in roughly one-fourth or fewer of the states with sufficient data.

Although African American students showed improvement in grade 8 math on both state tests and NAEP in every state with sufficient data, this has not translated into progress in narrowing gaps in every state. According to mean scores, the African American–white gap in grade 8 math narrowed on both NAEP and state tests in nine of fourteen states but showed mixed results on the two assessments in the other five states.

LARGE ACHIEVEMENT GAPS PERSIST ON STATE TESTS

Although progress has been made in raising achievement for all subgroups and, to a lesser extent, in narrowing gaps, sizable gaps remain between racial/ethnic groups and income groups.

Typical Size of Performance Gaps

Among racial/ethnic groups, Asian American and white students had the highest test performance in 2009. In reading, the Asian American and white subgroups performed at similar levels. In math, Asian American students outperformed white students in most of the states with sufficient data.

Other subgroups typically performed at lower levels. In many states, the gaps in percentages proficient between African American and white students and between Native American and white students amounted to 20 or 30 percentage points. The Latino-white gap in percentages proficient often totaled 15 to 20 percentage points. Gaps in percentages proficient also persisted between students from low-income families and those who were not low income; in many states, these gaps totaled 25 percentage points or more.

For each of the subgroups analyzed, the size of achievement gaps varied considerably from state to state. In grade 4 reading, for example, the largest Latino-white gap in any state was 38 percentage points in 2009, while the smallest gap in any state was 5 points. These variations may not be solely, or even mostly, due to differences in instructional quality but may also be attributable to state-by-state differences in where the cut score for proficiency is set, how difficult the test is, and other factors.

Differences in the Median Percentage Proficient for Various Subgroups

One way to gauge the relative performance of various student groups on a broader scale than a single state is to look at the median, or midpoint. Our study included calculations for each subgroup of the 2009 median percentages proficient across all of the states with sufficient data for that group. The results are shown in table 1.8 (reading) and table 1.9 (math).

Table 1.8
Reading: Median, highest, and lowest percentages proficient for subgroups across all states with sufficient state test data, 2009

	African American	Asian American	Latino	Native American	White	Low-income
Grade 4						
Median PP across states	59%	84%	62%	58%	83%	64%
Highest PP in any state	88%	95%	92%	86%	96%	92%
Lowest PP in any state	28%	44%	28%	36%	52%	29%
# of states with data	*41*	*36*	*43*	*19*	*50*	*46*
Grade 8						
Median PP across states	54%	83%	60%	59%	79%	57%
Highest PP in any state	91%	98%	92%	94%	96%	92%
Lowest PP in any state	27%	55%	34%	39%	56%	33%
# of states with data	*41*	*35*	*42*	*21*	*50*	*46*
High school						
Median PP across states	53%	79%	62%	54%	81%	60%
Highest PP in any state	95%	99%	97%	96%	98%	96%
Lowest PP in any state	18%	54%	30%	37%	48%	23%
# of states with data	*37*	*32*	*38*	*19*	*47*	*43*

Table reads: Across all 41 states with sufficient data, the median percentage of African American students scoring proficient in grade 4 reading was 59%. The highest percentage proficient in any state for the African American subgroup was 88%, while the lowest in any state was 28%.

PP = percentage proficient

Source: Center on Education Policy.

As these tables reveal, performance differed markedly by subgroup. In grade 4 reading, for example, the median percentage proficient ranged from 58 percent for Native American students to 84 percent for Asian American students. In grade 8 math, the medians ranged from 46 percent for African Americans to 84 percent for Asian Americans.

Tables 1.8 and 1.9 also indicate how much the percentage proficient for a particular group varies from state to state. In high school math, for example, the percentage of African American students scoring proficient ranged from 7 percent in the lowest state to 89 percent in the highest state, while the Latino percentage proficient ranged from 9 percent to 93 percent. For white students, the range was somewhat narrower but still substantial—from 33 percent in the lowest state to 97 percent in the highest state.

Table 1.9
Mathematics: Median, highest, and lowest percentages proficient for subgroups across all states with sufficient state test data, 2009

	African American	Asian American	Latino	Native American	White	Low-income
Grade 4						
Median PP across states	**58%**	**88%**	**67%**	**62%**	**84%**	**64%**
Highest PP in any state	90%	97%	94%	87%	97%	93%
Lowest PP in any state	21%	49%	25%	29%	51%	28%
# of states with data	*41*	*36*	*44*	*19*	*50*	*46*
Grade 8						
Median PP across states	**46%**	**84%**	**58%**	**51%**	**76%**	**51%**
Highest PP in any state	84%	96%	87%	79%	94%	86%
Lowest PP in any state	20%	38%	22%	28%	45%	25%
# of states with data	*41*	*35*	*42*	*21*	*50*	*46*
High school						
Median PP across states	**43%**	**81%**	**54%**	**46%**	**69%**	**43%**
Highest PP in any state	89%	98%	93%	92%	97%	84%
Lowest PP in any state	7%	33%	9%	18%	33%	12%
# of states with data	*37*	*32*	*39*	*19*	*47*	*42*

Table reads: Across all 41 states with sufficient data, the median percentage of African American students scoring proficient in grade 4 math was 58%. The highest percentage proficient in any state for the African American subgroup was 90%, while the lowest in any state was 21%.

PP = percentage proficient

Source: Center on Education Policy.

IT WOULD TAKE MANY YEARS TO CLOSE MOST GAPS AT CURRENT RATES OF PROGRESS

How long would it take to close achievement gaps of the size found on many state tests? We approached this question by first calculating the average yearly change in the gap for a specific subgroup in a particular grade and subject in each state with sufficient data. If, for example, the percentage proficient gap between Native American and white students in a particular state narrowed by 7 percentage points between 2002 and 2009, then the average yearly change in that gap would be 1 percentage point per year (there being seven year-to-year increases over the eight years of data). Next, we determined the median of these average yearly rates of change across all of the states with sufficient data for the subgroup in question.

Median Rates of Change in Gaps

Table 1.10 presents the medians of the average yearly rates of change for each subgroup. A bright spot among the data is the progress states have made since 2002 in narrowing percentage proficient gaps between Latino and white students. In most grade/subject combinations, Latino-white gaps narrowed more rapidly than gaps for other subgroups. In grade 8 reading, for example, the Latino-white gap in percentages proficient narrowed at a median rate of 1.4 percentage points per year across the states with sufficient data.

African American students tended to have the second highest median rates of progress in narrowing gaps, next to Latino students. In grade 4 math, the median change in the African American–white gap—1.3 percentage points per year—

TABLE 1.10

Progress in narrowing gaps in percentages proficient on state tests, in terms of median annual percentage point changes, 2002–2009

	African American/ white	Latino/ white	Native American/ white	Low-income/ not low-income
Grade 4 reading				
Median percentage point change	0.7	0.8	0.3	0.5
# of states with data	33	37	16	38
Grade 8 reading				
Median percentage point change	1.0	1.4	0.5	0.6
# of states with data	33	36	18	38
High school reading				
Median percentage point change	0.7	1.2	0.6	0.7
# of states with data	29	33	17	34
Grade 4 math				
Median percentage point change	1.3	1.2	0.4	0.7
# of states with data	32	36	17	39
Grade 8 math				
Median percentage point change	1.1	1.3	0.7	0.6
# of states with data	32	35	19	39
High school math				
Median percentage point change	0.7	1.2	0.5	0.6
# of states with data	30	34	18	35

Table reads: On state grade 4 reading tests, the median rate of progress in narrowing the African American–white gap in percentages proficient was 0.7 percentage point per year, across all 33 states with sufficient data for both subgroups.

Source: Center on Education Policy.

exceeded the median for the Latino-white gap. For some grade/subject combinations, however, the median change in the African American–white gap was less than 1 percentage point per year.

Other gaps have narrowed at a slower pace. The median rate of narrowing for the Native American–white gap ranged from 0.3 percentage point per year in grade 4 reading to 0.7 percentage point per year in grade 8 math. The gap between low-income and non-low-income students narrowed at a median rate that ranged from 0.5 to 0.7 percentage point per year, depending on the grade and subject.

The study also looked at the median rates of progress in narrowing gaps in mean scores, but the number of states with sufficient data was quite limited—ten to fifteen states, depending on the grade and subject. Fewer states provided the standard deviations needed to make these calculations than provided mean scores alone. In addition, these data did not always go back as far as the other data provided by states for this study. Because of these limitations, firm conclusions could not be reached about how quickly or slowly mean score gaps were closing.

Using the percentage proficient median, one can arrive at a hypothetical example of how long it would take to close a particular gap if the current rate of progress continued unchanged and if other critical factors remained the same. One could extrapolate that if a gap, such as the Latino-white gap in grade 8 math, were narrowing at a rate of 1.3 percentage points per year, it would hypothetically take 11.5 years to close a 15-point gap. If another gap, such as the Native American–white gap in the same subject and grade, were narrowing at a rate of 0.7 percentage point per year, it would take more than thirty-five years to close such a gap if all key factors remained the same. In reality, this is an unlikely scenario. Achievement trends for various groups rarely move at the same steady pace along a straight trajectory. In addition, the smaller a gap becomes, the more difficult it may be to close, as the very lowest performing students struggle to master more challenging knowledge and skills. Changes in tests, such as the adoption of tests that more sensitively measure the effects of good instruction, may also influence the rate at which gaps change.

Rates of Change in Gaps in Individual States

Another way of estimating how long it would take to close gaps at current rates of progress is to look at examples from individual states with typical-size gaps—not unusually large or small—for a particular subgroup. Since states with longer trend lines offer a better opportunity to look at progress over time, these examples were chosen from states with comparable data for the entire span covered by the study, 2002 through 2009. The following examples should be viewed as illustrations, not predictions, and should not be used to compare states given the differences in test characteristics, student demographics, and other factors, plus the fact that the data are not weighted for population size.

In Florida, a state with a typical-size gap, the African American–white gap in percentages proficient has narrowed in grade 4 reading at an average annual rate of 0.9 percentage point per year since 2002. In 2009, this gap remained at 25 percentage points. If the gap continued to narrow at the same rate and if other key factors remained unchanged, then hypothetically it would take twenty-eight years to close this gap. In Pennsylvania, it would hypothetically take seventeen years to close the gap between Latino and white students in grade 8 math at the current average rate of narrowing of 1.5 percentage points per year. In Colorado, the Latino-white gap has narrowed at an average rate of 2.0 percentage points per year, so it would hypothetically take 10.5 years to close this gap. But in the same state, the Native American–white gap in grade 4 reading has *widened* at an average annual rate of 0.4, so that gap would not close if that rate continued.

As these examples indicate, the average rate of change varies considerably among states with similar size gaps, but these rates may be affected by differences in testing programs, demographics, and other factors. It is encouraging that gaps in some states are much smaller in 2009 than they were in 2002. But it could still take many years to close most gaps if progress were to continue unchanged, and some gaps would not narrow, let alone close.

CONCLUSION

The requirements to disaggregate test data in the No Child Left Behind Act and related state statutes have produced a vast repository of data that document the persistence of wide achievement gaps between African American, Latino, and Native American students on the one hand, and white and Asian American students on the other. Large gaps also exist between low-income and more economically advantaged students. Data from state tests and NAEP—including average test scores on both assessments, the percentages of students scoring proficient on state tests, and the percentages scoring at the basic level on NAEP—indicate that although some headway has been made in narrowing achievement gaps, progress is inconsistent and incremental. Even for groups, such as Latino and African American students, that have improved at a fast enough pace to narrow gaps, wide disparities remain. More effective and innovative interventions and policies are needed at all levels of government to close achievement gaps.

ADDITIONAL INFORMATION ABOUT STUDY METHODS

The study of trends in subgroup performance and achievement gaps discussed in this chapter is part of a series of studies of student achievement conducted over the past four years by the Center on Education Policy with technical support from the

Human Resources Research Organization, its contractor for the study. The methodology was developed with advice from a panel of experts in educational testing and education policy. Several aspects of the methodology are worthy of mention, in addition to those described elsewhere in this chapter.[2]

Year-to-Year Comparability of Data

The trends analyzed on state tests alone (not in conjunction with NAEP) begin in 2001–2002, in states with comparable data going back that far, and end in 2008–2009, the most recent year of test data available at the time of the study. The year 2002 was chosen as the starting point because many states did not disaggregate their test results by student subgroup until they were required to do so by the No Child Left Behind Act.

Only trend lines that encompassed at least three years of comparable test data for a particular subgroup, subject, grade, and achievement level were included in the analyses. States that had at least three years of comparable data but fewer than the full eight years were included in the analysis of a particular grade and subject as long as their data extended through 2008–2009. Test data were *not* considered comparable if a state had introduced new tests, changed its cut scores for proficient performance, or made other major changes in its testing program; these types of "breaks" in test data make year-to-year comparisons invalid.

The comparisons of trends on NAEP and state tests covered the same time span for both assessments, 2005 through 2009. We focused on this period because a shorter trend line (2007–2009) would have been more subject to short-term fluctuations and therefore less reliable, and a longer trend line (2003–2009) would have excluded many more states. A maximum of twenty-five states had comparable state test data for 2005 and 2009 and could be included in at least some of the NAEP-state comparisons. All states had NAEP data for these years, but for most subgroups, the number of states with sufficient state and NAEP data was much smaller.

States Not Included in Various Analyses

Data used in the study were collected from all fifty states and the District of Columbia; state officials verified the accuracy of their test data. Some states were not included in one or more specific analyses for various reasons. First, as noted above, some states lacked sufficient years of comparable data. Second, not all states provided mean test scores, so the number of states in the mean score analyses was smaller. Third, states were omitted from a grade or subject analysis if the number of test-takers in a particular subgroup was fewer than five hundred, as this is too small to allow for a reliable determination of trends. For the NAEP analyses, states were excluded if the number of students in the NAEP sample for a particular subgroup did not meet the minimum size requirements for NAEP reporting. Native Americans were not included in the state-NAEP comparisons because in many states the NAEP samples of Native American test-takers were too small, or because fewer than five hundred Native American students took the state test at grade 4 or 8. Fourth, states were excluded from some analyses of achievement gaps if they did not provide data for students who are not low income, because a gap comparison could not be made with low-income students.

Use of Average Annual Changes

We determined movement in trend lines by using average annual changes in test results. These were calculated by taking the overall increase or decrease in the percentage proficient/basic or mean score and dividing it by the number of years of testing minus one (because the salient point is the difference between two years). To determine whether achievement gaps narrowed or widened, we compared the average annual gain in the mean score or the percentage proficient made by a lower-performing subgroup, such as African American students, with the average annual gain of a higher-performing group, such as white students, in the same state, subject, and grade level. If the average gain for the lower-performing subgroup was larger than that of the higher-performing group, this was counted as one instance of an achievement gap narrowing; if the average gain for the lower-performing group was smaller, this was counted as an instance of an achievement gap widening.

Means and Medians

As one indicator of achievement, this study analyzed mean scale scores for each subgroup. Mean scores were not included, however, in the analyses of the extent to which gaps narrowed or widened or the rate of change in achievement gaps. This was because only fifteen states (or fewer for some grade/subject combinations) provided both the mean score and the standard deviation data needed to calculate these changes. Any analysis based on this limited pool of states would have been insufficient to support or refute the findings from the percentage proficient analyses that included several more states.

Some of the analyses examined the medians of the 2009 percentages proficient for each subgroup across all of the states with sufficient data for that subgroup. Using the median made it possible to obtain a rough picture of the relative performance of different subgroups across multiple states in situations where state test results could not be averaged because they came from states with different sizes of student populations, diverse assessments, and different scoring scales and proficiency definitions.

NAEP and State Test Comparisons

The comparisons of state test and NAEP trends focused on results for each state from the main NAEP assessments in reading and math at grades 4 and 8. Because NAEP and state tests use different definitions of proficient performance, the study team determined, with advice from the aforementioned expert panel, that it was most appropriate to compare the percentages of students scoring at or above the "proficient" level of achievement on state tests with the percentages scoring at or above the "basic" level of achievement on NAEP. The purpose of the state test and NAEP comparisons was to measure gains at points on the achievement spectrum that were most comparable to each other; in most states, the median percentage proficient on state tests is much closer to the percentage scoring basic on NAEP than to the percentage proficient on NAEP. A 2009 study by the National Center for Education Statistics, which "mapped" states' proficiency standards onto the NAEP scoring scale, found that on most state tests, cut scores for the proficient level were less ambitious than the NAEP proficient level and were often closer to—or sometimes below—the NAEP basic level.[3] It could be said that for NAEP, "proficient" represents an aspirational goal for what students should know and be able to do, while on most state tests, "proficient" describes a level of performance that is good enough to be regarded as acceptable for a particular grade level.

The study counted an increase or decrease of any size as a gain or decline on both state tests and NAEP. Based on advice from the expert panel, the statistical significance of NAEP results was not considered in the comparisons of state test and NAEP results, so that trends on both types of assessments would be treated in the same way.

NAEP reports its results using tests of statistical significance because NAEP average scores and percentages are estimates, based on representative samples of students in a sample of schools in each state rather than on the entire student population in a state or the nation. Moreover, the collection of test questions used for each subject and grade level is just a sample of the vast number of questions that could have been asked. As such, NAEP results are subject to a measure of uncertainty.

Because of the sampling technique used, the NAEP program must compute statistical estimates of student performance in order to generalize results from this sample to the state's entire student population. NAEP reports its estimated results with a standard error, which is used to calculate whether a change in results is reliable—for instance, whether a state's average score in grade 4 math in 2009 is significantly different from the average score in a previous year.

If NAEP gains do not meet the NAEP standard of significance, this does not mean gains are necessarily nonexistent. Over a longer time period than the four-year span of our state-NAEP analysis, incremental gains that are not statistically significant could accumulate to become significant.

State tests results, by contrast, are not reported using tests of statistical significance. Checks for statistical significance are not routinely done because state tests are administered to virtually all students in a particular grade; therefore, the results do not need to be extrapolated from a sample and are not subject to uncertainty about whether the tested sample accurately represents the state's student population. There is still some possibility of measurement error in state tests due, for example, to the sample of test questions chosen, as mentioned above. However, states do not routinely report their test results in terms of statistical significance, and it would be very difficult to get estimates of appropriate standard errors for state tests.

Our study involved comparisons of state test and NAEP results. Because we treated small increases and decreases on state tests as changes, it would have biased the comparison to treat NAEP results differently and count only those changes on NAEP that met NAEP's strict standard of significance. This would have meant applying different rules to state tests and NAEP. However, because we counted even small changes as increases or decreases, it is possible that some of these changes on either state tests or NAEP merely reflect random fluctuations in some states.

## CHAPTER TWO

Reframing the Ecology of Opportunity and Achievement Gaps

Why "No Excuses" Reforms Have Failed to Narrow Student Group Differences in Educational Outcomes

ROBERT K. REAM, SARAH M. RYAN,
AND JOSE A. ESPINOZA

How are we to understand the long-standing expectation that public schools, all on their own, can remedy deep-rooted racial, social class, and linguistic disparities in educational opportunity and achievement? Is it indeed the case, as so much discourse surrounding education would imply, that all the work that needs doing can occur solely within the schools? In this chapter we argue that the current agenda for the reform of primary and secondary education in the United States needs to be altered. Our present path offers school-centered formulations of the problems and possible solutions, most often without weighing how other social institutions influence educational results. To continue on this path is to remain complicit in the perpetuation of the very student group achievement gaps that decades of reforms have been framed as being designed to eliminate.

In making our case, we begin by measuring the incidence and causes of the gaps in educational performance, taking account of the fluctuation in these gaps over time. Next we offer an account of how these gaps affect the lives of disenfranchised minority and poor students, but we also suggest that society at large has increasingly come to experience the repercussions of the disparate outcomes for students who are economically and culturally enfranchised and those who are not. It is clear to us, after taking a hard look at decades of research on this matter, that even though the standards and accountability reforms of the past twenty years coincided with increased achievement for the overall student population, that same "no excuses" approach has failed to narrow the differences in educational outcomes persisting at the group level and may have contributed to the perpetuation of this phenomenon. We can only conclude that the current tactics of holding schools almost entirely responsible for closing gaps, or rather for failing to close them, amounts to a kind of scapegoating, revealing if only by accident the "soft bigotry of low expectations"—not as pertains to what we expect of children,[1] but rather as concerns what we expect of ourselves as a society.[2]

In preparing the ground for an honest discussion of the occurrences, sources, and consequences of the educational problems now commonly referenced by the somewhat contentious label "the achievement gap," we first enter here into a discussion of the especially polemical issue of how it is that we as a nation find ourselves in this predicament.[3] Since the early 1970s, analyses of nationally representative survey data have documented an enduring history of achievement differences, which reveals that whites and especially East Asians enjoy relatively high average student performance, while African Americans and some Hispanic and Southeast Asian subgroups experience relatively low average student performance.[4] Moreover, children whose families are on the lower rungs of the social class ladder and/or speak a language other than English at home average far lower achievement and educational attainment levels than their wealthier, English-fluent counterparts. Thus, it is important to recognize that what is often characterized as a single unyielding gap between white students and all minority students is more accurately portrayed as multiple gaps that fluctuate between and within racial, social class, and linguistic groups. Yet, despite decades of school reform designed to eradicate glaring inequities in education, the gaps in educational outcomes now appear not only intractable but also (at least to some educators and policy makers) all but ineradicable. It is not an overstatement to say that the persistence of this problem has begun to undermine Americans' faith in the ability of public schools to confront the disadvantages faced by poor and minority students and to somehow "level the playing field" for all.

To shed light on what we see as the unrealistic expectation that public schools alone should be capable of remedying the gaps, we draw attention to how empirical evidence about the ebb and flow of educational inequities has shaped the education policy agenda. Such research goes a long way, we maintain, to dispelling some of the unrealistic expectations about what schools can do on their own, expectations that are deeply entrenched in the ways we talk about and have thought to bring about the convergence of majority and minority students' educational performance. Our ability to repair educational inequity will depend on an honest reckoning with evidence such as that presented here and may also require, we suggest, a thoroughgoing effort to mobilize the social institutions outside of school that play such a large—but still to this day often unacknowledged—role in students' educational experiences.

THE EBB AND FLOW OF THE GAPS ON THE POLICY AGENDA

James Coleman was a sociologist at Johns Hopkins University when his controversial 1966 report to the U.S. Congress, *Equality of Educational Opportunity*, became the first national study to offer a systematic description of racial/ethnic differences in academic achievement among children of various ages. Prior to the Coleman Report, investigations of this nature had been focused on educational inputs: school effectiveness was measured by the resources that went into schools, not the quality of the students who came out of them.[5] Coleman found that (1) although schools certainly influence student achievement—much of what tests measure must be learned in schools—and (2) although school quality varies widely in the United States, nevertheless, the large documented differences in the quality of schools attended by black and white children failed to explain most of the differences in average levels of achievement between blacks and whites.[6] These rather controversial findings have been cross-examined by many researchers.[7] Until very recently few, if any, disputed Coleman's fundamental claims.[8] Soon after publication of the Coleman Report, the federal government allotted substantial resources across multiple jurisdictions in an attempt to close family, school, and community input gaps. In fact, school desegregation in the wake of the 1964 Civil Rights Act combined with the Great Society's War on Poverty programs (including Head Start, compensatory Title I funding, the Safe Streets Act, the Economic Opportunity Act, and the Model Cities program) helped reduce glaring resource inequities and coincided with nearly twenty years of steady and substantial progress in reducing both the black-white and Hispanic-white test-score gaps since 1971, per figure 2.1.[9]

Paul Barton and Richard Coley of the nonprofit Educational Testing Service recently summarized much of the research on this topic.[10] They conclude that approximately one-third of the gap reduction during this twenty-year time period can be attributed to improved family conditions in minority households, such as increases in parents' education and income, relative to white families.[11] Nevertheless, it is clear that by the time U.S. Secretary of Education Terrel Bell released the landmark 1983 report to Congress, *A Nation at Risk*, concerns about inequality on the domestic front were pushed into the background, giving way to a growing preoccupation with educational efficiency, global competitiveness, and the politics of education productivity.[12] Thus, many targeted programs for the poor and compensatory education reforms were rolled back throughout the 1980s.[13] Some

FIGURE 2.1
Age 17 trends in average NAEP reading scores: 1971–2008

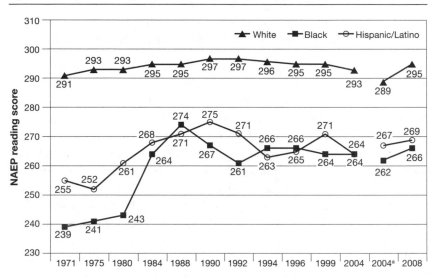

Source: U.S. Department of Education, Institute of Education Sciences, National Center for Education Statistics, National Assessment of Educational Progress (NAEP) 2008: Trends in Academic Progress, Reading, 1971–2008 (Report: NCES 2009-479).

Note: ªRevised assessment format baseline score

programs were completely eliminated.[14] By the late 1980s much of the progress in narrowing educational opportunity and achievement gaps had stalled.

The Bell Curve

The widening of test-score gaps in the late 1980s went largely unnoticed until 1994, when experimental psychologist Richard Herrnstein and political scientist Charles Murray published *The Bell Curve* to much fanfare and subsequent controversy.[15] Their conclusions about the genetic inevitability of the gap were deduced from the research of others and resurrected in particular the much-disputed claims of education psychologist Arthur Jensen, which were first published in 1969 in the *Harvard Educational Review*.[16] When a special task force of the American Psychological Association reviewed the data used by Herrnstein and Murray, they arrived at a much different conclusion: the paucity of direct evidence of the black-white differential in psychometric intelligence simply could not support the genetic hypothesis.[17] Richard E. Nisbett, a distinguished professor of social psychology at the University of Michigan, has charged the authors of *The Bell Curve* with having provided a "shockingly incomplete and biased" reading of the research.[18] Today what all psychologists agree upon is that a person's developed capacity for intelligent behavior often differs in predictable ways from his or her hereditary potential.[19] So-called intelligence or aptitude tests measure the *development* of innate abilities.[20] The collective research of American psychology leads one to conclude that the quality of the world that a person lives in explains far more of the variance in achievement than the number of blacks or whites in a person's family tree.[21]

The Standards and Accountability Movement

Though the effort to put achievement gaps on the policy agenda in the mid-1990s might once have seemed auspicious to educators, inequities in educational outcomes have persisted since that time. The shift to a policy focused on standards and accountability was already owing to, and since then has only been reinforced by, the belief that the work of narrowing or altogether erasing achievement gaps belongs solely to the schools. Unfortunately, achievement gaps remain a priority on the agenda to this day because they have not been effectively redressed by the standards and accountability policy. As Harris and Herrington write:

> The policies implemented before 1990, and recommended in A Nation at Risk, were based on the idea that schools needed greater capacity and that students needed to be pressured to take more difficult courses. By the earlier 1990s, some argued that the NAR recommendations had failed and therefore reversed the logic, assuming instead that it is the schools that need to be pressured.[22]

But those who single out schools as responsible for the persistence of unacceptable gaps in educational outcomes at the group level seem too often to be ignoring the fact that children spend the vast majority of their time in any given year outside the classroom—at home, in extracurricular activities, hanging with friends in the neighborhood—in short, somewhere other than in the formal academic setting.[23]

In taking account of the research on the gaps in outcomes and considering what might be done to eliminate them, in this chapter we draw on the work of developmental psychologist Urie Bronfenbrenner, whose *ecological systems theory* holds that the interconnectedness of several environmental systems, including families, peers, schools and communities, plays a major role in human development.[24] Educators and policy makers need not only to recognize the broad range of in-school and out-of-school factors that shape students' educational experience and their academic achievement, but they need also to deploy this knowledge, working collaboratively with persons from different but often overlapping social spheres of influence, to take action and alter the way we approach education in our society. The plain fact is that the gaps between minority or poor students and otherwise socially enfranchised children is already at roughly a year with regard to educational outcomes for math and reading by the time children enter kindergarten.[25] These differences at the group level remain fairly constant between the first and twelfth grades, so it is safe to say that it is not generally the schools themselves that create or even foster the inequity.[26] Indeed, while children are in school, the gap typically narrows, but when they're outside of the classroom, it widens.[27] In short, there is no getting around the fact that children are beings embedded in social networks, nested in families, navigating relatively complex social lives with peers, and functioning as members of neighborhoods and communities in which school is one important social institution among many shaping their reality. Schools may be charged with the formal education that is supposed to take place within the classroom, but the many competing and overlapping spheres of students' lives greatly influence their educational performance; and it is nearly impossible to isolate these spheres such that we might measure the influence of each as separate from the others.

INCIDENCE OF THE GAPS

However outcome gaps are measured—whether by preschool vocabulary, elementary school grades, middle school standardized test scores, or high school or college completion rates—the fact that there is a continuing history of race, social class, and linguistic differences in American education is not debatable.

Further Evidence About Test-Score Gaps from NAEP

Perhaps the best evidence is derived from the National Assessment of Educational Progress (NAEP), widely known as "the nation's report card." NAEP trend data demonstrate persistent, if somewhat fluctuating, racial test-score gaps going back to 1971. Although black-white and Hispanic-white gaps in mathematics and reading narrowed substantially between 1971 and 1988, trends toward test-score convergence reversed in the late 1980s. Some gaps stabilized and others actually widened throughout the 1990s.[28] Since 1999, however, black-white and Hispanic-white math and reading test-score gaps have held fairly constant across age groups—with the exception of a slight convergence in the Hispanic-white math gap and the black-white reading gap among nine-year-olds. This convergence has been trumpeted by the U.S. Department of Education as evidence of the impact of the No Child Left Behind Act (NCLB) of 2001.[29]

Figure 2.2 depicts cross-sectional analyses of fourth- and eighth-grade students' mathematics and reading results from the 2009 main NAEP. Asian Pacific Americans and whites score well above national averages at both grade levels. Asian fourth-grade students exceed the national math mean by .55 standard

FIGURE 2.2

Standardized NAEP mathematics and reading scores by race/ethnicity, grades 4 and 8, 2009

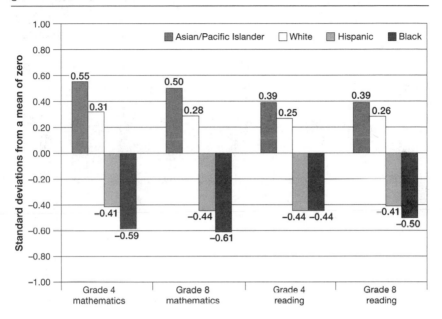

Source: U.S. Department of Education, National Center for Education Statistics, National Assessment of Education Progress (NAEP), 2009 Main NAEP Mathematics and Reading Assessments.

Note: Raw mean scale scores were used for all calculations. Each bar represents the number of standard deviations the mean achievement of each racial/ethnic group falls from (negative value) or exceeds (positive value) the 2009 national average at grades 4 and 8, respectively. Not accounted for in figure 2.2 are group variations according to factors such as social class, immigration status, English language proficiency, and gender. Adjusting the results accordingly would produce smaller mean NAEP test-score differences.

deviations (.50 SD approximates one year of academic growth), outperforming by .24 SD their white counterparts, who also score above the national average. Hispanics and African Americans score below the national average in fourth and eighth grade. The math gap is especially pronounced at approximately .60 SD for African Americans, whereas Hispanic students score approximately .40 SD below the national average in mathematics and reading at both grade levels.

Figure 2.3 depicts NAEP test-score gaps in 2009 according to student eligibility for the federally assisted National School Lunch Program (NSLP). We also account for English language learner (ELL) status in the test-score comparisons in figure 2.3.[30] Children whose families earn so little that the federal government chips in to provide a healthy lunch score approximately .40 SD below the average in math and reading at both grade levels. Even more pronounced are the gaps for

FIGURE 2.3

Standardized NAEP mathematics and reading scores by family income level and English learner status, grades 4 and 8, 2009

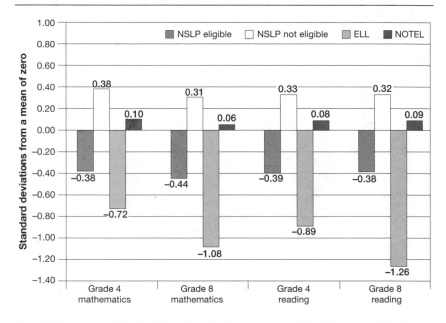

Source: U.S. Department of Education, National Center for Education Statistics, National Assessment of Education Progress (NAEP), 2009 Main NAEP Mathematics and Reading Assessments.

Note: Raw mean scale scores were used for all calculations. Each bar represents the number of standard deviations the mean achievement each falls from (negative value) or exceeds (positive value) the 2009 national average at grades 4 and 8, respectively. Not accounted for in figure 2.3 are group variations according to factors such race/ethnicity and gender. Adjusting the results accordingly would produce smaller mean NAEP test-score differences.

children not yet deemed proficient in English, most of whom (77%) speak Spanish at home.[31] Fourth-grade ELLs lag the national math test score average by .72 standard deviations. For ELLs to match the average eighth-grade math scores of their English-fluent counterparts, it would require an additional two years (1.14 SD) of academic growth. Reading gaps for English language learners are especially conspicuous.[32]

Gaps in High School and College Attainment

While standardized achievement data reveal students' relative mastery of specific knowledge and skills, still other data document differences in group-level educational attainment by alternative measures. For instance, according to the National

Center for Education Statistics, high school dropout rates for Hispanics and blacks substantially exceed those for Asians and whites.[33] Although gaps in high school attainment have narrowed in the past thirty years, the disparity in the graduation rates of Hispanics versus other racial/ethnic groups persists at double-digit rates.[34] The alarmingly high Hispanic high school dropout rate—1.2 million Hispanics between the ages of sixteen and twenty-four were dropouts in 2008— is nearly twice that of blacks and more than three times that of Asians and whites (see figure 2.4).[35] It should be noted, however, that Hispanics are also making real educational gains over generations. These improvements are obscured by the continuing influx of new immigrants.[36] Illustratively, while almost one-third of

FIGURE 2.4
Status dropout rates of 16- through 24-year-olds, by race/ethnicity: October 1972–2008

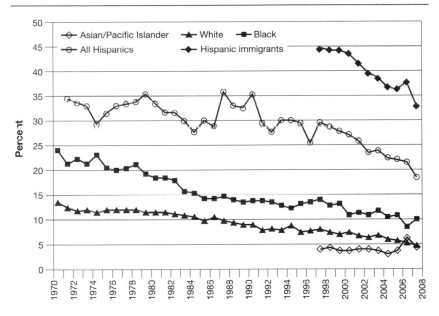

Source: Chris Chapman, Jennifer Laird, and Angelina Kewal Ramani, *Trends in High School Dropout and Completion Rates in the United States: 1972–2008 (NCES 2011–2012).* National Center for Education Statistics, Institute of Education Sciences, U.S. Department of Education, Washington, D.C.

Note: The status dropout rate indicates the percentage of 16- through 24-year-olds who are not enrolled in high school and who lack a high school credential. High school credentials include high school diplomas and equivalent credentials, such as a General Educational Development (GED) certificate. Beginning in 2003, respondents were able to identify themselves as being two or more races. The 2003 through 2008 categories for white (non-Hispanic) and black (non-Hispanic) contain only respondents who indicated just one race. The Hispanic category includes Hispanics of all races and racial combinations.

sixteen- to twenty-four-year old Hispanic *immigrants* were dropouts in 2008, approximately 14 percent of U.S-born Hispanics had failed to complete a high school degree.[37] Nevertheless, these numbers also prefigure problematic trends in educational attainment at the college level, where between 1971 and 2009, the gap in bachelor's degree attainment between blacks and whites increased from 12 to 18 percentage points, while the gap between Hispanics and whites grew even more, increasing from 14 to 25 percentage points.[38]

Since taking office, President Barack Obama has continued to reaffirm the goal that the United States produce an additional eight million college graduates by 2020 and reclaim the world's top spot as the country with the highest percentage of college completers. Several recent reports, expanding upon decades of similar reports, echo this message.[39] Although this rising tide of education has arguably lifted all boats, overall higher college participation rates for all demographic groups have directed attention away from enduring inequities along racial/ethnic and socioeconomic lines.[40] While the "college for all" ideology may not align well with the jobs available in an increasingly segmented economy in which, by one recent estimate, a college degree is required for only half of the jobs landed by new graduates, it remains the case that those who do not enroll and do not complete college degrees are precisely the underrepresented black, Hispanic, and Native American youth who have always experienced limited educational and social mobility in this country.[41] Therefore, before rapidly abandoning the goal for all students to be college educated, it is worth pausing to consider whether hastily doing so will further cloak unwarranted differences in *who* gets *what kind* of postsecondary education under yet more layers of rhetoric.

Consider, for example, the highly uneven distribution of college degrees in the biological sciences, where non-Asian minorities continue to be underrepresented despite a half century of national attention directed at strengthening and diversifying the scientifically and technologically trained labor force.[42] In 2004, blacks enrolled in undergraduate biology programs in proportion to their numbers throughout the United States. Yet among graduate students, the proportion of biology doctorates awarded African Americans fell 60 percent short of their demographic distribution throughout the nation. This inverse relationship between rigor and prestige in the biological sciences and the representation of blacks in that field also held true for U.S. Hispanics, who in 2004 were especially underrepresented in faculty positions, as shown in figure 2.5. Clearly, rates of science attainment decrease precipitously as underrepresented minorities move from undergraduate education to more prestigious and remunerative levels of higher education, including graduate school, postdoctoral work, and academic positions.

The rapidly increasing percentage of minorities in the U.S. population, with Hispanics constituting the vast majority of the growth, underscores the enormous

FIGURE 2.5
Representation in the biological sciences pipeline by race/ethnicity, 2004

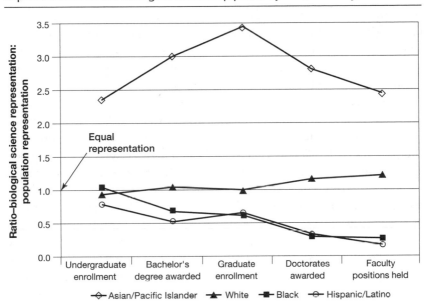

Source: James Lewis et al., "Rethinking Trends in Minority Participation in the Sciences," *Science Education* 93 (2009): 961–977.

Note: All estimates are obtained by dividing the percentage of representation in the biological sciences by the percentage of representation in the U.S. population in 2004. Conceptualizing representation this way, a ratio equal to 1.0 indicates *equal representation,* a ratio greater than 1.0 indicates *overrepresentation,* and a ratio of less than 1.0 indicates *underrepresentation.* As a ratio departs from 1.0, the magnitude of under- or overrepresentation increases.

significance of these gaps across all levels of education.[43] Thus, over the past two decades, many policy makers have redoubled their efforts (perhaps sometimes only symbolically) to achieve group-level equality of educational outcomes, if not inputs. Ironically, however, while official interest in these described gaps in American education may be at an all-time high, we have precious little to show for the past twenty years of reform efforts professedly designed to tackle the problem. Thus, America is confronted with a troubling reality: an increasingly significant portion of the eligible U.S. voting and working population is comprised of individuals drawn from groups whose academic achievement and educational attainment is significantly below the rest of the nation.[44] This presents a serious moral, civic, and economic challenge. Yet, before discussing in greater detail the implications of the vast inequalities we have depicted here, it is important to outline the manifold and overlapping sources of these disparities.

SOURCES OF THE GAPS

When we turn to an examination, then, of contextual factors contributing to gaps in education, the breadth and depth of their sources quickly becomes apparent. Since causes are layered and overlapping, they are best considered simultaneously across domains. From a top-down structural perspective, one might perceive broad economic conditions as being linked to, say, state and local tax rate policies that bear directly, if also differentially, upon community labor markets and housing values—which, in turn, dictate school finance schemes. There are indeed sizable gaps in educational resources in communities serving predominantly white and predominantly minority children.[45] From a less structural, bottom-up perspective, concentrated on student effort and family influence, one sees substantial variation in parents' approaches to child rearing. Whether children are talked at or listened to, how frequently they read and are read to, and whether or not they attend quality preschool and summer school are important factors that are conditioned by parents' effort and resources. Children's friends and peers pick up where families leave off, exerting increasing influence as students progress through schooling.[46] In short, there is a dynamic and sometimes transformative relationship between the practices of real people (including students, parents, peers, and teachers) and the structures of school, society, and even history.[47]

In figure 2.6 we offer a nested, albeit by no means exhaustive, depiction of the many structural and individual-level factors that have been examined to understand the causes of the gaps. The embedded domains are not mutually exclusive categories. Rather, they are composed of related factors that act upon one another in complex ways that are often difficult to observe and quantify.[48] One challenge, therefore, is to determine the extent to which the attributes of formal institutional settings and those of less formal student, family, peer group, and neighborhood and societal-level influences contribute to the gaps. A few of the better documented causes of these gaps are noted below.

Resegregation and the Distribution of Teacher Quality

In June 2007, a divided U.S. Supreme Court restricted the ability of public school districts to use race in determining which schools students can attend. Most voluntary desegregation efforts by school districts are now unconstitutional and most students are now assigned to schools based only on where they live. According to Gary Orfield and Chungmei Lee of the UCLA Civil Rights Project, the resegregation of American schools has accelerated since the early 1990s and continues to grow in all parts of the country, most conspicuously among African Americans and Hispanics.[49] Not since President Lyndon Johnson signed the Civil Rights Act have schools been as segregated as they are today. When we ask what it is about

FIGURE 2.6

Nested sources of gaps in opportunity and achievement

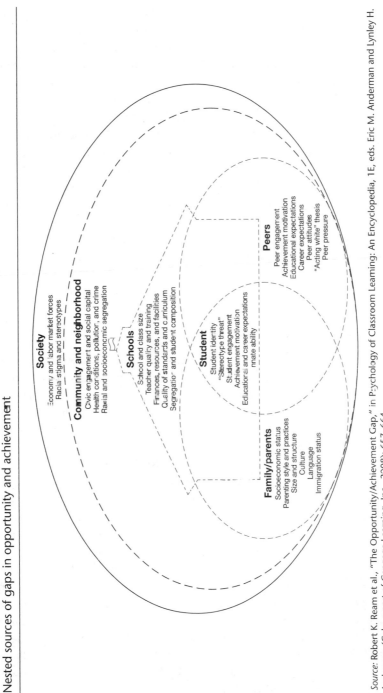

Source: Robert K. Ream et al., "The Opportunity/Achievement Gap," in Psychology of Classroom Learning: An Encyclopedia, 1E, eds. Eric M. Anderman and Lynley H. Anderman (Gale, a part of Cengage Learning, Inc., 2008): 657–664.

segregated schools that contributes to racial achievement gaps, many point to course offerings, the composition of the student body, and perhaps especially the "instruction gap."[50] In a 1991 study of nine hundred Texas school districts, Harvard University's Achievement Gap Initiative director, Ronald Ferguson, found that nearly all of the school-level variation in the gap in achievement between blacks and whites was attributable to systematic differences in the skills of their teachers.[51] The simple fact is that far fewer of the best-prepared teachers are teaching in schools where the vast majority of students are black and/or Hispanic. These disparities in access to high-quality teachers and teaching are large and growing worse.[52] Yet recent research shows that when low-income students of color are given the opportunity to live in middle-class neighborhoods and partake of the privileges that accompany schools serving more well-off students, they make gains that reduce test-score gaps.[53]

Although quality teachers are important, it is nevertheless the case that most of the group-level variation in student achievement outcomes can be attributed to factors outside of schools. As findings based on and replicating the Coleman Report have time and again demonstrated, other structured political, economic, and social conditions that envelope schools also impact gaps in achievement.

The Seasonality of Children's Learning

Among a broad range of studies that contradict the notion that American education is a failed enterprise and public schools are to blame, research on the equity implications of summer learning stands out.[54] For decades the sociologist Karl Alexander and his colleagues at Johns Hopkins University have been tracking a large representative sample of youngsters who began first grade in 1982 in twenty Baltimore City Public Schools.[55] Each student in the elementary school sample took the California Achievement Test (CAT) in September, just after summer vacation, and again in June at the end of the school year. Thus, it became possible to disentangle school-year achievement gains between September and June from the out-of-school learning that occurred from June to September (with today's proliferation of out-of-school programs, it would be much harder to reproduce a natural experiment like this). Figure 2.7 replicates a portion of Alexander's findings disaggregated by family socioeconomic status. Although first graders from higher-SES families start out with a 32-point advantage over the first graders from the poorest homes, both groups make markedly similar school-year gains in reading throughout elementary school. During third grade, high-SES children learn more, while reading gains in grades 2, 4, and 5 advantage low-SES children. In the formal school setting through fifth grade, poor children actually "outlearn" higher-SES children 191 points to 187 points. Over the summer, however, the reading scores of the low-SES children fluctuate around a flat trend line, while wealthier

FIGURE 2.7
California Achievement Test (CAT) gains by season and socioeconomic status

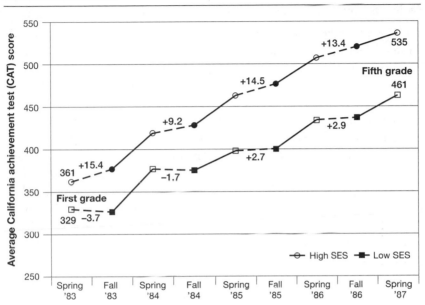

Source: Karl L. Alexander, Doris R. Entwisle, and Linda S. Olson, "Schools, Achievement, and Inequality: A Seasonal Perspective," *Educational Evaluation and Policy Analysis* 23 (2001): 171–191.

Note: Gains or losses in achievement made when school is in session are shown in solid-line segments, while gains or losses in achievement made when school is out of session (the summer months) are shown in dashed-line segments. The abscissa does not represent equidistant time intervals since fall to spring increments would present an 8-month time interval, while spring to fall would represent a 4-month interval. High-SES ($N = 150$) and low-SES ($N = 329$) groups are "relative to the sample's makeup" and represent a five-indicator composite that measures financial and intellectual resources available to each child. On average, mothers of students deemed High SES completed at least some college education (14.6 years of schooling), while very few High SES students qualified for free or reduced-price lunch (13.1%). The mothers of students in the Low SES group averaged only ten years of schooling (did not complete high school), and almost all Low SES students (95.1%) qualified for free or reduced-price lunch.

students continue to make much more substantial gains. They may learn more during the school year, but when it comes to reading skills, poor kids fall further and further behind over the summer. Thus, by the end of fifth grade, the initial reading gap between low- and higher-SES children has more than doubled, from 32 points to 74 points. This pattern indicates, first, that group-level differences in achievement at the elementary school level reflect conditions outside school far more than those inside school. Virtually all of the reading advantage that higher-SES students have over poor students is the result of differences they bring to school from home and the way that more privileged children learn when they are not in school.[56] Second, schools do not exacerbate unequal school performance across social lines. Instead, schooling mitigates inequality by limiting the expansion of the gaps as children progress through elementary school.[57]

Socioeconomic Status and Parenting

What is it about the out-of-school context that can account for summer advantage for some children and a summer slide for others? Myriad studies confirm that socioeconomic status as a measure of parental education, employment, and income is among the most powerful predictors of student achievement.[58] And many prominent social scientists have shown that the correlation between SES and race is inevitably linked to diminished access to quality education for underrepresented minorities, and thus, not surprisingly, to patterned racial inequality in educational outcomes.[59] While only 7 percent of white mothers in the Early Childhood Longitudinal Study of the Kindergarten Class of 1998–99 had failed to complete high school, a full 18 percent of black mothers and 35 percent of Latina mothers had failed to do so.[60] Likewise, only 15 percent of white children (and 11 percent of Asians) under the age of eighteen were living in poverty in 2005 compared to almost one-third of all black and Hispanic children.[61] Not only are black and Hispanic children more likely to have parents who have not completed high school and are poor, but they are also more likely to attend schools with other poor children. To the degree that both family poverty and school poverty affect academic achievement, Hispanic and black students are twice disadvantaged.[62]

Some understanding of how SES influences achievement is provided by psychologists who study the interactions between parents and children. The research of psychologist Laurence Steinberg at Temple University indicates that a lack of school-specific knowledge and a lack of opportunity (good parenting takes a lot of time) are what differentiate high- and low-SES parents in their parenting styles and approaches to raising children.[63] Other research conducted by Betty Hart and Todd Risley, child psychologists at the University of Kansas, links children's language development to parents' communication style. In a well-known 1995 study, they found that by age three the children of professionals had vocabularies of about 1,100 words—and the children of welfare parents had vocabularies of about half as many words.[64] Comparing children's vocabulary scores with their home life, Hart and Risley concluded that children's vocabulary correlated most closely to the number of words the parents spoke to their child. And the number and kinds of words that children heard varied markedly by social class. The most basic difference was in the number of prohibitions and words of disapproval heard by the child as compared with the number of encouragements or words of praise. Hearing fewer words yet many prohibitions had a negative effect on IQ, while hearing lots of words, especially affirmations and complex sentences, improved IQ. In short, early childhood parenting practices and communication styles matter greatly and are patterned along class lines.

To reiterate, only about one-third of the racial gap in achievement can be attributed to what goes on in schools. And there is an emerging research consensus that family socioeconomic status accounts for at least another third of the gap in educational outcomes.[65] While the effect of schools on a child's academic achievement is nearly impossible to isolate from other influences (including family SES), most researchers agree that even eliminating vast resource differences between schools and among families would not entirely close the racial gap in achievement. In fact, one of the most perplexing aspects of the racial test-score gap is its persistence among even middle-class students and among students at the top of the achievement spectrum—the very pool from which our nation's leaders are drawn.[66]

Wealth and Future Aspirations

However, it is possible that this puzzling aspect of the racial test-score gap may be related to the fact that researchers have largely relied on income as an indicator of class status, while the relationships that achievement and other important student outcomes share with household *wealth* has received far less attention in this body of literature.[67] Variously defined as assets, net worth, and ownership of financial products, regardless of how wealth is measured, ethnoracial wealth disparities are greater than those displayed by any other socioeconomic measure, and these differences persist at every income level.[68] Moreover, as Wei-Jun Jean Yeung and Dalton Conley assert, "there are ample reasons to suspect that race differences in family wealth levels may help explain differences in child outcome measures."[69]

Wealth may affect educational outcomes through a variety of mechanisms, in part depending on the sources of wealth and the age of the child. One way in which wealth may impact outcomes is by providing a safety net during times of income instability, underscoring the importance of liquid forms of wealth. It could also be that the social-psychological returns to wealth are just as influential through their effect on youths' sense of social class standing, security, and future aspirations that derive from the presence of visible manifestations of wealth throughout the course of family life. Yeung and Conley, sociologists at New York University, found a stronger association between family wealth and cognitive achievement among school-age children than among preschoolers, and within the school-age sample, a stronger association with math scores than with reading scores. In their concluding remarks, the pair speculate that the presence of wealth over time in a family may have a stronger impact by promoting a sense of economic security and future orientation. Specifically, they remark, "It is plausible that in young adulthood, wealth may become an even more critical factor in shaping one's path to college attendance, career success, or even the timing of marriage and choice of partners."[70] This position is supported by studies that have linked wealth to years of completed schooling, college enrollment, and college completion.[71] That being said, it should merit attention that at the same time that racial disparities in college completion have grown, so too have racial wealth gaps widened.[72]

Individual Identity and Stereotype Threat

The work of Stanford social psychologist Claude Steele also helps to interpret the persistent achievement gaps even among students who are enrolled in our nation's most competitive universities. In spite of the many obstacles that inhibit educational achievement among non-Asian minority students, many forge ahead to attain high levels of academic success. Some minorities within the academic vanguard, however, may encounter further achievement barriers corresponding to their relative identification with schooling. In his groundbreaking work on how stereotypes interact with students' identities to shape educational performance, Steele explains what he calls "stereotype threat."[73] According to Steele, stereotype threat arises when school-identified African Americans are in a situation or doing something for which a negative stereotype about one's group applies and must therefore be disconfirmed. Thus, stereotypes become particularly threatening for those who associate their identity and self-worth with success in a domain where their own group has been obviously stereotyped. So above and beyond the K–12 instruction gap and the socioeconomic and wealth inequality noted earlier, stereotypes about groups can influence the cognitive functioning and identity formation of individual group members. And this burden of heightened awareness about stereotypes and social stigma affects especially test-score gaps among students of color who are otherwise apparently advantaged.

THE CONSEQUENCES, AND SOCIETY'S INTEREST IN ELIMINATING THE GAPS

Policy makers are increasingly aware that the reasons for closing the gaps we have been discussing go well beyond presumed links between the improved academic performance of minority students and their future job prospects. There may be a moral imperative to addressing this problem, depending on the nature of one's political beliefs. But on a simply utilitarian rationale, we can also say that better-educated students earn higher incomes, live healthier lives, pay higher taxes, and prove less likely to be involved in crime.[74] On the premise that high school graduation should serve as a minimal threshold for being considered adequately educated, Columbia University economist Henry Levin has investigated and forecast the costs to society should we fail to succeed in providing students with this base level of education.[75] His report focuses on individuals who at the age of twenty in 2005 were not high school graduates, a group of approximately seven hundred thousand. The cost to society, as measured across the hypothetical lifetime of a single one of these students, runs to over $200,000, factoring revenue lost to society in federal, state, and local taxes and costs paid out in the public health-care and criminal justice systems. On aggregate, then, the fiscal consequences to society for this single group of students without high school diplomas is projected at the staggering sum of $148 billion—again, as measured by lost tax revenues and public expenditures for the care of these persons.

The implications of growing gaps in educational attainment beyond high school are equally troubling. Assuming no change in educational attainment gaps across racial/ethnic groups over time, the National Center for Public Policy and Higher Education forecasts a loss of $395 in annual personal income (inflation-adjusted dollars) between 2000 and 2020, with an annual decrease of 2 percent as opposed to the approximately 2 percent yearly *increase* between 1980 and 2000.[76] This decrease, impacting individual purchasing power, tax revenues, and demand for public services, would carry heavy consequences. Clearly it is in the nation's best interest to reduce dropout rates and to ensure that all children secure an adequate education.[77] Indeed, as job opportunities even for those with high school diplomas continue to decrease, the need to successfully complete some postsecondary education becomes paramount for young adults trying to increase their odds of finding work.[78]

Despite ominous projections such as these, we remain incapable as a nation of articulating how we expect to make good on the promise of the American Dream for *all* of our children. It is our contention, in concluding, that the failure to comprehend and take to heart the social consequences of the gaps in educational outcomes leads to complacency among educational policy makers. We also contend that the singular and repeated use of "the achievement gap" idiom obscures the nature and history of educational problems, therefore limiting the imaginable policy moves directed toward the design and execution of solutions.[79] Unless our society can develop a discourse of educational reform attuned to the diverse factors contributing to educational inequality, one free of jargon and clichés, our policy makers will continue to use worn-out concepts based on inadequate data in order to persuade themselves that they have fairly and adequately grappled with the problems in our education system when in fact they have not. Such complacency in public rhetoric and educational policy making, if it persists, will come at a dreadful cost to the nation.

MOVING FORWARD

Among the wide-ranging educational challenges facing American society, perhaps no issue is more important to the nation's civic and economic well-being than the inequity in achievement among diverse racial/ethnic, socioeconomic, and linguistic student groups. That test-score gaps, disproportionately high dropout rates, and low levels of college attainment among non-Asian minorities have reemerged on the policy agenda may seem relatively unsurprising in light of recent research demonstrating the steep costs exacted on the nation as a result of lost human capital productivity and associated forfeited tax revenues.[80] Baby boomers whose overall well-being depends on the productivity of subsequent generations are concerned that the population base of American voters and taxpayers will increasingly come to be made up of persons less educated than they themselves were. In response to the coincidence of dramatic changes in U.S. demographics and new information about gaps accompanying the standards movement, policy makers have increased pressure almost entirely on schools to demonstrate annual achievement progress for all students and to close "the achievement gap." Still, regardless of all we know about the incidence, causes, and consequences of these gaps, government policy has only partially and inconsistently responded to this ongoing crisis. Lamentably, the positive picture of narrowing gaps from the early 1970s until the late 1980s (when for some cohorts the gaps were cut by as much as half or more) has since been replaced by relatively small up-and-down changes along with periods of stagnation.[81]

What manner of democratic people are we, and what sort of progressive republic can we possibly envision, if persistent gaps in educational inputs and outcomes continue to differentiate large and expanding groups of Americans from mainstream society and its benefits?

If we as a society are to be moved to intervene in this state of affairs, we must first be able to properly recognize the nature of social inequities both within and beyond schools, before we can begin to conceive of ways to resist and overcome them. A good start would be to curb our current tendency to scapegoat schools and to stop using buzzwords and stock phrases such as "no excuses" and "the achievement gap" to reinforce well-worn but imprecise notions about the work schools do and the way children perform in them. The pervasiveness of such rhetoric places inordinate blame on schools and is often echoed uncritically in the media. This simultaneously limits the scope of the reforms our policy makers are willing to undertake, restricting the range of choices they imagine as available to them, diverting their attention from the array of social institutions and practices that condition formal schooling and influence its effectiveness. Even as most contemporary efforts in educational reform continue to ignore the structured underpinnings of inequality and focus almost entirely on school-centered efforts to eliminate differences in group-level achievement, the finding of the Coleman Report bears repeating: *No more than forty percent of the racial gap in educational outcomes can be attributed to the schools themselves (in isolation from other nonschool factors).*

We perceive a need for a much more strategic *alignment* between the larger social structures comprising the context in which schooling occurs and the goals for school reform as set forth in the preamble to the 2001 version of the 1965 Elementary and Secondary Education Act. These opening remarks explicitly state that the overarching purpose of NCLB is to finally bring an end to group-level differences in student achievement. We have here described many of the overlapping causes of the gaps (as depicted in figure 2.6) precisely because so many structural factors—from financial markets and the segmented economy, to deep inequities in health and nutrition, public safety, and transportation, to social environments and family circumstances—remain largely absent from the conversation about and therefore the scope of so-called comprehensive education reform. As we have insisted, then, the task of improving contemporary American schooling remains entirely necessary but not altogether sufficient for eliminating the gaps in outcomes.[82] If we are going to proceed as optimistically as possible within the academic setting, working as if there were no limit to schools' power to compensate for very real social disadvantage, we cannot pursue this course by putting on our blinders and refusing to respond simultaneously to a much more comprehensive range of factors that constitute the overall ecology of student development.[83]

Some of the message we are imparting here has already been disseminated and begun to take root. Local grassroots organizations as well as more formal policy-making institutions have begun to revisit and develop alliances that foster the cooperation of institutional representatives from the public, private, and independent sectors as a way of building civic capacity as a ground for educational interventions.[84] The Obama administration's Promise Neighborhoods competition puts federal monies to the issue, supposing that by meeting critical out-of-school needs we can begin closing the gaps in outcomes. In Massachusetts, city schools now compete for grants to establish "wraparound zones," which link the school, students, and their families to services provided by state health and human service agencies. The reformative agenda of Geoffrey Canada's Harlem Children's Zone connects Wall Street and venture philanthropists to the public problems of government housing and transportation as well as public safety and recreation. Much of this bottom-up grassroots work has been credited as the catalyst for integrative approaches seeking to develop civic capacity in an effort to spur education reform at the state and national levels. Such grassroots endeavors can spur systems-changing movements that provide a new impetus to meaningful comprehensive school reform.[85] And such strategies seem increasingly feasible as our notion about just who is responsible for schooling focuses not only upward on federal government but also outward from local school boards to general-purpose government officials, including city mayors, county supervisors, and state legislators.[86]

CONCLUSION

In this chapter, we have marshaled empirical data and theoretical arguments in order to puncture holes in both the public's and policy makers' overly rigid expectations about what is feasible, or *not* feasible, when it comes to options toward eliminating the very real gaps in opportunity and achievement. By challenging the characterization of these gaps as normal or natural occurrences somehow unrelated to societal inputs, we have grappled openly with how best to talk about the inequities that structure and perpetuate group-level differences, on average, with regard to diverse academic inputs and outcomes over generations. At the same time, we have attended to questions about the specific social institutions affecting students' disadvantages, while providing greater clarity about how and in relation to whom they are disadvantaged. Along these lines, we depicted those periods during the 1970s and 1980s in which gaps in outcomes narrowed significantly as encouraging, insofar as they give evidence of the pliability of the gaps. And yet we have argued that any significant progress in educational reform from here on will require us to talk about the problems differently, and we readily acknowledge that finding new language is always challenging. But it is imperative to reject Manichean and ahistorical and otherwise narrow conceptualizations of the sources of problems as well as the solutions if we wish, sincerely, to effect a rapprochement between the social structures shaping students' academic experience (often negatively) and the lofty achievement goals we continue to say we expect our schools to attain. Because the diverse causes of the gaps in outcomes overlap and are inextricably linked, we need an equally nuanced and integrative approach to solving these gaps (for a comprehensive review of organizational strategies that promise substantial impact on closing the gaps, see chapter 6). It is possible, we believe, to extricate ourselves from entrenched patterns of thought and policy practices that have worked, ironically, to perpetuate the inequality they were meant to redress. Our reflections here are offered in a spirit of optimism about what might be, not just what is, so that we can move toward greater alignment of what we expect of schools and what we expect of ourselves.[87] For what the democratic eruptions so far away in Cairo and Tunis and Tripoli portend about the essential unfairness in American education here at home, if nothing else, is that the capacity to conceive a newly structured reality is a powerful form of causation; and inequities in American education, no matter how firmly established and long-lasting, may give way before the will of people truly oriented toward changing such conditions.[88]

## CHAPTER THREE

Narrowing the Multiple Achievement Gaps in the United States

Eight Goals for the Long Haul

W. NORTON GRUBB

Differences in school outcomes among groups of students have been noted for a long time, at least back to the early nineteenth century, and some of these gaps—particularly those between immigrant and native-born students—were first quantified in the years around 1900.[1] Often these gaps have been defined in racial or ethnic terms, as they usually are now; sometimes as differences between native and immigrant students, or males and females, or students with and without certain disabilities, or (less often) differences due to family background. But the fact that these gaps are long-standing and have complex causes means that they are unlikely to be corrected quickly, or with a single policy like an accountability system. And achievement gaps take many forms, certainly in learning and test scores but also in progress through schooling, in attitudes and aspirations, and now in "college readiness." So narrowing the achievement gaps in this country will require many initiatives, carried out consistently over the long run.

In this chapter I outline eight goals or actions that could narrow many of the achievement gaps. This is my attempt to be relatively comprehensive, to outline the "landscape" of policies necessary for reducing achievement gaps. (In contrast, many existing analyses mention relatively few policies, and they cannot possibly reduce, never mind eliminate, the current gaps.[2]) Each of these eight goals is itself complex, and they are interdependent as well. For example, reducing dynamic inequality (Goal 1) requires enhancing and equalizing school capacity (Goal 2), as well as addressing the gaps due to race, ethnicity, and immigrant status (Goals 5 and 6); reducing racial and ethnic gaps (Goal 5) requires not only enhancing school capacity (Goal 2), but also providing a range of noneducational services in schools (Goal 7) and other social policies outside of education (Goal 8). Similarly, enhancing school capacity (Goal 2) must be done in different ways to address different types of gaps in outcomes (Goal 3).

Furthermore, all these goals require improvements in school resources. Usually this is interpreted as the need for more money—a view I call the Money Myth. But understanding the role that money does and does not play, and the kinds of resources (monetary and nonmonetary) necessary for successful schools, is a complex subject in its own right, and I return to this aspect of reducing achievement gaps in chapter 9.

The reforms outlined in this chapter are complex and politically difficult, and establishing priorities among them is no easy task. All of them are necessary to reduce achievement gaps substantially, and one purpose of this chapter is to clarify how large the challenge is. In light of these challenges, the many blithe statements about all students reaching proficiency by 2014 (in No Child Left Behind), or about *eliminating* (rather than *narrowing*) achievement gaps quickly, are simply foolish. Furthermore, different advocates will prefer some of these goals over others: advocates for students of color are likely to emphasize Goals 5 and 6; advocates for conventional and politically acceptable school reform will choose Goal 4 (improving interventions); and my own view is that the first goal—understanding and reducing dynamic inequality—is the most far-reaching. But even if there are disagreements over which goals to pursue in the short run, it will be necessary in the end to pay attention to all of them.

GOAL 1: DIAGNOSING AND REDUCING DYNAMIC INEQUALITY

At the outset, it is useful to have some conception of why achievement gaps are so pervasive in this country, and the conception of dynamic inequality helps explain this.[3] Children start their formal schooling, usually at kindergarten, with unequal capacities—both cognitive abilities (like knowledge of letters and numbers, vocabulary, and sophistication of language) and noncognitive capacities (like conceptions of what school is about and patterns of interactions with adults).[4] These differences are usually attributed to the effects of families and communities on young children, and narrowing these differences is the responsibility of early childhood and parent education programs. This explains why early childhood programs figure so prominently in most treatises on the achievement gap.

However, providing better and more widespread early childhood programs cannot by itself narrow achievement gaps.[5] Unfortunately, the differences that children come to school with tend to widen over time.[6] There are many reasons for this, including the psychology of learning (where "knowledge begets further knowledge"); the possibility that young students become discouraged by initial low performance and then become disengaged; the continuing effects of family background, where well-educated parents continue to be more effective teachers for their children than are poorly educated parents; the unequal allocation of school resources, where the most effective resources tend to be allocated to the best-performing students; and differences in the ability of teachers in different schools to keep up with grade-level norms and state standards. In addition, summer effects—where middle-class children continue to learn over the summer, while working-class children seem to lose ground—have explained some of the divergence in test scores in several districts, implying that year-round schools may help.[7] If all of these operate to some extent, *and* reinforce one another, this might explain why schooling outcomes diverge and expand over time so consistently.

Furthermore, there's no reason to think that learning trajectories are smooth and continuous. Instead, there are transitions where there may be sharp increases or "bursts" of inequality. At the transition into high school, for example, some students drop out and fail to learn further; some are placed in remedial or general tracks where their subsequent progress is low; some get into AP or honors tracks where their learning accelerates. The right-hand side of my NELS88 analyses illustrates such patterns, showing a burst of inequality from grade 8 to grade 10, with more modest increases thereafter.[8] But there are other points in the trajectory of schooling where such increases in inequality surely occur: at the transition from early childhood programs to kindergarten; sometimes in the third or fourth grade often called the "fourth-grade slump"), where many schools shift from "learning to read" to "reading to learn," leaving behind those students (including many English language learners) who have not yet mastered reading; and at the transition into middle school, where students encounter multiple teachers and subjects and are often assigned to different tracks.[9] So, the achievement gaps we see by grade 12 are the result of an extended process, with both different rates of learning and periods of transition with "spikes" of inequality. There is surely an even greater burst in inequality after high school, when about 60 percent of graduates enroll in a variety of colleges and postsecondary training programs, ranging from the best universities in the world to fraudulent trade schools.

In addition, dynamic inequality helps explain why we have a real crisis of remediation in this country. The lowest-performing students fall further and further behind grade-level norms as their schooling progresses. At certain points this gap becomes too large to ignore, and programs of remediation are created to help students catch up to grade-level (or college-level) norms—in programs called interventions in sixth and ninth grade, or in basic skills instruction or developmental education in the freshman year of virtually all community colleges and regional four-year colleges.

One worthy goal of the P-16 Councils established in many states would be to understand—through research and testimony—the dynamic process that creates the various achievement gaps by the end of college. Then a council could begin to create solutions that attack the problem at its causes—rather than, for example, waiting until students fail the early stages of high school exit exams, when test-prep courses might at best allow them to pass the exit exam but cannot in a short amount of time compensate for the gaps that have developed since the early grades. Some of these solutions would follow the subsequent goals in this chapter. For example, given the evidence that school resources contribute to greater inequality, enhancing school capacity (Goal 2) with multiple strategies (Goal 3) is necessary. Given the obviously widening differences by race, ethnicity, and language status, confronting these differences head on (in Goals 5 and 6) is necessary. A variety of support services (Goal 7) would be a strategy to counter the effects of low-income or inadequate access to health and mental health services.

A different set of solutions should focus on the transitions among levels of the schooling system and potential bursts of inequality at those points. For example, in the transition into kindergarten, the principal along with teachers can play a crucial role in creating welcoming environments and mechanisms of transition.[10] Some schools have devised programs where students in upper elementary grades who have not yet mastered basic reading and mathematical skills continue to be taught basic skills through techniques like differentiated instruction, even as they continue to they learn grade-level material. Some high schools have developed ninth-grade "academies" (schools-within-schools) or mentoring by upper-grade students to smooth the transition to the more anonymous high school, to provide basic skills instruction to those who need it, and to provide other services (especially guidance and counseling) to ensure that students understand high school requirements and the dire consequences of falling behind. But while remediation has been increasingly necessary and common, particularly in ninth grade and in both community and regional colleges, well-developed transition programs seem comparatively rare.

GOAL 2: ENHANCING SCHOOL CAPACITY AND RESOURCES

One reason for dynamic inequality is that low-performing students are typically in schools with fewer resources—not necessarily lower expenditures per student, but less qualified (or burned-out) teachers, weak leaders, unsupportive school climates, hostile personal relationships, and a lack of the systems that enhance learning and progression through education.[11] To summarize the argument of chapter 9, the resources that enhance educational outcomes include some simple resources that can be readily bought (as long as there are no budget constraints), like smaller class size, more experienced teachers, and more books and computer facilities and science labs. But they also include:

- *Compound* resources requiring several coordinated simple resources, such as class size reduction *plus* teachers trained to teach differently in smaller classes *plus* adequate facilities *plus* keeping the average quality of teachers high.
- *Complex* resources requiring extensive professional preparation and development, including innovative and "balanced" pedagogical approaches and specific practices to support racial and ethnic minority students, described in Goal 5.[12]
- *Abstract* resources, often embedded in a web of personal relationships within schools, like trust, curricular coherence, school climate, and stability.

All of these have demonstrable effects on different outcomes, but compound resources require coordination of several elements.[13] Complex and abstract resources cannot be readily bought—there's no store for improved instruction or a more supportive climate—and higher revenues per student do not lead to higher levels of these resources.[14] Instead, they must be constructed by teachers and school leaders—and often students and parents—working together in schools to create effective teaching, or to develop a supportive climate, or to coordinate approaches to an issue. Furthermore, as I will demonstrate in chapter 9, inequalities in these compound, complex, and abstract resources are generally higher than they are for simple resources and for spending per student—so reducing resource inequalities among students and thereby narrowing achievement gaps requires us to recognize the vast number of resources beyond money. In this approach to capacity building, Goal 2 requires first recognizing which of these resources affect schooling outcomes (and which do not), and then enhancing these effective resources in all schools.[15] I explore the variety of effective resources in chapter 9, but not surprisingly, they include various dimensions of teachers, leaders, climate, trust, stability, and organization.

A somewhat different analysis of what it means to build school capacity has emerged from the Chicago Consortium on School Research.[16] Based on the results from two hundred elementary schools between 1990 and 2005, the researchers' analysis separated schools into those with increasing levels of performance on reading and math tests, those with relatively steady performance, and those with declining performance. On examining these three groups of schools, they began to conceptualize five "pillars" of improving schools, each of which has several elements, and to develop statistical measures of each pillar. The first, and in many ways most important, pillar is strong leadership, which drives change in schools—then leaders concentrate on building a student-centered learning climate; a coherent *system* of instructional guidance; the professional capacities of teachers, teacher-leaders, and assistant principals; and strong parent-community ties. In my vocabulary, these "pillars" describe various kinds of compound, complex, and abstract resources, grouped in a way that clarifies the coherent systems of activities that need to take place within high-performing schools. Evidently, as for the effective resources in my analysis, the variation among schools in the strength of these "pillars" is considerable, helping explain why there are such great differences in schooling outcomes even in one district. Furthermore, as is true for virtually every analysis of schooling outcomes, family resources—measured here by the socioeconomic composition of neighborhoods and their racial/ethnic composition—influence outcomes (increases in average school test scores) directly; but in addition, schools in neighborhoods with greater social and economic resources are better able to develop the five pillars. The implication again is that narrowing the differences in schooling outcomes, and reducing the achievement gaps that come with them, requires building the capacities of schools by investing in the school resources described by the five pillars.

My emphasis on capacity building is an antidote to one of the great failures of the state and federal accountability systems of the past two decades. The existing accountability systems have certainly achieved one of their goals: schools are now paying attention to low-performing students as never before, and reducing achievement gaps is part of the vocabulary of school reform. Virtually all low-performing schools are obsessed with statistics on students who are below basic and far below basic, and most are targeting these students with special efforts—often called "interventions"—to improve their test scores. The problem, then, is not a lack of motivation to narrow achievements gaps, but a lack of capacity for many schools to help such students. Neither state nor federal accountability mechanisms come with the money and the other resources necessary to improve schools, and the result has been an "ordeal of inequality" in which schools have been under pressure to improve but don't have the capacity to do so.[17] The country's top priority should therefore be to enhance the resources in schools with low-performing students—understanding which of a broad range of resources matter—so that they can improve the quality of instruction and supporting environments for all students.[18]

GOAL 3: RECOGNIZING MULTIPLE GAPS AND MULTIPLE STRATEGIES

The achievement gap has most often been defined as differences in test scores, between blacks and whites or between whites and Latinos, on measures (often crude) of learning. However, there are other gaps that are just as if not more important, especially to the future abilities of students to earn their livings, participate politically, and become contributing members of their communities. Progress through schooling, as measured by suspensions and retentions in grade, is unequal among racial and ethnic groups; dropout rates from high school, which are particularly detrimental to future employment as well as college-going, are higher for Latino and African American students; attitudes toward schooling differ among groups, as does the desire for schooling past high school; more concretely, completion rates for the course requirements necessary for attending four-year colleges are unequal; and rates of college-going and completion are unequal as well. We should add a "college readiness gap" to the other gaps produced within the K–12 system.

Given different kinds of gaps, narrowing them may require different strategies. To be sure, some school resources affect virtually all types of outcomes; these include placement in traditional vocational, general, or remedial tracks; several dimensions of school climate; and access to counselors. But the majority of resources have *differential* rather than *common* effects: they influence some outcomes but not others. In particular, several kinds of evidence suggest that improving learning (and therefore test scores) requires explicit attention to the quality of teaching, including the use of innovative and "balanced" approaches. But improving the quality of teaching generally has little effect on progress through schooling. Conversely, progress through schooling is enhanced by resources that increase personal contact and student support, including more adults per student, help with academic subjects, and extracurricular activities. And student aspirations, including their assessment of whether they will continue their education past high school, are influenced by tracking and a school's climate, as well as several dimensions of family background such as maternal education and parental aspirations.

As corroboration, several whole-school reforms have been successful in increasing attendance, credits earned, aspirations, and other measures of student engagement, but they have not improved test scores. Only reforms that put special emphasis on reforming instruction, like First Things First, have been successful in improving both progress and learning.[19] So without *both* student support and personalization *and* the improvement of instruction, some of the many gaps will remain.

We can extend this argument to other kinds of gaps, particularly to "college readiness" now that college-going has become so necessary for personal advancement. In one of the most influential analyses, readiness includes: (1) basic academic preparation, often represented by the courses required for college admission; (2) conceptual understanding, cognitive strategies, and discipline-based ways of thinking, all poorly taught in conventional high schools but usually assumed in college courses; (3) "college knowledge," or information about the variety of colleges, their expectations, procedures for applying to college, and financial aid; and (4) behavioral capacities, including independence, initiative, flexibility, planning, and decision-making skills, all necessary for thriving in postsecondary institutions that provide few directives to students.[20]

Interviews with college students clarify that both the cognitive and the non-cognitive dimensions of college readiness are much more profound than many people realize. Many college students, especially those in community colleges, have had poor experiences in education and are understandably anxious—school is "not fun"—but their forms of fear management (like failing to seek help) are often counterproductive. Many have narrow conceptions of learning as information transfer, so the efforts of college instructors to engage them in discussion and argumentation are rebuffed, and they are often unfamiliar with the norms of academic approaches and literacies, which they disparage as "not relevant" or simply "stupid." Their lack of knowledge about what college-going involves makes it difficult to search for the right information, and many show little initiative in seeking out information and support. Their instructors often declare that they are "not ready to be college students"—that they don't do the reading, complete assignments, or come to class on time and lack basic academic skills—but the efforts to teach basic skills and "study skills" are either ineffective or fail to grasp the nature of the problem.[21] Therefore, narrowing the various gaps in college readiness—gaps often associated with poor academic preparation and counseling in high schools, to be sure, but also with the information and attitudes transmitted by parents who have gone to college versus those who have not—requires even greater resources than schools now provide.

The crucial point is that efforts to address only test score differences may leave other achievement gaps untouched. If our nation intends to narrow the many different achievement gaps, then it will need to support a broad variety of reforms.

GOAL 4: IMPROVING INTERVENTIONS AND RECOGNIZING THE LIMITS OF "PROGRAMMITIS"

Under recent systems of accountability, schools are under great pressure to improve the performance of low-performing students. In response, they have adopted a wide variety of practices to help these students. Unfortunately, the quality of these efforts varies widely from school to school and district to district.[22] Some schools have adopted relatively thorough reforms that have the potential for enhancing student success over the long run, and that improve the core instruction of a school rather than just adding small interventions here and there. For example, some schools have adopted a technique called differentiated instruction, which is intended to enable all teachers to reach students with a broad range of abilities. A few others have adopted a practice known as Learning Centers, which assess all students as they enter the school. Then the Learning Center team meets at least three times a year to consider the case of every student and develop plans similar to an Individual Education Plan (IEP) for all those who are below grade level. The impulse underlying Learning Centers has also emerged in the "movement" called Response to Intervention (RTI), which tries to provide early intervention to a subset of students by engaging in regular diagnosis, assigning students to different kinds of interventions (often called Tier 1, 2, and 3), with progressively greater specialization of services, smaller groups of students, and longer duration of intervention. Although some dimensions of RTI have been controversial, in theory it can create a coherent system of diagnosis and treatment extending to all students.

But many other schools, under pressure to improve test scores as quickly as possible, have adopted limited strategies and random interventions. Very often these are based on curriculum materials available from commercial publishers that promise to accelerate learning. Schools often choose such programs because of anecdotal evidence from nearby districts, or because the curricula are on the list of materials approved by the state board of education and are therefore assumed (incorrectly) to be "proven practices." While these interventions vary among schools—and therefore students receive inconsistent instruction of varying effectiveness—many are based on "remedial pedagogy," or drill and practice on limited subskills in reading and math, and neglect substantial evidence of the need for "balanced" instruction. Such students may be in four or five periods a day of English and math, and they will be unable to master the broader range of requirements necessary for college. This is a good example where one particular gap (in basic reading and math test scores) is emphasized to the exclusion of other gaps, including the ability to access public colleges (see Goal 3).

The strategy of adopting relatively self-contained interventions can also be labeled "programmitis," or the adoption of supplementary programs that leave the core of a school intact.[23] These are sometimes labeled "Christmas tree schools," with bright shiny baubles or "enrichment" programs hanging from a trunk and branches that are thoroughly rotten.

In addition, many schools with low-performing students have adopted after-school programs and tutoring efforts. However, these are usually taught or supervised by aides or volunteers, rather than well-trained teachers; they are voluntary, and may not reach the students most in need; and they are typically disconnected from "regular" classrooms, so their ability to reinforce the lessons of the classroom is limited. Although a consensus has developed on the characteristics of effective afterschool and tutoring programs, and some model programs appear to be quite effective, the lessons of this research have not been widely followed.[24]

There are, of course, sometimes good reasons for adopting specific programs—for example, when a school finds a weakness in second-grade math, or some students need additional time to master a concept, or a Learning Center or RTI evaluation identifies specific remedies for particular students. And there are similarly good reasons to continue evaluating self-contained programs, to see which of them work under which conditions. But "programmitis" should not be used as a substitute for systematic capacity building, as it sometimes is in schools that merely react to the pressures swirling around them rather than forging their own directions.

GOAL 5: ADDRESSING RACIAL AND ETHNIC ISSUES HEAD-ON

The conventional analysis of the achievement gap starts with differences defined in racial terms, particularly the black-white test-score gap, or the Latino-white gap. Then it moves to a number of potential remedies, but these remedies are almost always stated in race-neutral terms—for example, the need for improved teacher quality, or for more early childhood education—as if there were no specifically racial or ethnic dimension to the achievement gap.

Of course, some of the existing racial and ethnic gaps in achievement, progress, and college readiness can be attributed to school resources that need to be equalized (in Goal 2), and other racial/ethnic variations are due to differences in family background, some of which could be moderated by school services (Goal 7) or other noneducational policies (Goal 8). However, when I have tried to explain away racial and ethnic differences statistically—by attributing them to family background, to school resources, and to students' commitment to schooling—there remain differences that cannot be explained in any other way, equal to somewhere between 15 percent and 50 percent of the overall gap.[25] A knot of inequality related to race and ethnicity persists, even after careful analysis with the richest data set we have.

The first challenge this finding poses—to every educator, researcher, and policy maker—is to come up with some explanation for these gaps.[26] No doubt some will fall back on older genetic explanations, though recent research provides evidence that genetic differences are not to blame.[27] Others may point to dimensions of African American and Latino upbringing that are poorly measured in either quantitative or qualitative research, like the effects of violence in their communities and instability in their family lives.[28] However, when I look at the lives of children in schools, there is substantial evidence to suggest that some part of achievement gaps is caused by mistreatment in schools—mistreatment that is surely worse for racial minority students than for white and most Asian American students.[29] Mistreatment can take many forms. Sometimes it consists of paying less attention to some students compared to others. Sometimes it takes the form of lower expectations, something that has been well documented for African American and other minority students.[30] Sometimes it means there are fewer adults who can serve as mentors and sponsors. Sometimes students are corrected sharply for use of nonstandard English and behavior thought inappropriate to school. Discipline policies tend to treat black and Latino students more harshly than middle-class white students, and the overrepresentation of black males in retentions, expulsions, and special education has been a particular concern. Discipline, especially zero-tolerance policies, often reduces the amount of schooling available to some students as they are suspended, expelled, or subjected to further humiliation.[31] The concept of "stereotype threat" has documented the extent to which racial minority students turn inward and perform less well if they think they are being stereotyped; a related literature has examined the effects of perceived discrimination on school performance.[32]

The mistreatment of racial minority students is consistent with the steady alienation of some students from school, the kind of progressive disengagement that finally leads a disproportionate number of black and Latino students to drop out. If we believe that all students have the right to be treated decently in schools, then these patterns need to be changed. Fortunately, there are many ways of doing so:

- The practice of classroom observation—which appears to be increasing, especially in elementary and middle schools—can identify many kinds of teacher behavior, conscious and unconscious. Observation, reflection, and discussion of teaching patterns may allow some teachers to see where their behavior is inappropriate, particularly if this occurs within a school with high levels of trust and cooperation.
- Disciplinary policies are often the source of great conflict between educators and students, especially African American and Latino males. The analysis of discipline data has become more common. It often identifies not only which students are responsible for a large proportion of discipline problems, but also which teachers are responsible, potentially alerting administrators to examine their teaching and disciplinary practices.
- Techniques exist for correcting nonstandard English (including Black Vernacular English, or Ebonics) as well as teacher behaviors that avoid the harsh corrections of standard practices. These methods involve analyzing the differences in speech and behavior in many settings ("contrastive analysis") and then teaching children to code-switch, to speak and behave differently in different settings (as all adults do too), and to adopt repertoires of language practices for different purposes and settings.[33]
- Some schools have engaged in efforts to talk more forthrightly about racial issues as a way of clarifying not only the problems that students face but also the frustrations teachers feel, potentially leading to collective understanding about racial/ethnic dilemmas. These "courageous conversations" can replace the awkward "race talk" that often takes place in schools with greater

understanding of the norms of African American, Latino, and immigrant students and others likely to be mistreated.[34]

• A vast number of practices have developed under the umbrella of culturally relevant pedagogy and multicultural education.[35] Some of these—modifying the English literature selections in minor ways—are already widely practiced. Others—cultivating critical attitudes toward race relations in this country—go further than some schools and faculty may be able to go. But all these practices intend to create the schooling conditions in which racial minority students can do better, and they constitute a portfolio of options for schools that want to improve the learning of minority students.

To be sure, racial and ethnic issues are among the most difficult and contentious in our society, and it's not surprising that they are difficult and contentious in public education as well. Normally, these are issues that need to be diagnosed and addressed at the school level, among teachers and leaders who trust one another. Developing a culture of supportive classroom observations and inspections might also help, as would appropriate discipline policies.[36] But these are not issues that can be mandated or required, put into a state assessment system, or remedied overnight, and so—as important as it is to confront the issue of mistreatment—it is equally important to take great care in devising solutions.

GOAL 6: ADDRESSING THE ISSUES OF IMMIGRANT STUDENTS AND ENGLISH LANGUAGE LEARNERS

The United States has always been a nation of immigrants. Currently, immigrant students are a high and increasing proportion of public school students, and this trend is almost sure to continue.[37] The school performance of immigrant students is, on almost every dimension, below that of native-born students. So, it is impossible to narrow the achievement gaps in this country without addressing forthrightly the unique needs of these students.

A first problem is that many immigrant students and English language learners suffer from unequal resources—the issue in Goal 2 above. They have less access to teachers who are fully credentialed, who speak their language or understand their backgrounds, and who have specialized training in methods of second-language acquisition. Their schools have inadequate professional development to help teachers address the instructional needs of English learners. They suffer from inadequate time to meet a variety of learning goals, especially when they are pulled out of regular classes for English Language Development (ELD) or English as a Second Language (ESL) classes. They are more likely to be in dilapidated schools, and they are highly segregated in schools dominated by English learners, rather than having peers from whom they can learn.[38] Some of these problems could be remedied by enhancing the resources of their schools and paying special attention to the quality and professional development of teachers, the use of time, and physical facilities.

A second problem involves English language instruction, and the balance between the use of English learners' native languages (called L1) and English (the second language, or L2). An enormous range of practices now exists, including English immersion programs, English as a Second Language taught entirely in English, Specifically Designed Academic Instruction in English (SDAIE) focusing on subject-matter content taught largely in English, structured immersion with some support in the native language, two-way immersion programs where English learners and native English speakers learn in both languages, and bilingual/bicultural education designed to support a student's original language and culture *and* to promote fluid English and understanding of U.S. norms. These approaches vary in the relative use of L1 and L2, in the nature of teachers and other resources required, and in assumptions about language acquisition. Even for teachers using English-only approaches (like structured immersion), there are techniques like frontloading (teaching the linguistic demands of a task explicitly and up front), using illustrations, developing graphic organizers and word banks, and using vocabulary intentionally and strategically that help students learn more effectively.[39]

Not surprisingly, the effectiveness of these different approaches to second-language learning has been extremely contentious. However, the most recent review of the research suggests that a rough consensus has developed:[40]

- A student's native language (L1) and the language to be learned (L2, or English) are complementary to one another, not antagonistic, and specific aspects of L1 enhance oral and literary development in L2. In general then, English-only approaches are less effective than forms of bilingual instruction.
- Specific aspects of L1 are more influential in the development of L2—for example, basic literacy skills in the home language.
- The best teaching situations involve interactive classes with direct instruction of L2 that is focused on literacy and "academic" use of English rather than "everyday" English.
- Substantial differences exist among groups of English learners. Therefore, no one approach to language instruction can work well for all ELLs; instead, appropriate approaches must be developed at the *school* level to meet the needs of the specific groups of students each school has.
- The duration of special language instruction is significant since it takes considerable time to master a new language—from five to ten years, in one estimate.[41] Students who arrive in the United States in first or second grade may

catch up with their native-speaking peers by twelfth grade, but it is unreasonable to assume that students arriving during high school can catch up in a short period of time.

- The consistency of second-language instruction is important, and students exposed to a variety of approaches perform less well than those who have had the same approach.

Overall, these findings imply that educators need to use a portfolio of alternative approaches for ELL students, using both L1 and L2, with specific approaches geared to the needs of students and consistent over time. In contrast, the dominant practice is for ELL students to be in pull-out programs using ESL or ELD, which are "subtractive" approaches in at least two ways: students are unable to make progress in the subjects from which they are pulled out, and these English-only approaches tend to substitute English for native languages, rather than treating L1 and L2 as complementary.[42]

A third need for many immigrant students (and some second-generation students as well) is for support services to help with noninstructional aspects of progress through schooling, including knowledge of American norms, the value of and methods of access to college, and other cultural lore that immigrants don't automatically know—all part of Goal 7. Fourth, immigrant students—like native-born racial and ethnic minority students—suffer many of the forms of mistreatment mentioned in Goal 5.[43] The various mechanisms for addressing this issue—including classroom observations, discussions of race and immigration, and culturally relevant approaches (as in Puente programs in California)—would therefore help narrow the gaps between English learners and native speakers of English.

In a nation of immigrants, the roles of public schools have been crucial for their children, but the attitudes of American schools have varied: sometimes welcoming and supportive, sometimes assimilationist, sometimes hostile and rejecting. But immigration is a permanent part of this country. The public schools are virtually the only institution we have to welcome all children, including the children of immigrants, into our society and to enable them to become productive citizens, workers, and community members, and the nation should recognize its obligations to these groups.

GOAL 7: RECOGNIZING NONSCHOOL SOURCES OF ACHIEVEMENT GAPS AND PROVIDING SUPPORT SERVICES

Most of the initial differences among young students are due to elements of family background—especially, in my NELS88 analyses, variation in mother's education and in parental aspirations for their children. These and other aspects of families and communities also help explain why growth trajectories continue to diverge as students move up in grade level. Indeed, these noneducational sources of divergence are probably greater in the United States than in other developed countries, because our country is among the most inequitable of all developed countries, whether measured conventionally by the distribution of income or by other measures such as access to health care.[44] Many low-performing students therefore have unmet noneducational needs as well as educational needs, ranging from nutrition to health and mental health services to family support services. Adolescents in particular face a variety of perils, including drug and alcohol abuse, teenage pregnancy, family conflicts, and numerous mental health conditions.

A number of proposals have responded to the evident need for noneducational services—even though these have been controversial.[45] The vision of "full-service schools" views the school as a center where students receive a full range of support services.[46] The vision of community schools is similar, with public schools serving as hubs to provide a variety of supports and opportunities to children through community-based organizations. A more thorough approach has followed the Harlem Children's Zone, which provides a rich array of services along with schooling in a thirty-block area of Harlem. The Obama administration has vowed to replicate this model by funding a series of Promise Neighborhoods, concentrating many services in distinct neighborhoods, "building a college-going culture in the neighborhood; building a continuum of academic programs and family and community supports, from the cradle through college to career, with a strong school or schools at the center; integrating programs and breaking down agency 'silos.'"[47] In other schools and communities, school-based health centers provide a variety of physical and mental health services, depending on the funds available and on local norms (conservative towns are unlikely to support the distribution of condoms, for example).

Where funding for these comprehensive approaches is unavailable, many schools with low-performing students try to cobble together various support services, usually by identifying community-based organizations or public organizations willing to provide services either at the school site or nearby. In some communities, municipalities have teamed with the school district to provide these services; at others, "hero-principals" have managed through intense effort to scrounge up services, or foundations have contributed to various support services in individual schools or a network of schools. But all of these are inadequate ways to provide a full range of services. Some cities provide very little funding, there are not enough hero-principals to lead all schools, and foundation support is uneven at best. In addition, placing the burden for finding support services on schools and their principals is inappropriate: principals do not necessarily have the right expertise, and the effort takes them away from instructional improvement that should be their primary responsibility.

The first challenge, therefore, is to make the provision of support services systematic—by establishing Promise Neighborhoods in all high-need regions, for example, or providing comprehensive school-based health centers in all low-performing schools. Indeed, the prospect of universal health coverage may offer support in the future, particularly to school-based health centers. The legislation enacted in 2010 provides for funding of school-based health centers, though appropriations are still lacking and many administrative hurdles have to be overcome. But slowly, through different avenues, the idea of comprehensive support services for children and youth seems to be taking hold.

A second challenge is to integrate services into the fabric of the school. The conventional service model refers students to support services that are usually seen as external to the school, dealing with problems one student at a time, and assuming that *students* themselves (or their families) are the source of any problems. An alternative view, particularly in many urban schools, is that *schools* are part of the problem, especially in large, impersonal schools (like high schools) where it seems that "nobody cares," where students are alienated from their coursework, and where experiences of failure—exacerbated by high-stakes accountability exams and high school exit exams—are pervasive. In contrast, where schools foster feelings of connectedness and being cared for by teachers, other adults, and peers, students are less likely to experience emotional distress, use alcohol and drugs, engage in violent behavior, or become pregnant.[48] This implies that reforming a school's climate and instruction (part of Goal 2) may be a necessary part of alleviating some nonacademic problems, including mental health issues that interfere with learning.

In turn this suggests a tripartite division of responsibility, with school reforms, school-based health centers, and a rich array of afterschool activities supporting one another and providing the array of both instructional activities and noninstructional supports that students might need.[49] Such a tripartite approach might be resisted, particularly because public schools have historically been somewhat hostile to incorporating nonacademic supports into what has been an academic institution. But this model corrects some of the problems with other approaches to the provision of nonacademic services, and provides a stronger alternative for schools to embrace.

GOAL 8: RECOGNIZING NONSCHOOL SOURCES OF ACHIEVEMENT GAPS: OTHER NONEDUCATIONAL POLICIES

Although comprehensive support services alleviate some of the problems associated with poverty, high-stress neighborhoods, and other family and community influences, others cannot be so easily remedied by discrete services. For example, housing problems often lead to mobility as low-income families have to find new housing, and we know that mobility lowers school achievement.[50] The violence in some inner cities causes enormous stress among youth who live there, and reducing violence is surely a better approach than trying to create better coping mechanisms in mental health centers. As a result, countering the nonschool sources of achievement gaps requires noneducational policies that are complementary to schooling, that make the tasks of educators easier rather than harder. In particular, such an approach would require the following:

- *Housing policies to minimize the mobility of low-income students* whose parents have problems finding stable housing. Since mobility is detrimental to progress through schooling, housing subsidies and public housing should aim to maximize stability.
- *Urban development policies,* so that no student is surrounded by decay and violence. These in turn need to be complemented by locational policies that operate against the creation of ghettos, including regulation of housing loans and redlining, careful attention to exclusionary zoning, an increase in mixed-income housing and mixed-use development, and the careful location of public amenities.
- *Income-support policies* to help offset the effects of low income on learning and college-going. Specific ways to enhance incomes vary and include minimum wage legislation, tax and transfer policies like the earned income tax credit, and food stamps and other nutrition policies. The list of antipoverty mechanisms varies among advocates, but there are many from which to choose.
- *Labor market policies* to counter the hideous growth of inequality in this country. This might include more powerful minimum wage laws, real enforcement of antidiscrimination laws, efforts to make labor organizations easier to organize, and better accountability of obscenely paid managers to stockholders and regulatory agencies.
- *A full range of health services,* so that poor health does not compromise a student's education. Indeed, reforming health care could be one of the most important equity policies for a wide range of citizens.[51]
- *Family support and child welfare programs* to reduce violence against and neglect of children.

Of course, implementing these policies requires a resurrection of the welfare state, which has always been particularly limited in the United States and which is currently under attack from Republicans, the Tea Party, and others who have abandoned faith in government. But those who believe the popular rhetoric about eliminating achievement gaps, or making all students proficient, or addressing "the devastating waste of human potential and severe economic costs to our country" of failing to educate poor children, need to understand that the costs of doing so extend to reshaping policy in all spheres, not just in education.[52]

ACHIEVING THESE GOALS: RESOURCES, REORGANIZATION, AND CONSISTENCY

The reform agenda presented here is enormous, of course, and politically difficult. It couldn't be otherwise: achievement gaps have long been in existence, they have been extremely resistant to significant reduction, and they have been noted in many other countries (even if they take somewhat different forms). Clearly such gaps are rooted in the inequalities that affect most societies, capitalist and noncapitalist, even those societies that are relatively egalitarian and have stronger welfare states. That's the problem with inequality: it works in so many different and interrelated ways (as the analysis of dynamic inequality in Goal 1 clarified) that moderating it, never mind eliminating it, requires multiple and interrelated reforms.

Of course, achieving these eight goals will require resources. It helps, in a time of fiscal crisis, that these resources are not always monetary; as I clarify more completely in chapter 9, some resources can be constructed, by leaders and teachers working collaboratively. But by the same token, the constant withdrawal of funding, as we have seen in some states, makes reform impossible by burdening educators with too many roles and tasks, leaving them no time or energy for reform. Some of the resources necessary for reform include stability, slack (or some time and energy), persistence in reform efforts over time, and (as I will argue later in this section) consistency among the participants. If the current fiscal crisis undermines these kinds of resources, then we will need to wait for a complete economic recovery to address the achievement gaps.

Not only will reforms to close the achievement gap need various resources, they may also require organizational changes at various levels of the schooling system. Indeed, some evidence suggests that schools need to be reorganized to make *any* decisions at all leading to improvement. Many schools held up as exemplars have abandoned the conventional organization emerging from the Progressive Era, around 1900—where the principal makes most decisions and teachers are relatively isolated in their classrooms—with various forms of distributed leadership, where leadership responsibilities are distributed among teachers and formal leaders. Then teachers play active leadership roles as members or heads of committees, making crucial decisions about curriculum, budget, or other policies; parents and students also have important roles in the ongoing procedures.

A complementary vision stresses the nature of relationships within schools. Schools that are most successful in responding to *external* accountability—standards imposed by state and federal governments—are those that have developed *internal* accountability, of teachers and leaders to one another, of teachers to one another, of adults in the school toward students and parents. Still others have called this kind of school a learning community, stressing that collective decision making requires a community of practice. This approach is also consistent with the importance of "buy-in" from teachers, of trust in schools, and of the need to establish better personal relations, in place of the hostile relationships in many urban schools particularly.[53] It also reflects the fact that some of the most effective resources in schools are not simple resources, but instead are compound, complex, or abstract, all of which are collective resources that need to be constructed by a school community (see Goal 1).

Similarly, the evidence about high-performing elementary schools in Chicago, cited under Goal 2, indicates that successful schools organize themselves and operate in different ways.[54] Principals are crucial to reforms, but they work by enlisting teachers in the change effort; by cultivating a cadre of leaders, including parents and community members as well as teachers; and by establishing strategic priorities for using resources—distributed leadership by another name. Then these successful schools establish student-centered learning climates, including a safe and orderly environment as well as ambitious academic work; develop a coherent instructional guidance *system* incorporating learning tasks, assessments, materials, and instructional routines; and enhance the capacity of the school's staff—rather than, for example, investing in "programmitis." Finally, they establish strong parent-community-school ties. In every way, then, these successful schools organize themselves very differently from traditional schools with top down leadership, isolated teachers, idiosyncratic approaches to instruction, and relative distance from parents and community members.

To extend this argument further, some evidence indicates that high-performing *districts* also follow the organization of distributed leadership and learning communities. Several analyses of high-performing districts in California found the importance of having a coherent strategy for maintaining focus and for building capacity (see Goal 2), especially through professional development to enhance the instructional capabilities of teachers. These districts focused on instructional improvement, not political issues; they showed how district officials as well as principals can be instructional leaders. They also developed a balance between centralized policies and decentralized or school control—the district version of distributed leadership. Other analyses of districts outside California have confirmed many of these findings.[55] Districts able to respond to state policies depend on their capacity to learn new policy ideas, which in turn depend on a commitment to learning continuously about instruction, on relations of trust and collaboration within a district (sometimes described explicitly as a learning community at the district level), and on district willingness to engage in problem solving rather than controlling power. Similarly, a study of district responses to state accountability found that "enterprising districts" worked more actively with schools, got to know individual schools well enough to understand their strengths and weaknesses, and again served as problem solvers. "Slacking" districts used the same approaches for all schools and usually acted passively, waiting for schools to ask for help rather than clarifying central goals. Many studies have found that successful districts focus on instruction—the district equivalent of principals as instructional leaders—and on developing roles for the district office of guiding and supporting instructional improvements at the school level.[56]

Overall, there are many consistencies between these apparently successful *districts*—in their focus on improved instruction, their use of "balanced" teaching approaches, the ways they have developed interventions, the balance between district and school policy making, the efforts to operate in more collegial ways—and the *schools* operating in more "distributed" ways focused on instruction. Conversely, schools and districts operating in traditional ways have the most difficulty with reform, indicating that reorganization may be necessary, even though it may not be sufficient.

Above all, using resources and reorganization to achieve the eight goals outlined in this chapter provides the way to resurrect the promise of public education, articulated in the nineteenth century. When early reformers critiqued differences in student opportunities, and when Horace Mann called education "a great equalizer of the conditions of men, the balance wheel of the social machinery," they championed a form of schooling in which equity and democracy were the great benefits, not individual advancement to the detriment of others. The persistence of achievement gaps is an insult to this vision of schooling, but careful attention to its many causes and manifestations can bring us back to this noble ideal.

CHAPTER FOUR

The Achievement Gap
in California and Beyond

Context, Status, and Approaches
for Improvement

EVA L. BAKER, NOELLE C. GRIFFIN,
AND KILCHAN CHOI

This chapter describes the national achievement gap in education and, in particular, its relevance to California. We speculate with wavering enthusiasm what might be done about it in the realm of standards, measures, and relevant activities to mitigate our current status. The urgency of the U.S. situation is growing, as our nation's performance drops with most precollegiate international comparisons. Within the United States, as poorly as it generally sits in the international context, we look specifically at California, one of the lower-performing states. We provide shortened summaries of data to avoid overlap with other authors in the volume. In our commentary on California, we will consider outcomes and subgroup performance across a range of indicators, with most of our emphasis on the tested grades in elementary and secondary schools, although we have studied data from higher education and preschool levels for greater context.

DEFINING AND EXPLAINING ACHIEVEMENT GAPS

The charge to the authors of this chapter was to understand the gap in light of the measures and assessment policies now in place, which inevitably brings us to consideration of goals, now termed standards. The revision in state-by-state standards is being accomplished by the development of the Common Core State Standards (CCSS), developed under the auspices of the Council of Chief State School Officers (CCSSO) and the National Governors Association (NGA) and with funding from the new state consortia to measure CCSS standards. These standards are intelligently developed and carefully written, and suffer perhaps only in their ambition, an orientation in weak supply in much of U.S. education. The emergence of the standards will resolve into paperwork unless means are found to translate them into feasible instruction by well-prepared teachers. While policy makers see their development more strongly linked to high-quality assessment, considerable effort is required to assure that the standards will be assessed and interpreted as intended, and are written to support the extensive range of purposes they serve. Not only is the match of purposes, measures, and useful instructional interpretations essential, this reform cycle demands an as yet unrealized ramp-up of the quality and frequency of evidence of validity for each purpose. A new set of standards, with a wider geographical arc, calls for special attention to the transitions from older standards and tests, and technical quality indicators beginning with tests but addressing the entire system. These quality indicators include the balance between focus and comprehensiveness, creativity and accuracy, as well as fairness to all students, and evidence that the scores on assessments advance through means other than test practice.

What should be clear in the ensuing discussion is that the differences found among subgroups are not artifacts of measurement nor can they be ethically eliminated by simply changing measures, indicators, and cut scores. However, if measurement is a cue to practice, there may be important ways to create greater intellectual and social coherence in schools and to provide the everyday supports that teachers need so that all students, against many odds, may attain the knowledge, skills, propensities, and understandings that will help them succeed in school and beyond.

Defining Achievement Gaps

When two or more groups have severe, persistent discrepancies in formally measured academic performance, the phenomenon is commonly called an "achievement gap." A one-time moderate difference may not qualify as a "gap"; rather, differences should be obvious and relatively severe on a range of common measures and indicators. A second criterion, gap persistence, suggests that the discrepancies among compared groups are empirically intransigent; that is, they have not been overcome or moderated significantly by available interventions. The reality is that there is considerable overlap on a wide variety of measures, which documents that members of lower-performing subgroups do achieve in the higher ranges. In other words, overlap among groups is a fact and it is a mistake to assume that membership in a subgroup implies that individuals do not share strengths and weaknesses with members of other groups. Far more troubling is gaps' implacability in the face of interventions.

The language of "gap" is unsuccessful and simplistic. Metrics may be useful to determine progress rather than averages. To state the obvious, the rate of growth of lower-achieving groups needs to greatly exceed that of the higher-performing group(s). This suggests that gap mitigation could occur only when lower-performing students receive higher-quality, more-intense, and expanded instruction than they have experienced; in other words, they are taught what they need to catch up. This requirement rises above the frequent argument for *equivalent* "opportunities to learn" (OTL). The equal OTL position has been advanced because it has been clearly documented that poorer-performing students often have less well qualified teachers, fewer instructional resources, and more limited choices of content and courses. In later discussion we will suggest that lower- and higher-performing students have demonstrably different experiences. There is evidence that students in lower-performing groups show better rates of progress in schools that have higher-performing students in the plurality, a fact suggesting their responsiveness to higher-quality instruction. We also see greater variation within schools than between schools.

We suggest that a marker approach be taken to monitor progress on closing the achievement gap. We think it wise to consider the phases of progress that would need to be marked to indicate that substantial, sustained progress is being made. It is likely, and is historically the case, that closing the gap is too big a jump to claim in a three-year period, for instance. Core content and skills that underlie multiple requirements at a higher level should be the target of markers. The first marker would occur when rates of progress from different groups were shown to be equal (imagine groups of students progressing on higher or lower but parallel lines). A second marker would light up when lines of student group performance, or progress toward gap reduction, converge. Another marker would be triggered by the growth in the overlap of lower-performing groups with respect to other groups. This growth needs to be inspected not only in the frequency of students who move between categories (e.g., "Basic"), but also in the actual performance on subscales of the target examinations. In that latter case, we could tell if progress was being made that did not yet show up on overall student achievement classification.

To close an achievement gap usually comes at a cost. There are critics who argue that addressing the lower group's performance always comes at the expense of increasing the higher group's performance. As a consequence, parents may shop for better schools in either the private or public sectors. However, recent analyses of Programme for International Student Assessment (PISA) data show that bringing up poor-performing students to desired standards may occur without negative consequences for higher-performing groups.[1] The PISA data suggest that among higher-performing countries, differences can be reduced either when performance of high-performing students remains more or less equivalent and lower-performing students increase, or, in some cases, when both groups can continue to make significant gains.

This finding raises the question of the relevance of "gap" as a construct. Perhaps it is more appropriate to discuss fairness and focusing on balancing the interests of all children (and their parents). The U.S. economy in global competition needs all students to excel, including the very best. U.S. policy could make great strides by understanding international approaches and adapting those that fit our context. Unfortunately, in the United States, education and effort required to succeed are less prized, less a part of the endemic cultural values, vitiating the impact of imported approaches. Questions, although bald and uncomfortable, need to be confronted about celebrity, anti-intellectualism, the effect of politics, and the affection for the short term demonstrated in many sectors of society. If the United States has any chance to maintain or even rise above the midpoint in international comparisons, the question is what to do about values, not standards and tests.

Explanation of Gaps: International and National Context

Two contrary views are taken by experts considering seemingly intractable differences in achievement among subgroups. One view is that persistent and resistant gaps are caused *principally* by out-of-school factors, such as parental background, cultural values, and social capital, all linked to parental education and economic status.[2] The other perspective holds that differences in performance can be addressed significantly by management action within the education system; in other words, through dicta of educational policy, emanating from outside the school, at the district, state, or federal level.[3] If one buys into the first view, of the incontrovertible structural sources impinging on academic performance and attitudes, at least two inferences can be made: that early background plays an essential and invariant role, and that "catching up" is an unlikely outcome without fundamental social change.[4] This view argues that lofty notions of social justice can be operationalized by driving down the correlation between background and performance. The second view in the U.S. educational system, that educational policy can change performance, has operated for more than forty years. In the international community, educational policies have resulted in demonstrable change, while in the United States, policy-initiated interventions by the federal and state governments over the decades have yielded no dramatic effects (as discussed in chapter 11).

To the question "Is there a serious achievement gap?" between the United States and the rest of the world, the answer is yes. Although the research in the area of international comparisons is extensive and not without its critics, we summarize below the performance of the United States as documented in PISA findings.[5] PISA comparisons focus on the mathematics performance of fifteen-year-olds in more than forty countries, thirty of which are members of the Organisation for

Economic Co-Operation and Development (OECD).[6] Collaborative content math, science, and reading examinations were developed through iterative frameworks to guide test item and task selection, with an emphasis on problem-solving skills. Detailed OECD findings can be found on the agency's Web site (http://www.oecd.org/).

How did the United States perform? In a nutshell, the United States ranked twenty-fifth among the thirty OECD participating countries in 2006 in science, slightly lower than its twenty-three of twenty-nine ranking in mathematics in 2003.[7] At the top of the distribution were Taipei, Finland, Hong Kong–China, Korea, the Netherlands, Switzerland, and Canada. At the lowest end of performance were Kyrgyzstan, Qatar, Tunisia, Brazil, Colombia, Argentina, and Jordan. Not statistically different from scores of U.S. students were Croatia, Portugal, Spain, Azerbaijan, and the Russian Federation. In 2009, in reading, the United States fared somewhat better, performing around the average of all countries. In English-speaking countries, all except the United Kingdom scored above the United States in literacy. On the mathematics scale the United States performance was not significantly different from the average OECD score.

But note this: when 2006 science performance is adjusted for levels of gross national product, school expenditures, and responses to the economic, social, and cultural status (ESCS) scale, U.S. students' performance dramatically drops, underperforming their peers in countries with similar economic characteristics.

Furthermore, when comparisons are made on an "equity" dimension, where the effects of different economic status within countries are compared, U.S. school intake characteristics account for about 30 score points for each .5 standard deviation on the school characteristics measure (comparable to the OECD average), whereas individual status accounts for about 15 points on the mathematics examinations (high compared to OECD countries). In summary, using the equity data above, the U.S. performance is below the average rank of all countries, considerably below OECD member countries, and shows higher impact of individual student socioeconomic status; also, the United States does not show increasing performance by subsequent generations of immigrants to the point of approaching native-born performance. Australia, by contrast, with a small population but a high level of immigration, shows a difference between first-generation and native-born performance of three points, and of two points between native and second-generation students. In conclusion, we point to the obvious. The United States is not in a leadership position on the PISA measure, either in terms of overall student achievement or in the nature of achievement gaps.

Using the international context as a frame, we now turn to national findings regarding the achievement gap. The measure used nationally to monitor student achievement since the early 1990s is the National Assessment of Educational

Progress (NAEP).[8] NAEP assessments are implemented across multiple grades and subjects, but as part of the Nation's Report Card overall, and subgroup findings are reported for grades 4 and 8 in math and reading.[9] For key student subgroups, we will address overall trends in NAEP achievement gaps.

To summarize voluminous data—gaps persist, although they vary over time. African American students have the greatest gaps and only fitful progress. Can this intransigence be attributed to diversity within a state? Apparently not, where California scores below national averages and equally diverse states such as Florida and New York score above.

As with African American students, overall NAEP scores for Hispanic students have increased over time, but the gaps between white and Hispanic students persist, with no statistically significant change in the gap between white and Hispanic math scores from 2003 to 2007. In the area of reading, the score gap between white and Hispanic students also persists. It is also worth noting that overall levels of achievement differ widely for Hispanic students among states with large Hispanic populations. Hispanic students in Florida exceed California student performance in grade 4 reading by 23 points.

Comparisons between African American and Hispanic students add some additional information to the picture. For example, in grade 4 mathematics, there is no difference on NAEP scores found between the two groups, but, by grade 8, Hispanics outperform African Americans by 3 points. In reading, grade 4 African American students have a 5-point superiority, but the balance switches by grade 8 to a 2-point advantage by Hispanics. One could conclude from the data that there is a relative acceleration of performance for Hispanics when compared with African Americans in both reading and math.

CALIFORNIA: A CASE STUDY

As noted above, California's performance has been in the lower ranks of states overall in NAEP scores for the years examined for this report: 1990, 1998, 2002, 2003, 2007, and 2009. For example, the state was ranked 48th in grade 4 mathematics, 46th in grade 8 mathematics, and 49th in both grades 4 and 8 reading in 2007. It is also worth noting that California is in the lower ranks internationally. For example, in a recent analysis that equated international results from the Trends in International Mathematics and Science Study (TIMSS) with NAEP scores, California students scored at a level approximately one-third of the top country's score.[10] The purpose of this section is to examine as a case study trends in achievement gaps evident in existing California data based on its own state tests, as yet unchanged by the Common Core State Standards and attendant measures.

The foregoing discussion places the United States on a slide, with California near the U.S. bottom. Within the state, the principal measure of achievement is data from the California Standards Tests (CST). These tests are given in a range of content areas, but we focus on English language arts (ELA) and mathematics, which are completed by grades 2–11 and 2–9, respectively, and the California High School Exit Exam (CAHSEE) in math and language arts, offered to students starting in grade 10, with passing CAHSEE a graduation requirement.[11] The API (Academic Performance Index) is a school-level measure based on weighted state tests that provides both achievement targets and meaningful matched comparisons. Each of these measures is briefly discussed below in relation to specific student subgroups for two recent data years (2006–2007).

African American students scored lower than all other ethnic groups, across all grade levels and across both years on the API, although the gaps were slightly smaller in 2007 than 2006. There is some fluctuation in the gap across grade levels, but no linear increase. For example, in 2007 there was a 169-point gap between white and African American groups at grades 9–11, and a 178-point gap at grades 7–8. Although this shift suggests some consistency in the achievement gap, possible changes in the student population over time need to be considered when interpreting these results. For example, dropout rates (grade 9 and above) tend to be higher in student groups on the lower end of the achievement gap, such as Hispanic and African American students.[12] So it can be inferred that the African American and Hispanic student subgroups at the upper grades have disproportionately lost their lower-achieving students compared to other groups. Hispanic students show similar patterns using the API, with a slight decrease in the gap over the years. For example, in 2006 and 2007 there were 145- and 140-point gaps between Hispanic and white students, showing a small reduction trend.

Examination of data publicly available through the California Department of Education (CDE) Web site shows that the percentage of students proficient on CST tends to decrease by grade level across most ethnic groups and content areas, with students at the elementary level showing higher proficiency rates than students in middle school and, in particular, high school.[13] Thus, the gaps remain apparent across grades even though individual scores may change. For example, for test score year 2007, 66 percent of white students and 39 percent of African American students in grade 2 were proficient or above on English language arts, while only 55 percent and 23 percent, respectively, achieved proficiency at grade 10.[14]

Hispanic students have a lower percentage proficient than all other ethnic groups for English language arts, and for all groups except African Americans in math.[15] Growth over the years in the percentage of Hispanic students rating proficient was equal to or less than other ethnic groups in ELA, and only higher than African American and white students (by one percentage point) in math. Again, gaps between Hispanic students and higher-achieving groups start at the earlier grades, and persist through high school.[16]

Additional information can be gained from examining the most recent (2007) results available for students at the lowest levels of proficiency, that is, those in the "far below basic" category on the CST (California Department of Education, 2008). Across grades and content areas in math, language arts, and also science, African American and Hispanic students have the highest percentages of students in this group compared to other ethnic groups, with the percentage of "far below basic" African American students matching, and often exceeding, the percentage of Hispanic students.[17]

Looking at the end of California students' K–12 educational experience, a similar pattern can be found across multiple years of the CAHSEE. African American students have lower pass rates for both math and language arts across the years than white, Asian, and Filipino students.[18] CAHSEE pass rates for Hispanic students are similar to those for African American students in ELA, but slightly higher in math. For example, in 2006 approximately 50 percent of African American and Hispanic CAHSEE takers passed the ELA portion, while the numbers for math were 40 percent and 49 percent, respectively.[19]

RESEARCH ON ACHIEVEMENT GAP REDUCTION

There is a large body of research, theory, and debate about the impact and effectiveness of different instructional practices in improving general student learning and achievement.[20] A review of these practices and varying views regarding their effectiveness is beyond the scope of this chapter. More to the point is research investigating factors that have been associated with reducing the achievement gaps.[21] These studies tend to be based on case studies or to depend on correlations found naturally in the educational environments. As a group, they examine common practices and characteristics of schools that have shown to be effective in reducing achievement gaps for traditionally underperforming students or investigate factors that predict increased achievement among schools that predominantly serve these students. At present, there is neither a broad nor an empirically rigorous enough research base about the most effective approaches to reduce achievement gaps to infer useful and widely generalizable conclusions. However, given these limitations, there is some consistency across many of the existing studies about the common characteristics of schools that have reduced the typical achievement gaps. These commonalities tend to fall into three general categories, relating to types of school-level resources: (1) social capital (interpersonal factors such as shared trust, beliefs, goals, values, and expectations); (2) intellectual capital (shared knowledge, intelligence, and competencies); and (3) organizational capital (issues relating to broader resources and their employment).[22]

Social Capital

Across the studies described above, the shared beliefs and expectations at a school emerged repeatedly as factors distinguishing schools that showed evidence of closing the gaps. These beliefs are marked by feelings of trust and collaboration among school stakeholders as well as an identifiable shared vision/school mission that focuses on clear, measurable academic outcomes and goals. Academic expectations for the school and students are high within the school culture for all students, regardless of their previous academic background. Teachers are willing to share and support each other toward the achievement of school goals, and are open to feedback from their colleagues to improve their own practices. Families are part of these educational communities as well, with ongoing connection and communication between teachers/ administrators and parents about school vision, goals, progress, and outcomes.

Intellectual Capital

As with social capital, there were several trends across the studies in terms of knowledge/competency resources at exemplar schools. The school curriculum is coherent, consistent, and linked to the standards. Teachers have strong subject-matter knowledge for the content they teach, as well as a clear understanding of the standards and their connection to instruction. Professional development activities are targeted purposely to support the academic outcomes and goals of the schools (rather than individual teacher professional interests). Another consistent trend is the regular use of assessment data to examine current practices and improve instruction (i.e., use assessment information for formative purposes rather than only summative purposes).

Organizational Capital and Other Resources

Although less prevalent than the social and intellectual factors described above, other types of resources emerged across the studies. Most obviously, the schools had adequate classroom instructional materials (i.e., the needed instructional and classroom resources were available to teachers). These schools also tended to develop community partners/resources and use these partnerships toward targeted ends (i.e., programs and activities designed to promote academic achievement). Wraparound instructional support was accessible to students, including advisory programs, school counselors, afterschool and summer school programs, and early warning intervention activities (i.e., identifying students in need of extra help early, before problems may prove intractable).

Again, the number and design of these studies limit the conclusions to be drawn from these findings. The types of best practices identified are very often the same types of factors associated with quality practice at all schools. Additional research with larger samples and more empirically rigorous methodology would be needed to further tease out what factors specifically function to close achievement gaps versus those factors that improve achievement overall for all student subgroups within a school. In other words, as of yet there are no "silver bullets" with extensive empirical support for reducing a school's achievement gaps.

MEASURES

Part of our charge was to consider the standards and measurement system now in place and its role, if any, in reducing the gap. Our judgment is that the present system, while strong in a number of ways, is flawed if its principal intent is to provide information to improve the educational status of all students. We believe there are ways to repair or restructure it. In the next sections we provide an overview addressing standards, existing tests, and validity consequences and detail problems that could be overcome.

Standards

One deficiency is that the system depends on standards that are too numerous to teach well—that is, in depth. First, fewer standards, seriously measured, can streamline and improve the system and guide learning.[23] These standards would need coherence that could be provided in part by including skills such as application, problem solving, and adaptation of learning in content measures of cognitive readiness. To have fewer standards, we need a careful selection process to avoid the idea of minimum competencies. Instead they should include important content, domain skills, and individual cognitive skills, such as self-monitoring, that might cross subject-matter boundaries. Fewer standards would allow the careful analysis of prerequisite or supporting skills, features that might be measured and shared with teachers for use in classroom formative assessment. Fewer standards would permit a more robust assessment system, one that not only measured annual skill acquisition, but also retention, application, sustainment, and integration through periodic standard and nonstandard procedures.

The newly released Common Core State Standards in mathematics, literacy, and science raise the quality of the expectations for students, and provide very explicit logic, examples, and sequence for the standards. However, they also seem at this time not to include that many fewer standards. While one might expect some mitigation in performance gaps because the standards are clearly articulated and appropriately graduated, the number of standards may still be a barrier to significant change, especially in an era of lowered education spending, larger class sizes, and reduced teaching forces in some jurisdictions.

Testing Concerns

A system with as many standards as California's current set uses a survey test that by necessity must attempt to cover too much content with too few items per content area. This lack of depth for each standard may also be a factor in the new Common Core State Standards, although it is possible that new assessments will solve this persistent problem. For example, in our California case study, its tests included only one or even a third of an item to measure given strands or components of a standard. With accountability sanctions such as those in current No Child Left Behind legislation, and the intention of using test scores in teacher evaluation, enormous, if not excessive, pressure is placed on administrators and teachers to "get results" on any set of tests used for accountability.[24]

Suppose you were a teacher who took a lightly measured standard (i.e., few items covering it) seriously and invested a significant proportion of instruction there, because the subskills were needed for success in later, more complex tasks. However, because of inadequate measurement, your effort would not be rewarded by a significant gain in student performance. Both student and teacher effort on poorly measured but essential components of standards would count little toward a good test score. Low item frequency signals a lack of importance (seen by the policy maker) for certain content. Because salience on the test conveys meaning, it modifies the intention of standards. Instead of evaluating the importance of standards, the teachers and principals focus on the distribution of content included on tests. Education, in the last accountability epoch, has become test driven rather than standards focused, a satisfactory outcome only when the test items measure important content and skills in sufficient depth. The price of survey tests is relatively low, but their educational costs are high. They allow the public to believe that standards are adequately measured, and results are based on their design. In fact, they may give teachers impossible choices: either to drill on limited but adequately tested content, or to teach content and skills of importance without possibility of reward. Furthermore, because of excessive numbers of standards and an increasing reliance on specific pacing of instruction, little time is available to address students who need additional help to achieve prerequisite or desired knowledge and skills. Attention is instead given to moving numbers of students in the right classification, with less time available to promote deep and sustained learning for individual students.

An obvious statement is that to address gaps, either among groups or between U.S. students and their competitors, teachers need to redirect their efforts more to the learning of individual children than to the dictates of an accountability system. In the face of growing accountability requirements, teacher evaluation, and higher standards, they may not be able to achieve this goal. A small but bright light may lie in developing their skill in the use of formative assessment. If teachers are given an empowered role in the assessment system, with clear guidance about the intentions of standards, prerequisite skills, and sufficient time and resources, they can apply classroom formative assessments that give usable, significant diagnostic value. This diagnostic information then is translated into supportive instruction needed for the student(s) in question. Recent data demonstrate significant effects for students prepared by teachers applying formative assessments.[25]

As an aside, much of what goes by the buzzword *formative* does not function in this way, as it is not diagnostic, provides no rapid feedback, and is not connected to timely and effective instructional options.

Validity, Now and in the Future

While education authorities may be satisfied by the "alignment" of tests, standards, and content validity (e.g., there is a fragment, or one or more items that represent some aspect of the verbal standards), there is far less evidence that the current test results serve the intended purposes. Many educational purposes are claimed for assessments, including monitoring effectiveness of individuals and schools, measuring progress, providing diagnostic information for instruction, supporting overall system improvement, and communicating with the public and with educators and teachers regarding the important outcomes. Implicit in the testing sequence is the notion that passing a test at one level enables the student to approach the next level with confidence. In other words, there is a cumulative aspect to the measured order of content and cognitive demands. It is also assumed that the tests do not unintentionally include barriers that might result in unfair differential performance as a result of syntax, unfamiliar language, or context.

Yet, there is sparse validity evidence available about state tests used for accountability. For example, and clearly relevant to achievement gaps, it must be demonstrated that performance on the state tests can be affected by high-quality instruction (i.e., more than simply by practice on similar test items) for those students who have achieved necessary prerequisites. Tests that are sensitive to instruction imply that the test results will change because of instruction and that instruction will have a greater impact than irrelevant out-of-school activities, personal characteristics, and other factors external to the system.[26] Have there been clear studies that address this question in a way that disentangles student and school characteristics, teacher preparation, and a range of instructional options? Few or none.

For accountability systems to work, there needs to be evidence that what happens in classrooms considers and overcomes as much as possible differences in background, setting, and other correlates of poor performance. If such empirically rigorous evidence is not available, then it is questionable to claim that such measures accurately depict school effectiveness. If there is not clear evidence of the relationship of the tests to instructional effectiveness (nontautological evidence), then these tests should never be used to invoke sanctions on institutions and individuals.

Another purpose of tests beyond a snapshot of attainment at a point in time is to look at growth. Performance is used to mark the progress and status of schools and groups, and ultimately to foster individual monitoring of student progress so that each can ultimately improve. Is there evidence to date that data from tests can be used to develop high-quality instruction, or to improve or refine instruction? Are teachers and other educators using the standards and tests to diagnose and improve instruction? Has it been shown that teachers have a range of instructional tools at their disposal and can determine why students do poorly on certain standards or components of standards? Is there evidence about fundamental subskills that precede the desired performance at particular grade levels available for rapid instructional use? Are the test results timed and reported in a way that permits a serious effort? Overall, we would guess not. Instead, there is some evidence that preparation for the test itself (i.e., for the formats and content of the subject) occupies the attention of schools at risk for failing to meet their explicit performance standards. Evidence of this sort of practice includes the administration of interim or benchmark tests intended to predict student performance, without budgeting instructional time to remedy needed skills or content gaps. Nor is it evident that benchmark tests in use have rigorous empirical evidence or much evidence at all to support their appropriateness for formative assessment.

We also mention the concept of cognitive readiness, which can be incorporated into content-oriented assessments (the acquisition of important content, skills, and propensities to adapt to future requirements and opportunities in education and work). The United States, and each state, must bring its assessment system in line with changing expectations for cognitive readiness beyond K–12 education, especially by and for secondary students. Overall, any learning that is deliberately addressed in school must have a goal of transfer and generalization. Whatever the standard, students must be expected to demonstrate their achievement in a variety of ways, in different settings, and with varied constraints. Unless generalizing and adapting to new situations is valued in standards, in classrooms, and in tasks on tests, students will continue to learn in a noncumulative way. Validity studies are needed to demonstrate that accountability and formative purposes support the attainment of desired standards and that performance of students is robust across settings and constraints.

Frameworks

Implementation of standards and tests need glue to make them usable and coherent. It is no small irony that some states that performed well on NAEP compared to California used the frameworks developed by California, but no longer in use there, as a basis for their instructional system design. We believe it essential that we have frameworks that explicate curriculum, detail and explain skills and content, and give a range of usable instructional options and formative assessment guidance. These are key elements required to support the coherence of any proposed system. Given the Common Core State Standards, it is essential to determine which smaller set of goals can be emphasized in instructional frameworks to guide practice for teachers, parents, and students as well as educators in the community. These frameworks must be made available and clear and must address standards, content, instruction, and classroom assessment. They will stimulate the availability of interesting instructional materials and technologies, such as simulations and games.[27] Together, they form an essential basis for the design of teaching practices, instructional material, professional development, and preservice education, including subject-matter preparation in colleges and universities. The design and implementation of frameworks provide a demonstrable way to operationalize shared expectations for expected learning at every stage of the academic continuum.

Instructional frameworks can also be used to motivate and expand collaboration and connections between K–12 education and both two-year and four-year colleges. Agreement around shared frameworks could promote a better understanding between K–12 and higher education about the gaps in learning that many entry-level college students bring to both the two-year and four-year college experiences. At the National Center for Research on Evaluation, Standards, and Student Testing (CRESST), we have found sets of unachieved mathematics fundamentals that are exhibited by fourth-grade students all the way up to first-year college students. Such skills could be used as critical transition points in the process (elementary to secondary school, high school to two-year college, two-year to four-year college). The framework could also assist colleges in the development of college- and department-level student learning outcomes required for accreditation purposes.[28]

TOWARD A REVISED, BLENDED ASSESSMENT SYSTEM

Any useful testing system must address fairness for students who have underperformed, whether their lower performance is attributed to cultural, linguistic, or motivational reasons. Tests depend on uniform reporting. But to address individual differences, the balance between uniform reporting and individual needs, interests, and skills must be confronted and explored. Consider a blended approach that turns on its head the place of uniformity and diversity in learning goals. In the early grades we must make sure that fundamentals are learned in an applied context. As children develop, they are given further opportunities for choice. By the beginning of high school, students should be given multiple opportunities to demonstrate their core expertise and show how it transfers or applies to different situations. End-of-course examinations in secondary school can provide a deep dose of coherence by linking standards, frameworks, syllabi, and assessments together with sufficient flexibility and time to deal with individual student needs and preferences. Later certification options in secondary school might be expanded so that students could attain certifications in academic subjects (e.g., honors courses), AP classes, demonstrating specific applied skills (e.g., computer network manager), or by completing significant internships in areas of interest (e.g., environmental studies, graphic design). To accomplish this differentiation, schools would need to be aided by nonprofits, colleges and universities, businesses, and other community-based entities. Instead of passing only an exit examination, students could have the additional requirement to show their expertise in two or three separate subject matters or thematic areas, through either formal tests or personal evaluation.

SUMMARY

In summary, the evidence suggests that achievement gaps are pervasive and persistent at the national and state levels, and are unlikely to close in the foreseeable future. These gaps start early and are evident even at the highest levels of education. The causes of the achievement gaps are multiple and interactive, and there is limited empirical evidence about school-level changes that can reduce them. However, what we know about best practices in measurement and assessment can help us devise approaches to addressing the gaps. Based on these considerations, we contend that education must change from a school or group enterprise to an individual learning endeavor.

Schools should be addressing individual needs for acquisition of unlearned prior knowledge child by child, not group by group, grade by grade, or in any other summary matter. School management needs to monitor and support individual growth. To do so, schools must be given access, through technology, to options that allow students to learn on their own. This learning must have motivational, cognitive, and content excellence in order to reward persistence with real competence. If we start and end with the students, their particular learning needs and aspirations, our processes must inevitably change. Innovations start with changing the everyday experiences students have at school by supporting teachers and inventing better instructional opportunities.

Student and teacher learning needs to become paramount in assessment, rather than subsumed under bureaucratic requirements. Starting with children involves the full range and type of student—those learning English, those who are high performing (not mutually exclusive), those new to the school or the state, those with particular needs. This approach will cause dislocation at the outset as it is a shift from current practice. But starting and ending with children should resonate with educators. "Coherence" is a key underpinning of the system we are proposing. Coherence is different from more chiropractic notions of alignment, where objects like test items and bits of standards line up. Coherence operates more like a gravitational force that helps align elements without disturbing their own rotations or atmospheres. Coherence is something that grows from within a system rather than being imposed from without. Were individual learning valued and addressed coherently, states would need to provide different levels of instructional choices and support for different students. Coherence would be expected among standards, syllabi and tests, teacher development, and consequent in-service development. In many countries, vendors build in this coherence because they provide assessments related to a framework, detailed syllabus, instructional options, included materials, and professional development. Unfortunately, we have had a different, less integrated tradition in this country.

Also implicit in this coherent approach is the importance of the formative uses of assessment, linked with accountability outcomes, frameworks, standards, and student needs. This approach to formative assessment assumes targeted support for teachers—information and guidance to help teachers make instructional choices based on what they learn from the range of assessment results available to them.[29]

For such a coherent network to be effective, schools would be able to choose from among vetted vendors, and choice for students, teachers, and parents would extend to some standards as well.

The components of this discussion about measures, beginning with our thoughts on standards and assessments, lead us to consider a statewide system of assessment that reifies the pervasive rethinking of the standards that has occurred, the creation of instructional frameworks or syllabi to support them, and the design of tests that measure accomplishment. Such examinations will need to demonstrate their quality, utility, validity, and fairness empirically. Second, we have emphasized the importance of choice for children and youth, particularly as they approach adulthood. Third, our suggestions in many ways turn the system upside down, with an intense focus on children and youth rather than on the details of the accountability system intended to serve them.

CONCLUSIONS

The major conclusions of this analysis are stark and unrelenting. A first important conclusion from available data is that we are failing, and there are no harbingers of improvement on the horizon. U.S. students fall well below comparable countries in their achievement, which means they are at best average and sometimes in the lower reaches of world performance levels. In California, as an example, and nationally, membership in identifiable subgroups remains a strong predictor of level of success on examinations. The achievement gap seemingly endures. California is near the bottom ranks of the other states in this regard, and though we can argue for the uniqueness of our circumstances, they alone do not forgive our responsibility to educate all students well.

A second, inescapable conclusion is that learning is neither cumulative, well sustained in middle and upper grades, nor supported, repaired, or relevant enough to our youth to change their performance patterns. While potentially a testing artifact, California displays the national trend that academic performance decreases as students rise in the grade structure of schools, a fact persisting in the face of the differential dropout of lower-performing students.

Third, we conclude that educational policies have not been consistent or sufficiently coherent, and that most reform elements do not support coherence because they have been ill chosen, and most often are too remote from instruction and learning in classrooms.

In summary, the day-to-day learning experiences of students may have changed, but not for the better. We have neither designed nor applied widely effective instructional systems in which teachers have flexibility and sufficient content and pedagogical knowledge to address each student's need. We have not given a coherent and sustained approach to instruction, and we have not been effective in our approaches for underperforming groups. If we have spent much time and energy on the reform of educational structural and governance issues over the last two decades, it is now essential to shift the focus and renewed energy to the classroom and to students. We conclude that an overhaul is needed of our thinking and action on the achievement gap and its measurement. We need to change our attention to the performance patterns of individual students—within groups, if necessary—but the individual pattern of each student's strengths, interests, and needs must override thinking in great swaths about remedies for groups or institutions.

With regard to validity questions, including the urgent need to document the impact of instruction on assessments that evaluate the effectiveness of education, states and their consortia must require that vendors of examinations provide strong evidence for each intended purpose: accountability, accuracy, representativeness of standards, instructional sensitivity, diagnostic utility by teachers, and consequences overall for the educational standing and health of the schools. This is not at all unusual and a function of the speed and cost of implementing assessments.

In addition, we must overcome the factors that inhibit the rapid and intense engagement of all sectors of primary, secondary, and postsecondary education (i.e., grades P-16) communities. Unless we do, and achieve a serious understanding of the standards and their importance, we will never achieve social justice and intellectual parity for all U.S. students.

CHAPTER FIVE

Accessing High-Quality Instructional Strategies

EDMUND T. HAMANN AND JENELLE REEVES

Instructional strategies figure centrally in what happens in classrooms, are critical to educational outcomes, and are central to the narrowing of achievement gaps. However, broad improvement of schools, including the narrowing of these gaps, will depend on changes in instructional strategy and improved student access to educators using these strategies, as well as many other changes related to topics treated in the chapters in this volume.

Much of the research on instructional strategies identifies universal aspects of effective instruction that pertain across subject matter, grade level, and student characteristics. Other important findings from instructional strategy research are not as broadly applicable. Findings of this second kind are more specific to particular grade levels, topics of instruction, students' racial or ethnic affiliations, and like variables. It would be a mistake to overgeneralize the lessons from this second category, but it would also be a mistake to dismiss them.

As a final introductory point, it is crucial to remember Ladson-Billings's caution, from her 2006 presidential address to the American Education Research Association, that though much effort has been devoted in the last forty years to studying why certain groups of students struggle in school, such inquiries rarely provide large-scale relief. Ladson-Billings wants to see instruction change, but she challenges us: if much is known about what should be done to make schools more equitable and welcoming, why have the recommended strategies not already been made commonplace? She notes, "Emphasizing an 'achievement gap' can naturalize that gap, make it seem inevitable, and take attention away from the historical, economic, sociopolitical, and moral components" that have cocreated it.[1]

REPORT METHODOLOGY

This chapter is the product of a review of a two overlapping literatures: the literature on the general effectiveness of instructional strategies and the literature on effective instructional strategies for students from racial, socioeconomic, ethnic, and other groups that have historically fared less well at school. Our perspective mirrors that of the National Research Council: "Rarely does one study produce an unequivocal and durable result; multiple methods, applied over time and tied to evidentiary standards, are essential to establishing scientific knowledge."[2] We have attempted to substantiate findings through triangulation: if several different strategies of inquiry point to the same conclusion, then such a conclusion is particularly robust. Triangulation can be a result not just of comparing multiple articles, but also of finding articles that report the same effects at multiple sites—for example, Anderson-Levitt's comparison of literacy education in the United States, France, and Guinea.[3]

Information included in the chapter is the result of our systematic review of the last ten years of a number of leading education research journals—*American Educational Research Journal, Review of Educational Research, Educational Researcher, Harvard Educational Review,* and *Teachers College Record.* We also examined three meta-analyses on educational effectiveness and then selectively further reviewed studies that these sources pointed to.[4] The points raised in these three syntheses tended to echo (or triangulate) findings that came from other sources, while adding the explanatory power of effect sizes and multisite corroboration.

Aware that journals that focused on linguistic and cultural diversity or that examined effective school practices in other countries might provide particular illumination relevant to closing achievement gaps, we also systematically reviewed *Anthropology and Education Quarterly, Comparative Education Review, Journal of Education of Students Placed at Risk (JESPAR),* and *TESOL Quarterly.* The comparative perspective is important, because it reminds us that achievement gaps are not inevitable and instructional strategies are pursued in relational contexts laden with culturally informed expectations, hierarchies, and dispositions. For example, Korean-descent students can be consistent low achievers in Japan (compared to other groups of students) and consistent high achievers in the United States.[5] This suggests that low (or high) achievement outcomes are not an intrinsic property of a category of learners, but rather are a product of the interface between learners and educators, as informed by social expectations and stereotypes from the larger society.

THE IMPORTANCE OF TRUST IN A SUCCESSFUL INSTRUCTIONAL EQUATION

Underlying this chapter is the viewpoint that successful instruction requires trusting relations between children and educators, conditions that may be easier to create with some learners than others.[6] This perspective holds that trust is built (or impeded) based on how the participants in the relationship (i.e., teachers and students) learn to make sense of each other and of the task at hand. Do they feel competent? Does the task seem worthwhile? What are the social risks? According to this view, there is no such thing as a good instructional strategy apart from the context in which it is implemented.

Thus, part of what is critical with regard to any instructional technique is whether it either fosters or undermines the relationship of trust among those in the classroom, depending on how it is implemented. Trust is powerfully shaped by the teacher, but as the literatures on both cooperative learning and bullying suggest, other individuals figure into the trustworthiness of the environment as well. These are individuals whom the teacher can influence but not control. Learners' self-concept also figures centrally in their readiness and willingness to learn.[7] Teachers do not control this learner self-concept (it is shaped by previous teachers and many, many other sources), but they can attend to it directly and strategically. Failing to adequately instruct in relation to these issues can create or exacerbate low achievement.[8]

PEDAGOGICAL TECHNIQUE AND INSTRUCTIONAL STRATEGY

The academic task pursued sincerely in a trustworthy environment still needs to be rigorous and technically sound. One starting point for this review was the general literature on effective instructional strategies, a literature that has become more abundant and concentrated, as the standards movement has highlighted the need for academic rigor across content areas. Seidel and Shavelson's exhaustive review suggests three main domains of attention for instruction: learning processes, cognitive outcomes, and motivational-affective outcomes.[9]

A teacher's expertise and ability to apply effective instructional strategies consists of knowledge of content, pedagogy, and context. Shulman notes the role of pedagogical content knowledge in highly effective teaching.[10] Hammerness et al. observe that it is the unique combination of both teacher *innovation* and teacher *efficiency* that characterize the expert teacher.[11] Expert and effective instruction requires a professional who is prepared for the necessarily in situ decision making that is characteristic of teaching and who is ready with multiple tools to address the context specifics that pertain to a given learner, a given classroom, a given text, and a given curriculum at a given moment. In this section, we explore these instructional tools—these "promising strategies." Two categories of strategies deserve attention here: (1) the instructional habits that are generally wise and effective in all classrooms regardless of the discipline under study and (2) those that are more particular to a specific content area.

Effective pedagogical techniques address a range of learning outcomes. Seidel and Shavelson's meta-analysis categorizes these into three major areas. The outcome of developing "habits of mind" references students' capacity to think metacognitively, evaluate information, and self-regulate. Cognitive outcomes refer to gaining mastery of content—particularly content organized into the classic domains of the disciplines—and the literacy and numeracy skills necessary for disciplinary learning. Motivational-affective outcomes refer to learner disposition toward academic tasks. Converting each of these categories of learning outcomes into vehicles for guiding instruction, one could ask how teachers teach learners "how to learn" (learning processes), how they teach mathematical or interpretive understandings (examples of cognitive outcomes), and what strategies they pursue—for example, cooperative learning—to attend to learners' motivation and engagement (motivational-affective outcomes).

There is overlap among these categories and thus among the ways in which they might guide instruction. For example, Seidel and Shavelson report finding that "executing domain-specific activities [which has a big effect on cognitive outcomes] was also one of the most important factors for motivational-affective outcomes (e.g., interest or self-concept of ability)."[12] Acknowledging this overlap, the sections that follow are organized according to Seidel and Shavelson's three major categories, relabeled here as strategies that develop *habits of mind, content-oriented learning,* and *motivation and affect.*

Strategies to Develop Students' Habits of Mind

Most good instruction, including instruction that helps narrow achievement gaps, is good because it helps learners develop skills they can deploy successfully and purposefully as they learn, communicate with others, and negotiate the world. An example of such instruction comes from Gibbons's discussion of teacher-guided reporting, in which the teacher models how to orally report findings to the whole class (as from an experiment or small-group discussion)—a strategy that simultaneously delivers content well and builds habits of mind (e.g., presentation skills learners can use in multiple settings and other disciplines).[13]

Seidel and Shavelson actually use the term *regulative* in the same vein as "habits of mind." Whether it is the kindergarten social task of learning to raise one's hand to be called on, the weekly monitoring by a fifth-grade teacher who shares a sequence of activity guides with a pair of students collaborating on a science project, or the "think-aloud" modeled when an eighth-grade English teacher converts a student's question about whether to do a biography of Willa Cather, John Steinbeck, or Chinua Achebe into a public consideration of questions (such as length of texts to review and time to review them, text availability at the library, overlap with topics studied in social studies, etc.), all of these can include overt teaching of regulation, of what students need to consider as they pursue an academic task. The goal is for students to pick up and start enacting these self-monitoring, self-regulating habits of mind.

Of course, measuring the development of these habits of mind is a complex task and not one necessarily best executed by assessments of content-area knowledge. So, while it is important that students learn to be comfortable and adept at finding resources in a library, gain the self-awareness to know how much sleep allows them to operate effectively, and know how to evaluate the quality of information found through a Web search, attributing test results to the presence or absence of any of these habits is difficult.

As we consider culturally and linguistically diverse students (CLDs), a crucial habit of mind looms. The knowledge, ways, and language for talking and acting and the social expectations of school are often different from those that CLD students are familiar with. As Delpit has pointed out, the solution here is not to have CLD students be unaccountable for learning the knowledge and habits celebrated at school.[14] Rather, students whose home culture is not reflected in school culture need to learn how to "culture switch."[15] As Hamann, Zúñiga, and Sánchez Garcia have described the dilemma for transnationally mobile students, the task is not just to learn how to live and thrive in *this* place (where one lives), but also any new place (where one might be about to move).[16] These are habits of mind. A student who can recognize which rules, codes, ways, and so on apply will be a successful student. As Gibson (1988) eloquently described regarding the experience of Sikh immigrants at a California high school, one reason such students were academically successful is that school did not contest their preexisting identities. School honored existing habits of mind and, as needed, helped students build additional ones.[17]

Effective Content-Oriented Instructional Strategies

Many researchers have created lists of instructional strategies and guidance to teachers. Some come from meta-analyses, others from teacher education textbooks and professional development manuals. For example, in a practitioner-oriented book summarizing 1,400 studies on learning-related topics, the Northwest Regional Educational Laboratory (NWREL) made five recommendations related to instructional strategy:[18]

1. Orient students to lessons
2. Provide clear and focused instruction
3. Provide feedback and reinforcement
4. Review and reteach for mastery
5. Use probing, redirection, and reinforcement to promote metacognition

Echoing this chapter's introduction, NWREL authors emphasized that instructional improvements need concurrent reforms to be viable (e.g., teachers' content mastery, adequate formative assessment measures, and adequate time to revisit and reteach topics as necessary). The NWREL study also emphasized the cyclical nature of instruction and assessment—that effective instructional strategies are parts of an instructional cycle in which instruction is based on assessment of learners and that instruction is, in turn, assessed for its effectiveness in helping learners make academic gains. This is a cycle also utilized in the Sheltered Instruction Observation Protocol (SIOP), a popular research-supported professional development program for content-area teachers who teach ELL.[19] The relationship between instruction and assessment is symbiotic; effective instructional strategies go hand-in-hand with effective assessment strategies.

In this same vein of research synthesis on effective instructional strategies, Marzano, Pickering, and Pollock conducted a meta-analysis of more than a hundred research reports.[20] They identified nine instructional strategies that produced effect sizes ranging from 0.59 to 1.61. The larger the effect size, the greater the effect of the strategy on student achievement. From largest to smallest effect size, these were the identified strategies:

1. *Identifying similarities and differences.* Such strategies encourage students to compare and contrast items and categories and to use metaphors and analogies in presenting and assessing new material.
2. *Summarizing and note taking.* These strategies require learners to analyze information for the main points and to synthesize large amounts of information into concise statements.
3. *Reinforcing effort and providing recognition.* These strategies address student motivation and engagement through recognition of effort in others and self.
4. *Homework and practice.* Practice with information, through application strategies and homework policies, is key to students' comprehension and retention of new learning.
5. *Nonlinguistic representation.* Such strategies provide learners with extra-linguistic pathways into learning and include graphic organizers and other visual representations.
6. *Cooperative learning.* Cooperative strategies that pair or group students with their peers, utilizing strategic grouping configurations so that students learn from and depend on one another.
7. *Setting goals and providing feedback.* Meta-cognitive strategies like these invite learners to engage in and plan their own learning alongside their teachers.
8. *Generating and testing hypotheses.* Such strategies involve the application of knowledge and the prediction of outcomes based on prior knowledge and

observation. Moreover, these strategies engage learners as their own hypotheses are tested.

9. *Activating prior knowledge.* Techniques such as advance organizers, cues, and questions are strategies that invite learners to locate new knowledge in relation to what they already know.

Important as these strategies are, a challenge to practitioners who wish to apply the findings from both the NWREL study and the strategies identified by Marzano et al. is that they can read like a shopping list without regard to proportions, intertwining, or differences in implementation in one school environment versus another. The Center for Research on Education, Diversity and Excellence's (CREDE's) *Five Standards for Effective Pedagogy and Learning* offers an arguably more cohesive framework of effective instruction with its five "standards."[21] Each standard is a compilation of like strategies, and the standard itself is a synthesis of instructional strategies found to be effective in one or more of CREDE's extensive research projects in U.S.-based K–12 education between 1996 and 2003. The five standards are:

1. Joint Productive Activity: Teachers and Students Producing Together
2. Language Development: Developing Language and Literacy Across the Curriculum
3. Contextualization: Connecting Meaning to Students' Lives
4. Challenging Activities: Teaching Complex Thinking
5. Instructional Conversations: Teaching Through Conversation

Cutting across content areas, the CREDE standards attempt to address not only individual strategies but also the conditions in which learning is encouraged and facilitated (e.g., imploring educators to contextualize learning because this helps learners comprehend and engage with new knowledge). Each CREDE standard could be accomplished by any number of individual strategies, and teachers are called on to strategically use their knowledge of content, context, and learners to meet the standards.

Language, in oral and written forms, is the medium of school, and students' facility in comprehending, producing, and managing the language of schooling is crucial if they are to learn content knowledge well and develop the habits of mind needed for engaged participation in school. In their study of the instruction of reading, Mosenthal et al. compared the reading instruction practices of fifty-two elementary school teachers at six high-achieving elementary schools with the practices of twenty-five teachers at three demographically matched but less successful elementary schools. Strategies at the schools that were deemed effective at teaching reading included grouping and guided reading, student self-selected reading, reading aloud, writing story summaries, enabling students to solicit peers' perspectives, interpretive questions, use of phonemic-awareness computer games, keeping reading journal entries and working one-on-one with adult tutors (America Reads volunteers), and schoolwide use of the DEAR method (i.e., Drop Everything And Read). The authors also note:

> *The factors that the study singles out as imperative for "success" exist to some degree in every classroom: vision and commitment to literacy learning, coherence of approach, well-managed and paced instruction, and communication among faculty and administration. It is the combination and interplay of these factors that control the ultimate outcome.*[22]

Perhaps the key issues, then, are frequency and credible access to these factors. Through this research and a wealth of other studies on literacy, we know that how students comprehend texts is connected to who they are: their interests, their relationship with the teacher, the value they assign to the effort, and their self-concepts as readers.[23] In turn, both teachers' knowledge of who students are—their strengths, areas of challenge, and sociocultural backgrounds—and teachers' understandings about literacy affect the quality of their instruction.[24]

Learning strategy instruction may also play an integral role in developing students' literacy skills. We know that good readers might use up to thirty different strategies in working with a particular text and that weak readers can be taught the strategies used by stronger readers to favorable effect on reading comprehension.[25] We also know that good early reading instruction pursues a balanced approach, including instruction in phonemic awareness, but only as part of an integrated package that also teaches reading for meaning.[26]

According to Zolkower and Shreyar, the Vygotskian idea of verbal thinking, in which "the interconnection of thought and speech makes possible the planning function of the latter," draws a clear connection between the development of cognition and verbal language use.[27] In a sixth-grade class of culturally and linguistically heterogeneous students, they observed the use of think-aloud strategies as a successful strategy for advancing student understanding of algebraic functions. Gibbons, likewise, observed content-area instruction through oral skill building, in this case, the teacher-guided scaffolding of the academic register for reporting findings from experiments.[28] These studies are relatively small (with twenty-six and sixty students, respectively), yet their findings, taken in conjunction with the findings of similar studies, collectively point toward the effectiveness of instructional strategies that utilize and build learners' oral production skills to comprehend and demonstrate disciplinary knowledge.[29]

In some ways academic literacy is discipline-specific, and the literacy skills learners develop and use are distinct. In mathematics one learns that the last sentence in a word problem contains the pertinent question, while for social studies it is the first sentences in a newspaper article that provide the most important information. Such knowledge of the mathematical *register,* as well as the language registers used in all content areas, is critical for students' access to content-area instruction. A rich line of research into the language of content areas and how teachers might incorporate language instruction into content-area teaching is emerging.[30] These studies, typically using a systemic functional linguistic (SFL) approach to analyze disciplinary language, highlight the need for teachers to see disciplinary language use from the perspective of a newcomer or novice. With this new understanding, teachers can assist learners in gaining comprehension and eventual mastery of (or the ability to manipulate) these new registers. According to McDermott, part of what shapes the viability of educator/learner interaction and promotes trust in this relationship is the educator's demonstrated adeptness with the pedagogy and content of a discipline.[31]

Strategies That Stress Motivational and Affective Outcomes

Part of the craft of teaching is to figure out how to motivate and engage multiple learners, each with different interests, energy levels, and realized levels of attainment. Successfully doing this is often accomplished through what the literature refers to as student-centered or learner-centered instruction.[32] A learner-centered classroom is deliberately designed to maximize all students' chances for academic development. In such classrooms, teachers expect all students to actively use speaking, listening, and thinking skills across contexts. Interactive discussions and experiential learning regularly occur. A learner-centered classroom builds upon students' background, interests, and experiences. Research suggests that this emphasis supports reading comprehension, student engagement and motivation, and the development of positive academic identities. In such environments, the teacher is more typically facilitator, or coach, than lecturer.[33]

A key component of a learner-centered classroom is the effective use of collaborative learning experiences.[34] Two other aspects of an effective learner-centered classroom referenced throughout the literature are flexible grouping and a focus on inquiry-based learning, with or without computer support.[35] Used together, these three structures for learning enable teachers to be maximally responsive to students' literacy and learning needs. Based on her review of the literature, Curtis summarized that "the types of classroom environments shown to promote literacy development include ones that use a variety of approaches to skills instruction, integrate test preparation into instruction, make overt connections among in-school and out-of-school applications, enable strategy use, engage students in uses of their knowledge and skills, and incorporate collaborative work."[36] Curtis's summary seems to apply more generally to a classroom environment where a broad range of learners all have access to high-quality instruction.

Research reviews, such as two by Marzano and colleagues, indicate that cooperative learning techniques produce gains in student achievement.[37] It is worth querying why that is so. Likely, both time on task and the relevance and accountability to peers (i.e., relational factors) pertain. Peer review, peer tutoring, and response groups were also found to produce gains in ELLs' English language development.[38] In their study of peer tutoring, Xu et al. paired native English speakers and ELLs, increasing interaction across linguistic and cultural identities. Not only did ELLs benefit from peer tutoring by making gains in English development, but also an open, trusting community was created for all learners in the linguistically heterogeneous classrooms.[39]

SUCCESSFUL STRATEGIES FOR INSTRUCTION OF CULTURALLY AND LINGUISTICALLY DIVERSE STUDENTS

The observation that particular cultural groups are more likely to fall into an academic achievement gap than others suggests that instruction that has been identified as effective for all students may, in fact, not be so universal. Some groups of students have not been served well despite, as Ladson-Billings points out, years of research into effective instructional strategies.[40]

Fostering Connections Between Home and School Experience

Historically and currently, Latinos and African Americans fare less well in America's schools. It follows that instructional strategies need to change if these groups are to fare better. Studies of Latino student schooling and achievement in U.S. public schools suggest that their teachers play a significant role in Latino students' connection (or disconnection) to school.[41] Teachers' relations and interactions with Latino youth, for example, signal acceptance or rejection of a Latino identity. In *Improving Schools for Latinos*, Valverde notes that Latinos are advantaged when instruction and learning outside of the school are attended to, not as an extracurricular activity, but as a necessary and integrated part of a student's school learning (consistent with a holistic approach).[42] Ladson-Billings starts her profile of seven teachers who have been particularly successful with African American youth by first locating African American education historically and then noting that each of the successful educators she studied affirmed the histories and racial identity that African American youth bring to the classroom.[43] The use of Black English (or African American Vernacular English) within the academy is often discouraged or tolerated only as a lesser (or less legitimate) English than so-called standard English, and, as McCrary argues, the dismissal of Black English is read by black youth as a school's nonacceptance of black identities.[44]

Utilizing Learners' Background Knowledge

Activating learners' prior knowledge and utilizing their lived experiences in the instruction of new material can be highly effective, not just because of how it introduces content, but also because of the relational affirmation it offers. To value and support learners' background knowledge helps teachers engage learners during instruction. Too often the background knowledge of learners from nondominant linguistic and cultural backgrounds has not been received with the same legitimacy as that of non-CLD learners. Quite often educators know the historic, cultural, and linguistic experiences of nonwhite groups less well and thus have fewer starting points for engagement.[45] It follows that, absent active learning about these groups, these educators would know less well how to shape instructional environments that would seem familiar and trustworthy. There is a rich literature about the instructional strategies some educators have used successfully with Latino students, African American students, and/or students of other backgrounds. There is much, much more on these topics than is shared here. However, three core points are that learners' group identities were respected, teachers learned a lot about such students' backgrounds, and students were subject to high expectations.

Culturally Relevant Teaching Practices

Osborne's ethnology (i.e., a comparative examination of multiple ethnographies) of research on teaching practices that have proven effective with indigenous, minority, second-language, and other historically disadvantaged student populations in the United States, Australia, Canada, and elsewhere highlights the centrality of relationship cultivation in the production of successful learners (and the narrowing of achievement gaps). Based on his analysis, Osborne made nine assertions about culturally relevant teaching. Each has implications for increasing the likelihood of high-quality instruction:[46]

1. Culturally relevant teachers need not come from the same ethnic minority group as the students they teach.
2. Socio-historico-political realities beyond the school constrain much of what happens in classrooms and must be understood well by the culturally relevant teacher.
3. It is desirable to teach content that is culturally relevant to students' previous experiences, that fosters their natal cultural identity, and that empowers them with knowledge and practices to operate successfully in mainstream society.
4. It is desirable to involve the parents and families of children from marginalized and normalized groups.

5. It is desirable to include students' first languages in the school program and in classroom interactions.

6. Culturally relevant teachers are personally warm toward and respectful of, as well as academically demanding of, all students.

7. Teachers who teach in culturally relevant ways spell out the cultural assumptions on which the classroom (and schooling) operates.

8. There are five components of culturally relevant classroom management: using group work, controlling indirectly rather than confrontationally, avoiding "spotlighting," using an unhurried pace, and using the home participation structures of the children.

9. Racism is prevalent in schools and needs to be addressed.

Osborne's first assertion is welcome news given that the nation's teaching force and those entering the profession do not match the demographics of the student enrollment. Current U.S. teachers and those entering the profession are much more likely to be white and middle class than the students they teach. This means most education for CLDs will occur across a cultural boundary. As Erickson points out, cultural difference creates an additional, but not inevitable, chance for misunderstanding and the breakdown of a credible, learning-supporting relationship. In some senses, the remaining eight assertions Osborne identified in the literature then clarify how a cross-cultural teacher/learner relationship can be made viable.[47]

We offer as a caveat that Cazden and Mehan, among others, have warned that checklists about how to work with particular populations can reiterate stereotypes without offering much in terms of more efficacious instructional strategies.[48] That caution applies here, but it is also true that part of what makes classroom interaction and completion of tasks trustworthy are the racial and ethnic background of the learner, the history of their group's experience with school, and educators' understandings and expectations about learners related to their backgrounds.[49] As Pollock has memorably noted, educationally race matters when we talk about it *and* when we do not.[50]

ISSUES OF ACCESS TO HIGH-QUALITY INSTRUCTION

High-quality instruction is clearly partly a technical task, in that the research shows certain instructional techniques are more effective than others. Too often, however, wages and working conditions cannot attract and keep the well-qualified teachers who can employ these strategies—particularly in urban environments that have the largest share of CLD students. Thus, high-quality instruction is often a problem of access rather than, or in addition to, one of practice. Research indicates that novice teachers (those in their first or second year) tend to be less effective than their longer-serving peers.[51] Thus, the presence or absence of experienced, well-trained teachers needs to be on the table in any consideration of access to high-quality instruction.

Two examples from California illustrate this issue of lack of access to experienced, well-trained teachers for the students who need them most. The class action case of *Eliezer Williams et al. vs. State of California et al.* documented how CLDs were more likely to attend (or have previously attended) facilities in poor repair, to have instructors teaching outside of their certification area, to have emergency-credentialed teachers, to have long-term substitutes, and to have older and less well provisioned curricular materials.[52]

Another example is a California policy that should have helped close achievement gaps but may actually have exacerbated problems of access—the statewide effort to reduce class size in early grades.[53] As Gallagher notes, mandated class size reduction in California created a demand for a 43 percent increase in California's K–3 teaching force. The huge new demand enabled the movement of teachers with the greatest experience to more desirable positions (e.g., better paying, less stress related to student performance, lower student mobility). Most veteran teachers who relocated migrated to schools with fewer ELLs, minorities, and free-lunch-eligible students.[54] This meant less desirable schools had to staff classrooms with disproportionate numbers of teachers with emergency credentials, those teaching out of field, and novice teachers—all of whom are indicated in the research as less effective.

From the standpoint of access, it is also important to ask how much time students spend in classrooms where they have access to such high-quality instruction. There is a long-established instructional strategy literature that notes that the time students spend engaged in academic tasks relates to how much they gain academically.[55] In her classic study on tracking, Oakes famously noted that students in lower-track classes spent less time academically engaged.[56] Many dynamics (e.g., more time in those classes spent disciplining, less experienced teachers leading lower-track classes) contributed to this inequality, but her core point remains: those students who got less high-quality instruction made less progress. Given the preponderance of CLDs in lower-track classes, this often means CLDs get less chance to spend time on task and suffer academically in consequence.

Finally, there is research on teaching that indicates that teachers interact differently with successful and unsuccessful students and that low achievers have less access to high-quality instruction within the very same classrooms as more successful peers.[57] Good noted in his meta-analysis thirty years ago:

- Teachers tended to communicate less with low achievers and call on them less often.

- Teachers made less eye contact with low achievers when they did call on them and offered low achievers less time to respond.
- Teachers praised low achievers less than high achievers in instances when students were unsure of the answer.
- Teachers criticized low achievers more than high achievers for making inaccurate responses to questions.
- Teachers tended to provide fewer details and less precise feedback to low achievers.
- Teachers demanded less homework and less effort from low achievers.

In summary, high-quality instruction is accomplished by teachers with knowledge and skill to implement a range of instructional strategies that are known to be successful and adapt them to the needs of their students. However, CLD students often do not have access to such high-quality instruction for a range of reasons independent from teacher knowledge of effective strategies.

POLICY IMPLICATIONS

All the instructional strategies reviewed here point to a key and crucial governance question: What ways and means will give all students access to high-quality instruction? In this chapter we have endeavored to review what the research says. We have done so by distinguishing between universal or broadly applicable traits of high-quality instruction and those that are more particular to specific content areas and/or particular kinds of learners. We have located the whole review within McDermott's insight that high-quality instruction transpires only when the relationship between teacher, learner, and task at hand is trustworthy—that is, perceived by teacher and learner as credible and viable.[58]

Despite what we know about instruction, Ladson-Billings's question haunts: If we know so well the effective instructional strategies that could counter historic "educational debts," why have we not assured that such strategies are broadly implemented?[59] Teachers' lack of knowledge (vis-à-vis either content-area knowledge or instructional strategy) would be one explanation. Not understanding the centrality of cultivating a trusting relationship of patience and high expectations that makes both the learning task and the learning environment seem trustworthy to students would be another. It is also possible that teacher knowledge per se is not the main constraint. As Sizer noted in his classic volume *Horace's Compromise*, it is plausible that skilled veteran teachers know what they should do, but feel a disconnect between what they *should* do and what they *can* do.[60]

We should ask whether existing teacher education programs successfully cultivate the knowledge and dispositional qualities necessary for their graduates to succeed in classrooms with all kinds of learners. Here again, if the answer is no, if there are patterns regarding which students teachers are ready for and what areas they are ready to help with, then there will be patterns regarding which students get supported and in what areas. There were also patterns to who and what does not get supported. America's classrooms have changed enough in the last thirty years in terms of who is enrolling and what levels of mastery these students are supposed to attain that any expectation that preservice education alone could resolve all limitations related to teachers' knowledge of credible instructional strategies would be misplaced. In-service professional development likely matters in terms of teachers' content mastery (including in fields like technology and biology that are fast changing) and their capacity to well serve students from populations that teachers have never served before (or have been less successful working with).[61]

There is a body of research regarding instructional strategies that point to how to improve learning outcomes for some or all students—the policy task is to figure out the professional development strategy that will convince faculty of both the imperative of pursuing new learning and the viability of that learning for improving practice. But it is the learners themselves (in this case, teachers) who will have to concur that new ways are indeed viable. The promotion of self-regulation that Seidel and Shavelson note, and the habits of mind that Dewey alludes to, both remind us that many adults acquire the tools of lifelong learning and that, given tools and means (including time), they often have the capacity to self-guide much of their professional improvement.[62] Emphases on lesson studies, action research, and self-study all can be tools for developing the professional acumen needed to improve instruction and outcomes with a broad range of students.[63]

Much of the critique of the achievement gap is couched in terms of social justice. Osborne is particularly blunt when he asserts that "[r]acism is prevalent in schools and needs to be addressed."[64] Yet the guidance regarding what instructional strategies work best seems frequently to be based on a treatment-outcome logic where the instruction strategy is the treatment and grades, or more typically, standardized tests (the outcomes), are the measure of success (or lack thereof). In other words, the assertion of injustice, an assertion we agree with, is measured with standardized academic achievement outcomes. Clearly these outcomes matter, but they ignore any query about how credible or compelling the tested information is to the tested learner. Abedi writes, for example, about the inappropriateness of testing ELLs in English or their native language (if the native language was not the language of instruction).[65]

None of the instructional strategies reported here directly reviewed the capacity to help learners better advocate for justice, to gain a disposition for and skill at democratic participation. There may be one more policy domain for this report, then. Cohen recently argued that the goals of education need to be reframed to include social, emotional, and ethical competencies—in addition to academics.[66] It seems worth asking what instructional strategies might overcome any current gaps in teaching for participation in democracy and well-being.

CHAPTER SIX

Organizational Strategies for Addressing the Educational Achievement Gap

DOUGLAS E. MITCHELL, ROBERT K. REAM,
SARAH M. RYAN, AND JOSE A. ESPINOZA

Closing the gap must be more than a one-front operation. Educators must hold themselves responsible and accountable for improving schools when and where we can . . . we must recognize that the achievement gap has deep roots.[1]

This chapter presents a comprehensive review of organizational strategies, re- sources, and opportunities that promise substantial impact on improving student learning and closing achievement gaps. We do not address in any detail questions regarding instructional alternatives—our focus is on the organizational and opera- tional characteristics of schools and classrooms. We begin with the obvious but often overlooked fact that many factors—children's social and cultural backgrounds, physical well-being, socioeconomic status, natural abilities, and so forth—influ- ence achievement as much or more than school experiences. Environmental fac- tors like hunger, television watching, parent availability, and student mobility combine with school factors like curriculum rigor, class size, and school safety to shape student achievement.[2] As Tough summarizes, poor children will require not the same education as middle-class children, but one that is considerably better.[3] They will need more class time, better-trained teachers, and a curriculum that emphasizes psychological and emotional as well as intellectual preparation.

Adjusting school policies and practices alone cannot hope to fully close the deep and persistent achievement gaps separating rich and poor, white and non- white, English learners and English speakers in the public schools. As noted by Ream, Ryan, and Espinoza in chapter 2, long before children enter the public school system, substantial differences in academic readiness and ability are easily recognized. Thus, although our focus is on school policies and practices, we caution that policy makers can expect schooling adjustments to be only a partial solution. The gaps that need to be addressed are strongly linked to community and family characteristics that are beyond the reach of school changes alone.

OPTIONS, NOT PRESCRIPTIONS

In developing this chapter, we seek to avoid the usual tendency to argue for a definitive set of policy recommendations to "fix" the organization and governance of public education. We agree with the report of the California Governor's Committee on Education Excellence, which asserts, "For decades, we have pursued wave after wave of 'silver bullet' reforms, with shamefully little to show for billions of dollars of investment."[4] We offer, instead, a framework of organizational and governance options and an analysis of the results that might be expected from relying on some rather than others. Above all, our analysis indicates, it is important to link capacity, responsibility, motivation, and decision-making authority to the places where the battle for student achievement is being waged (and too often lost) in the public school system.

Change is needed on a very broad scale. The nation's public schools are not just failing to generate comparable educational outcomes for diverse racial, ethnic, social, economic, and linguistic student subgroups. They are underperforming for a substantial majority of the nation's children. They are understaffed, overregulated, and inadequately organized. Notably, they lack the infrastructure needed to constructively accommodate powerful state and federal policy initiatives.[5]

The body of our review distinguishes eight domains of organizational structure and explores the possibilities for reform within each. We begin with education's core technologies—curriculum, instruction, and assessment—and then expand the inquiry to include classroom, school, district, community, state, and federal policy options. Along the way we visit teacher professionalism and social capital policy options. We focus primarily on the extent to which organizational designs impact the development of educational achievement gaps and how restructuring might help to ameliorate them. The restructuring options under review involve fiscal and technical changes, of course; they also involve social, political, and symbolic changes.

Achievement Gaps Are Held in Place by Intersecting Social Systems

Although we focus on organizational structures, it is important to note that school achievement is held in place by the convergence of three basic social systems: (1) community and family culture, (2) school governance and policy frameworks, and (3) a professional ethos and organization that mediates the relationship between governance systems and communities. These three social systems operate with different logics, are under the control of different groups, and are engaged in a perpetual contest for control of the educational system.

No matter how committed one may be to eliminating achievement differences, policies must work through the people who teach school lessons and manage school operations. Thus, education policy analyses must be grounded in the study of *influence* over performance rather than direct action on the school problems.[6] Moreover, education is a relatively fragile business requiring confidence and trust among staff, students, and community members in order to operate effectively.[7] Harsh demands and threats of dire consequences for failure to produce needed improvements always run the risk of producing fear, confusion, and wasted efforts if staff do not recognize policy makers' expectations as legitimate, the attainment of established goals as realistic, and the resources available to produce expected results as adequate.

It is also important to keep in mind that policies exert influence over schools in diverse ways. In a widely cited paper, McDonnell and Elmore generate a list of influential policy mechanisms, including mandates, inducements, capacity building investments, and system-changing authority transfers.[8] In 2004, McDonnell expanded the list to include what she called "*hortatory*" jawboning policies.[9] Market strategies serve to supplement these governmental mechanisms.[10]

To be effective, these policy mechanisms must be used in ways that successfully offset what Williamson and House describe as "transaction costs"—costs that limit the willingness and ability to respond to policy and program changes enacted by school reformers.[11] Transaction costs are incurred whenever choices are made, routines are changed, or one tries to employ a new program or technique. They interfere with learning new programs or abandoning established practices. Recognizing, then, that policies aimed at closing school achievement gaps must influence stakeholders and accommodate transaction costs, we turn to a review of the eight structures that policy initiatives might address.

1. CORE TECHNOLOGY RESTRUCTURING OPTIONS

Education's core technologies are curriculum (which specifies the content of instruction), instruction (which facilitates the learning of curriculum content), and student assessment (which enables educators to monitor the efficacy of the curriculum content and instructional techniques used to deliver it). Research on examining ways of improving each of these core technologies is voluminous and, surprisingly, quite controversial.

Curricular reforms. Curricular reforms, particularly in reading, mathematics, and science, have been given very high profile support by state and particularly federal policy makers, with spectacular claims routinely made for both the successes and failures of these efforts. The "reading wars" have become legendary as practicing teachers have been alternately praised and castigated for relying on basal readers, "whole language" materials, or phonics curricula in the instruction of young readers. Many curricular innovations have apparently produced very large increases in student reading proficiency as they are exposed to one reading curriculum or another. But, after more than a half-century of serious, sustained, reasonably well resourced, and academically demanding curricular reforms, the achievement gaps between rich and poor, white and nonwhite, English language learners and native English speakers remain stubbornly resistant to changes in theory and practice. Individual teachers and individual schools have repeatedly produced very large student reading gains only to discover that these islands of excellence could not be consolidated into the green valleys of consistent and equitable reading achievement reformers expected.

Mathematics and science reforms have a similar history of lofty aspirations accompanied by serious professional disagreements about how to pursue them and a failure of highly successful programs to "scale up" or become replicable in new contexts at new sites. (For a detailed review of the history of curriculum debates from a national perspective, see Tom Loveless's 2001 edited volume, *The Great Curriculum Debate*.)[12]

In recent years, state and federal policy makers have shifted their curriculum reform focus away from trying to specify the scope and sequence of lessons to be taught in favor of defining "curriculum standards." The standards approach seeks to specify what children must know and be able to do, without trying to specify how to teach this content. As state and federal officials have moved toward standards, a significant group of reform activists and publishers of curriculum materials have been diligently trying to specify the content of classroom lessons—often with detailed scripts to be followed. It is too soon to tell whether either the standards movement or the scripted lessons reform efforts will substantially reduce the achievement gaps. Both have seen some notable successes and both have received substantial criticism.

Some recent research indicates that adoption of state standards does not easily translate into standardized classroom curricula. Despite the development, mandating, and widespread staff training in state standards, teachers often teach to different standards depending on the academic level of their courses and students, and tend to use instructional strategies that lower standards and emphasize basic skills for already low performing students.[13]

Instruction. Instruction, the second core technology, has been subjected to serious restructuring using several broad reform strategies. No doubt, the most promising approaches to instructional reform involve restructuring teacher preservice, induction, and in-service professional development. This approach to instructional reform is at the heart of efforts to enhance teacher professionalism— the reform strategy discussed in Section 3, below.

While giving substantial attention to teacher professionalism in recent years, policy makers interested in improved instruction have also relied heavily on monitoring outcomes and holding schools and teachers responsible for attaining specified outcome levels. Researchers have found, however, that whereas pass rates improve over time, the extent to which this is the result of improved teaching and learning is unclear. The results could be arising because students are becoming familiar with test formats, teachers are narrowing the curriculum to focus on tested items, states are making tests easier and/or lowering cutoff scores, or low achieving students are being removed from the testing program.[14] The removal of low-achieving students involves dropping out, "opportunity transfers," grade retention, reclassification of students as learning handicapped, or giving them inappropriate test accommodations. There have even been several cases of attempts to increase test scores through scoring manipulation rather than effective instruction.[15] In short, without a climate of trust and support, a coherent network of policies, and adequate resources, teachers can be expected to substitute test score production for comprehensive content teaching when their status or their jobs are put at risk under instructional outcome monitoring policies.

Assessment. Assessment is the third component in the public schools' core technology. Assessing student academic learning has a variety of important purposes. Teachers test students to hold them accountable for learning and to ascertain whether the curriculum and instructional techniques they are using have been successful in generating comprehension and recall of lessons. Schools use test data to ascertain whether programs are working and whether students need to be considered for placement in special programs for the gifted or learning challenged. School districts and state departments of education use student assessment data to characterize schools and, sometimes, even classrooms within schools as producing adequate academic growth rates. Researchers utilize assessment data to document the relative effectiveness of various programs and to determine what factors are actually responsible for variations in the rate of achievement and contribute to the development of achievement gaps among student groups.

Many policy makers assume that close monitoring of student achievement test scores, combined with accountability measures requiring failing schools to provide extra services, reorganize program and staff, and/or allow parents to opt out of the low-performing schools, will provide the leverage needed to secure substantial student achievement gains. Indeed, the No Child Left Behind Act relies on a theory which asserts that public education systems can produce large gains in achievement and equality of educational attainment without substantial new resources and without fundamental or long-term systemic organizational changes. Unfortunately, basic achievement trends remain almost exactly what they were before NCLB was adopted. Moreover, students are receiving less instruction in subjects not tested and may, therefore, be actually declining in overall academic attainment.

Though California is a notable exception, assessment reforms in many states are not very well coordinated with curriculum development efforts. As recently as 2000, research found that while many states are using high-stakes tests rather than standards to guide instruction, the tests have little overlap with what teachers actually teach. Reviewed state tests and curricula revealed that test-to-curriculum correspondence ranged from as little as 5 percent to only about 46 percent.[16] Fortunately, some states have begun to tackle the coordination of assessments and curricula quite energetically in recent years. California, for example, has one of the most thoroughly aligned systems, but this alignment is not accompanied by systematic comparison data regarding the extent to which the curricular standards most emphasized by teachers are the ones most central to high student scores on the state tests or how much the standards are contributing to any reduction in persistent achievement gaps.

Resnick and Zurawsky note that the reason many state tests are not well aligned to state curriculum standards is not because the tests do not include the standards, but because they don't test the full range of state standards and objectives.[17] Test developers tend to focus on simpler cognitive processes and teachers tend to teach to that expectation, neglecting curricular content that is of a higher order and harder to assess. California has tried to resist this tendency, but when it attempted to assess some harder-to-measure content in the early 1990s with the California Learning Assessment System (CLAS) test, the result was widespread public resistance to test content and form.

High-stakes testing programs typically encourage teachers to align instruction to the tests rather than to curriculum standards whenever they find divergence between these two strategies for core technology reform.[18] Students not meeting standards are typically moved out of courses with broader curricular goals to be given double or triple doses of the test-specific curricula.

Many scholars and policy makers see the National Assessment of Educational Programs (NAEP) tests as the appropriate benchmark testing system to assess whether states are making progress toward meeting common national achievement goals. On the NAEP tests, however, student performance has generally reached a plateau and even receded somewhat in the last few years. This raises questions about whether assessment-driven, standards-based reform and accountability can be expected to raise achievement and/or close achievement gaps.[19]

One criticism of NAEP testing is that it seeks to hold children to unrealistic standards. Rothstein argues that the NAEP tests are "excellent" but proficiency cut-points are not credible.[20] This is evidenced by the fact that 40 to 60 percent of Taiwanese students (who lead the world in mathematics achievement) would be scored as "below proficient" using the NAEP scoring system.

Summary. Linda Darling-Hammond summarizes reforms addressing the restructuring of schools' core technologies, finding them to be far from a perfect solution to issues of achievement improvement.[21] She argues that advocates of standards hoped they would spur other reforms, including high-quality curriculum frameworks and materials, and assessments tied to the standards, with resource equalization and professional development to assure that teachers would be able to help needy students. These reforms have not been well integrated and serious mid-course corrections are needed.

Mulcahy offers a blunt and dismissive assessment of the overall impact of restructuring at this level, saying that, "[c]entralized and standardized curricula and testing have ensured that a child's school day consists primarily of test preparation . . . an absence of education."[22]

California illustrates a common weakness in core technology reform efforts. Like many others, this state's system of school finance is not closely aligned to the basic premises of standards and accountability reform policies. Although the standards-based reforms promise to exchange increased flexibility in fiscal controls and governance for improved student outcomes, we find that a large proportion of education budgets continue to flow into *restricted* categorical accounts (approximately 35% in California), limiting how local school systems can spend scarce resources. Until very recently, the proportion of categorically restricted funds grew steadily, tripling in the last thirty years.[23] The recent fiscal crisis has, to some extent, reduced categorical restrictions—but the rationale for these reduced restrictions is based on cost cutting, not educational program development.

We have not seen promising new organizational or policy approaches to restructuring the core technologies of curriculum, instruction, and assessment. Standards-based, assessment- driven, research-guided core technology improvement has been at the heart of restructuring work for nearly a generation without showing signs of erasing basic achievement gaps. Indeed, over the last half-century an avalanche of changes, large and small, with and without research support, has been pushed by policy makers and pulled by professional leaders into the schools; but the achievement gap has remained large and intractable. There are, to be sure, hundreds of small-scale success stories showing that individual schools or school districts can, for various periods of time, overcome the odds and develop both high-quality and highly equitable local programs. Perhaps the most important core technology restructuring lesson lies in these oft-told stories—it seems increasingly likely that successful school program improvement lies not in standardization, replication, and "scaling up" of high-performance programs, but in local professional commitment to full engagement with families and communities to find unique solutions that match professional talent and capacity with local needs and interests.

2. CLASSROOM LEVEL RESTRUCTURING OPTIONS

There are many organizational dimensions to school classrooms beyond the ways in which they define and incorporate the core technologies of curriculum, instruction, and student assessment. How classrooms are organized can facilitate or deflect teaching and learning processes in important ways. The most important classroom structures are those that involve grouping students, specifying the timing and sequencing of their learning experiences, and establishing the controls needed to assure privacy, safety, and orderliness during the execution of instruction.

Schools have dozens of ways of differentiating classroom structures. Whole classes or instructional groups within them can be composed in ways that are homogeneous or heterogeneous with regard to race and ethnicity, prior academic achievement, family and student interest, specialized academic programming, and so on. Individual lessons can be made longer or shorter, the school day or school year can vary substantially in length, school calendars can be organized on a single- or multitrack year-round or traditional September to June calendar. Students can be strictly age or grade-level stratified, or they can attend combination grade classes with one to three grade-level differences among members of the class. Grade boundaries can be rigid, or student progress can be continuous.

At the extremes of academic achievement, classrooms are structured to segregate students—Gifted and Talented Education programs for the high achievers and special day classes for the learning disabled, emotionally disturbed, and mentally handicapped. These academic segregations were created to allow students to progress in their studies at different rates (compatible with their abilities and interests) and thus they virtually guarantee that 5 to 10 percent of the highest- and lowest-performing students will be exposed to classroom processes that exacerbate rather than ameliorate achievement gaps. In the middle ranks of student achievement there is also very widespread utilization of achievement tracking, embraced as a means of adjusting instruction to student needs and capacities, but again virtually assuring that continued schooling will reinforce achievement gaps for students so placed.

In their comprehensive summary of the literature, Gamoran and Long point out that classroom structural differences are more important even than fiscal differences in determining school effectiveness. They conclude that "[w]ithin-school studies have focused on the effects of processes such as tracking and exposure to learning material. Research on teacher effects reinforces the conclusion that within-school variation in achievement is partially attributable to schooling."[24]

Options for Restructuring Classrooms

A wide variety of classroom restructuring options are to be found in the professional and scholarly literature on this topic. We describe here eight of the most widely reported and most frequently supported with data.

1. *Tighten the system.* The dominant theme of recent efforts to restructure classroom operations has been to substantially restrict the autonomy of teachers. This is done by clarifying and mandating learning outcome standards, aligning curriculum and pedagogy with those standards, linking assessments to both curricular content and outcome standards, specifying curriculum sequencing and reteaching of unmastered elements, creating and enforcing teacher and administrator accountability for the specified outcomes, creating systems of teacher-centered and administrator-managed instruction, and placing students and staff at substantial risk of significant negative consequences if they do not follow guidelines or reach specified outcomes.

2. *Loosen the system.* Many observers recommend just the opposite strategy for raising achievement. Scholars like Oakes and Page see ability-group tracking as a primary mechanism for within-school achievement gap production.[25] And Linda McNeil found that teachers in Texas retreated from responsibility and adopted what she calls "defensive teaching" under the pressure of standards-based accountability systems.[26] Others observe that teachers opt for teaching to the test and focusing their efforts on students close to, but below, proficient in order to raise passing rates without actually closing achievement gaps. For such observers, the system-tightening reforms noted above exacerbate rather than ameliorating the achievement gap problem. These analysts urge detracking classes, giving all students access to high-quality materials, involving teachers and families in democratic decision making regarding instructional content and learning priorities, providing school programs of choice for families, and making instruction student and family centered. They see student motivation and parental support as major areas of concern and want schools to rely on interest and ambition to drive selection of high-quality learning opportunities.

3. *Disaggregate the system.* Jumping off from the well-documented research findings showing that students in smaller schools have higher achievement, some educators are enthusiastic about programs supporting the creation of

smaller schools and smaller classes within schools to provide a more intimate and engaging atmosphere.[27] They argue for reduced central control over curriculum content and teaching method on the grounds that—at least within smaller and intimate schools—personal commitments and family support will focus teaching and learning activities.[28]

4. *Desegregate the system.* American public schools are substantially segregated in ways that are certain to exacerbate achievement gaps. Poor, nonwhite and English language learners are concentrated in some schools and some classrooms within schools. These stratifications become all the more supportive of achievement gap production when instruction is simplified and slowed down for the students who are farthest behind. This suggests that policies should be formulated to ensure that the composition of each school and each classroom is balanced with regard to ethnicity, achievement, socioeconomic class, and other achievement-related factors.

5. *Professionalize the system.* Observers who see housing market–based segregation as politically irresistible and who support differentiated instruction for children with different learning needs urge professionalization of teaching as a primary mechanism for restructuring classrooms. They want policies that strengthen teacher training and certification, enhance induction support systems, encourage strong teacher professional development services, create differential pay and status based on teacher capacity to improve student outcomes, and reexamine teacher organizations, making them less protective of teachers and more supportive of professional standards development and enforcement.[29]

6. *Stabilize the system.* As much as 75 percent of the students in many urban classrooms change schools at least once during the school year.[30] Unfortunately, this student mobility tends to be worst among low-achieving students, compounding their learning problems and making it likely that achievement gaps will be exacerbated.[31] Teacher turnover and absenteeism is also typically higher in classes where achievement problems are the most pressing.[32] Observers focusing on these problems urge policies that will reduce student and teacher turnover and mobility: provide attendance incentives, report school-level cohort mobility rates, hold schools and school districts accountable for students who make nonpromotional school changes, bolster school guidance counseling by reducing the student/counselor ratio, and give teachers multi-year responsibility for student achievement so that they can really be held accountable for following individual student achievement trajectories.[33] Also, keep richer records of student achievement and have those records follow the students closely.[34]

7. *Strongly enforce the NCLB school safety policy.* A nontrivial number of families adopting home schooling or choosing to send their children to charter

schools do so because they do not feel that their children are safe in the schools to which they are nominally assigned.[35] Families not opting out are pressuring the schools to control bullying, violence, and harassment. They want policies that improve the attractiveness and quality of educational spaces and make schools more interesting places in which to spend a thirty-hours-plus work week for students and teachers.

8. *Integrate community social services.* Starting about two decades ago concerted efforts began to be made to combine educational programs with other social services—welfare, public health and mental health services, community development activities and adult counseling, and support and learning opportunities. Particularly prominent among these efforts have been the creation of before- and afterschool programs of nutrition, child care, and homework assistance to support families where the parent(s) are holding down full-time employment and cannot find affordable child care. Building on this base, advocates of this multisocial services model of schooling seek closer collaboration among community service professionals. Unfortunately, this cooperation is hard to sustain because most of the needed social services are organized on a casework basis, while public schools organize their work programmatically. The case-based professional workers are sensitive about privacy issues and have little experience in mounting or sustaining programs.[36]

At least as important as the specific direction taken in pursuing class-level instructional reforms is assuring that whatever reforms are undertaken, they be undertaken with relentless dedication to quality and consistency. The observations regarding English Language Development programs articulated by the authors of the September 2007 EdSource Report apply equally to all of the reform options discussed in this section of the chapter: "[T]he quality of . . . instruction matters more than a given number of minutes. Quality . . . instruction includes careful consideration of the content, the delivery, the amount and type of scaffolding (support) provided, and constant monitoring of student progress to intervene when needed."[37]

3. RESTRUCTURING OF THE TEACHING PROFESSION

A third broad array of restructuring opportunities involves changes in the way teachers are prepared, organized, supervised, evaluated, and compensated. Teacher training and certification have been undergoing three alternative, and not very compatible, restructuring processes. Preservice testing of teachers to assure that they have both the basic skills they are expected to teach and an array of pedagogical skills indicating that they know how to teach has become a major industry as states have adopted multiple screening tests. California has been a leader in this area, requiring that individuals seeking employment in this state pass multiple tests of their knowledge and skills. Accompanying these preservice screening tests have been adoption of fairly rigorous program standards to guide universities in the creation of training programs, and the strengthening of review processes to help assure that these standards are enforced. States have also strengthened their resolve to require that teachers at the high school level have more advanced training in the subjects they teach by requiring undergraduate college credits or rigorous tests and by monitoring and restricting teachers assigned to teach outside their subject-matter qualifications.

Even as this basic pipeline for teacher training and certification has become more rigorous and better monitored, however, states have been adopting and expanding alternative certification programs to overcome teacher shortages in hard-to-staff positions in rural and urban schools and in subject areas difficult to fill. In California, for example, an alternative certification (intern) program is currently being relied on to train about a third of all new teachers. About half the current crop of interns are working for certification in special education, which means that a majority of new special education teachers are being trained while they are working as full-time teachers of record in special education classrooms.

The third prong of current reform efforts involves enhancing professional induction, in-service training, and advanced certification. In an effort to strengthen the effectiveness of new teachers and prevent the very high attrition rates that plague most public school systems, many states have adopted formal induction programs to provide advanced training and support for new teachers. California's program, Beginning Teacher Support and Assessment, requires newly certificated teachers to spend two years in a close working relationship with an experienced support provider teacher and to undertake a series of training and development activities aimed at assuring increased competence and confidence. Recently this program, rather than university-based preservice training institutions, has been given responsibility for recommending teachers for permanent certification. This and similar programs are part of a broad movement, urged on by a cacophony of complaints about the quality of the nation's university-based education schools, to shift control over certification standards and processes toward practicing professional educators.

In addition to moderately expensive early-stage induction programs, teacher professional development and training programs have been undergoing serious scrutiny, with strongly worded demands for doing away with "one-shot" training programs in favor of team-based training organized by and supportive of local school site "professional learning communities." At the high end of this transformation of in-service professionalism is the National Board certification, which seeks to create a differentiated teaching workforce, with some teachers recognized as high-performance teachers capable of professional leadership.

Whether any or all of the teacher enhancements will work to significantly ameliorate persistent achievement gaps is quite uncertain. At one extreme, research seems to show that teachers with emergency credentials do about as well as those holding standard teaching credentials.[38] And there is little evidence that state testing requirements have an impact on teaching effectiveness.[39] There is evidence that students whose teachers are working outside of their certified field tend to perform less well on achievement tests in those subject areas. It is also clear from Linda Darling-Hammond's seminal work on teacher training that there are significant benefits for student achievement to be garnered from advanced teacher training.[40] Rivkin, Hanushek, and Kain find that there is no evidence that teachers with MA/MS degrees have greater impacts on student achievement.[41] They note important gains in teaching quality during the first year of teaching experience and smaller gains over the next few years, but little evidence of improvement after the first three years. There are significant negative effects on student achievement resulting from teacher turnover.

Some observers are quite confident that teacher training and work role restructuring will provide significant reductions in achievement gaps. Rivkin, Hanushek, and Kain, for example, argue that substantial differences in teachers' ability to facilitate student achievement make it likely that effective hiring, firing, monitoring, and promotion practices would significantly reduce the achievement gap.[42]

Teacher compensation is another factor that no doubt plays an important role in determining the overall quality of the workforce. School districts are quick to report that even modest differences in pay rates have a quite significant impact on the availability of qualified teaching candidates. At the same time, private schools, with their more select and committed student bodies, are able to staff their schools despite significantly lower salaries. Overall, though there is some dispute in the literature, it is evident that teachers are not particularly well paid when compared with similarly trained professionals. As Johnson and Liu report,

> *Analysts bring different assumptions to different sets of data and, therefore, reach different conclusions about whether teachers' pay is substantially lower than that of comparably trained employees in other fields. An analysis conducted by* Education Week *showed that the 1994 salary gap between teachers with bachelor's degrees and nonteachers with bachelor's degrees was $11,035 (in 1998 dollars). Just four years later, in 1998, this gap had risen 61 percent to $18,006.*[43]

Teacher Organization and Collective Bargaining

It is not much of an exaggeration to see teacher unions and the National Labor Relations Act (NLRA)–style collective bargaining they utilize as the proverbial six-hundred-pound gorilla in the school reform living room. Teacher unions have succeeded in organizing a substantial majority of public school teachers. They have negotiated significant job protection rights into most union contracts, and they have energetically accepted their legal responsibility to aggressively represent the interests of individual teachers who are accused of inadequate job performance.

This may all be changing as recently elected Republican governors and state legislators seek to repeal collective bargaining provisions in a number of states, but after a long history of periodic and unfair abuse by religious, social, political, and economic interests in local communities, public school teachers are not going to give up hard-won protections easily. There are, however, some creative possibilities that could work to strengthen union members' resolve to be more supportive of school reform and improvement. It is thinkable, for example, that public school teachers might shift from the NLRA model of industrial unionism toward the sort of model used by artist unions (e.g., for screen writers, musicians, etc.). The artist union model recognizes that individuals possess quite different levels of talent and ability and expect individuals to be rewarded for their unique talents. For this reason, the artist unions negotiate a base compensation that provides struggling artists with a living wage, but expect talented and skilled artists to be compensated according to their performance levels. More importantly, while artist unions insist that art production firms rely on union members, they are even more concerned about securing artistic control over their work and negotiate mechanisms for assuring that creativity will be recognized and control over its utilization be shared between artists and those who produce their work for public recognition. It is also thinkable that teachers might be willing to accept differentiated status and compensation in exchange for expanded artistic control over their work. By and large, teachers already recognize that their colleagues possess different types and levels of teaching talent. They already know that some teaching assignments are much easier than others and that there are insufficient incentives in the public schools to encourage teachers to take on the most challenging assignments.

Serious reform of teacher unionism will not be achieved easily, and it would require significantly expanding teachers' artistic control in the workplace. Moreover, schools and school leaders would have to play a significant role in recognizing the high performance of teachers deserving compensation beyond negotiated base rates, which would require a level of artistic "connoisseurship" that goes beyond the sophistication of many school leaders today. On the other hand, many parts of this reform are already being tried in various schools and school districts.

A number of local unions are trying to engage in "interest" rather than "rights" bargaining to create a more collaborative pursuit of schooling excellence. And the National Board strategy for advanced certification of professional teachers has already legitimated recognition of unusually effective teachers. Additionally, differentiated staffing, teacher career ladders, and merit pay schemes have been tried periodically for more than half a century. Each of these pieces has proven to be fragile and impermanent when tried alone, but they might work if a coordinated effort were made to link transformation of the compensation system to enhancing teachers' artistic status and control and recognition of the contributions of unusually dedicated, skilled, and talented teachers.

4. RESTRUCTURING SCHOOL ORGANIZATIONS

The fourth level at which restructuring and management changes might be expected to significantly impact student achievement gaps is in the structuring of schools as complex organizations and valued civic institutions. In many ways, this has been the mainstay of continuing efforts to address schooling effectiveness and equality of educational opportunity. As with other restructuring initiatives, the schools have seen a virtual avalanche of policy initiatives aimed at altering their structure in hopes of altering their performance. Grade configurations were the earliest targets of reform and restructuring policies. Secondary schools, then kindergartens were added; soon it became important to create unique school systems for students in the middle or junior high school grades. The boundaries between elementary, middle, and high schools have been shifted and shuffled. Vocational high schools were early forms of restructuring; more recently, career-oriented specialized schools and schools for students not performing well in the typical public school have been added. With the beginning of the first federal Elementary and Secondary Education Act (ESEA) in 1965, Title I, Head Start program preschools, and, sometimes, infant day-care programs were added in many places. School calendars have been shuffled, sometimes extending the school year by a few days or creating year-round programs with vacation periods spread across the year. School programs have been extended to include afterschool and summer offerings—often as voluntary programs and increasingly as opportunities for low-performing students to get special help. State regulations typically specify in great detail the number of days and hours that schools must operate and the amount of time that must be devoted to specific subjects.

In expert witness testimony prepared for the California *Williams* case, R. Mitchell reports that year-round educational calendars are clearly detrimental to student achievement.[44] Moreover, the use of multitrack year-round calendars to accommodate overcrowding in the schools is far from randomly distributed—the children most likely to be on the low side of the achievement gap are also most likely to be attending multitrack year-round schools.

Students who have difficulty maintaining good academic, behavior, and/or attendance records in mainstream schools are often assigned to alternative schools. These schools are often not very successful in providing needed support and educational services. Indeed, California is not atypical in reporting that while alternative schools comprise only 8 percent of the total high school enrollment, they account for 33 percent of all dropouts. And charter schools, with 4 percent of enrollment, account for 16 percent of dropouts. The high percentage of dropouts represented by students at alternative schools may reflect the fact that many of the students enrolled in these schools are already at high risk of dropping out when they enter.[45]

Average academic achievement among all students enrolled in each school is typically viewed by the news media, parents, and particularly real estate agents as the primary mechanism for assessing the quality of school staff and programs. Unfortunately, while achievement varies systematically across schools, "attempts to measure the school attributes that account for achievement variation generally fall short . . . only small portions of these effects have been attributed to specific teacher characteristics."[46] Moreover, the contributions of specific school and teacher characteristics are difficult to detect. The Coleman finding that social composition of the student body is more important than teacher characteristics or school facilities remains unchallenged.[47]

Family Choice and Creating Educational Market Structures

From the beginning of the twentieth century until the 1960s, business and political leaders concentrated reform and restructuring efforts on getting schools to emulate business practices. To produce what David Tyack labeled the "one best system," policy leaders throughout this period emphasized strong executive leadership (at the district rather than the individual school level), specialization of roles and functions throughout the school systems, and regimentation of class organization and operations.[48] By the 1970s, however, a number of key research findings began to coalesce to raise questions about the business/industrial model. It was noted that private and small schools often outperformed large public schools. It began to be believed that schools had monopoly control over educational service delivery and that this monopolistic control led to a system that was unresponsive to need and preference on the part of families and children. It was noted as early as the 1960s that business attitudes and pressures were making schools too impersonal and insensitive.[49] It was recognized that political pressure and especially court litigation were necessary to secure a more responsive school bureaucracy, one willing to address the needs of the poor, the nonwhites, the educationally disabled, the gifted and talented, the children at risk of failure, and even the equal treatment of girls and boys.

These findings set in motion a vigorous political campaign to provide families and children more choices and to subject schools to competitive market forces. Mandated client involvement began with the federal Elementary and Secondary Education Act (1965) when then senator Robert Kennedy insisted on Title I advisory councils to review program effectiveness and sign off on budgets.[50] Soon, however, advocates for families and students shifted toward private choice rather than regulated governance involvement. Open enrollment requirements, school vouchers redeemable at schools of choice, and charter schools were all developed with the expectation that schools would become more responsive to client needs and interests. More determined families opted increasingly for home schooling and enrollment in private and religious schools to realize their aspirations for choice of program content and pedagogical style.

As summarized by Gamoran and Long, evidence regarding the impact of family school choices exercised through reliance on private schools, publicly supported educational vouchers, and/or charter schools is mixed and highly controversial.[51] Some important studies find significant positive effects on student test score achievement; others of apparently equal quality find no achievement effects. Although no important studies have documented a negative impact on achievement test scores, there is evidence that these choice mechanisms are facilitating socioeconomic stratification of students—a factor that is often associated with increasing achievement gaps.

School choice does not lead to detracking of students. Student tracking continues despite extensive criticism of the practice. It is tied to larger issues of social inequality and racial injustice.[52] A case study by Alvarez and Mehan seems to prove that detracking can be achieved in at least some settings.[53] Teachers remain supportive of tracking practices, however.[54]

Integration: Attendance Boundaries, School and Classroom Composition

Racial, cultural, and socioeconomic integration in schools has been shown to have a significant impact on equalizing student achievement. Hanushek, Kain, Markman, and Rivkin find that peer average achievement has a highly significant effect on learning across the test score distribution.[55] Hence, differences in peer characteristics will have a substantial effect if sustained across a child's school career. According to Rumberger and Palardy, what matters most is the socioeconomic, not the racial, composition of schools and classrooms.[56] Average schoolwide SES is nearly as powerful as a student's own SES in predicting achievement test scores.

Unfortunately, however, segregation in U.S. schools outside the south has "nearly returned to the level in the late 1960s . . . This fact in part reflects changes in the U.S. population, which has a much greater proportion of minority students overall, but it also reflects the rollback of school desegregation policies."[57]

School Size, Class Size

The Tennessee STAR experiment represents the most sophisticated test of whether reducing class size can be expected to enhance student achievement. The results of this experiment were very promising—average achievement for the children in small classes rose significantly. Moreover, the achievement of minority children rose more than that of their white peers. Unfortunately, this positive result has never been replicated. Achievement effects arising from California's massive class size reduction program (adopted in 1995) were quite disappointing, and similarly modest and unsustained effects were found in other state programs.

Ehrenberg, Brewer, Gamoran, and Williams question whether external validity for the Tennessee STAR experiment was sufficiently established to warrant the generalizations typically made across populations and settings.[58] Additionally, they argue that using the money that would be spent on class size reduction to instead improve teacher pay in ways that might improve student learning—such as rewarding teachers for gaining subject-matter competencies, increasing student academic performance, or reducing teacher absenteeism or turnover—might ultimately be more effective. Moreover, a recent study by Northwestern University's Konstantopoulos finds that while the Tennessee STAR small classes outperformed the larger ones, they also expanded the dispersion in student achievement, making achievement gaps worse rather than better.[59]

With regard to school size, the positive benefits of smallness are less equivocal. Lee and Smith conclude that, while all (and particularly disadvantaged) students learn more in small classes, "the mechanism through which school size 'translates' to student learning is surely complex, operating primarily through its influence on how schools are organized.[60]

Bryk, Lee, and Holland concur, saying,

> *The coordination of work in larger schools typically imposes demands for more formal modes of communication and encourages increased work specialization and a greater bureaucratization of school life. In contrast smaller school size facilitates personalism and social intimacy, both of which are much harder to achieve in larger organizational contexts.*[61]

Research on school district policies creating procedures and criteria for student retention in grade has found that these policies operate quite differently in large and small school districts in ways that support the Bryk, Lee, and Holland finding that smaller schools are more personal and less competitive.[62]

At least one study indicates that school differences are not just expressions of the family cultures represented among the students who attend them. Rivkin, Hanushek, and Kain identified large differences in the quality of Texas schools that occur in ways that rule out the possibility that they are created by family factors.[63] Hence, it is appropriate to conclude that school policy can be an important tool for raising achievement, particularly by providing students with a succession of good teachers who can help close family income–related achievement gaps. However, achievement gains that are systematically related to observable teacher and school characteristics are generally small compared to the magnitude of the demographic achievement gaps that need to be corrected.

5. RESTRUCTURING SCHOOL AND DISTRICT GOVERNANCE

Although they are the basic structures for school governance and political control, local school districts have been largely bypassed by reformers seeking to directly change schools and classrooms. Upheavals in the nation's major cities may be changing this picture, however. Large urban centers from Seattle to Boston and from Atlanta to San Diego have seen their school districts make major governance changes. Mayors have been activated to seek district control in Boston, Philadelphia, Chicago, and Los Angeles. San Diego experimented with hiring a high-profile federal prosecutor as school superintendent, Los Angeles gave that job to the ex-governor of Colorado, and Seattle hired a retired general for the job. While the achievement gaps in these reform cities have not disappeared, the cities' demonstrated willingness to make dramatic and politically charged governance changes may be an indicator of renewed interest in how school districts should be reorganized and restructured to enhance achievement and reduce persistent achievement gaps. Virtually all of the big districts have created de facto subdivisions that are expected to act more or less like the smaller school districts found in the suburbs.

Scholars of school district politics have documented quite powerful links between political activism and policy change at the district level.[64] School district policy changes are most often made effective through key personnel changes. Like businesses incurring economic losses and athletic teams with losing records, school boards tend to rely on changing their chief executive officers to initiate significant change. Indeed, a line of research begun in the mid-1960s found that districts seeking changed policies and programs drive those changes by appointing outsiders (individuals recruited from other districts or even from outside the education profession). These outsiders make substantial policy, program, and personnel changes within their first year or two on the job. The changed policies are not always effective, of course. They can raise anxieties, waste resources, and create a kind of "policy churn" that is self-destructive, disappoints community groups, and wearies the teaching staff.[65]

In their work "Strengthening School District Capacity as a Strategy to Raise Student Achievement in California," Rumberger and Connell summarize the nature of effective district-level policies.[66] They see five basic elements in successful district reforms. These include (1) meeting "critical conditions" for teaching and learning, (2) effectively structuring participatory processes and timelines for meeting specified benchmarks in all schools, (3) providing adequate technical support and assistance, (4) maintaining comprehensive data systems capable of aggregating data to the levels where decisions are being made, and (5) sustaining relationships with external partners that provide new ideas, support, and professional development for administrators, teachers, and the data system.

Strong district leadership appears to be particularly important in reshaping high school operations, because "[p]ower in most high schools is organized into a clear hierarchy, with decision making about school policy severely limited at lower levels of the hierarchy." And, therefore, to make restructuring really "take hold," high schools require profound changes in "their most fundamental and entrenched features."[67]

Democratic Participation and Parent Involvement

For at least a half-century, reformers have been trying to create and refine mechanisms for direct democratic participation in school policy development and program design. As Amy Gutmann reminds us, schooling has as one of its central purposes the nurturing of democratic beliefs and the realization of democratic means of governance.[68] Educators have responded to pressures for democratic participation with enthusiasm when those seeking to participate embrace "boosterism" and act in support of current practices. With the maturation of the schools as archetypal public bureaucracies, however, responses to requests for participation, accommodation, and program revisions have often led to deflection and resistance. But as Ream and Palardy have noted, networking among parents whose children attend school together provides not only feedback on effective child-rearing but also gives access to information about school policies, teachers, and students, making it possible for parents to work collaboratively with their children and school staff.[69]

This process supports the development of "social capital" that enables parents to successfully challenge professional educator control and secure adjustments in school design and academic service delivery. Indeed, middle- and upper-class families are especially effective in using this information exchange process to "influence school personnel on behalf of their children . . . In exercising this strategy, [they] directly facilitate their children's educational and social growth through strategic institutional interventions."[70]

Parents on the lowest rungs of the class ladder are less likely to tap their social networks for the explicit purpose of exerting power over schooling practices.[71] Ream and Palardy elaborate: "[W]hile lower and middle class parents share similar educational goals for their children, their social networks tend not to overlap."[72]

Clearly, if the democratic purposes of education are to be realized, school district leaders will need to not only accommodate parental engagement, but also nurture and support it as a means of improving school effectiveness, particularly for those students and families least comfortable presenting themselves to public officials.

6. REORGANIZING INTERMEDIATE UNITS AND COLLABORATIVES

A sixth level of opportunities for reorganization and restructuring concerns the work of intermediate school organizations and school district consortia, which—along with a broad array of entrepreneurial organizations, education management groups, charitable foundations, voluntary associations, and "think tanks"—have sprung up around the public school system with serious intentions of altering their performance. The array of these intermediate-level organizations is almost too numerous and varied to catalogue, much less to evaluate and confidently distinguish those that are helping to ease achievement gaps from those that seek private ends and may well be helping to create and sustain student group differences.

In several states, the county office of education plays a number of very important roles. Historically, these agencies were merely the point of contact for teachers seeking recognition of their teaching credentials and thus their right to work at schools within the county. Although substantively this function has been relocated to the state level, the counties may be able to provide leadership in a number of important areas, especially for the hundreds of districts that are too small to afford administrators with a number of crucial capacities. The counties also play a major role in the provision of schooling services for special education and vocational education students. They also provide monitoring and oversight for local districts discovered to be encountering fiscal difficulties. They have major curriculum and staff development responsibilities and serve as the lead agency for many categorically funded programs.

Consortia. Consortia of schools and districts, often working with and through intermediate education agencies, have acquired primary responsibility for a number of important services that influence the character and consequences of student achievement gaps. Vocational and technical education, for example, have been largely eliminated from many high school programs as a result of rising pressure to meet state test score targets. Recent studies show, however, that collaboratively organized regional occupational and vocational programs play a significant role in raising motivation, improving academic performance, and facilitating access to both the labor market and postsecondary schooling successes for non-college-bound high school students.[73] In California, special education services are also greatly enhanced through the development of Special Education Local Planning Area (SELPA) agencies that organize data, monitor program performance, and provide technical assistance. The California Governor's Committee on Educational Excellence made explicit recommendations for strengthening the role of county offices in the areas of educational data management, district support, staff development, and problem solving.[74]

Entrepreneurial interventions. In his study documenting social network instability that accompanies high mobility rates among Mexican-origin youth, Ream examines some examples of organized program interventions that involve school consortia. Two described in his work are AVID and Puente. Of these, he says, "AVID identifies students of mid-range abilities in the 8th grade who demonstrate the potential," and enrolls them in college-preparatory classes "while also offering a system of social scaffolding to help ensure their academic success."[75] Some recent studies indicate AVID program successes.[76]

The Puente Project "targets Latino students across a wide achievement spectrum and within the first two years of high school," offering mentoring "to help them graduate and go on to college."[77] The Chicano/Latino Policy Project offers a thorough overview of AVID and the Puente Project, including cost-benefit analyses.[78]

Philanthropic foundations and education management organizations. Philanthropic foundations—such as Annenberg, Carnegie, Ford, Gates, Heritage, and Hewlett—have provided substantial off-budget resources and have been a major stimulus for program innovations and school restructuring experiments. King reports "[e]xpanded access to pre-kindergarten" due to the coordinating efforts of "private foundations, such as The Pew Charitable Trusts, Joyce Foundation, and David and Lucille Packard Foundation and national non-profit organizations."[79]

Unfortunately, foundations do not make permanent commitments of resources, and thus local schools and districts that use foundation resources as start-up money to get a program into operation must be careful not to cripple ongoing budget needs in trying to sustain the programs when the foundation resources are gone.

7. RESHAPING THE STATE POLICY AND GOVERNANCE SYSTEM

Over the last half-century education policy control has shifted dramatically away from local schools and school districts and into the hands of politicians and agency administrators at the state and federal levels. Historically, the state legislatures have often led the way in setting new policy directions. They have repeatedly upped the ante on teacher preparation and professional development. They adopted most of the recommendations of the *Nation at Risk* report, in some cases even before it had actually been written.[80] Many state agencies were early adopters of substantial student testing programs and have a belated but in some states reasonable record of creating programs for various special populations. Since the passage of California's Proposition 13 in 1978, financing public education in many states has moved substantially into the hands of the state government. The legislature and governor have not just controlled financing, they have adopted dozens of special programs and policies demonstrating their belief that with fiscal responsibility comes the right and obligation to exercise policy control.

States vary quite dramatically in the level of overall funding they provide to the public schools. With the budget crises following the 2007 economic recession, many states have found it necessary to dramatically curtail state investment in their schools.

In many states, educators have witnessed significant and protracted political conflicts among the major education policy initiators—the governor, the legislature, the state departments of education, and the major professional educator associations. As these agencies have wrestled with each other for power and authority over school policies, they have also had to interact with advocates for other core state programs—welfare, prisons, infrastructure construction, and so forth. Strong lobbying comes from business and industry, from environmental groups, from the medical community, from the state's largest school districts, and others. With substantial turnover among elected officials (especially in term-limit states) and the bevy of well-organized and highly paid lobbyists representing competing interests, state education policy leaders find it very difficult to formulate coherent policies and to maintain focus on their implementation. In this centralized and highly politicized policy environment, stability of policy direction, regulatory mandates, and fiscal support have typically been overrun by competing demands for state policy-maker attention and resources, by periodic crises in other public sectors, and by the demands of various special interests. Education policies have been rendered spectacularly unstable in many states by shaky tax revenue systems.

The judicial branches of both the state and federal governments have also dramatically expanded their influence through sweeping judgments regarding student rights, administrative responsibilities, and the statutory and constitutional responsibilities of state and local governments regarding the financing and regulation of public schools. California has provided much of the grist for the judicial intervention by federal courts. This state preceded the landmark *Brown* decisions (of 1954 and 1955) by using the state courts to strike down ethnic segregation with the 1943 *Mendez* case overturning the creation of "Mexican" schools (this case led California governor Earl Warren to commit to school desegregation well before he became the chief justice who articulated the *Brown* court decisions). California also led in the litigation of landmark state school financing with adjudication of *Serrano v. Priest* (1974). Most recently, in the *Williams* case settlement, this state has acknowledged its responsibility for assuring that students have equitable access to school facilities and instructional resources as well as to reasonably comparable funding levels.

Policy Coherence and Fiscal Stability

State budget and finance policies have, in recent years, substantially centralized control over local school and school district budgets as they have complied with and elaborated upon federal categorical program initiatives creating restrictive categorical program structures. Meanwhile, teacher union negotiations have substantially constrained the rest of the local district budget. Though it is certainly true that revenue variations do not translate directly into achievement differences, nevertheless, "international evidence shows that school resources do have a strong effect on student achievement for the poorest countries" but produce "a diminishing (though non-zero) marginal return" as additional resources are provided.[81]

In many states, schools have seen an unproductive collision between state revenue limits that restrict expenditures and state demands for innovations aimed at improving overall achievement and reducing academic achievement gaps. There is something quite ironic about seeing the report of the California Governor's Committee on Education Excellence urging major new policy initiatives covered in the same daily newspapers as announcements of draconian staff and program cuts sweeping across California's local school districts.[82]

8. FEDERAL POLICY AND RESEARCH DIRECTIONS

Federal education policy has long been the primary source of educational research and development funding, as well as the major source of resources aimed at improving educational opportunities for poor, minority, and non-English-speaking students. Though education is among the nation's largest business enterprises, federal research and development funds for education are quite modest when compared to the resources provided to other fields.

The three primary education initiatives in current federal policy—the NCLB renewal of the Elementary and Secondary Education Act, the Institute of Education Sciences (which replaced the Office of Educational Research and Improvement), and Race to the Top (the Obama administration's primary education policy initiative)—all mark a quite dramatic change in federal policy. These new federal policies place the federal government at the center of the standards-based accountability approach to educational research support, school organization and management, and the development of research-based approaches to program innovation and improvement. As Gamoran and Long summarize, "NCLB has its own theories about how gaps can be reduced," but "at present few programs and policies have rigorous evidence of causal effects.[83]

With substantial controversy surrounding the congressional renewal of NCLB, it remains to be seen whether the new directions taken in the Bush and Obama administration's primary education initiatives will survive the resurgence of Republican congressional leadership or the 2012 presidential election cycle.

Data Collection, Organization, and Analysis at Levels Above the School and Classroom

No doubt the most important contribution by state and federal administrative agencies is the development of data record-keeping and analysis systems that support both educators and their critics in their efforts to discern the effects of various factors influencing student achievement. Until recently, statistical data on educational programs, staff, resources, and actual operations have been collected in such delayed, disconnected, and inconsistent ways that it has been impossible to create real-time models of school operations and their outcomes. Over the next decade or so, this should change dramatically, allowing local educators to monitor institutional actions and their effects in ways that allow for timely adjustments in curricular content, instructional services, and assessment procedures. Only as new data monitoring and analysis systems become available is it possible to imagine that educators can move from their current fear that reliable data is primarily a resource for school critics rather than for school managers and program implementers.

CONCLUSION

The materials reviewed in this chapter support five broad conclusions about how policy makers might develop organizational structures and policies for addressing the very large achievement gaps separating poor, language-learning, and nonwhite students from their more advantaged peers.

1. *No single policy can hope to close the achievement gap.*

    The academic gaps in the public schools are large and persistent. And, except for the substantial progress made during the Great Society's War on Poverty programs, they have stubbornly resisted reform efforts for over half a century. There are examples of powerful policies that have closed achievement gaps in specific locations, for some populations, or for short periods of time. But locally successful programs have not been reliably "taken to scale." Changes in leadership or participant groups typically disrupt otherwise successful interventions, and repeated implementations of nominally identical programs do not have comparable effects. Thus schools, like other complex organizations, likely improve best through many, generally small, changes produced through persistent, well-supported efforts. In short, overcoming achievement gaps will not arise from "doing the right thing," but will require "doing everything right."

To get things right requires intense engagement, an emphasis on problem solving, and a dedication to team building. As Tough argues, schools with impressive results (1) require many more hours of instruction, (2) offer tutoring after school, on Saturdays, and in the summer, (3) leaven long hours with music classes, languages, trips, and sports even while spending extra time on reading and math, and (4) have an emphasis on team building, cooperation, and creativity.[84]

2. *Changes need to restructure family, school, and community relationships and redistribute achievement within the classrooms.*

The most optimistic projections of the extent to which school or district-level changes could reduce achievement gaps do not come close to solving the problem. More than two-thirds of the variance in student achievement is found *within* classrooms—less than one-third *between* classrooms and schools. School and district-level changes can be expected to substantially ameliorate achievement differences only if they systematically reorganize what goes on within the classroom.

3. *Classroom performance depends on (1) teacher professional capacity, (2) school and district leadership, and (3) school demographic composition.*

Several promising strategies for improving teacher professionalism have been identified. Recent research studies suggest that effective administrative leadership includes such moral imperatives as trustworthiness, interpersonal authority, the boldness that springs from deep personal commitment to a vision of social justice, and thoroughly grounded professional competence. As Coleman long ago documented, classroom composition is a very potent factor affecting student achievement, more important than teacher characteristics or school facilities.[85]

4. *Human and social capital formation is at the heart of educational success for all students, especially for children who have fallen behind.*

Overcoming achievement gaps does not necessarily mean developing educational systems that produce equal test scores for all students.[86] Provided with appropriate educational opportunities and given adequate social and psychic support, students often overcome very challenging beginnings. Moreover, the powerful influence of family and community factors in determining student academic performance confirms that academic achievement is, itself, one consequence of cultural integration and strong social support during childhood.

Meaningfully addressing the achievement gaps besetting the poor, English language learners, and nonwhite students depends significantly on intentionally designing a social support system that encompasses every student—a network of people who seamlessly link home and school so as to produce a countervailing force in the lives of at-risk youth. From their earliest years, children are embedded in interconnected networks of family, peers, and neighborhoods and eventually school and the mainstream culture. Efforts to reduce gaps must build on these networks, enlarging them and training and mobilizing network participants to work together on behalf of the students. The most promising strategies for success will be those that guide students in the most effective utilization of the social resources and support they already have at their disposal, including family members, school-oriented friends, school counselors, teachers, and engaged school administrators. Academic achievement is, in substantial part, a consequence of strong social support during childhood.

5. *There are promising strategies for improving classroom learning.*

While our review counsels against thinking that state or federal policy makers can formulate, mandate, and secure implementation of the comprehensive and detailed program and policy changes needed to overcome student achievement gaps, we can commend a half-dozen options promising to help schools learn from experience, nurture professionalism, and pursue continuous improvement. We don't see these as comprehensive strategies, but as good starting places. They directly address achievement differences and help to stir the sense of possibility that allows staff to elaborate and refine practices as they implement them.

- *Targeted high-quality preschool.* Studies of early education programs identify a variety of long-term benefits for participating children and their families ranging from lower high school dropout rates to decreased criminal activity. Model programs, such as the Chicago Child-Parent Center and Expansion Program, Abecedarian Project, and High/Scope Perry Preschool Project, indicate cost/benefit ratios.[87] Preschools are also good starting points because they attack achievement gaps where they first appear—before children experience discouraging difficulty mastering curriculum materials.

Preschool programs also invite close collaboration between educators and families.

- *Targeted school-community clinics.* Impoverished children suffer disproportionately from a lack of dental, vision, and overall health care.[88] Hence community health clinics housed in the schools serving impoverished students represent another promising mechanism for reducing a major cause of achievement gaps. There are challenges, of course. For example, health-care professionals rely on case-based rather than program-based approaches to organizing services and they have very different norms for protecting confidentiality and maintaining records. However, experience with the Individual Education Plans used with special education students have brought some of these norms into the public schools, encouraging case-oriented programming.

- *Targeted afterschool and summer programs.* Cultural and academic afterschool and summer programs are also likely to help. Effective schools often combine afterschool tutoring, Saturday classes, and summer programs with sports, music, and field trips to engage student interest. When properly targeted, such programs directly attack achievement gaps for children with the most challenges.

- *Targeted (and more substantial) class size reduction.* Reducing class size is the most expensive school reform strategy. Despite great popularity with parents and teachers, however, except for the Project STAR experiment in Tennessee, smaller classes have been largely unproductive. Quite likely this is because reductions have been too modest. According to a recent report, following California's massive class size reduction policy implementation, the average student/teacher ratio remained at about 21.4:1, still more than five students per teacher above the national average.[89] Disappointing results indicate that this level of reduction is insufficient. Policy makers serious about reducing achievement gaps are unlikely to find the money needed for comprehensive class size reduction, but might be able to find the resources needed for narrowly targeted reductions, addressing the needs of children who will otherwise not keep up with their peers.

- *Targeted school integration.* Although the Supreme Court has retreated from mandating ethnic integration in the schools, it is clear that educational ambition and motivation are contagious, and require that students experience schools where high performance is expected and manifestly visible. The social composition of the student body—who sits next to whom—is one of the most important factors affecting student achievement. Children need fully integrated educational experiences—social class and racial integration needs to be accompanied by academic, linguistic, and vocational integration.

- *Targeted "de-categorical" funding.* In most states, the system of school finance does not support the standards and accountability reform principle of exchanging program and staffing flexibility for improved student outcomes. A substantial part of every education dollar is restricted by mandatory budget categories. At one time, states articulated plans for ameliorating student achievement gaps by allowing greater flexibility in how schools and districts spend education money. This was the basic idea behind charter school development, but these schools have been increasingly subjected to similar fiscal constraints. There is a risk, of course, that significant innovation will lead to judgment errors and occasions when opportunism and unethical professional conduct abuse this flexibility. At present, however, it looks like the efforts to prevent errors and malfeasance are also preventing creativity and innovation.

In sum, exploration of the organizational and policy options available for addressing continuing achievement gaps in the nation's public schools makes it abundantly clear that leadership, flexibility, creativity, and multidimensional systems of action are urgently needed. The goal of producing educational equality has been almost completely overrun by relentless demands for the production of standardized adequacy in recent years. We may be marginally increasing average student performance, but the cost for doing so has been to institutionalize glaring gaps and leave them virtually untouched for two full generations of schoolchildren.

CHAPTER SEVEN

Improving High Schools as a Strategy for Closing the Achievement Gap

RUSSELL W. RUMBERGER

One of the most urgent educational challenges facing California and the United States is eliminating the large achievement differences among ethnic, linguistic, and socioeconomic groups of students.[1] Although this challenge has existed throughout the history of our country, it has taken on increased urgency in the current era of educational accountability. At the federal level, this urgency is perhaps best reflected in the landmark federal legislation, the No Child Left Behind (NCLB) Act, which requires annual testing of students and holds schools and districts accountable for demonstrating annual progress in improving the achievement of *all* students. In fact, NCLB explicitly states as a goal:

> *closing the achievement gap between high- and low-performing children,*
> *especially the achievement gaps between minority and nonminority students,*
> *and between disadvantaged children and their more advantaged peers.*[2]

Failing to address America's achievement gap is also costly. The consulting firm McKinsey & Company published a study in 2009 that estimated the achievement gaps between the United States and high-performing nations like Finland and Korea as well as the achievement gaps within the United States between black and Latino students and white students, between low-income and other students, and between low-performing and other states. Together these achievement gaps cost the U.S. economy more than $2 trillion, or 17 percent of the nation's gross domestic product, or GDP, in 2008.[3]

In California, the superintendent of public instruction, Jack O'Connell, made closing the achievement gap the top priority in his second term in office:

> *Now, it's true that the achievement gap exists nationwide, but in nearly every*
> *other state, it is viewed as a problem affecting minorities of students. In*

California, the students representing the achievement gap are the majority of our school population. In California, closing the gap is more critical than anywhere else in this nation and it is the way to help all students succeed. Closing the achievement gap will not only improve the lives and futures of our students, it will secure the future of our state.[4]

To address this priority, the superintendent created a P-16 Council with members from a broad array of backgrounds to help develop a strategy for closing the achievement gap.[5] The committee issued its report with a series of recommendations in January 2008.

Existing research demonstrates that the achievement gap is present throughout the educational pipeline, from preschool to the postsecondary level.[6] Moreover, achievement differences tend to increase as students progress through school.[7]

This chapter examines the achievement gap using data from California high schools. High schools play a critical role in preparing students for careers, college, and citizenship.[8] Thus, disparities in educational outcomes from high school may contribute to long-term inequality in educational, economic, and social outcomes throughout adulthood. At the same time, reducing these disparities can play a critical role in reducing unequal adult outcomes and improving the lives of the state's most disadvantaged student populations.

California is a useful state for studying the achievement gap in high schools. The state educates almost one out of every seven high school students in the United States.[9] It also has one of the most diverse student bodies, with racial and ethnic minorities representing almost three-quarters of all students.[10] Therefore, studying the achievement gap in California can provide useful insights in addressing the achievement gap in other states.

This chapter examines the nature of the achievement gap in California high school outcomes. It then reviews the research literature on features of high schools that have been shown to contribute to student achievement.

CALIFORNIA'S HIGH SCHOOL ACHIEVEMENT GAP

Existing data show sizable disparities in a number of achievement outcomes from California's high schools. One way to measure these disparities is by comparing the representation of student subgroups in schools with their representation on various outcome measures. Ideally, the two would be comparable. For example, if a subgroup represents 10% of the total population of students, then they should represent 10% of the students in the outcome category. If they are overrepresented or underrepresented, this suggests there is an achievement gap.

Figure 7.1 compares ethnic representation in high school enrollment (grades 9–12) in 2005–2006 with three educational outcomes: dropouts, high school graduates, and high school graduates who met the college preparatory course requirements (known as "A-G") for admission to California State University (CSU) and the University of California (UC). Asians represented 12% of all high school students in 2005–2006, but only 6% of dropouts.[11] Thus Asians were underrepresented in the dropout population. Conversely, Asians represented 15% of all high school graduates and 23% of all A-G high school graduates. In other words, there were twice as many Asians in the population of A-G graduates as in the population of all high school students. This indicates that Asians are doing better than other students. Similarly, whites were underrepresented among dropouts (21%) relative to their representation in the population of all high school students (34%). On the other hand, whites were overrepresented in the population of college graduates (40%) and even more overrepresented in the population of A-G high school graduates (45%).

Black and Latino students, however, are overrepresented among dropouts, but underrepresented among high school graduates and A-G high school graduates. For example, blacks represented only 8% of all high school students in 2005–2006, but 15% of all dropouts. Similarly, Latinos represented 43% of all high school students, but 56% of all dropouts. On the other hand, blacks represented

FIGURE 7.1

School enrollment, dropouts, graduates, and A-G graduates, by race/ethnicity, 2005–2006

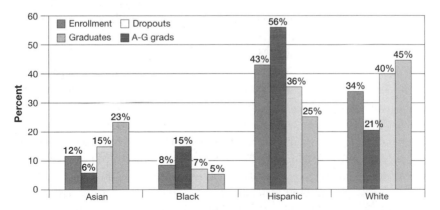

Source: California Department of Education, DataQuest. Retrieved June 13, 2011 from: http://dq.ade.ca.gov/dataquest/.

FIGURE 7.2
California Standards Test, English language arts, grade 11 results by race/ethnicity, 2005

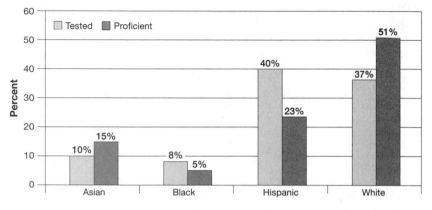

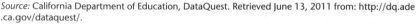

Source: California Department of Education, DataQuest. Retrieved June 13, 2011 from: http://dq.ade.ca.gov/dataquest/.

only 5% of all A-G graduates and Latinos represented only 25% of all A-G graduates.

Similar disparities are evident in test scores (Figure 7.2). Asians represented 10% of all students who took the California Standards Test (CST) in English language arts as eleventh graders in 2005, but 15% of all students who scored at or above the proficient level. Similarly, whites represented 37% of all test takers, but 51% of all students who scored proficient. On the other hand, blacks represented 8% of all test takers, but only 5% of all those scoring proficient . Latinos represented 40% of all test takers, but only 23% of all students who scored at the proficient level.

Disparities also exist for economically disadvantaged students, English language learners, and students with disabilities. For example, English language learners represented 16% of all high school students in 2005–2006, but 33% of all high school dropouts. Disparities appear to be even greater in terms of test score performance. For example, English language learners represented 15% of all CST test takers in 2005, but only 2% of the students who scored proficient. Students with disabilities represented 9% of all test takers, but only 1% of students who scored proficient. And economically disadvantaged students represented 39% of all test takers, but only 21% of all proficient students.

It should be noted that disparities in grade 11 test scores mirror disparities in grade 8 test scores three years earlier. For example, English language learners represented 20% of students who took the CST–English language arts test as eighth graders in 2002, but only 2% of all students who scored at the proficient level. Similarly, economically disadvantaged students represented 43% of eighth-grade test takers in 2002, but only 19% of all proficient students. These comparisons suggest that the large disparities that exist in high school test scores are similar to those that already exist by middle school. Thus, the achievement gap neither improved nor worsened in high school, illustrating not only the size of the high school achievement gap, but also its immutability.

There are large disparities in educational outcomes not only among students, but also among high schools. Dropout rates, for example, vary widely among schools. In 2005–2006, 1% or just twenty-five of the state's 2,486 high schools accounted for 21% of the dropouts.[12] College eligibility and entrance rates also vary widely by school: only 3.8% of high school graduates from the lowest-performing high schools (API Rank 1, the lowest level on the Academic Performance Index) attended the University of California in 2006, compared to 18.3% from the highest-performing high schools (API Rank 10).[13]

RESEARCH ON HIGH SCHOOLS

Although the research on high schools is extensive, much of it is limited in its ability to provide a rigorous answer to the question: What are the salient features of high schools that contribute to student success? The following discussion examines three basic types of research studies and their ability to provide rigorous evidence on high school effectiveness

Case Studies

One popular method for studying high schools is to conduct case studies of schools that have somehow been identified as effective. Sometimes schools are identified because they are simply using an innovative school reform model.[14] One recent case study of five high schools based selection criteria on a mixture of school practices, multicultural pedagogy, and a broad array of student outcomes not limited to student test scores.[15] Case studies can provide rich and detailed descriptions of the origins, practices, and outcomes of schools. But they cannot, by themselves, determine which features of schools are critical to student success. In fact, they cannot determine whether the school itself is effective in producing good outcomes for students—other factors could account for the schools' apparent success. For example, many successful schools, particularly charters and magnet schools, require students and parents to choose the school and perhaps fill out an application. They may also require some degree of parental involvement, such as volunteering in the school. In some cases, the school also selects the students based on criteria such as past performance or commitment to the school requirements. These so-called selection effects can result in a student body that is different from the student bodies of other schools. Thus, case studies are unable to determine whether the school outcomes are due to the characteristics of the school or of the students.

Correlational Studies

Another method for studying high schools is to use statistical models to test the relationship between student outcomes, such as test scores and dropout rates, and an array of student and school characteristics. These studies are often based on national longitudinal studies conducted by the federal government involving large national samples of students and schools, and a broad array of data based on student, parent, teacher, and administrator surveys, student test scores, and institutional data, such as student transcripts. In addition, because the data are collected over a number of years, the studies can examine changes in student outcomes over time. One of the most widely used studies is the National Educational Longitudinal Study of 1988 (NELS88), a federally-sponsored study of twenty-five thousand students who were surveyed as eighth graders in the spring of 1988 and followed throughout their high school and college careers until 2000, when most of the participants were twenty-six years old.[16] Many studies of high school effectiveness have been conducted using the NELS88 data.[17]

The statistical models used in these studies are able to control for differences in observed student characteristics to help determine to what extent differences in student outcomes may be attributed to differences in student or school characteristics. Because of the broad array of data in the datasets, the studies are able to determine which features of schools predict student outcomes, after controlling for other factors. This can help determine the relative importance of various factors. Also, recent advances in statistical modeling techniques allow these studies to estimate causal effects in ways that have not been possible in the past.[18] However, not all correlational studies use these more sophisticated techniques, so not all studies can establish a strict causal connection between school characteristics and student outcomes. And despite the wide array of data collected in these studies, they may not be able to identify all of the factors related to student success. Nonetheless, these studies do provide valuable evidence on the effectiveness of high schools.

Evaluation Studies

The most rigorous evidence on the effectiveness of high schools comes from evaluation studies. Evaluation studies are used to study the effectiveness of a wide variety of interventions, from single interventions, such as small classes, to comprehensive school reform (CSR) models.[19] Various research designs can be used for conducting evaluation studies, and the rigor of the design dictates the ability to determine a causal connection between the intervention and student outcomes. The "gold standard" in evaluation studies is the randomized experiment, more formally referred to as a randomized controlled trial (RCT), where students are randomly assigned to the intervention (experimental group) or to the regular or nonreform program (control group). For single interventions, such as small classes, it is possible to randomly assign students to the treatment or control condition. One well-known example is the Tennessee class size reduction study, where students in grades kindergarten to grade 3 were randomly assigned to small (15 students per class) or regular (25 students per class) classes.[20]

Because it is virtually impossible to randomly assign students to schools, an alternative design for evaluation of CSR models is to randomly assign reform models to schools, but this, too, is difficult. A review of the research evidence on the effectiveness of CSR models found only seven studies of three CSR models, or about 3 percent of all studies examined in the review, that were based on randomized experiments.[21] Another review of 197 studies of 18 secondary CSR models found only 16 with rigorous evaluations.[22] A more common evaluation design is the quasi-experimental design that is not based on random assignment, but instead uses statistical techniques to control for differences in the characteristics of students attending experimental and control schools. Several techniques can be used to estimate causal effects from quasi-experimental studies.[23]

Results from rigorous evaluations can determine not only whether a particular intervention is effective, but also the magnitude of the effect, known as the effect size (ES). Although there are no absolute standards for judging the magnitude of effect sizes, one prominent statistician argues that an ES of at least .2 should be considered a small effect (which corresponds to increasing the likelihood of graduating from 50% to 58%), an ES of at least .5 should be considered a medium effect (which corresponds to increasing the likelihood of graduating from 50% to 69%), and an ES of at least .8 should be considered a large effect (which corresponds to increasing the likelihood of graduating from 50% to 79%).[24] To illustrate, an evaluation of the Tennessee class size experiment found that students who were enrolled in small classes from kindergarten through third grade had high school graduation rates that were 11 percentage points higher than for students who were enrolled in regular-size classes, which is an effect size of about .25.[25] The effects were even stronger for low-income students—those in small classes had graduation rates 18 percentage points higher, which is an effect size of .50. A review of 232 evaluation studies of the effects of twenty-nine different CSR models on student test scores found an average effect size of .12, although interventions that had been implemented for eight years or longer had an average effect size of .50.[26]

Although evaluation studies are able to establish a causal connection between the intervention and student outcomes, evaluations of whole-school or CSR models are not able to determine the specific causes responsible for the outcome. CSR models typically involve a series of components, from structural features, such as creating small learning communities, to specific instructional components. Consequently, it is impossible from a whole-school evaluation to determine which components are critical to the models' effectiveness—some components may be critical and others not, but the evaluation is unable to make this determination unless it was implemented in such a way that the effectiveness of specific components could be determined.

Each method for studying the effectiveness of high schools has limitations. In general, it is most useful to draw on all three types of studies and look for confirming evidence from many studies to help determine which features of high schools are most critical in contributing to student success.

Measures of High School Performance

High school performance can be measured in different ways. Test scores are the most common measure of high school performance. California's state accountability system, the Academic Performance Index (API), is based completely on test scores. But other measures are also important, such as dropout rates, graduation rates, and college-ready graduation rates. One reason for using multiple indicators of school performance is that some schools may perform better on one type of outcome than another. This may be especially true if the features critical to raising performance in one area are different from the features critical to raising performance in another area. For example, if teacher resources are more critical in raising test scores, but other resources, such as school counselors, are more critical in keeping students from dropping out, then schools may have to choose where to focus scarce resources. Some features of school performance may be effective in improving performance in all areas.

For example, one recent correlational study of 912 U.S. high schools found that schools that were effective in promoting student learning (growth in achievement) were not necessarily effective in reducing dropout and transfer rates.[27] Moreover, the study found the same features of schools had different effects on those outcomes: larger high schools had higher dropout rates, but also larger gains in student learning. Finally, the study found that measured school characteristics had a greater impact on dropout rates than on student learning, suggesting that schools have more potential impact on dropout rates than on improvements in student achievement. A more recent correlational study of sixty-three public high schools in California confirmed these findings: two measures of high school performance—test scores and graduation rates—were not correlated, and schools had more potential to improve graduation rates than to raise test scores.[28]

FEATURES OF EFFECTIVE HIGH SCHOOLS

This section reviews the research on features of effective high schools. To guide our discussion, it is useful to consider a conceptual model of the schooling process.

A Conceptual Model of Schooling

The most common conceptual model is based on an economic model of schooling, which focuses on two distinct aspects of schools: school *inputs* and school *processes* (policies and practices).[29] School inputs represent the features of schools typically provided from outside the school itself, usually the school district where the school is located. School inputs include the characteristics of the student body, such as their academic background and socioeconomic status; structural features, such as type of school (public, Catholic, other private) and size; and school resources, such as teachers and textbooks. Many research studies have attempted to identify which school inputs are related to differences in school outputs such as student test scores, graduation, and college-ready graduation.[30]

The second aspect of schools concerns the processes and practices that take place within them. They include such things as leadership and decision-making practices, instructional practices, and the overall academic and social climate of the school.[31] Many studies of school effectiveness have sought to understand which school practices affect student achievement and the extent to which they explain how and why school inputs make a difference. For example, studies have demonstrated that Catholic schools are more effective than public schools because of their strong academic climate and the strong social relationships or social capital among parents and school personnel.[32]

A large body of empirical research has demonstrated that a number of specific school characteristics within these two domains can explain differences in school performance, particularly as measured by test scores and dropout rates. Yet the research findings are far from consistent. In some cases the impact of school characteristics on the same outcome varies across studies. In other cases the impact of school characteristics varies across outcomes. Below I provide a brief summary of this research and highlight a few of the inconsistencies.

School Resources

While it is obvious that resources are required to produce any desired educational outcome, there is considerable uncertainty and disagreement concerning the amount and types of resources that are necessary. Scholars have identified four types of resources that may impact student outcomes: (1) fiscal or monetary resources, (2) material resources, (3) human resources, and (4) social resources. Although these types are clearly related (e.g., fiscal resources can be used to purchase material and human resources), they remain conceptually distinct and have been distinguished in both the theoretical and the empirical research literature.

Fiscal Resources. Researchers have long debated whether fiscal resources make a difference.[33] In a major review of 187 studies that examined the effects of instructional expenditures on student achievement, Hanushek concludes: "There is no strong or systematic relationship between school expenditures and student performance."[34] Other reviewers conclude, however, that school resources can make a difference.[35] Critics of the efficacy of fiscal resources point out that real expenditures per student have risen dramatically in the United States over the last few decades, while student achievement has changed very little.[36] According to these critiques, the problem is not a lack of resources, but how resources are used:

> *The fundamental problem is not a lack of resources but poor application of available resources. Indeed, there is a good case for holding overall spending constant in school reform. Not only is there considerable inefficiency in schools that, if eliminated, would release substantial funds for genuine improvements in the operation of schools, but there also is a case for holding down funding increases to force schools to adopt a more disciplined approach to decisionmaking. Schools must evaluate their programs and make decisions with student performance in mind and with an awareness that trade-offs among different uses of resources are important.[37]*

Material resources. Fiscal resources can be used to purchase an array of material resources in order to produce educational outcomes, including facilities (buildings, science and computer labs, etc.), smaller schools and classes, instructional materials (textbooks, computers and software, Internet services, etc.), and personnel (teachers, support staff, and administrators). Economists attempt to determine what material resources contribute to educational outcomes by estimating educational production functions. By attempting to measure all of the resources used in the educational process and estimating the relationship between each of these resources and educational outcomes, these studies attempt to find which resources matter. Educational production function studies have a number of methodological limitations, including inadequate measures of all of the factors that might contribute to educational outcomes and the fact that the estimated relationships between inputs and outputs are correlational, not causal. Despite the fact that more than four hundred studies have been conducted, there is very little consistent evidence on which particular material resources affect student outcomes.[38]

One of the most studied and controversial resources, and the one that represents the largest expenditure, is teachers. More than half of public school expenditures go directly to instruction.[39] Yet while most scholars agree that teachers have a considerable influence on student achievement, they disagree on which specific teacher characteristics matter. Two types of teacher characteristics have been examined in the literature. The first has to do with teacher background characteristics, including degrees and coursework, credentials, and experience. These characteristics are typically used to make hiring decisions and determine teacher salaries; thus they can be considered material resources because schools have to spend more fiscal resources to hire teachers with more experience and advanced credentials. Although a large number of studies have examined the impact of teacher background characteristics on student achievement, many of these studies suffer from methodological limitations, including a lack of control for student background characteristics prior to entering the classroom.[40] A recent review of the research, which focused on only twenty-one studies that controlled for students' prior achievement and socioeconomic status, found evidence that "students learn more from teachers with certain characteristics," particularly teachers who attended higher-ranked colleges and who earned higher test scores, but the evidence is inconclusive regarding the effects of degrees, coursework, and certification, except in the case of high school mathematics.[41] This study suggests that the teacher background characteristics typically used to determine salaries have little systematic relationship to student achievement.

Two California studies provide mixed support for the role of school resources on student achievement. One recent California study found that several resource variables—the student-teacher ratio, the proportion of teachers with full credentials and with bachelor's degrees in the subject area that they taught, and the mean teacher salary in the school—had no significant, independent effects on high school graduation rates after controlling for student demographics.[42] Nonetheless, there is at least some evidence that certain background characteristics affect student achievement in California. A large study of student achievement in California found that teacher experience, credentials, and, in the case of math, subject-matter authorization were positively associated with middle and high school achievement.[43]

Teacher resources can also be used to reduce class size, which requires hiring more teachers. A recent review of the research literature found that small classes generally improve student achievement, although the impact varies in a nonlinear fashion.[44] There is also little research on the effects of small classes in high school. A major study of student achievement in California found no effect of smaller classes on student achievement in high school.[45]

Another material resource is school facilities. Fifteen percent of California high school students attend overcrowded schools.[46] Overcrowded high schools are more likely to use year-round calendars to accommodate all their students. A recent study of California high schools found that the odds of graduating for students who attended year-round high schools were half those for students who attended high schools on regular calendars, controlling for the family and academic backgrounds of these students.[47] This finding is consistent with two recent studies of year-round schools in California that found differential resources and outcomes in multitrack, year-round schools.[48] These findings are at odds with a recent review of the national research literature, which found that districts with modified calendars generally have higher performance than comparable districts on traditional calendars, although the same review found little effect at the secondary level.[49]

Human resources. The existing research literature finds limited support for the impact of fiscal and material resources on student outcomes. Yet if there is widespread agreement that teachers and schools vary widely in their effectiveness, there must be other types of resources that distinguish between more effective and less effective teachers and schools. Cohen, Raudenbush, and Ball argue that conventional school resources—such as teachers' formal qualifications, books, facilities, and time—are indicators of the capacity to improve teaching and learning, but to actually make these improvements requires teachers' *personal resources*, which Cohen et al. define as their will, skills, and knowledge:

> *The instructional effects of conventional resources depend on their usability, their use by the agents of instruction, and the environments in which they work. When added conventional resources appear to directly affect learning, it is because they are useable, because teachers and students know how to use them, and because environments enable or did not impede their use . . . If these ideas are correct, then when added resources lie outside the range of teachers' and students' knowledge, norms, and incentives, they will have no discernible effect.[50]*

Similarly, Newmann argues that teachers need to have a range of commitments and competences to guide practice and improve student achievement.[51] The concept of human resources is consistent with the economic concept of human capital, which includes cognitive and noncognitive (perseverance, motivation, and self-control) skills.[52] It is also consistent with the literature on policy implementation, which has found that "policy success depends on two broad factors: local capacity and will."[53]

Social resources. A final type of resources critical for effective teaching and learning are the resources embedded within schools that provide the institutional norms, incentives, and supports necessary for human resources to be realized or activated. A number of case studies have found that social resources, which represent the social relationships or ties among students, parents, teachers, and administrators, are a key component of effective and improving schools.[54] In their in-depth study of Chicago school reform, Bryk and Schneider argue that one particular social resource necessary for school improvement is relational trust, which represents the reciprocal, social exchanges among all the participants in the schooling enterprise that depend on respect, competence, personal regard for others, and integrity:

> *We view the need to develop relational trust as an essential complement both to governance efforts that focus on bringing new incentives to be bear on improving practice and to instructional reforms that seek to deepen the technical capacities of school professionals. Absent more supportive social relations among all adults who share responsibility for student development and who remain mutually dependent on each other to achieve success, new policy initiatives are unlikely to produce desired outcomes. Similarly, new technical resources, no matter how sophisticated in design or well supported in implementation, are not likely to be used well, if at all.[55]*

Hoy, Tarter, and Hoy suggest that three social resources in schools affect student achievement, all of which reflect the collective views of teachers: an academic emphasis, collective efficacy, and trust in parents and students.[56] Other institutional characteristics and resources may be necessary to develop and sustain an adequate level of social resources in schools, including a small size, more participative organizational structures, effective leadership, and district support.[57]

Student Characteristics

The social composition of students in a school, sometimes referred to as contextual effects, can influence student achievement above and beyond a student's individual social background.[58] Studies have found that the social composition of schools predicts school engagement, achievement, and dropout rates even after controlling for the effects of individual background characteristics of students.[59] One measure of school composition, the mean SES of the student body, has generally shown a positive and significant effect on student achievement.[60] However, its impact on dropout rates has been inconsistent—some studies show similar impacts, while others find no significant impacts.[61]

One California study found two measures of student composition—the percentage of students who receive free or reduced-price lunch and the percentage of English language learners—were associated with lower student achievement in grade 11.[62] Another California study found that students attending high schools with higher proportions of low-achieving students were less likely to graduate.[63]

Structural Characteristics

Structural characteristics also represent features of schools that are generally determined by forces outside of the school itself. These include the school's location, size, and type of control, such as whether the school is a comprehensive high school, charter school, or alternative school.

One structural characteristic is school location. One California study found that the percentage of eleventh-grade students scoring above the 50th percentile was 5 to 6 percentage points higher in reading and 4 percentage points higher in math for students attending suburban schools compared to students attending either rural or urban schools, net of other inputs such as teacher characteristics.[64]

There has been a great deal of recent interest in creating alternative structures to the comprehensive high school. California operated 1,425 schools with some kind of alternative structure in 2005–2006.[65] One category of such schools consists of an array of alternative schools, which include magnet schools, continuation high schools, and alternative day schools run by county offices of education. Some of these schools serve students who, for a variety of reasons, are not successful in the traditional comprehensive high school. Another category consists of charter schools, which were first established in California in 1993 as way to establish public schools that could operate exempt from most California state laws governing other public schools and districts.[66] In 2005–2006, there were 271 charter high schools in California, enrolling 76,463 students, a dramatic increase from 2000–2001 when there were 87 charter high schools serving 30,444 students.[67] Despite the growth of nontraditional high schools both nationally and in California, there is no research evidence that these structures are more effective than traditional high schools after controlling for the characteristics of the students served.[68] One recent California study found that neither alternative schools nor charter schools had significantly higher high school graduation rates after controlling for the characteristics of students.[69]

More recently, there has been considerable interest in another structural feature of schools—school size. While some correlational studies have found that large schools have significantly lower test scores and higher dropout rates than midsized or smaller schools, other studies report no significant impact of school size overall or a significant impact only on lower-SES schools.[70] One recent study found that while dropout rates were higher in larger schools, students in larger schools also had higher achievement growth rates.[71] Interestingly, schools that were effective in raising achievement growth were not necessarily effective in reducing dropout rates. A recent California study found that high school size had no effect on student achievement.[72] Although correlational studies are mixed, evaluations of a number of comprehensive school reform models have found that they all are based on "small learning communities" of students and teachers, suggesting small schools at least contribute to effectiveness.[73]

School Practices

Despite all the attention and controversy surrounding the previous factors associated with school effectiveness, it is the area of school processes that many people believe holds the most promise for understanding and improving school performance. Although increasing school inputs that improve student performance may be costly and difficult, it may be relatively easier to improve school practices—how they are organized and managed, the teaching practices they use, and the climate they create for student learning.

A number of school policies and practices have been shown to affect school performance. Some studies have found that school organizational practices, such as decision-making practices (including teacher and parental involvement in decision making), impact student achievement in middle and high schools.[74] Other studies have found that teachers' expectations and efficacy as well as their instructional practices impact student learning in high school.[75] Still other studies found that an array of indicators related to the social and academic climate of schools—such as the number of advanced academic courses students take, the amount of homework they do, and teachers' interest in students—impact a number of school performance indicators, including student achievement, engagement, and drop out rates.[76]

WHAT FEATURES OF HIGH SCHOOLS CAN ADDRESS THE ACHIEVEMENT GAP?

Research has found that a wide array of factors predict high school outcomes. But knowing these factors alone is not sufficient to reduce the achievement differences among schools. To reduce achievement gaps, it is also necessary to find the answers to two questions: (1) What is the relative importance of these factors? and (2) What is the relative distribution of these factors among high schools?

The need to answer the first question is straightforward. It is clearly useful to know which factors have the most influence on school performance because they can then be targeted for improvement. Of course, some factors may be easier and less expensive to change than others. It may be easier to improve school resources, for example, than to change the social composition of schools. Yet because many of these factors are related, it may not be easy to change one factor independently of the other. For example, both school resources and some school practices are highly correlated with student composition, as shown below. To the extent that such characteristics are "triggered" by the social makeup of the students served—that is, educators and school officials consistently respond to high concentrations of poor and minority students with lower expectations and a less challenging curriculum—then attempts to alter those characteristics absent changes in student composition may be difficult at best.

The need to answer the second question may be less straightforward. To alter achievement differences among schools, it is not only necessary to know the relative importance of factors that influence school performance, but also the relative distribution of those factors among the schools. For example, even if teacher resources have a powerful impact on school performance, they may have little impact on the achievement differences among schools if they are distributed fairly evenly among schools. Similarly, even if some factors are distributed unevenly among schools, those factors may contribute little to achievement differences if they have a relatively weak impact on school performance. Sociologist James Coleman made this observation more than forty years ago: "[E]quality of output is not so much determined by equality of the resource inputs, but by the power of these resources to bring about achievement."[77]

In the largest and most widely known study of school effectiveness, Coleman examined three types of school inputs—the characteristics of the student body, the characteristics of the teachers, and the facilities and curriculum of the schools.[78] The study found that the distribution of these inputs among schools was in reverse order of their importance in affecting student achievement: the input that mattered most—the characteristics of the student body—was the least equitably distributed among schools in the United States, whereas the input that mattered least—the facilities and curriculum—was the most equitably distributed; the distribution and impact of teachers were in between.

A California Example

One recent California study provides a useful example and recent replication of Coleman's analysis.[79] The study first examined the distribution of several school inputs and practices—students, school and class size, teacher preparation, and high school curriculum—among high schools in California. The study then analyzed the extent to which changes in the distribution of these factors would produce changes in on high school student achievement in eleventh grade in 1998.[80]

Figure 7.3 shows the distribution of several inputs and practices. The three points on each bar represent the bottom quarter (25th percentile), middle (50th percentile), and top quarter (75th percentile) of the distribution of regular high schools in California. For example, the data show that the "average" high school had an enrollment of 12.7% ELL students, but schools in the bottom quarter of

FIGURE 7.3
Distribution of selected high school inputs and curriculum

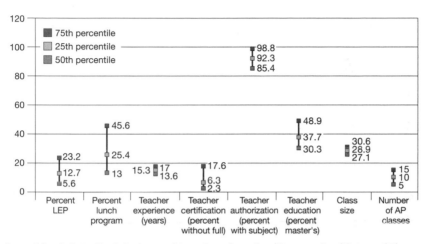

Source: Julian R. Betts, Kim S. Rueben, and Anne Danenberg, *Equal Resources, Equal Outcomes? The Distribution of School Resources and Student Achievement in California* (San Francisco: Public Policy Institute of California, 2000).

the distribution enrolled 5.6% ELL students and schools in the top quarter enrolled 23.2% ELLs. Schools also varied widely in the percentage of students who participated in the school lunch program—from 13% in the bottom quarter to almost 50% in the top quarter. Schools varied less widely with respect to teacher resources. Teacher experience, for example, ranged from 13.6 years in the bottom quarter of high schools to seventeen years in the top quarter of high schools. There was more variability in the percentage of teachers without full certification—ranging from 2.3% to 17.6%. There was little variation in class size, but substantial variation in the number of AP classes—a school at the bottom quarter offered five classes, on average, while a school in the top quarter offered fifteen.

What would happen if the distribution of these inputs and practices were more equal? Again, the answer depends on the relative impact of these factors on student achievement. To explore this question, the second part of the study estimated how much student achievement might change if schools at the bottom of the distribution looked like schools at the top. More specifically, the authors estimated the change in the percentage of students scoring above the 50th percentile on standardized achievement tests in reading and math associated with a change in the level of school inputs and practices from the 25th to the 75th percentile. The results are shown in figure 7.4.

FIGURE 7.4
Achievement impact of altering high school inputs

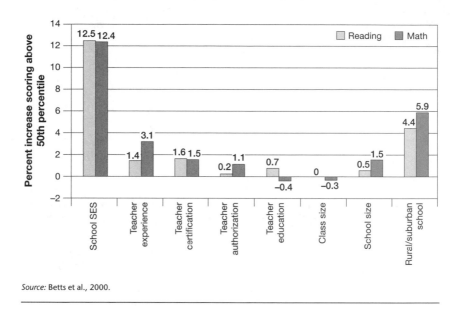

Source: Betts et al., 2000.

The results show that the biggest change in student achievement was associated with a change in the percentage of students participating in the school lunch program. A change from a low-SES to a high-SES school would increase the percentage of students scoring above the 50th percentile by more than 12 percentage points. The next biggest change in student achievement was associated with changing school location from an urban setting to a suburban setting (5.9 percentage points). Of course, schools have no control over their location and little control over the demographic characteristics of their students.

What can be altered are the teacher resources. The estimates suggest that for math, the biggest impact would come from increasing teacher experience, which would raise student achievement by 3.1 percentage points. The estimates suggest that for reading, increasing the percentage of teachers with full certification would have the greatest impact. It is interesting to note that the estimates suggest increasing school size would increase student achievement, especially for math. This could reflect the fact that, as the study found, there were more college preparatory courses in larger schools than smaller schools, and those differences were larger than the differences in the number of college preparatory courses between low-SES and high-SES schools.[81]

In summary, this study's results were similar to those of Coleman's 1966 study: the factor that had the largest impact on student achievement—the socioeconomic status of the student body—was the most unequally distributed feature of the high schools in California, and the factor that had the least impact was class size, with teacher resources in between.

It should be pointed out that this study only examined differences between schools at the 25th and 75th percentiles. The data show much larger differences between schools at the 5th percentile—the roughly forty-five high schools at the bottom of the distribution—and the schools at the 95th percentile—the top forty-five high schools.

In addition, other features that affect school performance may also be unequally distributed. For example, a recent study of learning conditions in California high schools found that schools with high concentrations of underrepresented minorities (blacks, Latinos, and Native Americans) were almost three times more likely to be overcrowded as schools with low concentrations of such students.[82]

CHALLENGES AND LIMITATIONS

This chapter examined a host of factors that influence high school performance. Identifying those factors is an important first step in developing a strategy for reducing the high school achievement gap. Yet some of the most powerful factors may be beyond the ability of policy to readily address. In particular, an analysis of data from California found that the most powerful factor influencing high school performance appears to be the socioeconomic status of the student body. This mirrors the conclusion reached by sociologist James Coleman in his landmark 1966 study of school effectiveness years earlier. It is also consistent with more recent studies, both nationally and in California.

Yet other factors may be more readily addressed by public policy. In particular, efforts should focus on providing more experienced and fully certified teachers in the most disadvantaged high schools. In the case of math, providing more teachers with authorization to teach math would also improve student outcomes in those schools.

Beyond altering school inputs, research also suggests that changing school practices could improve student outcomes. Rigorous evaluations of comprehensive high school reform models suggest a number of features of effective high schools:[83]

1. A personalized learning environment for both students and teachers
2. Rigorous and relevant instruction
3. Supports for students that address both social and academic needs
4. Connections to the real world to better engage students

The challenge is to get these practices into schools, especially schools with high concentrations of poor students, racial and ethnic minorities, and English language learners.

A number of large-scale initiatives have been undertaken over the last twenty years by government agencies, foundations, and independent developers to improve high school performance and reduce achievement gaps. A recent review of these efforts found that they have been largely unsuccessful, although there was widespread variability in both the implementation and impact of the initiatives across schools, districts, and states.[84] The study found that the will and capacity of both individual educators and institutions were key in engaging in and sustaining improvement efforts. It then recommended a number of actions the federal government could undertake to move away from short-term, test-based accountability, which a recent National Research Council report found has not improved school performance, to long-term capacity building:[85]

1. Support the development of broader indicators of student progress and outcomes, and include these indicators in the National Assessment of Educational Progress.
2. Help build the capacity of state governments and technical-assistance providers to support improvement efforts and capacity building in districts and schools.
3. Develop guidelines to ensure that states do a better job of matching reform strategies to the capacity of schools and districts in need of improvement.
4. Improve coherence among federal policy initiatives, between federal and state initiatives, and between government and foundation initiatives.
5. Support the development of more comprehensive state and local data systems that not only measure educational inputs and outputs, but also district and school readiness and capacity to initiate reform as well as progress toward improving student outcomes.

States could undertake similar actions.[86]

Finally, there are limitations to how much high schools can do to address the achievement gap. There are large disparities in achievement long before students enter high school. In fact, there are already large disparities in achievement when students first enter kindergarten.[87] To address the achievement gap will require a concerted effort not only to reduce disparities in resources and opportunities within all levels of the educational system, but also to reduce disparities in family and community resources.[88] This is an immense challenge, one recognized by James Coleman:

> *In some part, the difficulties and complexity of any solution derived from the premise that our society is committed to overcoming, not merely inequalities*

in the distribution of educational resources (classroom teachers, libraries, etc.), but inequalities in the opportunity for educational achievement. This is a task far more ambitious than has even been attempted by any society: — not just to offer, in a passive way, equal access to educational resources, but to provide an educational environment that will free a child's potentialities for learning from the inequalities imposed upon him by the accident of birth into one or another home and social environment.[89]

## CHAPTER EIGHT

Teaching All Our Children Well

Teachers and Teaching to
Close the Achievement Gap

JULIE MAXWELL-JOLLY AND
PATRICIA GÁNDARA

Students of color comprise the majority of students in all the major urban centers of the United States, and about 38 percent of students nationwide.[1] Moreover, one of every ten students is an English language learner (ELL). In the large states of California and Texas, the majority of the school-age population is also composed of students of color, and up to one in every four students is identified as not yet proficient in English. Far too many of these culturally and linguistically diverse (CLD) students are faring poorly in our nation's schools. Increasingly, the success of American education will be defined by our success with these students.

Achievement gaps can be attributed to myriad factors and types of disadvantage. Addressing many of these is outside the ken of schools and arguably requires social changes and policy reforms in arenas beyond education alone (see, for example, chapter 2). A key disadvantage experienced by many CLD students in this country that is within the realm of education is their teachers, who often lack the appropriate preparation, skills, and characteristics to meet the unique educational needs of these students. Research demonstrates that having teachers who are better prepared to teach CLD students will contribute to narrowing gaps in achievement. There are, of course, other aspects of schooling that can contribute to better outcomes for CLD students, but the bulk of the evidence suggests that teachers have the most impact. Therefore, this chapter focuses on that critical resource. We address what is known about effective teachers overall, as well as more specifically, the skills, characteristics, and preparation of teachers who are particularly likely to be able to help CLD students achieve at higher levels, and thus to narrow achievement gaps.

Although questions remain, education research provides substantial evidence regarding the placement, preparation, recruitment, and retention of well-prepared teachers who can contribute to the greater success of all students and of CLD students in particular. Moreover, there is evidence that current education policy does not routinely incorporate what is known in this regard. Failing to act on this knowledge shortchanges these students and robs the nation of critical human capital. If state and federal leaders do not more consistently support policies that incorporate this evidence regarding what is known about the best teachers for diverse students, we are ignoring an important strategy for closing achievement gaps.

THE SCOPE OF THE CHALLENGE

Unfortunately, there are large chasms between the academic performance of students of different ethnic and linguistic groups. For example, a third to a quarter as many African American and Latino students score proficient in either reading or mathematics in the fourth grade as white and Asian students. By the eighth grade, these gaps grow even wider in most cases. For English language learners, the gaps are chasms, with only 3 percent of ELL students able to pass the reading test at the level of proficient and only 5 percent able to meet this level in math. (See figures 8.1 and 8.2.)

FIGURE 8.1
NAEP percent of 4th graders proficient or advanced by ethnicity and language, 2009

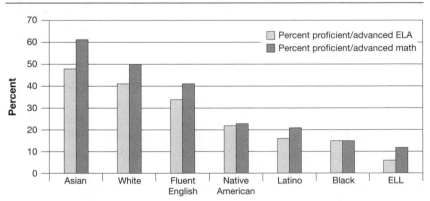

Source: The Nation's Report Card, National Center for Education Statistics, U.S. Department of Education, www.nationsreportcard.ed.gov.

FIGURE 8.2
NAEP percent of 8th graders proficient or advanced by ethnicity and language, 2009

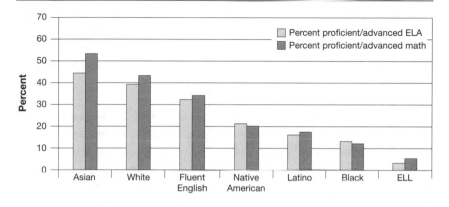

Source: The Nation's Report Card, National Center for Education Statistics, U.S. Department of Education, www.nationsreportcard.ed.gov.

TEACHER EFFECTIVENESS

Many characteristics, such as compassion, patience, and sincere interest in the well-being of students, are difficult to capture and impossible to quantify.[2] Cohen, Raudenbush, and Ball have argued that teachers' personal resources, defined as their will, skills, and knowledge, while difficult to measure, may be essential to effectively implementing other, more conventional teaching resources such as curriculum and general pedagogical knowledge.[3] Bryk and Schneider, comparing more and less effective schools, have convincingly shown that trust built among teachers, students, and parents may be a *sine qua non* to effecting significant positive change in schools serving low-income and minority youngsters.[4] Yet, we do not have good measures of the set of dispositions that teachers must have to foster such trust, nor do we have a test of "will" to be an excellent teacher.

In addition, some measurable indicators are time consuming and costly to assess. For example, how well teachers facilitate learning experiences, engage students, and value student interests can only be understood by observation at the school or classroom level.[5]

Quantifiable Measures of Teacher Effectiveness

A growing body of research demonstrates that teacher skill can affect student achievement over the long term—sometimes dramatically.[6] Moreover, these teacher impacts can be long-lasting, so that having a highly effective teacher in one year can contribute to greater student learning in a subsequent year. Unfortunately, this long-term effect applies in the case of ineffective teachers as well: having an ineffective teacher can contribute to decreased learning in subsequent school years.[7] Detractors of the value-added methodology (VAM) that results in the above conclusions warn of the instability of VAM measurement and of its potential for misuse.[8] Despite the challenges and caveats regarding quantitative measures of what makes an effective teacher, there is credible evidence of the contribution of certain factors to teacher effectiveness.

- *Experience.* There is reasonable agreement in the education research that teachers with several years in the classroom outperform new teachers, as measured by student standardized test results.[9] In addition, research indicates that teachers who stay on the job continue to become more effective, but this growth flattens out after three to five years.[10]
- *Standardized test scores.* Other research has found a positive relationship between teachers' scores on standardized tests during their undergraduate years and the success of their teaching as measured by student test scores.[11] Verbal ability, as indicated by standardized tests, appears to be another indicator of teacher effectiveness.[12] Research also finds a positive link between higher teacher test scores in a particular content area and greater achievement of their students in that content area, particularly in math.[13] There is also evidence that higher teacher test scores on professional certification tests—most likely as a proxy for content and/or teaching knowledge—can be predictive of higher student scores on standardized exams in specific subject areas, especially in math.[14]
- *Teacher undergraduate education.* Teachers' undergraduate majors have also been linked with increased student achievement in the area of secondary mathematics and science: students of teachers who were math majors did better in math; likewise with regard to science.[15] In addition, some studies report a positive relationship between the selectivity of the undergraduate institutions teachers attended and their students' achievement.[16]
- *The contribution of pedagogy courses.* Research indicates that in addition to teachers' content expertise, their pedagogic knowledge contributes to their students' learning. Several studies of teacher effectiveness show a positive relationship between teacher certification (for which they learn about pedagogy) and student achievement.[17] However, based on a review of the literature, Jacob found that in urban settings, certified teachers were not consistently more effective than uncertified teachers.[18] Jacob's work does not refute the contribution of pedagogic coursework to teacher effectiveness; rather, it highlights that what makes a good teacher in a given situation is nuanced and bears careful consideration.

In summary, although understanding the relationship between specific teacher characteristics and effectiveness presents certain measurement challenges, the educational research literature has found that several characteristics are related to student success. Overall, this research indicates that the quality and content of teachers' undergraduate and teacher preparation work has an impact on student learning and that, on average, students of teachers who have some years of classroom experience outperform students of beginning teachers.

Placement of the Most Effective Teachers

Although it is evident that those students who have the greatest academic challenges need the most qualified teachers, in reality teacher distribution is quite the opposite. Urban schools with large proportions of low-income students of color and English language learners are actually less likely to have highly qualified teachers than suburban schools that educate more advantaged students. There is considerable research revealing that experienced and credentialed teachers are not equally or equitably distributed across schools and districts.[19] Lankford, Loeb, and Wyckoff studied the unequal distribution of highly qualified teachers across regions, districts, schools, and classes.[20] Their research, using datasets that in a typical year held information for approximately 180,000 New York State teachers, found variation in the distribution of quality teachers at each of those levels. Ultimately, the researchers concluded that urban schools have less qualified teachers and that low-income, low-achieving students of color, particularly those in urban schools, find themselves in classes with many of the least skilled teachers. While many factors contribute to the outcome of unequally distributed teaching expertise, including salary, working conditions, and where teachers live, this does not change the negative effect on students. The Center for the Future of Teaching and Learning has reported similar findings in its annual assessment of the quality and placement of the California teaching force.[21]

Teacher absenteeism has also been shown to have a highly disproportionate impact on the schools serving Latino and African American students. Based on a study of all high schools in a large California school district, crossing school district data with geographical information systems (GIS) to map the relationship between teacher absenteeism and school location, Bruno found that absenteeism was much more prevalent in urban schools and those with the lowest median family incomes.[22] He notes that teacher absenteeism lessens a school's resources in various ways. For one, it lowers the quality of instruction. It can also have an instructional "ripple effect": when a substitute teacher cannot be found—a frequent condition in urban schools—teachers at the school must fill in (thus shortchanging students in their classrooms as well). Moreover, absenteeism is extremely costly since substitute teachers' salaries must be paid in addition to regular teachers' salaries.

ATTRIBUTES, SKILLS, AND KNOWLEDGE OF
HIGH-QUALITY TEACHERS FOR CULTURALLY
AND LINGUISTICALLY DIVERSE STUDENTS

The research discussed above identifies characteristics of effective teachers overall. Additional research explores the question of which teachers may be most effective with culturally and linguistically diverse (CLD) students, including ELL students.

Characteristics of Effective Teachers from the Same Ethnic and Linguistic Background as Their Culturally and Linguistically Diverse Students

Research using quantitative methods to determine whether teachers of the same racial and ethnic backgrounds as their students are more pedagogically effective exhibits a pattern of support for such teacher-student matching. However, the number of studies is small and not all are equally conclusive.[23] For example, analyzing a sample of 130,000 tenth-grade students in North Carolina, Clotfeldter et al. found that African American students had higher standardized test scores in classrooms taught by African American teachers, as did male students of male teachers and female students of female teachers.[24] A smaller-scale study of Latino students found a positive correlation between Latino student learning and the presence of Latino teachers in the classroom in twelve Florida school districts.[25] Dee analyzed data from Tennessee's Project STAR class-size experiment, which randomly matched students and teachers, and found that own-race teachers significantly increased the math and reading scores of both African American and white students.[26] On the other hand, an earlier study using test scores of approximately two thousand high school students from the National Education Longitudinal Study of 1988 (NELS88) found no such relationship between teacher and student race, ethnicity, and gender, although researchers cautioned that the sample size when disaggregated by teacher ethnicity was small and thus problematic.[27] Research in other traditions, discussed below, indicates that teachers from backgrounds similar to those of their students are likely to have a greater understanding of these students, to be particularly motivated to help them, and to have higher expectations for them.

Serve as role models. Ethnographic, observational, and interview studies reveal several areas in which teachers from the same ethnic or linguistic background may be more effective for students of color and English language learners. The work of some researchers explores how teachers from backgrounds similar to those of their ethnic minority students serve as role models. One finding is that many minorities who opt for a career in teaching had a teacher who inspired them to continue their education and become teachers themselves.[28] Gloria Ladson-Billings suggests that

African American teachers can play a critical role by assisting students to "choose academic excellence yet still identify with African and African American culture."[29] She also proposes that one reason having successful teachers of color is particularly important for students of color is to counteract low academic self-concept that can lead to schooling difficulties:

> *Not seeing one's history, culture, or background represented in the textbook or curriculum or by seeing that history, culture, or background distorted. Or they may result from the staffing pattern in the school (when all teachers and the principal are white and only the janitors and cafeteria workers are African American for example) and from the tracking of African American students into the lowest-level classes.*[30]

Use knowledge of student background to inform classroom and school decisions. A critical attribute of effective teachers of culturally and linguistically diverse students is the ability to make the best educational decisions for students of color based on a wide range of information, including knowledge of a student's linguistic and cultural background. Lisa Delpit characterizes teachers whose background is similar to their students' as able to use their knowledge of their students' culture to ask hard questions about the suitability of dominant paradigms for these children and to challenge the wisdom of a "one size fits all" approach [31] This hypothesis is supported by Meier, who found that Latino teachers from the same ethnic heritage as their students, and thus with a greater understanding of their students' language and background knowledge, were less likely to place Latino students in remedial programs, and were more likely to identify them as gifted.[32]

Knowledge about students' culture also helps teachers understand student behavior. Meier found that Latino students with Latino teachers were suspended or expelled significantly less often than Latino students in other classrooms across the twelve districts he studied. Downey and Pribesh documented how teachers from different backgrounds than their students can misinterpret ways of acting that are acceptable in students' home cultures as "bad behavior" in the classroom.[33] Using data from a behavior measure among two large-scale samples—one of kindergartners and one of adolescents—they found that African American students in both age groups consistently received lower ratings of classroom behavior, but that this poor rating disappeared among African American students who had African American teachers.

In addition, there is an advantage to a linguistic match between teachers and students, no matter what the program of instruction. Clearly, teachers from the same language background as their students can communicate with students and their families, which can help teachers understand students' academic, social, and other needs, and can foster a positive home-school relationship.

Counteract negative teacher expectations. There is a substantial, and disturbing, strand of research that focuses on teacher expectations for culturally and linguistically diverse students. Several of these studies find that mainstream teachers and counselors of low-income and minority students are more likely to perceive these students as having low ability and, therefore, to hold lower aspirations for them.[34]

Such low expectations can have powerful effects on student achievement. A series of studies conducted by the psychologist Robert Rosenthal found that students tend to perform better or worse according to teachers' positive and negative expectations.[35]

Teachers habitually communicate their expectations in behaviors that send nonverbal messages about the amount of confidence they have in students' abilities Not only do teachers call on favorite students more often, but research has shown that they wait longer for an answer from a student they believe knows the answer than from one they view as less capable. Teachers are more likely to provide students in whom they have little confidence with the correct answer, or move on quickly to another student.[36] Students have been shown to be very sensitive to these subtle teacher behaviors and to "read" their teachers' attitudes quite accurately.[37] Thus, there is a great likelihood that students will confirm the expectations of teachers who do not believe that they are capable of excelling.

Reinforce higher teacher expectations. The reverse of this aspect of low expectations is the potential for higher expectations from teachers of the same cultural background. Based on interviews with successful African American teachers, Foster reports that study subjects said that their own school experiences with African American teachers had an important positive influence. They reported that their African American teachers always had high expectations for their success and didn't let them "get away" with doing less. Foster's discussion with study subjects led her to conclude that these teachers dispelled "the pernicious myth that without access to white culture, white teachers, white schools, and white leadership, black people could never adequately educate their children, nor hope to create a decent future for their race."[38] A counterexample comes from Ream's multimethod study of Mexican American students and their teachers.[39] He found that teachers, from either the same or different backgrounds, who are knowledgeable about the multiple challenges these students face can lower expectations in an effort to shield students from potential failure, thus undermining their academic self-concept.

Characteristics of All Effective Teachers of Culturally and Linguistically Diverse Students

The research discussed above indicates that teachers from the same backgrounds as their culturally and linguistically diverse students may be particularly effective with these students. However, the reality is that there will not be enough of these teachers to match with all CLD students anytime soon. While there has been a slow increase in the percentage of teachers who come from communities of color, and therefore more closely resemble their students in urban areas, still, nationwide, 83 percent of teachers in 2004 were white, 8 percent African American, and 6 percent Latino. In addition, teachers' tendency to migrate back to their own communities when opportunities become available contributes to a constantly revolving door of teachers in the schools that serve primarily black and Latino students, as these majority white teachers return to teach in communities like those in which they grew up.[40]

None of the research discussed above signifies that white teachers cannot be very effective with culturally and linguistically diverse students, but it does mean that they will need to learn a great deal about the students in their classrooms—knowledge that will probably not be readily available in their own communities. It is also unlikely that they will speak the home language of many of the children in their classrooms.

Preparing teachers to meet the needs of all students is imperative for closing existing achievement gaps.[41] It requires both a broad understanding of social, cultural, and linguistic differences and specific knowledge of subgroup differences that can have powerful effects on learning. Given the demographics of our nation's schools, all teachers need expertise in the instruction of diverse students; therefore, it is critical to specify what the research says about effective teaching of diverse students.

Ability and Desire to Include Families and Communities in School Life. Students' parents are their first and most important teachers and should be collaborators in their schooling; thus teachers need to communicate with parents. If they share a language and culture, this is made easier. If they do not, then teachers must have the desire and disposition to find ways to make connections with the home. The importance of making these connections is well supported. In a study of fourteen urban schools with high minority populations, Taylor, Pearson, Clark, and Walpole found frequent teacher-to-home communication to be a common factor in classrooms where students' academic achievement was highest.[42] Ladson-Billings's 1994 ethnographic study of eight African American and white teachers who were successful with African American students also found that these teachers cultivated a relationship with students and their families beyond the classroom.[43] In addition, research has pointed to the high correlation between various kinds of parental involvement and minority students' positive academic outcomes.[44]

Different types of schools, families, and communities require different strategies for involving parents.[45] In low-income and largely minority schools, teachers commonly complain of a lack of parent involvement and therefore perceive a lack of caring on the part of the parents.[46] Yet with little connection among parents, teachers, and schools, and an increasing number of parents and teachers who literally do not speak the same language and/or who come from vastly different socioeconomic and cultural backgrounds, it is difficult for parents to create a role for themselves in their children's schooling, thus handicapping these students academically. Moreover, the ways that parents express their aspirations for their children and the ways in which they support their children's educations may not be evident to teachers who are unfamiliar with students' cultural backgrounds.[47] This is especially true in the case of immigrants, who may have little understanding of the operations and demands of American schooling.

View of Students' Homes as Assets and Background for Learning. Another aspect of this willingness and ability to connect with students' homes and families relates to teachers' ability to appreciate the culture of their students, to call on students' experiences and knowledge in that culture to promote learning, and to view students' families as a valuable resource.

With regard to English language learners, research on the most successful English language strategies highlights the role of tapping into students' experience, the importance of understanding what students know, and being familiar with their background knowledge in order to facilitate learning. A 2007 report for Carnegie's Alliance for Education Excellence compiled a list of nine strategies that promote simultaneous content and language learning for ELLs.[48] Among these strategies is instruction that builds and activates background knowledge. The role of knowing students' backgrounds for successful instruction is also an important feature of the English language Sheltered Instruction Observation Protocol model (SIOP), a planned instructional model that includes a wide range of English language strategies and has proved successful in promoting both content and English language learning for ELL students.[49]

Teachers can also foster CLD student achievement by tapping into home and community resources, or what Gonzalez, Moll, and Amanti have termed the "funds of knowledge" that these students bring to the classroom.[50] In a synthesis of the research on characteristics of teachers whose culturally and linguistically diverse students achieve academic success, Zeichner concluded that successful teachers include contributions and perspectives of a variety of ethnic groups in the classroom and link the curriculum to the cultural resources that students bring to school.[51] Ladson-Billings found that successful teachers of African American students explored and utilized students' previous knowledge to help them achieve, and helped them make connections between their local communities and the national and global context.[52] The Center for Research on Education, Diversity, and Excellence (CREDE) standards for effective teaching practice also suggest the importance of the connection between teaching and curriculum to the experiences and skills of students' home and community. CREDE standards are based on a synthesis of recommendations from literature "that is in agreement across all cultural, racial and linguistic groups as well as all age levels and subject matters."[53]

Monolingual English-speaking teachers routinely note the problem of the language barrier in attempting to engage parents of ELLs. In a study of more than 5,300 educators of ELLs in California, the single most frequently mentioned challenge for elementary teachers was the inability to communicate with the students' parents.[54] Bilingual teachers clearly have an advantage in this regard in that they share a language with ELL parents. Hopkins also found that bilingual teachers emphasized their desire to develop strong personal connections with ELL parents and to work with them to promote student achievement, whereas monolingual teachers more often preferred that parents reach out to them rather than vice versa.[55]

Ability to Accurately Diagnose Students' Academic and Language Needs. Delpit argues that mainstream teachers sometimes overlook or misinterpret the needs of students who are different from them.[56] She notes that considerable research has documented mainstream teachers' failure to appreciate the unique educational challenges that minority students face. The CREDE standards also include teachers' ability to conduct meaningful assessments of student learning as one of their essential teacher competencies.[57] This research supports an argument for a linguistic match between teachers and students whenever possible. Teachers who can communicate effectively in both English and the primary language with English learners and with students who speak a language other than English at home are more likely to gain the fullest understanding of these students' learning needs.

This is especially important in the case of teaching English language learners, because a major task of all teachers of ELL students is to be able to distinguish between students' language proficiency and their competence in the subject matter being taught. Thus, it is critical that teachers have the ability to understand and implement ongoing meaningful assessment of students' English language and academic abilities in order to provide instruction aimed at an appropriate level above what students currently know and to integrate into instruction the students' mix of academic level and degree of English language proficiency.[58]

Special education research highlights the importance of assessment knowledge as an essential teacher skill. Overrepresentation of culturally and linguistically diverse students in special education is a well-documented problem.[59] Based on their research on such overrepresentation in eleven California school districts, Artiles et al. report that patterns of overrepresentation vary by age group and language proficiency status, and that school and classroom patterns often differ from statewide or even district statistics.[60] They conclude that schools (and teachers) need to attend to the nuances of student need in order to monitor the possible misdiagnosis and misplacement of these students.

Capacity and Desire to Grow Professionally and to Learn to Teach CLD Students Effectively. Haberman studied teachers in urban schools whose students demonstrated significant learning on test scores and work samples to determine what might be contributing to their instructional success.[61] He noted that capacity for professional growth was a critical attribute of these effective teachers. He found this to be manifested in teachers' ability to generate practical, specific application from the theories and philosophies they learned and, conversely, to infer principles and "derive meaning" from their classroom experiences. Another feature of this capacity was teachers' recognition and admission of their mistakes and a belief that their teaching could always improve. Zeichner's synthesis of the attributes necessary for quality teachers of culturally and linguistically diverse students revealed the critical importance of teachers' personal commitment to achieving equity both within and outside the classroom.[62] These teachers firmly believed that they could make a difference in their students' lives and they established a personal bond with students rather than viewing them as "the other."

High Teacher Expectations for Their Own Performance and That of Their Students. In a study of six high schools where linguistic minority students were achieving particular success, Lucas and Henze provided concrete examples of how teachers, administrators, and counselors made their high expectations for these students clear through consistent schoolwide and classroom-level practices.[63] These practices included the ways in which courses were designed and scheduled; the resources devoted to counseling and ensuring parent and student information about college requirements; and hiring of administrative and teaching staff who reflected the backgrounds of students, thus providing an example of professional success. Zeichner also discusses the critical importance of teachers' high expectations for the success of all students and the ability to communicate this belief effectively. He finds that teachers demonstrate these high expectations in their practice with culturally and linguistically diverse students by using an academically challenging curriculum that incorporates higher-level cognitive skills.[64] CREDE also includes high standards and challenging instruction that requires thinking and analysis to be among the most effective teaching practices for CLD students.[65]

Zeichner adds the finding that these teachers have high expectations of *themselves* and firmly believe that they can make a difference in their students' lives. Similarly, Ladson-Billings notes that teachers who are successful with African American students, instead of aiming for slight improvement, aim for excellence, and rather than shifting responsibility for the learning of struggling students (to special education, for example), accept that responsibility themselves.[66]

Ability to Call on and Use Resources Appropriately and Effectively. One of the characteristics and attitudes that Haberman found among outstanding teachers of diverse students was an ability to work within the school system to protect and support their students and themselves.[67] He described this as an ability to negotiate with authority to protect learners and learning. He cited as examples teachers' insistence, to the principal and others, on the protection of classroom time in order to enhance students' involvement in meaningful learning activities. Haberman also noted the ability of effective teachers to learn how to function appropriately within the school and district bureaucracy to gain the widest discretion for themselves and their students. Finally, he found that these teachers learned skills and habits that helped them avoid burnout, including setting up networks of like-minded teachers that they used as support systems to help them function within the bureaucracy.

With regard to teaching English language learners, this ability to call on and use district resources includes teachers' ability and willingness to act as advocates for their students, and as advocates for the field of ELL education in general, and to work cooperatively with colleagues and with small communities of inquiry designed to advance learning for ELLs.[68] Milk, Mercado, and Sapiens describe this as the ability to collaborate with others at a school to get the best mix of services for ELL students.[69] Because the education of English language learners has so often been fraught with controversy over appropriate instructional models, this is particularly critical for teachers of ELL students.

UNIQUE TRAITS, SKILLS, AND UNDERSTANDING OF EFFECTIVE TEACHERS OF ELLS

While the factors discussed in earlier sections pertain to effective teachers of all culturally and linguistically diverse students including ELLs, there is a body of research that explores specific characteristics and abilities of successful ELL teachers. Short describes the triple task of ELL students. She argues that these students have the academic task of learning the English language at the same time they are learning content knowledge and how to complete the academic tasks of the classroom.[70] This means, of course, that teachers have a triple task as well, and no matter what the method or program of instruction, teachers of ELLs require specific skills and training to effectively accomplish this task.

With respect to English language learners, the research on teacher effectiveness is closely tied to studies of instructional type. If the goal of the program is to produce biliterate students, then it goes without saying that a bilingual teacher will be more effective in this regard. But if the goal is an increase in English language test scores, the same assumptions cannot be made. In a recent study, Hopkins found significant differences between the pedagogical practices of bilingual and monolingual English-speaking teachers based on over five hundred teacher surveys.[71] While the monolingual teachers emphasized language forms (i.e., vocabulary), the bilingual teachers reported emphasizing both form and function by using strategies that explicitly built on ELLs' language and culture, and that provided ELL students with opportunities to practice using language and new vocabulary in context. These are important differences, given that research indicates that using students' primary language and culture can promote achievement, and second-language learning research indicates the importance of both form and function in effective ELL instruction.[72]

Different ELL Teacher Skills for Different Program Contexts

Clearly, teachers in different contexts need different skills and abilities: a teacher using students' primary language in instruction needs a different set of skills than a teacher using English only. Likewise, a teacher of English as a second language (ESL) or English language development (ELD) needs different skills than a mainstream teacher who is teaching both English speakers and ELLs. And, elementary teachers need some different skills than secondary teachers. Nonetheless, all teachers of ELL students need skills and knowledge about teaching students whose first language is not English.

Effective ELL Teachers Need Language Skills and Knowledge. Teachers of ELL students need extensive skills in teaching the mechanics of language—for example, phonology, syntax, semantics, and writing conventions—and how language is used in different contexts and for different purposes.[73] They also need to know about first- and second-language acquisition.[74] In addition, teachers require a deep understanding of language in order to help ELL students learn the level and type of English required for them to be successful in content subjects, often called academic English. The development of such academic language is crucial for the academic success of second-language learners.[75] For students to become proficient in academic language, the language of schooling, students need to develop their skills to deal with new genres and tasks and to build from oral to written language.[76] ELLs and other students who speak another language at home are unlikely to have exposure to these grammatical styles in English; thus, mastering academic language is a particular challenge. As Schleppegrell points out, even the earliest of school tasks, such as kindergarten sharing time, require an oral style involving intonation and careful speech that is not characteristic of conversation.[77]

Effective ELL Teachers Need Strategies for Content-Area Literacies. Success-ful teachers of English language learners need strategies that can help them promote academic literacy among ELLs in all subject areas. These strategies include:[78]

- Examining curricula not just from a content perspective but also from a lan-guage perspective to determine the aspects of English that students need to know and apply.
- In addition to planning content objectives in subject-area lessons, planning language objectives related to key vocabulary, reading or writing skills, and listening or speaking tasks, and making both language and content goals ex-plicit to students.
- Emphasizing academic vocabulary to include words crucial to conceptual un-derstanding of a topic and giving students multiple opportunities to practice using these words orally and in print.
- Activating and strengthening students' prior knowledge and applying it to lessons or building background knowledge for ELL students who may have different background knowledge than that of students whose primary lan-guage is English.
- Promoting well-planned oral interaction that can help ELLs acquire literacy skills and access new information.
- Pointing out the key concepts and associated academic vocabulary in a lesson that ELL students might miss because they can lose focus as a result of being constantly engaged in the mentally exhausting task of attending to a new language.

These types of strategies can be helpful in the instruction of all students. However, they are critical for the successful learning of students who are not yet fully English proficient.

Importance of Ability of ELL Teachers to Communicate and Motivate. ELL students can benefit from having teachers who can communicate with them— who speak their primary language and who know about their home culture for all of the reasons addressed in earlier sections of this chapter. The advantage to ELL students of having these expert teachers is supported by research evidence from a study of the effect of the best-prepared teachers on ELL student learning con-ducted in the Los Angeles Unified School District. In this study, researchers found that the students of teachers who had specialized training and who also spoke the students' language showed greater academic gains than those with teachers who lacked such preparation.[79]

Meeting the Particular Needs of Secondary-Level ELLs

Secondary-level ELLs face unique educational challenges that are often over-looked. As older children near the end of their K–12 careers, they have fewer years left to acquire both English and the academic skills they need to get ready for high school graduation and to prepare for postsecondary options. A frequent approach to this urgency is a curriculum that is narrowly focused on basic skills and English, but research shows that this strategy can be counterproductive. Callahan found that when teaching basic English is the major focus of the curriculum, secondary ELL students tend to achieve poorly.[80] Thus, teachers and schools have the chal-lenging task of delivering a curriculum and instruction that is motivating and stimulating, and that addresses necessary content and students' English language needs, which range from basic to advanced.

Issues of identity development and adolescent transitions also complicate ed-ucational motivation and focus among this age group. Adolescent students are more likely to suffer embarrassment over their lack of competence in English.[81] Furthermore, secondary teachers often lack expertise in teaching basic skills such as reading—skills that may be necessary when working with older students who do not know how to read in English, or do not know how to read at all. Nor are pedagogical strategies and educational materials used with younger children al-ways appropriate for older students.

Based on an extensive review of the literature on both ELL literacy education and adolescent literacy learning, Meltzer and Hamann concluded that student motivation is key to the effective teaching of literacy for ELLs, especially at the secondary level.[82] Given the limited curriculum offered to these students, the lack of preparation of most secondary teachers for instructing ELLs, and the challenges of learning English, passing high school exit exams, and meeting coursework re-quirements for graduation, these students often become discouraged and give up. Meltzer and Hamann found that certain instructional features, summarized below, can keep ELL students motivated.

Making connections to students' previous learning and experience—to what students already know, what they need to know, and what excites them—is critical to their academic motivation, but is often ignored in instruction for ELLs. There-fore, teachers of these students need to regularly assess students' interests as well as subject-matter knowledge. And, while teachers need to build new learning based on what students already know, they must also avoid assuming that things are universal for all students from a particular group. Teachers should also call on stu-dents' first language when possible and appropriate: students' first language can contribute to their advanced literacy in English because second-language learners can produce more sophisticated second-language text by doing some of the planning in their native language.

ELL students in particular need to feel safe and accepted in the classroom environment, especially since many already feel marginal to U.S. society and adolescents are often anxious about doing or saying the wrong thing, particularly in a new social environment for which they do not know the rules. Having a relationship of trust with a teacher contributes to this feeling and thus to their success. Therefore, a strategy for improving the success of ELL students is establishing and fostering such relationships and providing adequate time for them to flourish. For students who speak little English, this is likely to be a teacher who speaks their home language, so schools need to use teacher resources in ways that promote this type of student-teacher connection.

It is a decidedly difficult challenge to address the content and academic needs of older ELL students. Many times these students are placed in ELL tracks with the intention of providing access to appropriate instruction.[83] However, evidence indicates that this often limits students' possibilities for more complex interaction with peers, with the teacher, and with text. Many English language learners need their instruction to be sheltered in English, but this should not translate to a watered-down curriculum or academic content. Meltzer and Hamann note that when ELLs are placed in lower-track classes they have fewer chances to read, reflect on, ask questions about, and discuss a variety of text—the very tasks in which they need to engage in order to learn both language and content. The authors also note that writing and reading may be particularly useful for ELLs because these language modes lend themselves to review both before and after expression. When a task is unfamiliar, the ability to review textual information is helpful to ELLs. Meltzer and Hamann found that ELLs need many opportunities to practice their English skills but are given few opportunities for this practice in mainstream classrooms.

INCREASING THE POOL OF EFFECTIVE TEACHERS OF CULTURALLY AND LINGUISTICALLY DIVERSE STUDENTS

There is both good news and bad regarding the state of teacher preparation for working with diverse students. The bad news is that looking across a number of reviews of research in the area, Hollins and Guzman conclude that "there has been remarkable consistency in the conclusions of previous reviews: basic changes in teacher education for diversity are necessary, but have not occurred despite 25 years of attention."[84] The good news, then, is that there is ample room for improvement. As discussed above, most teacher candidates tend to be a homogeneous group who do not reflect the diverse profile of their students.[85] Nonetheless, these mostly white, middle-class, and female candidates from suburban or rural backgrounds often express a willingness to teach in urban environments.[86] Thus, teacher education programs have the charge of preparing candidates who are most likely from homogeneous white, suburban, or rural backgrounds to teach children who most likely are not.

Teacher education programs take two general approaches to increasing the pool of teachers who are well-prepared to work effectively with diverse children and youth: recruitment of candidates of color, and activities to try and develop or change the attitudes and knowledge of white candidates about working with diverse students.[87]

Recruitment Approaches to Increasing the Pool of Effective CLD Teachers

Based on a research review, Sleeter found that most of the studies of recruitment strategies were program descriptions rather than evaluations of program success in preparing the recruits. The many studies did, however, "demonstrate that it is possible to recruit and prepare many more teachers of color than we do currently."[88] Two programs designed to recruit and prepare paraprofessionals to become teachers provide examples. The Norfolk State University provided professional preparation for paraprofessionals, most of whom were later employed as teachers. Graduates said positive aspects of the program were (1) strong support services; (2) a good collaborative relationship between the university and the public school system; (3) a dedicated and accessible staff and advisors; and (4) an attitude of respect for the prospective teachers on the part of school district personnel and university faculty.[89] The University of Southern California Latino Teacher Project prepared paraeducators, most of whom were Latina, to become teachers. It had a low attrition rate (as did Norfolk) and all but one of the graduates became teachers in local (Los Angeles area) hard-to-staff schools.[90]

Another recruitment strategy is to bring into the field individuals with personal profiles that might better equip them to teach diverse students successfully. Haberman describes the behaviors and ideologies of outstanding teachers in urban schools whose students demonstrate significant learning through test scores and work samples.[91] Based on these characteristics, he devised a profile and screening interview questions designed to select teachers who could be successfully prepared for the job of teaching in urban schools. The profile he created differs from the traditional teacher education graduate—young, white, and middle-class. Rather, these individuals were often nonwhite, either were in or had been from low-income circumstances themselves, and were likely to have attended urban high schools, so they were familiar with the kinds of communities they would teach in and the students they would find there. These teachers were often preparing specifically with the intent to teach in urban schools. Haberman stressed the importance of selection rather than preparation because, in his words, "Teachers' behaviors and the ideology that undergirds their behaviors cannot be unwrapped. They are of a piece."[92]

The importance of recruiting teachers from the communities with the greatest shortage of high-quality teachers is underscored by research on teachers' geographical preferences.[93] Since teachers prefer to work either in, or near, areas that have similar characteristics to their hometowns, and currently most teachers come from suburban or rural districts, we need to generate more teachers who are originally from these urban areas. Currently the number of prospective teachers from urban areas falls far short of the number of teachers needed in urban schools, so these schools must attract teachers from other areas. This issue of teacher preference adds to the already heavy burden of urban schools that "must overcome these preferences in addition to addressing the considerations typically identified with recruiting teachers to difficult-to-staff urban schools, such as salary [and] working conditions."[94]

Coursework Approaches to Preparing Effective CLD Teachers

A major strategy to prepare a white middle-class population of prospective teachers to work with diverse students is through coursework, either stand-alone courses or courses that include field experience. Studies of these courses are virtually all small-scale and very often the researchers are the faculty members who teach them.[95] These courses usually center on a variety of activities designed to reduce prejudice. Based on their review of research reporting results of studies of prejudice reduction activities, Hollins and Guzman find generally positive impacts on teacher candidates' attitudes and beliefs, with variation in results depending on the teacher candidates' experiential backgrounds, course content, and pedagogical strategies.[96] Zeichner provides a discussion of strategies used in these courses.[97] One frequent approach in these courses is autobiographical exercises to help teacher educators develop and clarify their own ethnic and cultural identities as a necessary precursor to cross-cultural understanding. Another strategy is the use of case studies and readings written by people of color about their personal schooling experiences. Strategies to learn about the historical and contemporary contributions of different ethnic groups to all aspects of life in the United States, and about the unique characteristics and learning styles of these groups, are also frequently employed.

Zeichner finds that programs that are successful in preparing teachers for diversity also provide teachers with strategies that enable them to draw on the particular knowledge and backgrounds of the students in their classrooms as a way to design the most appropriate instructional experiences.[98] These programs help teachers learn how to discover what students already know and how to use students' learning strengths, knowledge, and experience as a foundation for building new learning.

Another major approach to preparing teachers for classrooms with diverse student populations is fieldwork.[99] Generally, field experiences are either short-lived, with prospective teachers working in a school or community situation, or longer and more intensive, involving relocation and immersion in an urban setting. The studies of longer-term field experiences generally showed benefits, including "a better understanding of diverse populations and learning how to communicate and build relationships with those from cultures different from their own."[100] However, based on a study of programs in which teachers are immersed in communities in Mexico, Hamann concludes that effects may not be sustained after teachers return to their U.S. schools in which there is little support for the practices teachers learned during their immersion experiences.[101]

McDiarmid provides a caution about the importance of depth and sensitivity when designing courses that include generalized information about ethnic and/or linguistic groups. His survey study of 110 prospective teachers revealed that their multicultural professional development courses reinforced previously held negative stereotypes.[102] He concludes that there is a paradoxical problem inherent in programs that seek to disabuse prospective teachers of stereotypes about cultural groups with whom they have no experience or knowledge because part of the curriculum of such programs includes information (and generalizations) about those same cultural groups.

The Imperative of Ongoing Professional Development

An increasingly prevalent idea in the literature is that becoming an effective teacher for linguistically and culturally diverse students is an ongoing process rather than the result of a discrete learning period after which one is an expert. This concept is not unique to teachers of CLD students but it may be even more critical in the preparation of effective teachers of these students. In a report on the role of coursework, field experiences, cooperating teachers, and university supervisors in preparing teachers for linguistic and cultural diversity, Zeichner comments:

> *The implication is that prospective teachers need to learn how to be and do all of the things that are discussed in this report by the time that they begin their first year of teaching. Given what we know about what student teachers bring to teacher education (e.g., the lack of interracial experience), and about the complexity of the process of teachers' learning to teach across cultures, this is probably an unrealistic expectation.*[103]

Current professional development research describes two major approaches: "reform-oriented" and "traditional."[104] Traditional in-service professional development is a term used to denote single, one-time workshops that often happen in isolation. Reform-oriented professional development, on the other hand, represents in-depth engagement, including mentoring and coaching, and participation in committees or subgroups.[105] There is general agreement in the educational research literature that the practical and specific professional development that is more prevalent in a reform-oriented approach is more helpful than theoretical and general professional development when seeking to make change in classroom practice a reality.[106]

There is evidence that professional development of any kind that is specifically focused on English language learners is lacking for many teachers. A survey of over five thousand California teachers of ELLs found that few had received professional development designed to help them work with ELL students.[107] For example, almost half of the teachers with 50 percent or more ELLs in their classrooms had received either no professional development that focused on the instruction of ELLs or only one ELL-focused in-service workshop during the five years previous to the survey. Moreover, while this one in-service consisted of multiple hours for some teachers, for others it was limited to a single after- or before-school workshop. Earlier work indicates that teachers in California, on average, received only about two hours of in-service training annually that was focused on ELL issues.[108] Yet the potential benefit of such professional development was signaled in this study as well. Teachers—at both the elementary and secondary level—who had professional development specifically focused on the teaching of ELLs rated themselves significantly more able to teach ELL students in both English language development and content than teachers without such training. The fact that elementary and secondary teachers found different professional development subjects to be most useful is a reminder that the "one size does *not* fit all" approach for students is also true for teachers. Over half of the high school teachers found a focus on cultural insights that helped them understand their students to be useful, while elementary school teachers just as often cited professional development that provided practical classroom skills that could *realistically* be used with ELL students as most helpful.

RECOMMENDATIONS

This chapter has presented a brief review of the knowledge base regarding the effectiveness, availability, preparation, and distribution of qualified teachers for diverse students, including English language learners. Research explored in this review supports an argument that the need for highly qualified teachers is particularly acute for these students and leads us to a series of recommendations that we argue can make a difference in the academic outcomes for groups of students who currently underperform at significant levels.

Recommendation One: School and Local Approach

A tension exists between the preparation that every teacher needs for teaching students who come from a range of cultural and linguistic backgrounds and the preparation that individual teachers need to work with the specific diverse students in their classrooms. Certain general areas of expertise can help every teacher address the needs of diverse students, and these are discussed in this chapter along with the general kinds of knowledge that teachers might need about the specific subgroups of students in their classrooms. We support the need for every teacher to receive preparation for working with culturally and linguistically diverse students through teacher preparation and induction programs. Nonetheless, we believe that even these well-prepared teachers need extra support, as it is virtually impossible for all teachers to have deep expertise in all areas, for all students in our diverse society.

We argue, therefore, for a schoolwide perspective on addressing the needs of cultural and linguistic minority students and for viewing the school as a team that has within it the expertise to meet those needs. The foundation of this team should consist of classroom teachers—teachers who have varying degrees of expertise for working with CLD students. The team should also include some school experts who can work with students and teachers to fill some of the inevitable "expertise gaps." A key part of this team is a principal who knows about diverse students and their needs and who therefore knows what kinds of additional expertise are needed at the school and how to use this expertise. Another source of such expertise is bilingual teachers. These teachers' specialized skills in the instruction of ELL students, their ability to communicate with parents and students, and their ability to informally assess ELL students make them critical resources in schools regardless of the program of instruction. Teacher induction and support programs struggle to provide appropriately trained mentors for new teachers who are willing to teach ELL students because there are so few teachers with solid preparation in ELL instruction to serve as mentors. Bilingual teachers are critically needed in this capacity but in many parts of the country their numbers are dwindling.[109] This view also argues for a local approach: the extra expertise at one school might be very different from what is needed at another. In addition, the professional development that teachers need is likely to vary by site, or perhaps groups of sites, within a district, and should be allowed to vary so that teachers gain the skills that will benefit them and their particular students.

Finally, the research supports the importance of ongoing teacher support and professional development. A single workshop or even a set of sessions on a topic is unlikely to lead to instructional change. Rather, successful professional development has been shown to be reiterative and to include ongoing reinforcement, classroom follow-up, and high-quality coaching.

Recommendation Two: Recruit Teacher Candidates with the Disposition and Skills to Teach CLD Students

We argue that it is especially urgent to recruit teacher candidates with the disposition and preparation to become excellent teachers of CLD students, as well as the propensity to remain teaching in the communities where these students live and go to school. Inasmuch as the research has demonstrated that teachers from students' own communities are most likely to remain in schools in those communities, gaining important experience and expertise and providing critical continuity for students, it makes sense to recruit from these areas. It cannot be assumed, however, that just because teachers come from the same community as their students, they will be able to tap into the cultural and linguistic resources of their students. The need for these teachers is unquestioned, but they must also be assisted in both their teacher preparation programs and their induction experiences, to recognize and develop these resources.[110]

Talented young people from communities of color, with college degrees and often with competence in additional languages, can usually find attractive jobs that pay better than teaching. Therefore, it becomes necessary to provide attractive incentives for becoming a teacher. One such incentive would be to provide either loan forgiveness or upfront scholarships for students with the characteristics mentioned above who want to become teachers in diverse communities. Analyses by Vernez, Krop, and Rydell of the RAND Corporation show that the cost of educating African American and Latino students to the same levels as their Asian and white counterparts would more than outweigh the benefits in tax dollars collected for recruitment incentives.[111] This, combined with the critically important service such individuals would provide to the education of CLD youth, argues strongly for a state program of total scholarships for teacher candidates from underserved communities.

Recommendation Three: Define Critical Competencies for the Field

Even with the best incentives and teacher preparation, the majority of teachers in the United States will continue to come from middle-class suburban communities in which young people come of age with little contact or knowledge of the circumstances in which inner-city youth grow up. It is imperative, therefore, that the field define and categorize the critical competencies of teachers of specific subgroups of students and that the federal government include this information in its definitions of "highly qualified" teachers for diverse urban students. A priority should be placed on state and federal government support for research on how these critical competencies could best be taught and measured. This codification of essential skills could provide a critical tool for teacher preparation and professional development, allowing for more consistency of training. Furthermore, with regard to skills for teaching English language learners, these competencies must address the particular challenges of teaching and learning for secondary students.

Recommendation Four: Develop Centers of Teaching Research and Excellence Focused on CLD Students

Evidence presented in this chapter indicates that the nation requires a deeper capacity to address the learning needs of diverse students. We must develop a better understanding of what is essential for teachers of diverse students to know and be able to do, and how to best provide these skills and knowledge to the current and future teaching force. One way to do this would be through centers of teaching and research excellence that would be designed to help answer these questions, serving as incubators for teacher preparation and professional development with a focus on teaching CLD students. In addition to researching and designing professional development, such centers could also build the cadre of well-prepared professionals who have deep knowledge and skill in teaching diverse students to carry out this professional development activity. Often the recommendation given to schools and districts to improve the performance of their African American, Latino, and ELL students is to provide teachers with good professional development. But expert trainers, coaches, and mentors are in short supply. There are some excellent teacher research centers in existence today around the country, and some have studied issues raised in this chapter. However, there has been no systematic national focus on the identification of the specific skills and abilities of teachers to serve this growing proportion of the nation's students, nor has there been sufficient focused attention on how to teach these skills or measure them.

## CHAPTER NINE

Narrowing Achievement Gaps in Tough Times

Rethinking the Roles of Money and School Resources

W. NORTON GRUBB

The current rhetoric about eliminating achievement gaps is the latest in a long series of concerns about the poor performance of some students compared to others. In the early nineteenth century, concern about the children of the poor led to charity schools. Later in the century, one of the impulses underlying the founding of free, universal public schools was to create an education common to all children, one that would be "beyond all other devices of human origin, a great equalizer of the conditions of men, the balance wheel of the social machinery," as Horace Mann declared. At other times educators have been worried about the differences between boys and girls, or between immigrant and native children, or—as is usually the case now—among children of different racial and ethnic backgrounds. Of course, public schooling has never been the "great equalizer" that Mann envisioned—African Americans and American Indians were often left out, as were lower-class boys and girls who needed to work—and the quality of schooling (as distinct from simple access) has varied enormously. Perhaps what is remarkable is that, in a country of high levels of inequality compared to other developed countries, equity has still been a persistent goal.

The primary challenge in the nineteenth and early twentieth centuries was simply to cobble together enough money to provide teachers, buildings, and materials for the increasing numbers attending public schools, including the mass of immigrants throughout the nineteenth and into the twentieth century. Horace Mann—often considered the father of public education—strained to convince districts and states to cough up enough money, and lambasted opposition to taxation as "embezzlement and pillage from children." Small wonder, then, that school improvements all seemed to require additional funding, and that without additional money improvement might not be possible. As Ellwood Cubberly, one of the first to identify variation in spending among rich and poor school districts as a barrier to equity, declared in 1905: "One of the most important administrative problems of today is how properly to finance the school system or a state, as the question of sufficient revenue lies back of almost every other [educational] problem."[1]

Ever since, what I call the Money Myth has dominated thinking about school improvement and reform—the idea that more money is more effective than less money, and that the solution to any educational problem requires increased spending. For those who are currently seeking to reform schools, including those trying to reduce achievement gaps, the Money Myth is a real challenge because it implies that, in periods of fiscal decline like the present, it is impossible to make much progress on equity goals.

However, there is evidence that the Money Myth is false, and that we need to think in different ways about school spending. Even during the nineteenth century, as reformers struggled to expand tax support, some argued that taxation alone could not solve problems such as mediocre teaching by untrained schoolmarms, decrepit physical facilities like log cabins and decaying privies, instruction in a limited variety of subjects, and poor-quality textbooks—or, in the language I develop, ineffective resources. Since the 1960s, other challenges to the Money Myth have emerged. One is simply that expenditures per pupil have increased—in real or inflation-adjusted terms—relatively steadily; they have more than trebled since 1960, doubled since 1970, and increased by a quarter since 1994–1995. Yet education is still beset by problems familiar from the 1960s—gross inequalities among students, dilapidated conditions in some schools, ineffective teachers, teacher shortages in some fields, achievement gaps among different groups of students—implying that simply increasing spending cannot resolve all school problems. A second is that, when researchers examine the relationship between spending per student and outcomes, they have generally failed to find any simple relationship. Eric Hanushek summarized this literature in 1989, and found that only 13 of 65 studies reported spending per pupil to be positively and significantly related to student outcomes; a later reanalysis found only 27 of 163 estimates statistically significant— not exactly rousing support for the Money Myth.[2]

On a smaller scale, many specific reforms that have spent great sums of money have failed to produce any demonstrable effects on the average. So again, spending more money, even in ways that are carefully thought out, does not automatically lead to improvements.[3] And when we consider urban schools, where many achievement gaps are concentrated, the problem is not simply one of funding. In 2003–2004, for example, central city schools spent $7,812 per pupil compared to $7,542 in suburban schools (and $7,268 in all public schools), but this slightly higher level of spending did not lead to more real resources: central city schools had higher numbers of students per teacher (15.0 vs. 14.6), lower teacher salaries ($45,400 vs. $46,100), a higher proportion of schools with temporary buildings (37.7% vs. 34.4%), and a higher proportion of schools using common spaces for instruction (21.3% vs. 19%).[4] These kinds of findings have been replicated in other countries as well, so there's no reason to think that American schools are uniquely wasteful.[5]

Thus we need a different way to think about spending, the resources that money can only sometimes buy, and outcomes. Only then will we be able to understand how to reduce the various achievement gaps in American schools and colleges, particularly in periods when revenues are generally declining. In the first section of this chapter I present a new approach, one that—unlike conventional school finance, which emphasizes *spending and revenue* per student—focuses instead on a variety of different *resources*. The second section shows why spending and outcomes are so weakly related to one another, and along the way provides some strategies for distinguishing effective but relatively inexpensive resources from those that cost a great deal of money.

The final section outlines various strategies to continue narrowing achievement gaps, even when schools cannot count on additional funding. These strategies are considerably more complex than simply reducing class size, or increasing teacher salaries, or hiring reading or math coaches, or adding an afterschool program, or finding new curricula—examples of typical reforms that both cost additional money and, under many conditions, are likely to be unsuccessful. The strategies I present have the potential to increase the capacities of schools in more substantial ways, and to do more with the resources that schools already have.

SHIFTING FROM MONEY TO RESOURCES

Rethinking the role of money starts with the banal observation that dollar bills do not educate children. Instead, the resources that money can (sometimes) buy might be teachers with particular capacities, leadership building to fulfill certain responsibilities, materials like books and computers, labs and libraries. But as we shift our thinking from money to resources, we need to think expansively about the variety of school resources responsible for outcomes. No typology can be perfect, but I have found it useful to think of resources in four categories:

- *Simple* resources are those that show up in the simple identity between expenditures per pupil and the components of spending:

$$\text{Expenditure per pupil} = (\text{Teachers/Pupils}) \times \text{Average teacher salary} +$$
$$(\text{Counselors/Pupils}) \times \text{Average counselor salary} + \text{Admin\$/pupil} +$$
$$\text{Materials\$/Pupil} + \text{Capital outlays/Pupil} + \ldots$$

Simple resources include class size, teacher salaries, and spending on other inputs or resources (including spending on counselors, subject-matter coaches, afterschool programs, and other interventions thought to influence test scores or other outcomes). Simple resources are the ones most people think of when they consider school improvement, and they are the resources most likely to show up in production functions relating outcomes to inputs.[6] By using data on district spending patterns, it is clear (as well as obvious) that increasing simple resources costs more money.[7]

- *Compound* resources require two or more simple resources. Class size reduction provides an obvious example: when California spent $1.5 billion for several years to reduce the K–3 class size ratio to 20:1, the experiment had no effect on the average because many districts hired teachers on emergency credentials, reducing their quality; many districts did not have appropriate spaces for the additional classrooms required; and the legislation provided too little for professional development that would train teachers to adjust their teaching for smaller classes.[8] In this case, the appropriate resource was smaller class sizes *plus* keeping teacher quality constant *plus* adequate facilities *plus* appropriate staff development. Similarly, providing computers without professional development and maintenance is unlikely to be effective because the computers are apt to go unused or become dilapidated; computers are simple resources when a compound resource is necessary. Other examples of compound resources are the lower-status tracks in high school, like traditional vocational education, the general track, and the remedial track dominated by drill and practice on basic skills: they incorporate several elements, including less demanding teachers, watered-down curricula, unmotivated peers, and lower expectations for college. And almost any reform requires professional development to be effective, so again compound rather than simple resources are necessary.
- *Complex* resources, especially those associated with instruction, are resources that are complex by their very nature and also complex to change. Various dimensions of instruction are complex resources, particularly difficult to change at the high school level. So is guidance and counseling since, contrary to common practice, this requires more than the usual "information dump," and more than simply increasing the counselor: student ratio (though in many schools that would be valuable too). We might consider preparation for college, or college readiness, a complex resource, not only because it requires many different capacities among youth but also because some of these capacities—independence, initiative, and planfulness, for example—are difficult to "teach."

- *Abstract* resources refer to aspects of a school that cannot be seen or touched, though they can be perceived by asking participants; often abstract resources are embedded in the web of personal relationships in a school. School climate—both in the positive sense of a climate supportive of academic performance and in the negative sense of an atmosphere of distrust, poor personal relations, and distractions like drugs, violence, and gang activity—is one of the most commonly cited abstract resources. Others that have been empirically examined include curricular coherence and trust.[9] Stability is yet another abstract resource, and anyone who has seen the extreme instability in some urban schools—with students turning over (often as they experience housing problems), teachers and principals coming and going, and superintendents changing frequently and bringing in new policies as they do—should recognize how detrimental instability is to consistent reform.

There are at least four reasons for recognizing this array of resources. The first is that it forces us to recognize a larger number of resources; while it may be simpler to think about class sizes and counselor-pupil ratios, some complex resources like the quality of instruction and some abstract resources like stability may be much more important. Second, and confirming the value of this four-part typology, all four of these resources affect student outcomes in various ways. Among the simple resources that affect outcomes are teacher salaries (which enhance quality and reduce turnover) and the staff-pupil ratio, not a measure of class size but (in my interpretation) a reflection of the possibilities for adult contact and personalization with a school. Among the compound resources that prove ineffective are different tracks—the traditional vocational track, the general track, and the remedial track for those who are behind, all of which have consistent negative effects (even after controlling for selection in the form of prior test scores). In addition, teacher experience specifically in secondary schools, teaching in the field of a teacher's education, and planning time all have positive effects on learning and test scores, as one might expect. The compound and complex resources that influence different outcomes include teachers' use of time; departmental encouragement of innovation; teachers' control over their own classrooms; constructivist or balanced pedagogy, especially in math; a positive school climate; and negative events like drug-dealing and fighting. Furthermore, these school resources increase the explanatory power of equations explaining variation in test scores, more than any other set of variables do.[10] With rich data like the National Educational Longitudinal Study (NELS88), we can see that it simply isn't true that "school resources don't make a difference"; this is true only with impoverished datasets that include little more than simple resources.

Third, it turns out that many compound, complex, and abstract resources are more unequally distributed than are simple resources, especially in comparison to expenditure per student—the source of inequality that has led to many lawsuits in this country. Table 9.1 describes a simple measure of inequality—the coefficient of variation, or the standard deviation divided by the mean—for a number of resources, all of them effective in enhancing one outcome or another. The coefficient of .234 for expenditure per student is among the lowest levels of inequality in the table. Inequality in both low and high teacher salaries is about the same as inequality in spending, while other simple resources—the pupil-teacher ratio, teacher certification, and teacher education levels—are more unequal. But in general, inequalities in compound, complex, and abstract resources are much higher still. In particular, the resources linked to innovative instruction—teacher use of time, overall innovative teaching, innovative math (and science) teaching, teacher innovation as noted by the principal—are highly unequal, at least as compared to the distribution of spending per pupil. Both positive and negative aspects of school climate are also very unequal. So to understand the inequalities of school resources—the inequalities that contribute to inequality in outcomes and to achievement gaps—it's necessary to consider a much wider range of resources than has been customary.

Finally, many resources cannot readily be bought, and schools with higher expenditures per pupil do not generally have higher levels of these resources. This is not, of course, the case for simple resources, which require additional funding in direct and obvious ways. Similarly, compound resources can often be bought, as long as educators remember to buy all the components of a compound resource. However, there is no simple way to buy improved instruction, or a more supportive climate; there are no stores or markets in which to spend money for these resources. Instead, they require leadership, vision, cooperation from teachers or "internal alignment" among teachers and leaders, and consistency in implementing new practices.[11] Small sums of money may be necessary—for teacher release time, for example, or for outside consultants—but more expenditures do not lead to better instruction, more supportive climates, better personal relationships within urban schools, or—to take the most difficult resource of all—greater stability.

The distinction between resources that can be bought and those that must be *constructed* by a school community provides a way to enhance schooling and close achievement gaps even in periods of fiscal austerity. Evidently, one part of the solution is to focus on those effective resources that do not cost inordinate sums of money—like improved instruction and climate. When I return in the final section to the range of policies that could be used to reduce achievement gaps, even in a period of scarcity, this will be one of the important insights of my approach to funding and resources.

TABLE 9.1
Variation in resources

Variable	Coefficient of variation
Financial resources	
Current expenditure per pupil (adj.)	.234
Instructional expenditures per pupil (adj.)	.244
Parental contributions per pupil (adj.)	3.19
Simple resources	
Pupil/staff ratio	.427
Low teacher salary	.159
High teacher salary	.213
Teacher certified	.366
Teacher education	.321
Compound Resources	
Teacher experience in secondary education	.545
Teacher teaching in field of preparation	.294
Planning time	.370
Staff development	.530
Student in general education	1.42
Student in vocational education	2.89
Student in remedial education	1.72
Complex resources	
Teacher time use	.765
Conventional teaching	?39
Innovative teaching	.497
Teacher control	.183
Teacher sense of efficacy	.194
Teacher innovation	.951
Conventional math teaching	.255
Innovative math teaching	.421
Abstract resources	
Positive school climate	.234
Negative events	1.483
College pressure	.244
Staff responsibility	.193
Principal control	.221
School attendance rate	.059
Percent school lunch	1.037
School problems (admin.-reported)	.523

Source: NELS:88, second follow-up, senior year, calculations in Grubb (2009), table 1.1. W. Norton Grubb, 2009. *The Money Myth: School resources, Outcomes, and Equity.* New York: Russelll Sage Foundation.

Note: "Adj." refers to adjustments for cost of education differences across districts.

MONEY AND ITS AMBIGUOUS EFFECTS ON OUTCOMES

The expanded conceptions of resources in the previous section still do not explain why the Money Myth is wrong—why the relationship between spending per pupil and outcomes is so weak. Clarifying this relationship—clarifying when money matters to outcomes, and when it does not—provides some other clues about how schools can continue to improve, to become more equitable, and to reduce various achievement gaps, even in the absence of great spending increases.

When Money Does Matter

In several direct and indirect ways, money does matter to outcomes. In the broadest sense, modern schools are not the informal places of the eighteenth century, where an otherwise unemployed woman would teach students in her own home, in places called dame schools. Schools are now much more formal institutions, and they demand specifically prepared teachers, updated textbooks, computers, and programs, and increasingly elaborate facilities. These all require money, especially as we integrate special education students, create programs for English language learners, and provide computers and multimedia centers. But such spending provides *access* to schooling, not necessarily enhanced *outcomes*.

A few effective resources, improving learning or progress through school or student attitudes and values, require additional spending—some of the *simple* resources noted in the previous section. Based on my statistical results, teacher salaries improve outcomes, since they allow districts to attract a larger pool of applicants from which they can choose. The staff-pupil ratio—not a measure of class size like the teacher-pupil ratio, but a measure of personalization, including staff like counselors, specialist teachers, coaches, and assistant principals—also affects progress through high school. Teacher experience in secondary education enhances a number of outcomes, and higher salaries affect teacher persistence. Access to counselors enhances a variety of outcomes, and requires funding. When a simple resource is effective *and* requires money in obvious ways, then money makes a difference to outcomes.

In a more diffuse way, my results suggest that personalizing high schools enhances progress and completion. Having more adults and counselors, closer contacts in advisories, other adult relationships in internships and service-learning, and better working relationships with teachers in theme-based approaches make schools more welcoming places—and some of them cost money in obvious ways. Not all of these can be readily measured, and some of them require better working relationships rather than additional forms of spending, but many of them do have effects on progress through high school.

Finally, some negative consequences of low spending affect other dimensions that are hard to measure. In many states, years of cuts have imposed more duties on teachers and administrators. Many schools cannot improve because their teachers and leaders have no more time and energy, and have become weary of "reforming again, again, and again."[12] This consequence emerges only over time, and this "resource"—reform fatigue—cannot be readily detected in conventional statistical analysis. But hoping that low-performing schools can remake themselves as "lighthouse" or "turnaround" schools can't work if there is no time or energy or "slack" for reform.

What Undermines the Positive Effects of Money

Although money affects outcomes in several ways, many examples of increased spending leave outcomes unchanged, or lead to *worse* outcomes:

1. *Money is wasted.* Money can be embezzled, or spent to hire friends and relations. More often it is spent on ineffective resources—incompetent teachers, weak afterschool programs, or teacher aides without clear plans. Money may be spent without changing practices, such as when ineffective professional development—Friday afternoon one-shot workshops—is used for complex changes like improving instruction. Money is often spent piecemeal, buying whatever categorical grants or foundation grants dictate without an overall plan, or spending year-end money wildly. Legislatures often fail to pass budgets early enough for districts and schools to plan well. All too often, principals and other school leaders know little about the funds they control and about using resources effectively.[13] Perhaps worst of all, money gets spent on potential long-run benefits, like improving school climate or changing instruction; then a new principal or a superintendent with different priorities reverses course, and the resources already spent go to waste.

   The conditions for waste seem more serious in urban districts because of sharper political debates, racial and ethnic conflicts, disagreements over reforms, the difficulty of educating students from low-income families, and the instability of mobile students, turnover of teachers and principals, and new superintendents. Not only do many urban districts lack additional revenues for high-need students, then, but they also seem more likely to misspend the money they do have.

2. *Some ineffective programs cost more money.* Some expensive practices actually *reduce* test scores or progress through high school. In my NELS88 results, this is most obvious for traditional vocational education (which costs more than academic programs), the general track, and the remedial track dominated by

drill and practice on basic skills. Special education represents another program with high spending but with minimal effects on conventional outcomes. While we have as a society decided that inclusion is preferable to exclusion, these equity goals have negative effects on the relation between spending and outcomes. High-cost continuation schools and alternative education have similar problems. And some spending looks "ineffective" because its goals are not measured by conventional outcomes. For example, spending on campus security, especially high in urban districts, is intended to keep students safe, but has no effect on test scores or graduation rates.

Urban districts spend a great deal of money on second-chance efforts—alternative education, remediation for low-performing students and those who have failed exit exams, and interventions of an infinite variety. Such practices reflect a commitment to equity and reducing achievement gaps, and to the responsibility of schools (rather than families alone) for academic performance. But by definition they operate under difficult circumstances. Students who have experienced earlier failure or mistreatment may be reluctant to intensify their schooling. Peer effects work in counterproductive ways since second-chance programs concentrate low-performing students. Second-chance programs are often asked to make several years of gains in one year or less, and there is little evidence about which programs work. Spending money on second-chance programs may be the only justifiable response to underperforming students, but it undermines the relationship between money and outcomes.[14]

3. *Many reforms fail to understand that compound rather than simple resources are necessary.* Class size reduction provides a clear example: the billions spent in California were on average ineffective because districts hired lower-quality teachers, funded inadequate professional development to facilitate different instructional methods, and provided insufficient space.[15] Other examples are new curricula, or approaches to assessment, or computers, all of which require professional development before they can be effective. Professional development is itself a complex resource, requiring sustained attention to pedagogical issues by a faculty working collaboratively.[16] When districts try to provide simple forms of professional development—isolated lectures by outside experts, for example—that approach is ineffective and therefore wasteful. When districts or states provide money for simple resources, the money is often wasted unless it can be combined with complementary resources—a case where money is *necessary but not sufficient.*

4. *Many effective resources cannot be bought.* As I argued in the previous section, many complex and abstract resources cannot be bought, but have to be

constructed by school communities. The need to *construct* certain resources clarifies why conventional approaches to school finance—equalizing spending per student, or litigation to force more equitable spending—do not guarantee effective schools. The emphasis on allocating money and simple resources usually ignores complex and abstract resources whose money costs are often indeterminate, and which depend on other resources—leadership, vision, cooperation—that may be in short supply. Indeed, these missing resources often require changes in the capacities of teachers and leaders, as well as organizational changes. Again, these are compound and complex resources that must be constructed, not simply bought.

5. *Closing the achievement gap can't be done with money alone, since it must confront racial dimensions.* Current demands for reform often focus on the achievement gap, almost always stated in racial terms—the differences among white, black, and Latino test scores, or the dropout rates of Latinos compared to white and Asian students. Then the conventional analysis recommends improvements in teachers, smaller classes, or intensification like afterschool classes. However, most policy recommendations ignore the glaring fact that these "gaps" are related to race and ethnicity.

In my NELS results, the profound differences in many kinds of gaps among African American, Latino, and American Indian students on the one hand and white and Asian American students on the other cannot be explained, even by many variables describing family background (or "class"), unequal school resources, and students' behavior and commitment to schooling. These measures fail to explain between 45 percent and 61 percent of the black-white differences in test scores; 25 percent to 40 percent of white-Latino differences; 45 percent of the black-white difference in earning a high school diploma; and 2 percent of the white-Latino difference.[17] An irreducible knot of racial/ethnic inequality remains after controlling for everything conceivable, in the richest data set I know.

Anyone who is serious about eliminating achievement gaps has first to explain these differences, and then come up with solutions. My own hypothesis is that many students are mistreated—based on class differences, sometimes, but most often based on race and ethnicity. There's substantial testimony from African American and Latino authors writing about their own schooling, from ethnographers describing particular schools, from critical race theory and its personal stories, and from my own observations in schools and community colleges. Mistreatment takes many forms, sometimes overt and conscious, as in the physical abuse of students, but more often covert and unconscious "micro-aggressions" that are individually small but collectively relentless.[18] Racial minority students are less likely to find adults who can serve as mentors and sponsors; they are more likely to be the victims of lower teacher expectations; and they are more likely to be suspended or expelled for infractions for which other students are not punished. These practices start early: in Ann Ferguson's ethnography *Bad Boys*, the trajectory of school practices that set students up for failure begins in fourth grade.[19]

To combat these forms of racial/ethnic mistreatment head on, advocates have developed an enormous range of strategies. These include finding more teachers of color; explicit attention to code-switching for immigrant students and speakers of Black Vernacular English; culturally relevant pedagogy and multicultural education that bring new curriculum materials, new subjects (like the role of race in American society), and new pedagogies with more critical perspectives; systematic classroom observation so that teachers can learn if they are unconsciously mistreating students of color; different approaches to discipline; and nonteaching support from same-race counselors and mentors. In my vocabulary, these are complex and abstract resources, which again must be constructed by teachers and leaders working together within specific schools. Sometimes money is necessary—for outside experts, facilitators of difficult racial conversations, release time, or curriculum materials. But other abstract resources are more important, including clear diagnosis, vision, cooperation, persistence, and above all, trust among the members of the school community while discussing the explosive issue of race. Once again, money is necessary but not sufficient.

The overall effect of money on outcomes is therefore the sum of several effects—some positive, in the case of simple resources that prove to be effective; some negative, as with tracking mechanisms and special education; and some neutral, as in cases of waste. In addition, some forms of spending—for security in urban schools, for example, or for transportation in rural areas—may look like waste because they are unrelated to student outcomes, but they are nonetheless necessary. And the failure to recognize the nature of compound, complex, and abstract resources means that some opportunities to improve schools and reduce achievement gaps are unrealized, something that shows up in schools being less effective with the funding they do have.

NARROWING ACHIEVEMENT GAPS IN A PERIOD OF SCARCITY

The analysis of resources and money in the two previous sections provides a number of clues for how educators can continue to improve schools and make them more equitable, even in the absence of new revenues. Six strategies in particular seem worth pursuing. Most of these would be worthwhile even in boom times, but they become all the more important given fiscal constraints.

Eliminating Waste

One of the most obvious strategies is to first identify and then eliminate the waste of funding that now affects many schools, especially (it seems) urban schools. This is hardly a novel idea. Several researchers and educators have addressed this problem recently in articles like "What Money Can't Buy," "Using Resources Effectively in Education" and "Solving the Funding-Achievement Puzzle."[20] Henry Levin excoriates the waste of classroom time, the difficulty of firing obviously incompetent teachers, ineffective professional development, and most remediation. Mike Schmoker critiques the waste of time on ineffective instructional practices like worksheets and movies, and exhorts educators to replace them with purposeful lessons and coherent curricula—one dimension of instructional improvement. Marguerite Roza, Dan Goldhaber, and Paul Hill also identify layoffs based on seniority (rather than teaching ability) as a waste, along with paying teachers with master's degrees more; based on earlier research where they found most district and school leaders ignorant of how they spend money, they recommend "frank assessments of spending in district budgets," or more careful fiscal audits. Ben Levin and Nancy Naylor, from Canada where the same conditions hold, suggest new forms of professional development, reallocating resources from specialists to regular classroom instructors, replacing remediation with prevention, and enhancing efficiency—again, reducing the waste that comes from ineffective forms of professional development.

A more general approach is to conduct a "waste audit" to uncover the different forms of waste. A format for doing so is presented in Grubb and Tredway, and this is something that teachers, school leaders, and district officials can all do.[21] Identifying the sources of waste, as distinct from the fact of waste, may be more difficult, particularly for teachers (and sometimes for principals) who are often unaware of what funding streams are responsible for certain forms of spending; in such cases waste audits need to be conducted by combinations of teachers, school-site leaders, and district officials responsible for the allocation of funds to schools.

One of the common forms of waste is what I and others call "programmitis."[22] In response to evidence of low performance, many schools add little programs—an afterschool program or other effort to extend the amount of time in classrooms, an intervention of some sort, literacy or math coaches to help teachers, a new curriculum that promises "proven results!!" What characterizes programmitis is that these programs generally leave the core teaching alone; they are add-ons, and are often poorly integrated with the rest of the school—as when afterschool programs have little contact with classroom teachers, or interventions are independent of the rest of the curriculum. Because they are often peripheral to the school, they are often ineffective; in addition, they are likely to be fragmented and episodic—a reading coach for second and third graders, math enrichment for fourth graders. Schools with a lot of these "little programs" are often labeled "Christmas tree schools," with shiny baubles hanging from a trunk and branches that are quite rotten. No Child Left Behind and state accountability mechanisms have propelled desperate districts and schools into adopting many ineffective programs. As a result, a great deal of waste has occurred.

Identifying common forms of waste should be relatively easy. Any school or district can undertake a "waste audit" quite simply, as I clarify in the last section. However, even if eliminating waste is conceptually easy, politically it collides with the interest groups, union rules, legislative regulations, and bureaucratic mechanisms that created it in the first place. Furthermore, eliminating waste doesn't tell anyone what to do instead of wasting resources; this requires deeper understanding of how resources might be effectively spent.

Undertaking Resource Audits

A second strategy is for a school to undertake a "resource audit," in place of the fiscal audits that are much more common. Again, a mechanism for conducting a resource audit is presented in Grubb and Tredway.[23] Like a waste audit, the idea underlying a resource audit is simple even though its execution may be difficult. Budgets describe only revenues and spending, so at best they can describe simple resources, and sometimes compound resources—though conventional line-item budgets typically don't clarify even these resources since they typically identify spending on teachers, staff, books, and materials, but not how these resources are being used. A resource audit is intended to help school (and district) leaders examine compound, complex, and abstract resources as well as simple resources, to see if they are overlooking resources that might help them improve outcomes and equity. To be sure, a resource audit is only as helpful as the information that goes into an inventory of *effective* practices, so information about effectiveness is necessary as well.

Providing a Repository of Information About Effectiveness

A corollary of carrying out a resource audit is providing better information on effectiveness. For example, the federal government has established a What Works Clearinghouse, presumably to provide information about effective (and ineffective) programs to schools and districts. Unfortunately, the current What Works Clearinghouse is pretty much a failure. It includes only a narrow range of random-assignment and statistically sophisticated studies, ignoring a wider range of evidence. It reports individual studies, rather than synthesizing results across topics of interest to schools (like the use of time, or afterschool programs, or ninth-grade remediation). Its results are accessible only to researchers, not to busy principals and school councils without research expertise. It has been accused of political bias, particularly in favoring pedagogically conservative curricula over others. And, like most evaluations based on random-assignment and statistical methods, it generally confines itself to discrete programs that can be compared to the status quo in which such a program is lacking—another form of "programmitis." More general forms of capacity building cannot be evaluated with random-assignment methods or complex statistical techniques because the "treatment" or "program" is not self-contained, and its effectiveness and implementation vary with the nature of leadership, the teachers in a particular school, and the history of previous reform efforts. It's practically unimaginable to control for all these potential influences.

A better alternative would be a network of What Works Institutes, perhaps established at the state or regional level, that could synthesize research on topics suggested by districts, schools, and state policies. Such institutes could be demand-driven rather than researcher-driven. The institute would then present the results in research briefs and conferences, as one way to bridge the divide between research and practice, something that would benefit both researchers and practitioners.

However, there are good reasons to believe that *any* repository of information is inadequate to translate research and evidence into practice. The study of innovations and their diffusion suggests that a knowledge base is only the first of six or seven steps, including the following:

1. The creation of a knowledge base, or an innovation
2. The diffusion (relatively passive) or dissemination (more active) of this knowledge to more practitioners.
3. The persuasion of educators that a research- or knowledge-based practice is superior to existing practice.
4. A decision to adopt rather than reject a practice, which involves many more factors than research conclusions: the superiority of the innovation, economic considerations, compatibility with existing practices, the complexity of the innovation, the uncertainty of benefits, political positions, and the ability of organizations to absorb new practices.
5. The implementation of a practice. In agriculture this may be as simple as using a new seed or plowing technique, but in education this always involves the capacity of teachers, leaders, and schools to put changes into place—so capacity building may be a prerequisite for this step.
6. Making a practice sustainable, or institutionalizing it so that it doesn't blow away with a new wind (or fad, or principal, or superintendent).
7. Evaluating the practice, adding to the knowledge base, and creating possible revisions—and, in a virtuous circle, returning to number one.[24]

The implication is that a more complex process is necessary to translate research, or a knowledge base, into practice. Many agree that the Agricultural Extension Service has been the most successful organization in the United States to do this, relying particularly on extension agents with one foot in practice and one in research.[25] Indeed, several educational reform organizations more or less follow this model, like Success for All and America's Choice, with their full-time facilitators or "linking agents" to support implementation.[26] So, developing a series of state or regional Educational Extension Services, with personnel akin to extension agents, would help facilitate the movement of knowledge about effective practices into school. Of course, such a development would also require significant expenditures, over periods of time, to create anything like the Agricultural Extension Service, so this is not a proposal to develop in tough times. Still, the potential usefulness of such an extension service clarifies that, while schools clearly need access to expertise about effectiveness, an inert repository of information following the What Works Clearinghouse is almost certainly not the right approach.

Increasing the Capacity for Schools and Districts to Allocate Resources Well

One way to do this is to decentralize decision making about resources to the school level, and adopt school-based budgeting so that principals and school-site councils have the fiscal resources to develop and implement their own improvement plans. Currently, districts make most funding allocations, and schools have neither the incentives nor the funds to develop their own resource plans. However, school-based budgeting creates the opportunity and the resources for principals and school councils to develop the resources that are effective at *their* schools, with *their* students and *their* teachers. Along the way, school leaders necessarily become more knowledgeable about "where the money goes," or which resources are enhanced, since they are the ones allocating and developing these resources.[27]

Two elements of state funding formulas would help increase the capacity of schools to allocate resources. One would be to reduce the amount of categorical funding, which inevitably reduces the discretion of districts and schools. Another would recognize the category of expenditures that are necessary but not intended to affect student outcomes—expenditures like security in urban schools and transportation and parental contact in rural schools—and then fund them separately. This would, among other things, help people see that some forms of spending are absolutely necessary, but educators should not be faulted if they don't improve outcomes.

A necessary corollary of school-based budgeting, or any system that gives schools greater control over their own resources, is professional development to make school leaders and school-site councils more sophisticated about the range of resources, and about *effective* resources. Many existing school-based budgeting systems provide inadequate professional development to enable schools to make better decisions. For example, an examination of New York's Performance-Driven Budgeting (PDB) initiative found that low-performing schools whose principals lacked knowledge and experience, and suffered from instability due to staff turnover, had only limited capacity to implement PDB.[28] So districts that implement school-based budgeting in order to give schools the resources and autonomy to make their own resource decisions must give them the capacity to make such decisions as well.

Instituting Planning Mechanisms

Finally, and perhaps most importantly, schools and districts cannot spend their funds wisely on *effective* school resources if they do not have planning mechanisms to create coherent instructional plans and then allow these plans to determine spending and resource patterns—rather than reacting to crises, whims, fads of the moment (to spend on computers, for example, or class size reduction), or desperate efforts to increase test scores quickly through stand-alone programs. In addition to implementing school-based budgeting, some apparently exemplary districts have developed more collegial and cooperative relationships with their schools, with more deliberation about the resources schools need—rather than having districts dictate curricula and allocate materials that then end up being wasted when schools don't use them. Some districts have created "tiers" of schools, allocating more attention and resources to schools that have been especially ineffective, including attention to enhancing the capacity of these schools to plan for themselves—rather than taking away school-level discretion through a district takeover.[29]

State Policies

Similarly, some states have experimented with mechanisms of helping both schools and districts spend their resources wisely, by providing consultants to low-performing schools and districts, adopting continuous-improvement practices in low-performing schools, trying to enhance the capacity of low-performing districts, and adopting a "tiering" system to identify both schools and districts in need of special attention.[30] These somewhat novel state efforts all require the capacity for technical assistance in the state department of education, which some states lack, and the effectiveness of these state initiatives is not yet clear since they are so new. But if we as a nation are willing to learn from experiments in states, there are many practices that could help both districts and schools learn to allocate resources more effectively.

So there are many ways to continue making progress on school reform and improvement—including efforts to enhance equity and reduce the various achievement gaps—in the absence of money during periods of fiscal constraint. In effect, these efforts require mobilizing other resources not in such short supply: understanding more carefully the effectiveness of various resources, including the *inef*-fectiveness of resources that are being wasted and the potential effectiveness of complex and abstract resources often ignored; mobilizing the cooperation (or "internal alignment") of teachers and leaders; developing clear visions or plans for a school, and making sure those plans are adhered to; enhancing the basic capacity of both teachers and leaders through carefully designed professional development to enhance instruction, school climate, and stability of policies and personnel—rather than engaging in "programmitis." But there's no reason to continue believing in the Money Myth, or to give up on narrowing achievement gaps just because money is scarce.

## CHAPTER TEN

Partnering with Families and Communities to Address Academic Disparities

NANCY ERBSTEIN AND ELIZABETH MILLER

The experiences of schools that have decreased or eliminated racial, socioeconomic, and linguistic disparities in academic performance and high school graduation rates suggest that that while there are no hard and fast recipes for their success, family and community partnerships are essential.[1] However, community and family engagement are rarely an integral aspect of school reform discourse, policy, and practice. This chapter elucidates dimensions of school-community partnership that should be central to strategies intended to promote stronger, more equitable academic outcomes. Conditions that enable widely shared characteristics of promising practices are identified as an important focus for education policy.

The chapter is organized in three sections. The first provides an overview of partnership strategies employed to decrease the "achievement gap," drawing on implementation and outcomes studies of partnership strategies as well as research on school reform and factors associated with student academic achievement. We organize the overview of strategies according to their focus on strengthening four aspects of student experience that contribute in pivotal ways to academic achievement: academic instruction, the school environment, school resources, and community contexts. We draw on this implementation research and research syntheses in the second section to summarize widely shared qualities of effective partnerships and key enabling supports for them. Finally, based on this review of the research, we discuss key steps for the field of education toward fostering the necessary conditions for successful family and community partnerships.

We focus here primarily on partnerships that most directly shape students' day-to-day experiences and learning opportunities. However, we acknowledge the importance of partnerships and collaborations that shape student opportunity by targeting policy and political contexts (e.g., community-driven efforts to create new schools and promote school choice, desegregation strategies, community mobilization to build political will to tackle disparities, etc.).[2] Indeed, in many cases, the effective forms of practice described in this chapter are predicated upon these latter forms of organizing and community engagement.

The empirical basis for these various partnership strategies is embedded in disparate education and related literatures that together present several challenges. Partnership research and practice reflect multiple hypotheses about the causes of academic disparities. One of five broad explanations tends to dominate any given initiative: (1) student, family, and/or community deficits produce barriers to school performance; (2) differences or mismatches between students' home/cultural group and school cultures and expectations affect academic achievement; (3) school practices and policies disadvantage students and families of particular ethnic, language, or socioeconomic backgrounds and/or underrecognize and underutilize their strengths; (4) local and regional institutions, policies, social dynamics, and political economies together produce disparities in educational opportunities and affect political will to address them; and (5) complex interactions among school, family, peer, and local factors account for differences in academic performance.

This range of hypotheses reflects distinct theoretical frameworks and corresponds to a multiplicity of partnership practices. However, the hypotheses and practices that have been rigorously studied are limited, with most large-scale studies focusing on strategies that reflect a deficit or, to a somewhat lesser extent, a cultural mismatch orientation to families and communities.[3] A lack of consistent approaches to defining and operationalizing partnership strategies makes it difficult to aggregate knowledge across studies. Some strategies have also been studied primarily via small-scale qualitative case studies. Longitudinal, comparative, mixed-methods research appears to be underutilized, yet it is a critically important direction in light of the localized and complex nature of partnership strategies and their relationship to academic outcomes.[4] To date, this broad and emergent area of scholarship does not yet provide definitive findings regarding the relative importance of different partnership strategies and how those patterns might vary across contexts, or the mechanisms through which individual and combined strategies affect academic outcomes.[5]

In this context, we sought to identify high-quality studies that used experimental methods, and primarily focused on research conducted since 2002.[6] Studies that employed quantitative methods (quasi-experimental, comparative-population, and correlational studies, as well as a small number of surveys) were selected according to a number of methodological criteria: assumptions and definitions were described and applied consistently, and research designs employed statistical controls, isolated effects, and used validated and reliable measures. Studies that employed qualitative methods, including evaluation reports and case studies, were also included as these reflect much of the available research on this topic and often raise critical theoretical questions. As with the quantitative studies, we considered specific methodological issues, including the extent to which assumptions and definitions were described and consistently applied, the studies' grounding in theory, and the use of sound qualitative methods. Finally, we examined several literature reviews and meta-analyses that address the links among family involvement, school-linked services, and academic outcomes.

PARTNERSHIP CONTRIBUTIONS

Family and community partnerships are highly visible at schools that successfully serve students most vulnerable to disparate educational opportunities and outcomes.[7] They involve a variety of collaborators, including local institutions, parents/caretakers, other community members and leaders, and local youth. While there is no evidence that a family and community engagement approach, or combination of approaches, alone eliminates racial, socioeconomic and linguistic disparities, partnership strategies appear to contribute to effective overall efforts in critical ways. In particular, they focus on dimensions of student support that *together* appear to be key factors in student academic success, including (1) strengthening academic teaching and learning; (2) providing social supports to create a healthy learning environment; (3) building school leadership and resources to ensure adequate support of teachers, students, and their families; and (4) fostering neighborhood and community development to promote school engagement. (See figure 10.1.)

FIGURE 10.1
Contributions of school-community partnership strategies to academic achievement

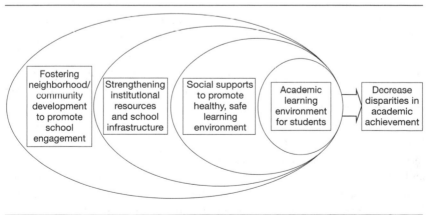

The remainder of this section describes how partnerships are being employed with respect to each of the above dimensions of support to:

- eliminate barriers and disparate levels of support disproportionately experienced by low-income students, students of color, students learning English, and their families;
- recognize and build on the strengths of these young people and their communities; and
- generally strengthen each element of support for student learning.

We conclude with an overview of efforts to integrate work across these four dimensions.

Strengthening Academic Teaching and Learning

Multiple approaches to school-community partnerships focus directly on academic achievement by addressing factors closely associated with teaching and learning. In particular, these strategies use local knowledge and resources to promote high expectations of students, foster student engagement, offer rigorous curricula, and extend student opportunities to develop strong academic skills.

Successful schools promote high expectations for academic achievement early and consistently, explicitly challenging widespread, inaccurate, and damaging beliefs that African American, Latino, Native American, and economically poor children are intellectually inferior and/or uninterested in education.[8] Establishing respectful, caring relationships with students' families helps reinforce school staff and leaders' understanding of families' high hopes and dreams for their children and the types of resources they can contribute to school efforts. In turn, schools work with parents/caregivers in multiple ways to foster and enact these expectations, countering a trend of low-income and language-minority families experiencing more limited outreach from their children's schools,[9] building on a substantial body of developmental research demonstrating the impact of parent involvement on children's school trajectories,[10] and addressing barriers to family engagement. Strategies include (1) explicitly communicating high expectations and academic norms to families,[11] (2) engaging parents in constructing and communicating school norms,[12] (3) communicating with families regarding their children's academic progress through key educational transition points and ensuring families have the capacity to advocate on their behalf,[13] and (4) partnering with local and state postsecondary institutions and systems to offer parents multiple and early opportunities to learn about postsecondary requirements and resources.[14] In some settings, community partners such as mentoring programs, colleges and universities, faith organizations, health-care providers, and local businesses are also enlisted in reinforcing these expectations, which bolsters family support and offers a critical source of encouragement for young people whose parents' capacity to provide this is limited.[15]

Student engagement in their learning is a key condition of student academic achievement. Although there is significant debate among researchers about the factors that constrain classroom engagement (e.g., social identity, prior academic achievement levels, cultural mismatch, teacher practices[16]), there is broad agreement that building on student and community funds of knowledge[17] and offering opportunities to develop and hone skills in meaningful, real-world contexts[18] are powerful mechanisms for promoting engagement. Successful schools and teachers recognize that the language and cultural knowledge of their students and families offer a rich and powerful foundation for building new skills, knowledge, and interests. For example, a study of eight south Texas border schools that outperform most in attaining state standards found that math teachers across all grade levels employ community cultural knowledge as a context for teaching skills and concepts. In serving a K–12 student population that is predominantly Latino, low-income, and native Spanish-speaking, these teachers used local music as the basis for songs about math concepts, taught measurement through cooking and carpentry projects familiar to many families, generated word problems referencing the local environment, built on students' inclination to work collaboratively, and engaged family members at home and school as educators and audiences.[19] More broadly, teachers who are familiar with local communities and make use of local resources appear to increase student engagement in curricular material.[20] Strategies such as place-based curricula, service learning, internships, career academies, and projects that engage youth in complex research focused on local community issues offer opportunities to tap student interests, energy, and insight; develop skills and knowledge; and understand their real-world application.[21] In addition, schools pursue academic rigor through collaborations that tap the specialized expertise and resources of local individuals and organizations, in some cases offering accelerated learning opportunities through local colleges and universities.[22]

In recent years, research has documented the effects of wealthier students' greater access to a range and depth of out-of-school opportunities to develop academic and social skills associated with academic performance. Over time, this appears to result in a pattern of accumulated gains for wealthier students, accumulated losses for poorer students, and a growing gap between the two.[23] School, community, and/or family partnerships confront this pattern in several ways. First, they offer supports (e.g., project ideas, materials, curricular information, family programs) for parents and caregivers to further support academic learning at home. Accessible, affordable, and high-quality tutoring and other afterschool programs provide learning opportunities that are engaging, meaningful, developmentally appropriate, rigorous, and built on funds of knowledge. Similar opportunities are offered during the summer.[24]

Specific approaches to partnerships focused directly on academic learning vary across grade levels to reflect young people's development, as well as developmental shifts in parents' roles.[25] Approaches also vary according to school staff capacities, student and family interests and needs, and local resources. However, schools that are succeeding appear to employ some form of partnerships to build and communicate high academic expectations, foster student motivation to pursue rigorous work, and increase student access to the academic support they need.

Providing Social Supports for a Positive Learning Environment

Studies of schools that have successfully reduced or eliminated disparities inevitably comment on the climate of care and respect that permeates these institutions. Schools where all students attend regularly and focus on learning are places where young people feel physically and emotionally safe and respected, which also contributes to school engagement. Partnership strategies are often an important factor in shaping this environment.

School-community partnerships can foster students' sense of connection to school by helping their families feel comfortable engaging with school personnel and processes, and helping schools become welcoming and accessible places for families and community members.[26] Approaches to establishing trusting and trustworthy relationships in some cases entail school partnerships with intermediary organizations that bring cultural capacity and established local networks.[27] Enlisting the support of families, students, community members, and school staff familiar with the community can help foster a climate of respect among students and between youth and adults of different backgrounds.[28]

At some schools, efforts to create an effective learning environment are linked to broader health promotion strategies, reflecting the advice of the Carnegie Council Task Force on Education of Young Adolescents: "School systems are not responsible for meeting every need of their students. But when the need directly affects learning, the school must meet the challenge."[29] When students and families experience extreme poverty, violence, and/or neglect, fostering a climate conducive to meeting high academic expectations and negotiating the social demands of school life requires ensuring that students' basic needs are met. School-community partnerships are often central in pursuing these objectives.

Health inequities exist largely among socially and economically disadvantaged and linguistically isolated families, populations that also experience inequitable educational opportunities and outcomes.[30] Poor health (both physical and mental) of children and their caretakers is closely correlated with lower educational achievement,[31] and school failure is associated with significant health consequences, offering a strong rationale for collaborative efforts across education and health systems. For example, recent research on the relationship between childhood mental disorders and educational attainment has highlighted the impact of attention deficit, hyperactivity, and impulse control on completion of high school; targeted interventions and treatment early in the course of a disorder are likely to have an effect on educational attainment.[32] Similarly, exposure to traumatic events (including high levels of community violence) affects learning; innovative school-based mental health interventions have demonstrated reduced stress levels and improved academic outcomes.[33] Several strategies have emerged to foster student health and well-being in coordination with schools, and to bring evidence-based programs and promising practices to schools, including coordinated school health, school-based health centers, school-linked services, and comprehensive case management and mentoring approaches.

Coordinated School Health (CSH) was intended to address the nexus of health status, health risk behaviors, and academic success.[34] These programs involve coordination across multiple key school-based stakeholders, including school district staff, school boards, administrators, school nurses and counselors, health assistants, teachers, and food service employees. Parent and community participation are a necessary component to this schoolwide effort to address the health and well-being of students.[35] Anecdotal descriptions of successful CSH models include multiple ways in which health (including health promotion efforts such as "walk to school" day) has been incorporated into school activities and instruction and enhanced by community partnerships, but the most rigorously evaluated interventions focus only on one or two components of CSH. Despite this limitation, studies demonstrate that CSH approaches do appear to be associated with improvements in academic achievement. For example, where schools provide asthma education and there are schoolwide efforts to increase awareness of asthma triggers, students demonstrate improvements in grades, science performance in particular.[36]

School-based health centers (SBHCs) use evidence-based strategies to provide comprehensive primary, preventive, and mental health services to children and adolescents, with documented improvements in access to care as well overall health knowledge.[37] SBHCs provide easy access to developmentally and culturally appropriate services by collaborating with parents, educators, and the primary health care providers of students to develop an array of services. SBHCs are often located in schools where students are likely to be at greater risk for experiencing both physical and mental health-care inequalities and may have limited access to care due to lack of health insurance, underinsurance, or undocumented status. In rural communities, SBHCs are often the primary source for all students' health services. While data suggest that improving the overall physical and mental health of students (including provision of health services on-site at schools) would have some effect on academic achievement, research on the effects of SBHCs on school academic performance is more limited, and it is difficult to isolate the effects of SBHCs on academic outcomes. The primary outcomes that have been assessed in studies looking at the potential effects of SBHCs on academic outcomes are absences and dropout rates.[38]

School-linked services allow for a coordinated, integrated approach to addressing the complex needs of socially and economically disadvantaged students and families by offering a single point of entry. Services may be provided on- and/or off-site from the school, with the school as the central clearinghouse. With a primary goal of fostering local interagency and community collaboration and communication to provide holistic support for children, youth, and families, these initiatives attempt to reduce duplication of effort and fragmentation of care. Services may include youth development activities, gang risk intervention programs, youth and family counseling, emergency food and shelter, access to clothing and laundry facilities, provision of school supplies, medical and preventive care, tutoring, assistance in finding stable housing, legal services, and employment training. Programming often draws upon the knowledge and networks of staff and volunteers who have local roots or have navigated conditions similar to those faced by students and families. Implementation of these school-linked services varies widely, which limits rigorous evaluation and the ability to look at specific effects of particular elements. However, evaluation reports of two California school-linked initiatives, Healthy Start and Beacon Schools, demonstrate some improvements in academic outcomes.[39]

Partnerships not only enable provision of locally responsive programs and services, but also mechanisms for assessing student and family resources and needs, and for connecting to existing resources and addressing gaps while supporting and monitoring students in an intensive and ongoing way. For example, via Check & Connect, paid mentors—often from the communities in which they are working—work with students and families over a period of at least two years, following them across programs and schools. These "monitors" serve as mentors, advocates, and service coordinators, with an emphasis on building trusting relationships with the young people they support.[40] Similarly, *ALAS* (Spanish for "wings"), an intervention for middle and high school students, is designed to address student, school, family, and community factors that affect school persistence. Each student is assigned a counselor/mentor who monitors attendance, behavior, and academic achievement. The counselor/mentor provides feedback and coordinates interventions and resources for students, families, and teachers. Counselors/mentors also serve as advocates for students and intervene when problems are identified. Students are trained in problem solving, self-control, and assertiveness skills. Parents receive guidance on parent-child problem solving, how to participate in school activities, and how to contact teachers and school administrators to address issues. *ALAS* was found to have potentially positive effects on staying in school and potentially positive effects on progressing in school at the end of the intervention (ninth grade).[41] While such initiatives do not necessarily reduce the structural fragmentation of local support systems and programs, they do increase coordination for individual students and facilitate families' capacities to navigate them.

Findings regarding the effects of specific health and well-being interventions on school completion rates (as well as related measures of academic achievement) have some shared general characteristics.

- Programs are school-centered, with schools serving as a central locus for connection to multiple services (both school-based and in the community): these include coordinated school-health programs, school-based health centers, mental health programs, substance abuse treatment, and targeted services for pregnant-parenting teens.
- Successful interventions and integrated services occur in partnership with local community agencies (e.g., community mental health agencies, public health departments, and local businesses) that assist with program development and implementation (including securing funding sources outside of education).
- Some of the health interventions, in addition to direct effects on health outcomes, appear to have additional effects on school climate and student connectedness (to school and other caring adults) that may have an indirect effect on academic outcomes.
- Targeted interventions and services that focus on marginalized populations (e.g., youth who are in foster care, homeless, pregnant/parenting, and/or involved with the juvenile justice system) support youth to continue with their education, while providing much needed wraparound services.

In summary, the coordinated school health framework, school-based health centers, and school-linked services all offer models for provision of supports and services to improve the health and well-being of students and their families and foster a school climate that facilitates attendance and engagement. School-community partnerships that recognize and build upon local partners' insight and expertise are integral to each of these models of health promotion that are intended explicitly to create a positive learning environment for students. Attending to the overall school environment and student and family well-being is not a sufficient strategy for eliminating ethnic, linguistic, and socioeconomic disparities in academic performance. But, implemented well, it is a powerful strategy for reducing significant barriers to school engagement disproportionately faced by low-income students, students of color, and English language learners.

Partnerships to Cultivate School Leadership and Resources

Thus far we have described how partnerships with families and community organizations directly support academic learning and foster a healthy environment for student achievement. In many successful schools, partnerships also build core institutional resources such as school leadership, a highly skilled staff, and school infrastructure as well as funding to support partnership strategies.

School leadership is a critical element of school success.[42] Shared or distributed leadership strategies (including engagement of parents, community members, and/or local institutional leaders) are employed in some cases to marshal the assets of nonschool staff to strengthen the school program and ensure cultural relevance, to expand services and capacities that cannot be offered by the school alone, and to build community-wide support for school and district reform efforts.[43] Reform efforts in the New York City New Century Schools are an example of such partnerships. In some cases, community institutions are lead partners, resulting in innovative school curricula, integrated youth development practices, and increased family involvement. Meeting the needs of youth and families is regarded as integral to the school, and in some cases, schools play an active and integral role in broader community development efforts.[44] Underlying this strategy is the understanding that such partnerships offer knowledge, resources, and opportunities that schools alone are not equipped to provide. While longer-term outcomes are yet to be documented, formative evaluation and descriptive studies demonstrate that community integration encourages innovative curricula and pedagogy, school climate change, service provision, family involvement, and healthier neighborhood environments.[45] Initial outcomes assessments tracking attendance rates, dropout rates, and graduation rates are promising.[46]

School leaders at many New York City small schools have been supported by nonprofit intermediary organizations that assisted in implementing school designs. Intermediaries typically helped identify human resources and manage external pressures, provided materials for school planning and assessment, and built professionals' knowledge and skills through coaching and networking.[47] In other cases around the country, schools and districts are working with college and university partners to provide a range of professional development opportunities for school leaders and teachers, employ research to inform ongoing planning, and creatively draw upon the multiple resources of higher education.[48]

As part of reform and ongoing developmental processes, successful schools often demonstrate creativity in partnering to provide space and other infrastructure to support student learning. For example, small schools in some cases co-locate with community organizations; career partnership academies may employ the facilities of local businesses and organizations as teaching and learning venues.[49] Others enter joint-use agreements with municipalities or counties around access to parks, pools, libraries, and other community facilities.[50]

In this climate of school funding cuts and growing rates of child and family poverty, it is especially critical to both use existing resources well and find additional resources to promote student success. Implementation analyses of school-linked services suggest that collaboration with community partners may offer a powerful mechanism for reducing duplication of services and for leveraging additional private and public funding.[51]

Fostering Neighborhood/Community Development to Promote School Engagement

The previous three foci of partnership practices—supporting academic learning, fostering a learning environment, and building institutional capacity—reflect efforts to reduce barriers to and increase support for academic learning at school and home. Over the past three decades scholars have increasingly sought to understand how local social, economic, and built environments shape student opportunity and learning.[52] Related research and practice move beyond a focus on utilizing locally available services to explore how local individuals and institutions can mobilize to build social capital and civic capacity, marshal local assets, and transform community conditions that are barriers to well-being and school success.[53] While studies suggests that school leaders in low-income neighborhoods typically work to improve schools in isolation from larger community-development projects, in some cases localities have pursued a comprehensive focus on community development, with educational reform positioned as both contributing to and benefiting from such efforts.[54] One of the best known examples is the Harlem Children's Zone, which has both focused on community revitalization within an area of approximately one hundred city blocks and constructed an infrastructure of support for families living there. Supports include schools for children and youth from preschool through high school, afterschool programs, mentoring for students focused on higher education enrollment and persistence, parenting support, physical and mental health promotion programs, and advising services focused on issues such as housing, employment, and legal issues. Community beautification and the development of grassroots leadership are also core activities. Community organizing is a central tool for building social capital, identifying local interests and assets, and connecting families with resources.[55] Preliminary assessment of student outcomes suggests that while community investments alone may not drive student success, when coupled with high-quality schools, such innovative community supports may contribute to improved performance.[56]

The Chicago-based research of Bryk, Sebring, and Allensworth suggests the need for further attention to when and where investment in community development may be especially integral to educational reform.[57] Their analysis reveals that some schools serve "truly disadvantaged school communities": attendance areas that stand out based on extremely high concentrations of economic poverty, racial segregation, social disorder (as measured by crime rates and rates of child abuse and neglect), and a more limited institutional base for building social capital (e.g., vital business community, nonprofits, churches, etc.). These schools saw fewer gains in overall academic performance and faced greater challenges with family community engagement in comparison with schools in somewhat less disadvantaged neighborhoods.[58] Their findings raise the question of whether there are certain thresholds of neighborhood well-being below which school capacity to promote academic performance becomes more seriously compromised; if so, it might follow that in these settings educational reform would especially benefit from coordination with a broader community development strategy.

While many such community strengthening efforts are focused in areas with high concentrations of economic poverty and racial and/or linguistic isolation that have experienced disinvestment over time, more affluent districts with strong average academic outcomes have also identified the importance of community scale work to address ethnic and socioeconomic disparities.[59] In the absence of many of the challenging conditions that often become the primary focus of community building in economically poor urban and rural settings, some local partnerships have drawn explicit attention to how opportunities for individuals and groups are shaped by structural racism—"a system of linked public policies, institutional practices, cultural representations, and other norms often reinforce the perpetuation of racial group inequity."[60] Such partnerships focus on understanding and addressing factors such as school practices that (often inadvertently) disadvantage students and families of color and somewhat lower income families, policies and social dynamics outside school that produce racialized and unequal experiences for local youth and families that affect their education, and beliefs that are used to justify differential expectations of young people and their families based on their race and/or immigration background.[61] For example, in Davis, California, local high school students, community activists, and school and district staff have worked for more than six years to promote an honest and constructive community discussion of race and racism; by generating, reviewing, publicizing, and responding to data reflecting students' disparate school experiences across racial and ethnic groups, they have taken up teacher and counselor expectations, peer expectations, discipline policies, GATE program access, hiring practices, and curricula, among other issues.[62]

This area of research and practice draws attention to the shared fortunes of schools and their communities. While a great deal remains to be learned about the relationship between community development and reduction of academic disparities, promising practices, as well as the persistent failure of school-centered efforts, suggest the importance of further experimentation and assessment.

Integrating Partnership Strategies

Partnership practices and development of supporting policies are often pursued in a disjointed manner. The conceptual umbrella of "community schools" offers one approach to linking such efforts. The Coalition for Community Schools defines community schools as "both a place and a set of partnerships between the school and other community resources."[63] The coalition pursues an integrated focus on academics, health and social services, youth and community development, and community engagement, with the goal of promoting improved student learning, stronger families, and healthier communities. The continuum of community schools extends from the limited addition of support services within schools to highly intertwined institutional and neighborhood/community reform.[64] These schools and their strategies also reflect varying orientations to community partnership, positioning families and communities as recipients of services and interventions, providers of services, partners in change, and/or drivers of change.[65] While some sites take up fundamental challenges to partnerships and educational reform such as structural racism, others do not.

Despite the fragmented nature of partnership research, five broad areas of scholarship referenced here together underscore that multiple forms of family and community partnerships will be required to eliminate disparities that produce the academic achievement gap: (1) developmental research demonstrating the role of multiple ecological contexts in children's well-being, with families as a key factor in children's academic success, (2) medical research highlighting health disparities and revealing an association between child and family health and school outcomes, (3) analyses linking community and regional development and school success, (4) partnership strategy studies revealing associations with academic learning, and (5) comprehensive school reform research identifying family and community engagement as a factor in promoting stronger, more equitable academic outcomes. The absence of research providing direction on the relative efficacy of individual partnership strategies and various combinations of strategies, as well as how those patterns might shift according to local needs and resources, places a high level of responsibility on local schools, families, and communities. Together they must assess local contexts and adapt strategies that address barriers to strong and equitable academic achievement in ways that build upon local strengths and resources.

SHARED QUALITIES AND ENABLING CONDITIONS
OF SUCCESSFUL PARTNERSHIPS

Although many specifics of partnership work must necessarily emerge from localities, implementation research across this diversity of partnership strategies suggests that promising practices share some fundamental qualities.[66] Achieving these qualities appears to be facilitated by several enabling conditions that depend upon schools and school systems. These shared qualities and enabling conditions together offer an important foundation for education planning, practice, and policy development.

As noted earlier, schools that foster academic success among economically poor students, students of color, and English language learners employ a variety of approaches to partnering with students' families and other local individuals and institutions. Whether partnerships are focused on engaging parents as educators and advocates of their children, promoting school attendance and engagement by supporting young people's development and overall well-being, building school capacity to offer relevant and rigorous learning opportunities, or building communities that support children, youth, and families well, the following qualities and practices tend to characterize successful, sustainable efforts (see table 10.1).

Implementation studies across various types of family and community partnerships together suggest four common conditions that are associated with the qualities listed, reflecting a combination of capacities and commitments:

1. Partnerships are normative
2. Partners are prepared
3. Resources are sufficient and sustained
4. Planning and practice reflect ongoing evaluation

These conditions appear to be widely shared, necessary precursors of effective, sustained implementation, and therefore offer an important basis for planning and policy development.

Partnerships Are Normative

At schools where students benefit from multiple successful partnerships, education leaders and practitioners view partnerships as a core element of school—not an optional add-on. Rather than relegating partnership activities to peripheral silos, they are embedded in school and district structures, cultures, and practices. A framework of policies promotes partnerships that reflect the full diversity of the student population. The work of partnerships is embedded in job descriptions and accounted for in workloads. Districts and schools work with potential partners to articulate comprehensive and sustainable visions of community

TABLE 10.1
Qualities and practices of successful school-community partnerships

Quality	Practice
Focused	The experiences and success of young people—especially those most negatively affected by patterns of disparity—are at the center of planning, implementation, and evaluation.
Systemic	School boards, district leaders, principals, and leaders of other engaged systems provide active and ongoing support.
Respectful	Treatment of partners reflects their great value to schools, and processes are in place to acknowledge and act upon the challenge of working across different ethnic, language, and cultural backgrounds.
Tailored	Strategies are tailored to reflect the changing needs and interests at preschool, primary, and secondary school levels; differences among cultures; and local priorities and resources.
Inclusive	Personal, culturally sensitive, and proactive outreach and engagement are normative, as are the input and leadership of stakeholders in partnership strategies (especially those most often underrepresented).
Cultivated	Resources are allocated to strengthen school staff members' and partners' capacity to work together effectively.
Creative	Solutions are pursued to overcome logistical, informational, and regulatory barriers to partnerships.
Supported	Stable—or at least sustained—sources of funding are identified.
Reflective	Partners regularly use evaluation data to strengthen efforts and refine strategies.
Realistic	Partners and supporters maintain a sense of urgency while recognizing that it takes time to build needed trust and see evidence of large-scale effects.

partnerships that reflect local needs, interests, and assets and that evolve based on experimentation.

Partners Are Prepared

Successful partnerships require that partners have the insight, knowledge, and skills needed to collaborate effectively. This has implications for the preparation of school staff, leaders, and community partners. Specific capacities required of school-based staff and leaders include:

- A sense of responsibility for learning to work effectively across ethnic, language, cultural, and class differences, as well as differences in partner organizations' cultures and policies
- Cultural capacity/cultural humility, cross-cultural communication skills, and an appreciation that schools might need to repair relationships with communities in light of perceived and real past wrongs[67]

- Knowledge of partnership practices and strategies that promote stronger, more equitable outcomes for children, youth, and families
- Knowledge of local and regional networks and resources
- Understanding of relevant policy arenas and institutional actors in related fields such as public health and community development, and ways of blending funding streams to support partnerships (particularly among school leaders)
- Willingness to share leadership and power

These capacities are actively cultivated in schools that partner successfully to promote equitable learning opportunities and outcomes. Professional development, coaching, and orientation of credentialed and classified staff are important ways of augmenting individual staff skills and fostering a family- and community-oriented school culture, as are hiring processes that incorporate these qualifications.

Long-term institutional partners benefit from cultivating similar qualities. Potential family and institutional partners also often face a steep learning curve regarding how schools operate and the policies and institutions that guide and regulate their activity—a knowledge base that can easily be taken for granted by people working within school systems. In addition, community constituencies that could bring critical insights, knowledge, and expertise to schools are sometimes constrained by their isolation, communication barriers, and fear and mistrust rooted in a history of real and perceived mistreatment by the education system. School-community partnerships benefit when community partners have opportunities to expand their skills, knowledge, and networks in ways that strengthen their ability to work with schools and advocate for young people.

Resources Are Sufficient and Sustained

Although partnerships can provide crucial capacities for supporting school success, partnership activities also depend on organizational resources. Pivotal resources include physical space, staff time, and sustained funding.

Accessible physical space is often an important aspect of partnership activities; for example, school-linked services research is particularly clear that school-based program elements are critical to the seamless provision of needed services. Collaborative schools demonstrate a willingness to be creative about addressing space needs.

Enacting partnerships, planning and assessing partnerships, funding partnerships, and building the relationships that form the foundation of successful partnerships all take time. Engaging with working parents and caretakers as well as local youth partners requires time outside the typical school- and workday. Partnership strategies that rely on short-term, inadequate funding and heroic school staff members are unsustainable; when resources disappear, programs do as well, contributing to the perception and practice of partnerships as peripheral. Transiency of partnership efforts—especially if they are making a critical difference for students, their families, and their neighborhoods—cuts against foundations of trust and shared knowledge that can serve as a basis for further collaboration. Dedicated, full-time partnership coordination appears to be crucial in both facilitating the work of partnerships and sustaining a flow of funding.[68] While many initiatives struggle to maintain programs launched with philanthropic funding, there are important lessons to be learned from localities such as San Francisco, Multnomah County, Oregon, and New York City, which have found ways to braid resource streams and sustain full-service school initiatives.[69]

Planning and Practice Reflect Ongoing Evaluation

Schools that successfully reduce disparities in academic outcomes maintain a laser-like focus on identifying and addressing barriers to their students' learning. Formative and outcomes evaluations of partnership contributions are a critical source of information for ongoing planning. Evaluations should be carefully designed to produce accurate information about young people's experience and outcomes, account for the language and cultural background of students and families, limit burdens on frontline staff and participants, employ indicators that partnerships are designed to directly affect, produce findings on a timeline and in a format that can inform collaborative work, and promote accountability for student success. Student data should be broken down by subgroups such as age/grade, socioeconomic status, racial/ethnic background, home language, English language abilities, and place of residence to assess strategies' effectiveness for various student populations and ensure that typically marginalized populations are well served.

Alongside more traditional approaches to evaluation, participatory methods offer the opportunity to engage youth and community members in developing indicators, collecting and analyzing data, and generating recommendations. While such strategies can be resource intensive, this approach appears to be a powerful mechanism for gathering meaningful information, building capacity to work with data, strengthening partnerships, and generating momentum for action based on findings.[70]

Enabling Strategic Partnership

In sum, while a wide variety of partnerships can contribute to school and student success, partnerships that help reduce academic disparities appear to share some important qualities. These qualities are fostered by four critical conditions: partnerships are normative, partners are prepared, resources are sufficient and sustained, and planning and practice reflect ongoing evaluation. Therefore, steps toward bringing about these conditions must be an integral aspect of an agenda to create a more equitable system of K–12 education.

FOSTERING THE CONDITIONS FOR
SUCCESSFUL PARTNERSHIPS

Fostering the conditions required to promote successful, widespread implementation of school-community partnership strategies will likely demand education policy and regulatory attention at the federal, state, and local levels. Professional development, school finance, school and district planning, school facilities/transportation, and evaluation and data management are also areas in which challenges must be resolved.

Professional Development

Teacher and administrator credentialing programs and ongoing professional development must cultivate the knowledge, skills, and commitments that together comprise the civic capacity necessary for creating and sustaining strong partnerships between schools, families, and communities.[71] To date this has been a limited focus of training, reflecting a widespread orientation to partnerships as a peripheral element of the work of schools.[72]

Simultaneously, educational opportunities for community partners and families showing how schools and the educational system operate are needed to build a shared vision and language for school-community partnerships. State- and school-sponsored partnership initiatives, businesses, faith networks, unions, city government, and so on are all potential sponsors of such efforts. Existing resources to support school, community, and statewide efforts, such as federally supported Parent Information Resource Centers (PIRCs), must be strengthened and consistently publicized.

School Finance

Fostering strong partnerships that promote more equitable outcomes for children and adolescents may ultimately require additional financial resources. For example, success stories such as the Harlem Children's Zone depend on the annual infusion of millions of dollars beyond regularly available funds.[73]

Increased flexibility coupled with adequate support and accountability mechanisms might yield greater ability to also leverage existing resources.[74] Steps to facilitate more strategic *braiding* of resource streams across areas within the public sector (e.g., education, health services, public health, community development, transitional assistance, juvenile justice, parks and recreation), and within and across scales (local, state, federal) are a needed direction. For example, recent federal health reform legislation includes the provision of school-based preventive and clinical services (including funding for equipment and health information technology), which school districts can marshal in partnership with local health care systems. Making such nontraditional funding sources more easily accessible to school districts and providing incentives to schools for increasing community partnerships may also increase the sustainability of school-community partnerships. However, for any individual school district to identify these relevant funding sources and create a strategic and sustainable funding stream to support school-community partnerships remains a daunting task. The multiplicity of programs and reporting requirements places a tremendous demand on local partnerships, and inhibits development of comprehensive partnership strategies and outcomes.

Over the past decade, additional public and private funding for partnership strategies has become available, primarily through competitive grant programs. For example, in the public arena, 21st Century Community Learning Centers, Service Learning grants, the Full Service Community Schools Act, Promise Neighborhood grants, Nell Soto Parent/Teacher Involvement Grants, and SAHMSA grants offer opportunities to partner with local community members and organizations. The allocation of many of these resources through competitive grant programs presents a significant challenge; although this system helps facilitate school and district planning and effective use of public funds, schools and districts with great need but more limited grant-writing capacity may be denied access to support. Requiring reporting to the state on education budgets and expenditures at the school level (rather than only at the district level in the case of California) would enable increased oversight to ensure that partnership resources are utilized and maximized, and reach the most disadvantaged neighborhoods and communities. The balance of partnership funding available through competitive grants versus regular allocations deserves further exploration, as do approaches to fostering small rural school and district access to grant funding.

School and District Planning and Leadership

Multiple policy mechanisms require schools and districts to involve parents or community members in governance (e.g., through School Site Councils, English Learner Advisory Committees), engage parents (e.g., under ESEA provisions, Title I, Migrant Education Program), and submit formal plans for parent engagement (Title I School Site Plans). Schools and districts should be encouraged and supported to develop comprehensive plans for explicit, strategic family and community partnerships by building upon these and existing state requirements. Comprehensive needs assessment and planning will be especially critical as funding mechanisms become more flexible and schools identify nontraditional funding streams to support community partnerships. School organization and staffing should accommodate the demands of planning and implementing partnerships. Education and other local leaders must position such partnerships as central to the work of their schools and communities.

School Facilities and Transportation

Beyond being creative with existing school facilities, addressing the space needs of various school-community partnerships may require designing and locating new facilities with partnerships in mind and addressing regulatory challenges of using school buildings during off-school hours. Cases where school-based space is unavailable or undesirable may necessitate developing transportation strategies that facilitate student and family access to other community locations, suggesting the importance of increasing links between education and community and regional planning and of developing incentives that encourage land use and transportation planners to adopt a youth focus.

Evaluation and Data Management

Learning from new innovations and ensuring that school-community partnership initiatives are implemented well and address the needs of student populations most affected by the achievement gap will require high-quality evaluation at both state and local levels. This requires data management strategies that allow for tracking of key indicators that programs are designed to affect. Mixed-methods designs with attention to intended and unintended consequences of the effects of community partnerships on students, school environments, teachers, and families are necessary to develop a greater body of evidence on the role of such partnerships in academic success. Given the variation of intervention effects among different student populations, careful data collection and subgroup analyses should be included in evaluations (including analyses based on age/grade, socioeconomic status, racial/ethnic background, home language, English language abilities, and place of residence). The ability to track such data will be greatly enhanced in states with statewide systems for monitoring individual student data.

Ensuring coordinated evaluation requirements among funding entities is an important step in streamlining the work of comprehensive partnership strategies. Because such efforts typically rely on multiple funding streams, contending with associated and varying demands for data documenting progress and outcomes can rapidly overwhelm local initiatives.[75]

Strategic and Coordinated Advocacy

While the constituency that stands to benefit from stronger school, family, and community partnerships is large and the knowledge base in this area is broad, efforts to learn about and promote partnership strategies in education and related fields remain relatively undercoordinated. Local, state, and federal policies to encourage, incentivize, and enable integration and coordination across education and related systems (such as health and human services, law enforcement, juvenile justice, child welfare, transportation, and housing) are needed.

In addition to these shifts in the education arena, associated fields such as public health, community planning and development, law enforcement and juvenile justice, family and child welfare, workforce development, the arts, and parks and recreation have significant roles to play in a comprehensive strategy to build conditions for partnerships. While an analysis of their potential contributions is beyond the scope of this chapter, increasing communication and coordination across these areas is a vital direction for future research and practice.

CONCLUSIONS

Partnership strategies appear to be critical elements of serious efforts to reduce disparities in K–12 student success associated with ethnicity, language, and socioeconomic status. Such strategies contribute to improved academic outcomes through four interrelated domains: strengthening academic instruction, providing social supports to create a healthy learning environment, building school leadership and resources to ensure adequate support of teachers, students, and their families, and fostering neighborhood and community development that promote school engagement.

The fragmented development and implementation of policies that foster the conditions for partnership make it difficult to assess the overall effects of such school-community partnerships with respect to eliminating disparities in academic outcomes. In addition, rigorous research on the effectiveness of school-community partnerships is constrained by multiple factors, including the difficulty of maintaining similar interventions across many different sites, the tendency to randomize interventions at the level of schools rather than students (limiting the power of a study), large variations in the community institutions and community contexts involved, and inconsistent definitions of outcomes and measures across studies (e.g., "family involvement" has differing definitions across studies). However, as noted earlier, assessments of school-community partnerships have indicated positive effects on students and families in terms of both health and academic outcomes. Partnerships are also one important feature of schools that produce more equitable learning outcomes.

Building effective school-community partnerships requires enabling conditions that necessitate policy change at multiple scales, in education and other policy areas. There are several challenges to policy development in this area, all of which are exacerbated by a climate of scarce resources.

First, implementing comprehensive school partnerships with families and communities appears to require additional resources, at a minimum to cover costs associated with coordination. A variety of financial and technical supports for partnerships are available to schools and districts via a combination of requirements, allocations, and competitive grants that vary state by state; while some of these resources are based in education, others are offered through public and private funders associated with other fields. However, pursuing these funding streams and knowing how to braid funding requires focused effort and trained personnel. In addition, the challenges of working across public agencies at state, county, and local scales defy the kind of coordination that is likely to amplify resources and facilitate partnership processes for school districts, schools, and their community partners. Thus, state and federal policies to streamline information and funding mechanisms and to incentivize partnerships that build on existing assets are essential.

Second, the current emphasis on standardized assessment may work against investment in partnership-based strategies that foster relevance, personalization, and meeting basic needs, despite the apparent importance of these factors in addressing academic disparities associated with ethnicity, language, and socioeconomic status. Because it is difficult to produce data demonstrating clear causal relationships between many partnership strategies and higher standardized test scores, and well-researched intermediate indicators are lacking, making the case for sustaining investment in partnerships may be difficult. In addition, based on a narrower vision of the role of schools that precludes the provision of supports for students that are not directly educational, some communities and policy makers appear resistant to school-community partnerships.

Finally, establishing and maintaining partnerships that address disparities in young people's academic learning opportunities and outcomes requires grappling with challenging social dynamics around race, class, culture, place, and, ultimately, power. Engaging in what Singleton and Linton call "courageous conversations," and the subsequent actions they suggest, demands a significant commitment to their importance on the part of individuals, institutions, and communities.[76] Committed, sustained leadership is essential.

Despite these challenges, the United States has many components of an infrastructure to promote and support school-community partnerships. Strengthening, coordinating, and building upon them are crucial next steps in efforts to foster stronger, more equitable educational outcomes for children and youth.

CHAPTER ELEVEN

Reframing Policy and Practice to Close the Achievement Gap

THOMAS B. TIMAR

Beginning with the *Brown v. Board* decision and later accelerated by the Great Society reforms initiated during the Johnson administration, eliminating disparities in educational opportunity, achievement, and attainment between African American and Latino children on the one hand and white and many Asian children on the other has been a central and persistent policy objective of American education. Policy makers have acted on the premise that school desegregation, finance equalization, compensatory education, elaboration of legal rights, and an array of targeted interventions would eventually close the historically wide educational, social, and economic chasm that has separated those groups.

However, some forty-five years after enactment of the federal Elementary and Secondary Education Act of 1965, which incorporated wide-ranging policies to address unequal student access to education and disparate achievement, significant group differences persist. Black and Latino children face very different life chances than white children. For instance, a study by the California Council on Science and Technology found that there was only a 1 percent chance that a Latino child entering kindergarten would obtain a college degree in mathematics, science, or engineering.[1] Also in California, the Governor's Committee on Education Excellence concluded that only 60 percent of Latino and 56 percent of black students graduate from high school in four years.[2] Moreover, among those who do graduate, only 14 percent of Latino and 16 percent of black students are considered "college ready." On both the California Standards Test and the National Assessment of Education Progress, students classified as economically disadvantaged—most often students of color—are much more likely to perform at the basic or below basic level in language arts, reading, and mathematics than their nondisadvantaged counterparts. As figure 11.1 shows, since 1975, there has been some narrowing of the achievement gap, but on the whole, the results are discouraging for school reformers who had hoped to see greater progress over a twenty-year period.

FIGURE 11.1
Trend in NAEP Test Scores, 1975 to 2004

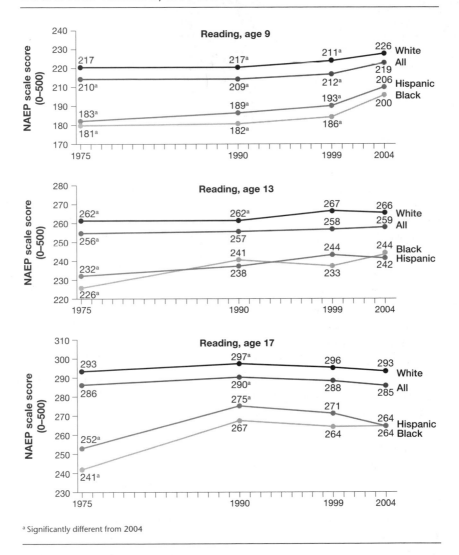

^a Significantly different from 2004

Lack of marked improvement, however, is not for lack of trying. Since the publication of *A Nation at Risk*, which was the impetus for the current school re-form movement, the federal government, states, local education agencies, foundations, universities, and think tanks have put considerable investments of money, time, and energy into reducing the achievement gap. Nor has there been a

FIGURE 11.1 *continued*
Trend in NAEP Test Scores, 1975 to 2004

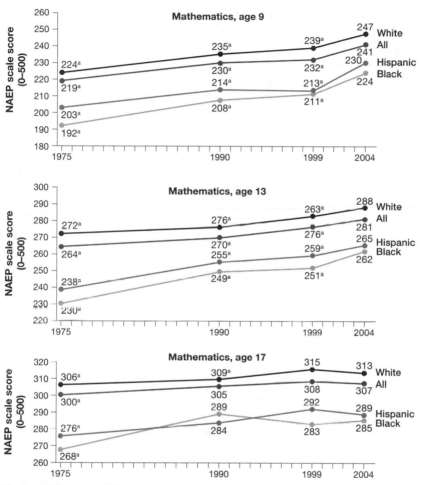

[a] Significantly different from 2004

Source: Marianne Perla, Rebecca Moran, and Anthony D. Luticus, NAEP 2004 Trends in Academic Progress: Three Decades of Student Performance in Reading and Mathematics (NCES 2005-464), U.S. Department of Education, IES, NCES, 2005.

shortage of proposed fixes: increasing professional development for teachers and administrators, revamping teacher preparation programs, incentive pay schemes, teacher evaluation based on student achievement, charter schools, privatizing school management, school restructuring or reconstitution, standards-based accountability, mayoral control of schools, small school communities—and the list goes on. Foundations and governments have spent tens of millions of dollars on research. Think tank and university researchers have produced volumes of studies related to the achievement gap. The whirlwind of reforms in schools over the past thirty years is also well documented. It is not unusual for schools to have several simultaneous reforms where individuals associated with one effort know nothing about the other. Many reforms have short lives—two or three years—and then the school moves on to the next good idea.[3] Under such conditions, it is easy to understand why teachers and administrators grow wary of the latest "good idea" flowing from centralized bureaucracies. Charles Payne notes that "[a]fter a couple of decades of being energetically reformed, most schools, especially the bottom-tier schools, and most school systems seem to be pretty much the same kind of organizations they were at the beginning. 'We've seen 'em come,' teachers say of reforms, 'and we've seen 'em go.'"[4]

Given the investment, why is there so little in terms of student achievement to show for thirty or more years of intensive school reform activity? Why has closing the achievement gap remained such an elusive policy objective? This chapter proposes several reasons why policy strategies to close the achievement gap have had meager results in spite of the magnitude of efforts.

One reason is that although schools can be held accountable for some of the educational disadvantage these students experience, they have been given the entire responsibility for closing the achievement gap. Yet the gap is the symptom of larger social, economic, and political problems that go far beyond the reach of the school. Much like medical professionals dealing with cancer, educators are expected to fix problems of teaching and learning by treating symptoms of the problem, though they have only imperfect knowledge and no control of its causes. While schools are part of the solution, they alone cannot solve the problem of educational disparities.

The second reason is that predominant policy strategies over the past thirty years have been mostly misdirected and ineffectual. Although school reformers have kept schools in a constant state of "policy spin," they have not touched the critical areas of teaching and learning that matter. As one observer puts it, "Most discussion of policy and practice is dangerously disconnected from the daily realities of urban schools, especially the bottom-tier schools; most discussion fails to appreciate the intertwined and over-determined nature of the causes of failure."[5] Rather than helping, policy may have undermined efforts to close the achievement gap by focusing attention on the superficial dimensions of schooling. Like the old joke about searching for a lost button in the kitchen not because it was lost there, but because the light is better there, it is easier to focus on schools than on the broader social, economic, and political conditions that shape schools. Even under the guise of "systemic policies," reformers failed to create the necessary learning infrastructure in schools and failed to create the social capital that forms the critical foundation of effective instructional systems.[6] Not only can they not create the necessary infrastructure, they can't overcome the irrationality, dysfunction, and negativism that characterize the gritty reality of life in many low-performing urban schools.

Finally, I argue that closing the achievement gap will require a new kind of leadership, a new politics of education that embraces a broad community of interests, and a new policy paradigm that places the school at the center and builds policy from the inside, from the school, rather than from the outside, by distant policy makers, as has been the prevailing policy strategy in education for the past forty years.

SCHOOLS CAN'T DO IT ALONE

In 1951, historian Henry Steele Commager observed that "no other people ever demanded so much of schools and of education as have the Americans."[7] However, Schrag writes,

> [H]e could not have dreamed how much more would be demanded. Win the Cold War; beat the Germans and the Japanese in the battle for economic supremacy; outduel the Chinese and Indians in the training of scientists and engineers; Americanize millions of children . . . from a hundred Third World cultures; . . . make every child proficient in English and math; educate the blind, the mentally handicapped, and the emotionally disturbed to the same levels as all the others; teach the evils of alcohol, tobacco, and marijuana, cocaine, heroin and premarital sex; prepare all for college; teach immigrants in their native languages; teach driver's ed; feed lunch to poor children; . . . and serve as the prime (and often the only) social-welfare agency for both children and their parents.[8]

To that list, we should add also the elimination of racial segregation.

As with other large social problems—whether related to desegregation or the Cold War—fixing disparities in social and economic equality between racial and ethnic groups has been relegated to schools, even though the problems originate outside the schools. Cuban and Usdan, for instance, note that reform agendas targeted at fixing low performance, especially in high-poverty, urban schools, are usually restricted to governance, organization, curriculum, and instruction:

> Avoided are mentions of race and poverty in dealing with issues of housing and access to jobs as they relate to schooling. To include families, neighborhoods, and city agencies in the reform agenda would entail major

expenditures such as re-conceptualizing schools as youth-serving agencies rather than places where the single most important job is to produce higher test scores. It would mean reorganizing existing city cultural, civic, medical, housing, employment, and social services. Contemporary urban school reformers stammer when faced with the scale of such changes.[9]

While manifestations of the achievement gap are to be found in rural, suburban, and urban areas, the evidence is rather compelling that the achievement gap is largely a problem of urban education. As such, it is a problem of racial isolation, concentration of poverty, crime, drugs, and a long, well-known litany of other urban ills. In a report on urban schools, *Education Week's Quality Counts, 1998* found that conditions in urban schools were quite different from those in the average school in the United States. Specifically, the study noted these discrepancies:

- Black children are more likely to live in conditions of concentrated poverty. In seventy-five of the nation's largest cities, 63 percent of children live in extremely poor neighborhoods.
- Child poverty rose in nearly every city from 1970 to 1990. In some cities the rate doubled. For the U.S. as a whole, the rate remained steady at 5 percent.
- Urban students are more than twice as likely to attend high-poverty schools. In urban districts, 53 percent of students are in high-poverty schools. In nonurban schools, 23 percent of students are in high-poverty schools.
- In 1990, the child poverty rate for the United States as a whole was 18 percent. For the ten worst cities, it was between 40 and 58 percent.
- The percentage of fourth-grade students proficient in reading and language arts in high-poverty schools was 23 percent compared to nonpoverty schools, where it was 68 percent. In math the differences were 33 percent versus 55 percent.[10]

While pressure on schools to diminish the achievement gap has intensified, the indicators of student poverty and isolation have worsened. In 1990–1991, 45 percent of black and 51 percent of Latino students were in schools with a minimum of 75 percent enrollment of minorities. By 2006–2007, the percentages were 52 and 57. In 2007–2008, 40 percent of black public elementary school students attended schools in which a minimum of 76 percent of students were eligible for the free or reduced-price lunch program. For the same period, only 5 percent of white students went to schools in which the number of students eligible for free or reduced-price lunch exceeded 75 percent. Among elementary school students, 75 percent of white students were in schools with 25 percent or fewer poor students.[11]

According to the International Monetary Fund, the United States ranks among the top three of thirty-four developed nations for income inequality; only Singapore and Hong Kong have greater income inequality. The official unemployment rate is also among the worst, as is a measure of food insecurity—defined by the percentage of individuals who answered yes to the question, "Have there been times in the past 12 months when you did not have enough money to buy food that you or your family needed?" U.S. life expectancy at birth is also among the lowest in this group, as is student performance in math and science. Where the United States rates the highest among the thirty-four developed countries is in its prison population (743 per 100,000 citizens, compared to the next highest nation, Israel, with 325 per 100,000 and 59 for Japan).[12]

Because all of these conditions are closely related to student academic achievement, improving student performance becomes a moving target. Efforts to close the achievement gap have played out against a backdrop of changing demographics, globalization, rising levels of crime, and high rates of incarceration (especially among African American males), the collapse of urban neighborhoods, increased economic inequality, and, especially among the poor, an increase in single-parent households. As Geoffrey Canada with the Harlem Children's Zone argues, achieving significant improvement in the education of poor African American children requires a much broader reform agenda, one that addresses housing, jobs, crime, child neglect and abuse, and isolation.[13]

While policies to eliminate the achievement gap have focused almost exclusively on schools, it is clear that many of the important factors that influence student achievement fall outside the scope of schools. Policy makers pay scant attention to these factors in crafting policy strategies aimed at closing the achievement gap. On a daily basis, schools are essentially on their own in dealing with some of the more severe problems associated with urban life. In a study published by the *Journal of the American Medical Association,* researchers estimated that as many as one-third of children living in high-poverty, high-crime urban neighborhoods have witnessed serious acts of violence.[14] Citing other studies related to children exposed to violence, researchers found that "the majority of children exposed to violence, defined as personally witnessing or directly experiencing a violent event, display symptoms of posttraumatic stress disorder" (PTSD).[15] In a series on children who survive urban warfare, San Francisco journalist Jill Tucker examined the impact of violence on children and their schooling. "Los Angeles Unified School District officials conduct annual surveys, finding similar rates of PTSD within the schools in the city's most violent neighborhoods," she wrote.[16] Efforts to deal with the problem have been sporadic at best. In California's San Francisco Bay Area and in most areas in the nation, "PTSD in urban children is undiagnosed, untreated, and almost completely off the radar for policymakers and education officials." According to a poll administered by school officials in one San Francisco school, nearly a third of the 105 sixth-grade class have seen or know someone killed with a gun.[17]

In addition to the violence and its effects, which spill into the school lives of urban children, poor children are educationally disadvantaged long before they enter kindergarten. According to a policy study by the Educational Testing Service, significant education-related disparities exist between the children of high-SES, professional families and lower-SES families. By age four, the average child in a professional family has heard about 20 million more words than the average child in a working-class family and about 35 million more words than the average child in a family that receives welfare. As a result, children of professional parents have a recorded vocabulary size of 1,116 words, while children of parents on welfare have 526.[18] The study points out that well before entering kindergarten, children are vastly different in their readiness for school. Researchers looked at differences among children entering kindergarten for their ability to recognize the letters of the alphabet and found that, here again, race, ethnicity, and socioeconomic status play an important role. Eighty percent of Asian American and 71 percent of white kindergartners could identify the letters of the alphabet. On the other hand, only 57 percent of black and 50 percent of Latino children could do so. The results were similar on all other measures of reading proficiency. The results for math proficiency showed equally significant disparities between groups. Measured by race/ethnicity and SES, researchers found that 69 percent of Asian American and 64 percent of white kindergartners, in contrast to 41 percent black and 43 percent Latino kindergartners, could understand relative size. Measured by SES alone, 77 percent of children in the top quintile and 31 percent of children in the bottom quintile could do so.[19]

In an effort to bring greater national attention to the broader dimensions of the achievement gap, the authors of "A Broader, Bolder Approach to Education" argue that "[d]espite the impressive academic gains made by some schools serving disadvantaged students, there is evidence that school improvement strategies by *themselves* cannot close the gaps in a substantial, consistent, and sustainable manner.[20] Yet, in spite of the evidence, policy makers continue to pursue a blinkered version of school reform—exemplified by No Child Left Behind—that makes the achievement gap a problem for schools to solve. As the evidence clearly shows, achievement gaps appear at a very early age, and because schools cannot fix the conditions that caused those gaps, the gaps simply grow wider and wider the longer children stay in school—a phenomenon Norton Grubb refers to as "dynamic inequality."[21]

Given the evidence connecting the school performance of poor and minority children to the conditions of their lives, it is notable how little attention that relationship has received in policy circles. Based on statements by President Barack Obama and Secretary of Education Arne Duncan, reauthorization of No Child

Left Behind (NCLB) seems to take as a given that low student achievement in the nation's five thousand lowest-performing schools can be fixed by changing how teachers are evaluated, by better use of data, by creating charter schools and "turn-around" schools—that is, hiring all new teachers and administrators. This focus on the same narrow range of "fixes" is echoed around the country in state efforts to reform education—in part because the task set for teachers and administrators by state leaders reflects the same limited vision.[22]

Several factors may explain what seems to be such an obvious oversight. The separation of powers is a cornerstone of American political culture. As a result, federal, state, and local governments operate in their own spheres of authority. The federal government does, for instance, require states to create standards-based accountability systems and mandate that all teachers be "highly qualified," but does not tell states what "highly qualified" means in practice and does not set the substance or rigor of assessments. Because of the fragmented nature of government institutions, the history of cooperation and collaboration among various levels and sectors of government is rather limited. California, for instance, not unlike other states, is a jumble of overlapping counties, cities, and districts. Within the city of San Jose alone there are a dozen school districts. Even though the state has taken greater responsibility for local government funding since the 1978 passage of Proposition 13, the initiative that limits property taxes, state, regional, and local governments maintain separate funding streams. There are some areas in which school districts and counties share costs and services (in special education in rural areas, for instance, where economies of scale make it very costly for each school or district to provide services). Another area where state policy has created incentives for local agency cooperation is school truancy. However, the efficacy of these ventures tends to be hit-or-miss, and even exemplary programs are often not sustained.[23] The fragmented nature of government creates difficulties in determining who is responsible for oversight of programs, who has budgetary and management authority, and a host of other issues that make multiagency collaboration difficult.

Efforts to bridge government fragmentation vary. They range from changing urban school governance to "civic capacity building."[24] A number of cities—Chicago, New York, and Washington, D.C., among them—shifted control over schools to mayors. One argument for such a governance shift is to create a broader base of political support and to enhance communities' abilities to effectively coordinate various services to children. Another reason is to create a more powerful political base for schools, to bring politics back into school governance. However, these strategies have not been uniformly successful. What works in one city does not necessarily work in another. Effective leadership strategies that are effective in one city may be feckless attempts at reform in another.

POLICY VERSUS REALITY: LIFE IN LOW-PERFORMING SCHOOLS

Researchers from the Chicago Consortium on School Research (CCSR) conclude that "the job of school improvement appears especially demanding in truly disadvantaged urban communities where collective efficacy and church participation may be relatively low, residents have few social contacts outside of their neighborhood, and crime rates are high."[25] Community factors, they find, are important, but in many of these communities the relevant factors—high social capital as measured by low crime, abuse, and neglect rates—are missing.[26] The irony is that the greater the student needs, the less likely that the critical community factors will be present. For that reason, they write, "in communities where there are few viable institutions, where crime, drug abuse, and gang activity are prevalent, and where palpable human needs walk through the school doors every day, a much more powerful model of school development is needed—one that melds systemic efforts to strengthen instruction with the social resources of a comprehensive community schools initiative."[27]

Beginning in the mid-1960s and intensifying in the mid-1980s, there has been no shortage of policy initiatives aimed at reforming low-performing schools. As a result, few areas of schooling remain untouched: finance, governance, teacher preparation and certification, instructional materials and curriculum, student discipline, teacher pay and working conditions, and much more. The passage of No Child Left Behind catalyzed the greatest shift in school governance since the early part of the twentieth century. The balance of power shifted from local education agencies to the states and federal government. Sanctions against federally and state-defined "failing schools" are imposed through centralized bureaucratic processes. However, after more than a decade of intense and perhaps the most far-reaching and intrusive federal and state activism since the creation of a system of common schools in the first half of the nineteenth century, the achievement gap persists.

There are several reasons why. Chief among them is that high-quality education does not result from a fixed set of policies that can be implemented under a variety of circumstances and yield predictable results. As research has shown, simply having the parts or components of high-quality instruction—high expectations for students, mentoring for new teachers, principal leadership, and the like—does not guarantee or necessarily translate into higher student performance. A long body of research on effective organizations has made clear that organizational elements such as high expectations, teacher professionalism, and community support must be woven into a complex social fabric that connects all these parts into an organic whole. The current approach is akin to dumping all the parts of a car in someone's driveway and expecting that person to be able assemble the car and drive it away.

The prevailing theory of action among education policy makers has been that a combination of regulations, incentives, and/or structural changes will lead to better educational outcomes. However, this approach overlooks the fact that a wide range of behaviors, attitudes, and incentives lies beyond the purview of state policy. Thus, the effects of schooling are dampened by various factors. As this chapter and others argue, poor children who live in deteriorated neighborhoods and who do not encounter role models committed to education and a middle-class work ethic will generally not benefit as much from schooling as a child from an upper-middle class suburban family. Some schools clearly do a better job teaching poor, urban school children than others. But, a handful of success stories does not amount to predictable, systematic, and sustained change. Policy makers lack the resources to change people's lifestyles, health habits, and associations. *A Nation at Risk* told parents that they "bear a responsibility to participate actively in their child's education . . . they should encourage more diligent study and discourage satisfaction with mediocrity." The commission report also told parents to monitor their children's study; encourage good study habits; nurture the child's curiosity, creativity, and confidence; and, above all, "exhibit a commitment to continued learning in your own life." And finally, it urged parents to "help your children understand that excellence in education cannot be achieved without intellectual and moral integrity coupled with hard work and commitment. Children will look to their parents and teachers as models of these virtues."[28] True enough. But who were they talking to? Did commission members even remotely understand what it would take to realize these recommendations in most urban schools?

Increasingly, research on effective organizations shows that they are shaped organically from within.[29] They are not cobbled together by combinations of policy initiatives, be they mandates, inducements, capacity building, or system changing.[30] One of the features of centralized, top-down policies is that policy makers have a limited repertoire from which to draw. They can manage what they control. They control macropolicy—funding, curriculum, assessments, standards, teacher credentialing standards, and the like. But they have limited control over the daily operations of schools and classrooms. The most important of those, the critical interactions among teacher, student, and instructional materials, fall outside the sphere of policy manipulation. Consequently, state efforts to engineer school improvement represent only one, albeit the most visible, dimension of school reform. Two other dimensions, though less apparent, are equally important.[31]

The first dimension of the overall reform is what might be labeled the *authorized* movement. This is the official version of reform. It is the world of state mandates, legislation, formal structures, and directives. The authorized dimension comprises macropolicies such as state accountability systems, regulation of teacher training and evaluation, resources allocation, high school graduation standards, and specific curriculum content.

The second dimension of reform might be called the *localist* dimension. This comprises the array of local and regional school improvement activities. It represents local interpretations and responses to the official version of reform. Like the authorized dimension, it is structured and regulatory, but its various changes are masked by their dispersion. It is into this morass of projects that reform efforts such as Comer Schools, the Coalition of Essential Schools, AVID, the National Writing Project, and Accelerated Schools—to name only a few—are rooted. Although understanding this dimension is difficult, research findings from the CCSR, Richard Elmore and his Instructional Rounds Network, Michael Fullan, and the California Collaborative on District Reform are mapping the dimensions of that landscape in an effort to understand the complex dynamics of educational improvement. While the importance of this dimension has been largely undervalued by state and federal policy makers, it is a critical aspect of reform. School improvement is not what state policy makers say schools should do, it is what schools actually do, and the two may be quite different. As Berman and McLaughlin showed many years ago, local conditions, not state policy makers, determine the quality of implementation.[32] It is in the localist dimension where school improvement efforts succeed or fail.

The third dimension of reform is *social capital*. It is the dimension of education that has become increasingly significant.[33] This dimension determines the most critical elements of teaching and learning: how teachers and administrators think about their jobs, how they think about the students they teach, and how they relate to the communities those schools are meant to serve. But it is also about students—the dispositions and attitudes about schooling that they bring to the classroom each day. Finally, it is about social relationships within communities—how safe people feel, how much control they have over their lives, how they relate to one another, how they relate to the public agencies that ostensibly serve them. Charles Payne, among others, provides a lens into what it is like to teach or be an administrator in an urban school and how personal and professional relationships interact to shape the quality of schooling. What he shows is that the most important elements of schooling—those that determine the quality of teaching and learning in schools—fall through the gaps of policy. Increasingly, researchers are documenting what James Coleman said in the 1960s: social capital is a critical determinant of the outcomes of schooling. Most importantly, social capital is the glue that binds disparate elements of reform efforts together.

Social capital, however, is a rare commodity in urban school settings.[34] A major impediment to school improvement is a prevailing mood of demoralization that typically exists in low-performing schools. Payne's list of "social barriers to school change," for instance, includes the following:

- Lack of social comfort among parents, teachers, and administrators
- Low mutual expectations
- Predisposition to suspicion of "outsiders"
- Generalized belief in program failure
- Distrust of colleagues
- Tensions pertaining to race, ethnicity, and age cohort; predisposition to factions
- Generalized anger, consequent withdrawal as major coping strategy
- "Happy talk" culture, tendency to put the best face on everything
- Poor internal communications
- Institutional inability to learn from experience, intensified by a tendency to particularize, to treat one's school as if were unique, making the experiences of all others irrelevant
- Ego fragility, touchiness, emotional fatigue
- Disproportionate leverage for most negative teachers
- Inability of teachers to share professional information[35]

The conditions that Payne describes lie outside the boundaries of policy. State policy makers can't force teachers to be civil to one another, to have high expectations of students, to trust their colleagues and cooperate with them. Nor can policy address problems of ego fragility, touchiness, or emotional fatigue. The social barriers that Payne lists are products of demoralization conditioned by years of failure in systems that have simply stopped working. Teachers and administrators can do little to nothing about the pervasive lack of resources, the conditions of children's lives, and the overwhelming sense of hopelessness. As Fukuyama, Putnam, and others have argued, government does not create social capital.[36] Social capital is what makes government possible. Good ideas and intentions simply dissipate in dysfunctional organizations.

Studies coming from the Chicago consortium find that the quality of relationships within schools is among the most important factors associated with improvements in teaching and learning. That is to say, effective organizations are built on strong social relations. Trust turns out to be critical. In Chicago, teachers in the top improving schools were able to cooperate, discuss problems and concerns with colleagues, and rely on other teachers for support. In the bottom performing schools, "teachers perceive much less respect from parents and report that only about half of their colleagues really care about the local community and feel supported by parents."[37;38] Finally, in reviewing the data from the CCSR, Payne concluded that "neighborhoods with strong social capital are four or five times as likely to have high-functioning schools as neighborhoods where the residents feel disconnected from one another. At the neighborhood level and at the school level, our most vulnerable students are vulnerable precisely because they are surrounded by adults who cannot cooperate with one another. Schools in the ghetto become schools *of* the ghetto."[39]

A study of state policies to improve student achievement in the lowest-performing schools in California also found that organizational factors trumped specific policy strategies.[40] The common features of improving schools were a high degree of social capital and trust, stable teaching staff, stable and competent leadership, developing leadership among teachers, focus on schools as organizations rather than collections of classrooms, organizational coherence, ongoing assessment and evaluation, and coherent program funding tied to strategic plans. Here again, schools that improved did so because they were able to *take advantage* of the state program, not *because* of the program.

Among the things that mattered, organizational stability and continuity were at the very center. It is impossible to build organizational coherence, community, leadership, and trust when there is constant turnover of faculty, administrators, and students. In improving schools, teachers focused on the importance of cooperation and collegiality. Teachers trusted the professional judgment of administrators, regarded them as knowledgeable about school improvement, and looked to them for professional support. A consistent theme among improving schools was the importance of teachers taking responsibility and leadership for school improvement. Its forms were varied. One was a sense among teachers that school improvement is a collective responsibility and cooperative effort. Common planning time, school- or, in the case of high schools, department-specific and teacher-planned professional development activities were another. Teachers, administrators, and staff working together to achieve a common goal was a consistent theme throughout the study findings.

In low-performing schools that did not improve, conditions were quite the opposite. Most notable among their features was their instability and incoherence. Most schools had had a succession of principals. In one high school, the longest-serving principal in thirty years lasted almost three years, but was demoted to vice-principal for refusing to hire a school board member's relative. The average principal tenure in the school was two years. The constant turnover at the school, moreover, mirrored the turnover of superintendents in the district. The school board fired principals at will just as it did superintendents. In another district, a high school had had six principals in eight years. That it was a huge school with year-round attendance tracks made the need for stability and continuity even more acute.

The lack of continuity and stability meant that schools were in a constant state of churn. One principal invested all of the school's state program improvement funds in handheld computers. The next principal had another idea for school improvement, so the handheld computers went into storage. In one large high school with over 250 faculty, the principal could not get teachers to participate in school improvement planning activities, not even by offering to pay them an additional $1,000 per month. And because there was no collective vision and strategic plan for school improvement, state funds targeted to improvement dissipated among a wish list of items that faculty wanted—whiteboards, LCD projectors, travel to conferences, and the like.[41]

The antithesis of dysfunctional schools were those in which there was stable leadership. (Among the schools in the study, the principals had been at the school for ten or more years and in some instances had been teachers at the school.) There was a sense of purpose, a coherent plan, and individuals with responsibility to coordinate and implement the plan. Teachers worked collaboratively to improve teaching and learning across the entire school curriculum. "Writing across the curriculum," for instance, meant that students wrote in physical education classes as well as in their English classes. School improvement wasn't something being done to them (like some sort of medical procedure), but a collaborative undertaking. Students also realized that the school's engagement in school improvement activities was meant for them, for their benefit.

RETHINKING EDUCATION POLICY AND PRACTICE

Since 1970, policy efforts to reduce the achievement gap in education have evolved through two stages. The first was born of early federal and state efforts to target resources to poor children. The Elementary and Secondary Education Act (ESEA) Title I was the most prominent among them and served as a model for states. Federal funds flowed to schools, and schools were required to make certain that those funds were used to provide services to eligible students. While the ostensible goal of Title I (and similar state categorical programs) was to provide programs that "contribute particularly to meeting the special education needs of deprived children," it was also meant to address broader social, political, and economic problems by making schools the instrument for fixing those problems.[42] Education became part of a larger struggle to eliminate poverty and to achieve greater social and political equality. Such efforts centered on new programs and funding streams targeted to "special needs" student. To assure that resources flowed to their intended beneficiaries, policy makers created an elaborate regulatory structure that enveloped schools in rules and bureaucratic procedures.[43]

The regulatory framework created for Title I implementation bore the weight of the civil rights movement, constructed in large measure around the educational system. The moral and legal impetus of Title I came from the federal government's championing of the rights of individuals—most importantly the rights of children—who were marginalized by local governments. Although in retrospect it seems naïve, federal policy makers believed that creating a regulatory superstructure could overcome the incapacity, ineptitude, or indifference of local schools in serving poor, low-achieving students. In some instances, regulatory rigidity was necessary to compel schools to use funds for the benefit of disadvantaged children. But such policies proved to be wrong-headed for a couple of reasons. It treated all school officials with mistrust. As one observer noted,

> *The new regulations were rooted in distrust of the motives and the capacity of local school officials: "We treated every state as if it were Mississippi," Congressman Albert Quie remarked. Early scandals concerning expenditures of compensatory education funds . . . fueled this suspicion. Regulation came increasingly to entail control, and supervision displaced the encouragement and assistance that formed part of the initial federal strategy. At the state level . . . officials grew to share Washington's belief in the necessity for stressing compliance, as distinguished from assistance.*[44]

The federal approach shifted attention from pedagogy to regulatory compliance. Title I developed its own culture, one that favored uniformity and procedural regularity over innovation, experimentation, and the exercise of professional judgment. Schools could be sanctioned for not following rules, but they could not be sanctioned for failing to teach students. "Doing the right thing" had much more to do with rule adherence than with instructional practice. One could argue that rules displaced the program's original purpose, to improve the education of low-income, low-achieving children.

Another major flaw of policy was the implication embedded in policy that schools, as organizations, didn't matter. Title I service delivery was predicated on the assumption that local compliance with federal mandates was sufficient to secure sound educational results for those students who were the most challenging to teach. Also underlying Title I was the assumption that Title I programs could do for students what schools could not. Regulations implementing Title I created a cleavage between Title I and the rest of the school and exacerbated the isolation of Title I students and services. The effect was to fragment schools organizationally. It should be remembered that Title I was only one of a panoply of special-purpose programs. A number of federal and state programs on behalf of handicapped, learning-disabled, English language learner, and gifted students, along with other programs, piled rules on top of rules to make certain that schools served the various target populations. But just as schools were programmatically fragmented, so were students. Students came to be regarded as objects of special services. In retrospect, what seems even more naïve about the capacity of Title I to improve educational achievement is the underlying assumption that good programs could exist in bad schools.

The second stage of policy began in the 1990s and coincides with "systemic" reform and its progeny—standards-based reform. It was an important change, as it shifted the focus of reform from programs and students to schools. Schools were held accountable for student outcomes. Enactment of standards-based accountability was also the first time in the history of American education that schools would be held accountable for the educational achievement of students by race, ethnicity, and wealth. While it represented a major turning point in education policy, it has failed to achieve its intended effect—closing the achievement gap. Test scores, based on NAEP, have increased somewhat for all groups, as Kober, Chudowsky, and Chudowsky show in chapter 1, but significant differences between groups remain. In contrast to its intentions, NCLB as the principal driver of performance-based accountability may have the opposite effect. It may be creating a two-tiered system of education: one for low-SES and minority children, another for high-SES white and Asian children.

The Center for Education Policy (CEP) has shown that the same low-performing schools that serve large numbers of poor minority students are also the ones where the curriculum has been narrowed to those subjects that are tested.[45] In California, there is no shortage of anecdotal evidence to support CEP's findings. In one low-performing high school in the Bay Area that serves mostly poor African American and Latino students, students are enrolled in three periods of remedial language arts and two periods of math courses in order to improve their scores on mandated state tests. About thirty miles down the freeway, in a nearby suburban high school serving the children of Silicon Valley's tech industry professionals, students have many options, including nearly a dozen advanced placement courses. Thus, even if group test scores in language arts, math, and science were to converge, it would not mean that all groups were getting the same education. Even if all African American and Latino students in low-performing schools scored at the proficient level, the quality of their education wouldn't be comparable to that of high-SES students in suburban schools.

Eliminating the achievement gap through high-stakes accountability is predicated on the assumption that the right combination of incentives and sanctions, the right governance structure, parental choice, or better data will cause schools to improve. But why should they? Creating charter schools as the solution to low-performing schools won't fix the problems associated with urban schools. Charter schools will have to teach the same students who will continue to live in the same urban conditions. Charter schools won't eliminate joblessness, crime, drugs, child neglect and abuse, and urban decay. Noting that isn't meant to absolve schools of their responsibility for providing quality education to all students. Nor does it ignore the fact that some charter schools are more successful than others. The Harlem Children's Zone and KIPP schools, for instance, have shown remarkable results with low-SES students. But among KIPP schools, the burnout rate for students and faculty is over 40 percent. Again, this does not mean that some charter schools are not successful, but it does mean that charter schools are not a predictable fix for all low-performing schools.[46] Research has shown that what works in one school is not a formula for success in another. What KIPP schools do well may not be possible to replicate in the five thousand low-performing schools that Secretary of Education Duncan has targeted for "turnaround." There are common practices, instructional supports, and the like that form the foundation of effective instructional systems in schools.[47] But those are simply the necessary conditions for constructing high-quality systems of teaching and learning. They create the opportunities. By themselves, they are not sufficient. Absent the kinds of social relations, social capital, and civic capacity that researchers find to be essential to effecting and sustaining school improvement, creating charter schools and, thereby, freeing them from a host of regulations and union contracts may well create opportunities for innovations and experimentation, but they are unlikely to be of sufficient magnitude to eliminate existing achievement gaps.

Firing teachers and administrators whose students and schools fail to make sufficient academic progress won't turn bad schools into good schools either. As we have found, there are many ways for local school officials to game the testing system. Schools develop strategies for showing "adequate progress" (among them identifying the "bubble kids," the students most likely to show adequate progress on achievement tests) in meeting achievement growth targets. The latest tales of a testing scandal in Washington, D.C., Atlanta and other urban districts are a good example. Of course, if school officials were to fire all the teachers whose students fail to show progress, it is doubtful that those teachers could be replaced. But even if they could be replaced, firing teachers won't solve the problem. Whoever takes the place of those teachers will still be working in the same conditions and with the same students.

CREATING A NEW POLICY PARADIGM

Given the limited scope and pace of change over the past thirty years of education reform, it might be time to rethink the capacity and reach of policy to engender and sustain school improvement. While reform policies have changed the institutional landscape of schools in many ways, the impact on student achievement has been meager. To be sure, handicapped students have access to services that they did not have before; Title IX has opened possibilities for females to participate in school activities that were previously not available to them; non-English-speaking students have to be instructed in a language that they understand; there is greater access to college for poor children and children from underrepresented minority groups. But in spite of these gains, gaps remain. If, as a society, we are committed to equalizing educational outcomes among racial and ethnic groups in the United States, we need to think differently about our policy strategies with that goal. The next sections discuss both long- and short-term strategies to that end.

Long-Term Policy Strategies

There is no doubt that the organizational life of schools is inexorably intertwined with the social, political, and economic context of schools. Therefore, eliminating or significantly diminishing existing achievement gaps necessitates a more comprehensive set of policy strategies than those of the past. Some of those strategies are based outside of schools and require long-term policy commitments. Problems of unemployment, incarceration, child abuse, and all the rest require coordinated, multiagency efforts to resolve. Consequently, eliminating the achievement gap argues for a coherent, comprehensive strategy that targets multiple problems endemic to urban education.

One example of such efforts is the Initiative for a Competitive Inner City (ICIC) started by Michael Porter at the Harvard Business School. It provides research and strategy support to businesses, governments, and investors for urban development and market opportunities. It is just one example of the types of economic development initiatives that might be institutionalized in urban areas. An urban development strategy is essential both for rebuilding an urban middle class and connecting education to jobs and careers. It is nearly impossible to imagine that children living in the kinds of urban conditions described earlier in this chapter see education as leading to much of a future. Under present circumstances, it is difficult to see how doing well in school is even remotely relevant to the lives of children in high-poverty urban schools.

However, rebuilding an urban middle class in the United States goes against the prevailing trend of the past thirty years of increasing income inequality.[48] As observers of this trend have pointed out, income inequality in the United States is the greatest that it has been since the 1920s. As noted earlier in this chapter, the International Monetary Fund ranks the United States as among the worst of thirty-four developed nations in terms of income inequality.[49] Turning that trend around would require a very different kind of politics than what exists today. In

1947, the year that began a nearly thirty-year period of the greatest income equality in the century, the top 10 percent of income earners received about 30 percent of the nation's total income. In 2007, the top 10 percent of earners took home 50 percent of total income.

Short-Term Strategies

In addition to long-term urban development strategies, there are promising short-term organizational strategies. As discussed earlier in this chapter, the strategies of the past thirty-plus years have been top-down strategies. Most, though not all, have been regulatory strategies, accompanied by some additional resources targeted to specific student needs. NCLB has raised the ante by further bureaucratizing the process of school improvement and turning it into a chase after high test scores. Standards-based assessments and the sanctions and incentives that accompany them are intended to be the engines that drive good teaching and learning in the nation's lowest-performing schools. For reasons already discussed in this chapter, the strategy has not been successful. NCLB and its state variants have not made schools more stable, coherent, better led, or professional. If anything, it has undermined professionalization. In short, NCLB and its state variants have not built effective instructional regimes in those schools where they are most needed. In fact, some would argue that they have had exactly the opposite effect.

A promising alternative to past strategies would turn the existing structure on its head. The new paradigm is a grassroots model of change. The new model focuses on schools as the unit of change. Instead of relying on new programs, regulations, resources, and structural reconfiguration, the new model emphasizes the development of professional communities, of collaborative and cooperative networks. This theory of change engages those who work in schools, from the superintendent on down, in the business of improving teaching and learning. There are several models of this type of reform; the Comer Process, Accelerated Schools, the Coalition of Essential Schools, and the Co-nect schools are only a few that have been in place for some time. Other, newer efforts are also under way. Richard Elmore's Instructional Rounds Network engages district superintendents in problems of instructional practice. It brings together superintendents from several districts to solve problems of teaching and learning in a collaborative relationship with teachers and administrators. Begun in the Boston area, this model of professional collaboration and networking for improving teaching and learning is gaining currency nationally. The School of Education at the University of California, Davis, for instance, is developing the model to work with school superintendents in Northern California.

The improvement strategies described above are in contrast to the prevailing model of change in California, which is school by school, one school at a time. For example, schools designated as "program improvement" schools—that is, those that haven't made adequate progress toward proficiency goals—work with an "external provider" (consultants) to develop and implement strategies to improve teaching and learning. But this isolates school districts, in a one-on-one relationship—the local education agency on the one hand and the state and consulting agent on the other. A departure from this model is the partnership between Fresno Unified School District and Long Beach Unified School District[50] which was established in 2008 with the purpose of improving achievement of all students and to "close achievement gaps by capitalizing on shared systemic capacity-building across two high-need districts."[51] As the report of the two-school partnership notes, it may be possible for districts to make progress without the kind of collaboration of the two districts, but "the Partnership is one important factor that contributes to the pace of improvement in both districts."[52] Seven districts in California that applied and did not receive Race to the Top funds decided to form a consortium to continue their reform efforts collaboratively.

The Obama administration's Promise Neighborhoods initiative is modeled on the Harlem Children's Zone for the purpose of building systems of community and family support for education. Its avowed purpose is to break the cycle of inner-city, intergenerational poverty. The *Wall Street Journal* reports that the Obama administration is currently seeking $210 million in fiscal year 2011 for implementation.[53] Funds would support initiatives boosting early-learning-to-college education, as well as health, safety, and other support services. One of the program's goals is to break down existing silos among agencies so that community, health, social services, and education can be integrated into a seamless system of services to students and their families. Combining the Promise Neighborhoods and ICIC models might prove to be an effective strategy for rebuilding urban centers and for making schools relevant and important pathways for children's futures.

REFRAMING THE RELATIONSHIP BETWEEN POLICY AND PRACTICE

Closing the achievement gap will require a fundamental reframing of the roles of centralized—state and federal—policy makers in the process of school improvement. As I have argued in this chapter, much of what comprises the panoply of school improvement is a hodgepodge of good ideas fueled by modest to lofty expectations that "something" will eventually work. And, indeed, there are schools that have succeeded in closing the achievement gap. But they represent a very small percentage of Secretary Duncan's five thousand "turnaround" schools. For every anecdotal story of success, there is one of failure. In the spring of 2011, San Francisco Unified School District announced the closure of one of its charter schools, the Willie L. Brown Jr. College Preparatory Academy. Despite being part of the Dream Schools program and receiving millions of dollars in special aid, the school is closing due to student underachievement and high truancy.[54] The school is located in San Francisco's Bayview district, a largely poor, black neighborhood with high crime (including murder) rates and gang violence, drugs, and not much in the way of jobs.

What policy makers and foundations, who are part of the policy churn, miss is that it doesn't matter how many new programs and resources they provide to schools. Turning those programs and resources into high-quality teaching and learning depends on the capacity of teachers, administrators, students, and local communities. Programs and funding streams are nothing more than opportunities. They are the raw materials. Turning raw materials into effective instructional regimes is something that only a few—the Harlem Children's Zone is the most notable, though not by any means the only—have succeeded in doing. The reason that some schools are successful while others are not is because they have the social capital—the internal professional and external community networks and collaborations.

An alternative to prevailing policy approaches is to engage schools in collaborative professional and civic networks. As noted earlier, several collaborative efforts are under way in California and in other states. The purpose of these collaborative activities is to engage administrators and teachers in problems of practice. Reframing policy in support of professional and civic collaboration places the school at the center. Improvement is not about evaluating or training teachers, more or different instructional materials, one kind of reading or math program as opposed to another. It is about building professional organizations in which teachers are responsible not just for their classrooms, but for the entire school. The theory of action is based on the principle that high-quality instruction is everyone's responsibility. According to a recent study, about 64 percent of the variation in student score gains from one year to the next is explained by differences among teachers.[55] It is hard to imagine how the achievement gap can be reduced in such an unpredictable environment. The high level of variation emphasizes the rampant randomness of the education system. In the present system, how much academic progress a student makes in the course of a year depends in large measure on the luck of the draw, to which teacher the student is assigned.

In creating a policy system in support of instructional improvement, policy makers must focus on the role that the state and federal governments can play in supporting and strengthening collaboration and professional networks. Networks for improvement and the professional and civic collaborations that they might engender are essential to building communities of school reformers who can help and support one another. The first step to closing the achievement gap is to build school cultures that focus on organizational effectiveness and competence. The second is to build civil capacity in the communities in which the schools operate. The third is a broader, more ambitious, and long-term investment in rebuilding urban centers.

Notes

Introduction

1. Lorraine M. McDonnell and Richard F. Elmore, "Getting the Job Done: Alternative Policy Instruments," *Educational Evaluation and Policy Analysis* 9, no. 2 (1987):133–152.
2. David K. Cohen and Susan L. Moffitt, *The Ordeal of Equality: Did Federal Regulation Fix the Schools?* (Cambridge, MA: Harvard University Press, 2009).

Chapter 1

1. High school trends were not included because NAEP only recently began reporting state-level data for grade 12 in a limited pilot, so trends cannot be determined. In addition, NAEP is administered in grade 12, while most state high school tests are administered in grade 10 or 11.
2. A detailed discussion of methodology for this study is contained in the appendix of Kober, Chudowsky, and Chudowsky, *State Test Score Trends Through 2008–09, Part 2: Slow and Uneven Progress in Narrowing Gaps*, (Washington, DC: Center on Education Policy, 2010), http://www .cep-dc.org.
3. Victor Bandeira de Mello, Charles Blankenship, and Don McLaughlin, *Mapping State Proficiency Standards onto NAEP Scales: 2005–2007* (Washington, DC: National Center for Education Statistics, U.S. Department of Education, 2009).

Chapter 2

1. Of course, when President George W. Bush coined that education slogan he was referring to our expectations of children and, in particular, eschewing low expectations of historically underrepresented minority children. See Nicholas Lemann, "Testing Limits: Can the President's Education Crusade Survive Beltway Politics?," *The New Yorker* (July 2, 2001):28-34.
2. It is not our intention to assert that effective schools that adopt promising practices cannot improve disadvantaged students' chances for success against steep odds. They most certainly can and do: see Ronald Edmonds, "Effective Schools for the Urban Poor," *Educational Leadership* 37 (1979): 15–18, 20–24; L. Scott Miller, *An American Imperative: Accelerating Minority Educational Advancement* (Binghamton, NY: Vail-Ballou Press, 1995); and Paul Tough, "What It Takes to Make a Student," *New York Times Magazine*, November 26, 2006. Nor are we inclined to make alibis for schools that do not work well and that do little to bolster student performance. Yet as debate over the series of Education Trust and Heritage Foundation reports asserting that there are plenty of what they call "high-flying" schools makes abundantly clear, the question of how to replicate ideal case schools on a meaningful scale is far from settled. See initial study by Patte Barth et al., "Dispelling the Myth: High Poverty Schools Exceeding Expectations" (Washington, DC: Education Trust, 1999); and critique by Douglas Harris, "High-Flying Schools, Student Disadvantage, and the Logic of NCLB," *American Journal of Education* 113, no. 3 (2007): 367–394.
3. In point of fact, "the achievement gap" idiom is considered a problematic misnomer—not only because this phrase implies just one inequity rather than many, but also because its emphasis on achievement outcomes works to deemphasize a long history of discriminatory gaps in educational inputs. Gloria J. Ladson Billings, in her 2005 presidential address to the American Educational Research Association, asserted that the so-called achievement gap is more accurately portrayed as

a historically accumulated "educational debt" still owed minority and poor students; see Gloria Ladson-Billings, "From the Achievement Gap to the Education Debt: Understanding Achievement in U.S. Schools," *Educational Researcher* 35 (2006): 3–12.

4. If U.S. Hispanics/Latinos are asked to choose between these panethnic terms, Hispanic is preferred to Latino by a 3 to 1 margin. Thus, we tend to employ the term Hispanic, although we use both labels interchangeably. Neither adequately acknowledges the diverse ethnic and cultural heritage in the populations they describe, however. National Research Council, *Multiple Origins, Uncertain Destinies: Hispanics and the American Future* (Washington, DC: The National Academies Press, 2006).

5. Patrick McGuinn, "Swing Issues and Policy Regimes: Federal Education Policy and the Politics of Policy Change," *Journal of Policy History* 18 (2006): 205–240.

6. James S. Coleman et al., *Equality of Educational Opportunity* (Washington, DC: U.S. Government Printing Office, 1966); R. Rothstein, *Class and Schools: Using Social, Economic, and Educational Reform to Close the Black-White Achievement Gap* (Washington, DC: Economic Policy Institute, 2004).

7. Adam Gamoran, "American Schooling and Educational Inequality: A Forecast for the 21st Century," Sociology of Education, extra issue: *Current of Thought: Sociology of Education at the Dawn of the 21st Century* 74 (2001): 135–153; Christopher Jencks et al., *Inequality: A Reassessment of the Effects of Family and Schooling in America* (New York: Basic Books, 1972).

8. There were, of course, limits on the school-level data available for these early studies and in the statistical techniques that could be used to examine school-level data in concert with out-of-school characteristics. Gregory Borman and Maritza Dowling, "Schools and Inequality: A Multilevel Analysis of Coleman's Equality of Educational Opportunity Data," *Teachers College Record* 112, no. 5 (2010): 1201–1246, in a new study that reanalyzes data from the Coleman Report, report findings that contrast somewhat with Coleman's original findings about the impact of schools on student test-score performance. The results of the new study suggest that the joint effect of the fiscal and social resources found in families and schools appears to be much greater than either considered alone.

9. David Grissmer, Ann Flanagan, and Stephanie Williamson, "Why Did the Black-White Score Gap Narrow in the 1970s and 1980s?" in The Black-White Test Score Gap, eds. Christopher Jencks and Meredith Phillips (Washington, DC: Brookings Institution, 1998), 182–226.

10. Paul E. Barton and Richard J. Coley, "The Black-White Achievement Gap: When Progress Stopped," Educational Testing Service Report No. PIC-BWGAP (Princeton, NJ: Educational Testing Service, 2010).

11. Explaining the large proportion of the narrowing gaps that are not accounted for by demographic and family variables proved much more challenging, however, since the causes must (1) have changed significantly for adolescents in 1970–1975 versus adolescents in 1990, (2) have significantly affected black and Hispanic test scores but not the scores of non-Hispanic whites, and (3) be disentangled from the aforementioned changes in family characteristics. See David Grissmer et al., *Student Achievement and the Changing American Family* (Santa Monica, CA: RAND Corporation, 1994); Mark Berends and Roberto V. Penaloza, "Changes in Families, Schools, and the Test Score Gap," in *Steady Gains and Stalled Progress; Inequality and the Black-White Test Score Gap*, eds. Katherine Magnuson and Jane Waldfogel (New York: Russell Sage Foundation, 2008); and Larry V. Hedges and Amy Nowell, "Changes in the Black-White Gap in Achievement Test Scores," *Sociology of Education* 7 (1999): 111–135.

12. James Cibulka, "The Changing Role of Interest Groups in Education: Nationalization and the New Politics of Education Productivity," *Education Policy* 15 (2001): 12–40; Larry Cuban, *Why Is It So Hard to Get Good Schools?* (New York: Teachers College Press, 2003). National Commission on Excellence in Education, *A Nation at Risk: The Imperative for Educational Reform*, (Washington, DC: U.S. Department of Education, 1983).

13. David Macarov, "Welfare as Work's Handmaiden," *International Journal of Social Economics* 8, no. 5 (1981): 21–30.

14. Linda Darling-Hammond, "The Flat Earth and Education: How America's Commitment to Equity Will Determine Our Future," *Educational Researcher* 36 (2007): 318–334.

15. Richard Herrnstein and Charles Murray, *The Bell Curve: Intelligence and Class Structure in American Life* (New York: Free Press, 1994).

16. Arthur R. Jensen, "How Much Can We Boost IQ and Scholastic Achievement?" *Harvard Educational Review* 39 (1969): 1–123, argued that programs like Head Start, which tried to boost the academic performance of minority children, were doomed to failure because IQ was so heavily genetic and therefore impervious to environmental influences.

17. Asa G. Hilliard III, "Excellence in Education Versus High-Stakes Standardized Testing," *Journal of Teacher Education* 51 (2000): 293–304.

18. Richard E. Nisbett, "Race, Genetics, and IQ," in Jencks and Phillips, *The Black-White Test Score Gap*, 86–102.

19. Richard E. Nisbett, *Intelligence and How to Get It: Why Schools and Cultures Count* (New York: W. W. Norton, 2009).

20. E. Turkheimer, A. Haley, M. Waldron, B. D'Onofrio, and I. Gottesman, "Socioeconomic Status Modifies Heritability of IQ in Young Children," *Psychological Science* 14 (2003): 623–628.

21. Ibid.; U. Neisser et al., "Intelligence: Knowns and Unknowns," *American Psychologist* 51 (1996): 77–101.

22. Douglas N. Harris and Carolyn D. Herington, "Accountability, Standards, and the Growing Achievement Gap: Lessons from the Past Half-Century," *American Journal of Education* 112, no. 2 (2006): 227, citing John Chubb and Terry Moe, *Politics, Markets and Schools* (Washington, DC: Brookings Institution, 1990).

23. David C. Berliner, *Poverty and Potential: Out-of-School Factors and School Success* (East Lansing, MI: Great Lakes Center for Education Research & Practice, 2009); R. Stevens and J. Bransford, "The LIFE Center's Lifelong and Lifewide Diagram," in *Learning In and Out of School in Diverse Environments: Life-Long, Life-Wide, Life-Deep*, ed. J. A. Banks (Seattle, WA: UW Center for Multicultural Education, 2007).

24. Urie Bronfenbrenner, *The Ecology of Human Development: Experiments by Nature and Design* (Cambridge, MA: Harvard University Press, 1979).

25. Jencks and Phillips, *The Black-White Test Score Gap*; Roland G. Fryer and Steven D. Levitt, "The Black-White Test Score Gap Through Third Grade," *American Law and Economics Review* 8, no. 2 (2006): 249–281.

26. Meredith Phillips, James Crouse, and John Ralph, "Does the Black-White Test Score Gap Widen After Children Enter School?" in Jencks and Phillips, *The Black-White Test Score Gap*.

27. Karl L. Alexander, Doris R. Entwisle, and Linda S. Olson, "Schools, Achievement, and Inequality: A Seasonal Perspective," *Educational Evaluation and Policy Analysis* 23 (2001): 171–191.

28. Ibid.; Jaekyung Lee, "Racial and Ethnic Achievement Gap Trends: Reversing the Progress Toward Equity?" *Educational Researcher* 31 (2002): 3–12.

29. U.S. Department of Education, "No Child Left Behind Act Is Working (press release, December 2006), http://www2.ed.gov/nclb/overview/importance/nclbworking.pdf.

30. English language learner status indicates students who speak a language other than English at home and who range from students just beginning to learn English to students who are approaching proficiency in English but may need additional assistance in schooling situations. Among ELLs, Spanish is by far the most common home language. Second in frequency of use is Chinese, which is spoken by roughly 3.8% of ELLs, followed by Vietnamese (2.7%). While English skills obviously matter more for reading comprehension than for mathematics test score performance, research shows that lack of English proficiency also inhibits student performance on standardized math tests; see Jamal Abedi, Carol Lord, and Carolyn H. Hofstetter, "Impact of Selected Background Variables on Students' NAEP Math Performance," Center for the Study of Evaluation Technical Report No. 478 (Los Angeles, CA: University of California, National Center for Research on Evaluation, Standards, and Student Testing, 1998). Being able to distinguish a math expression like "the sum of the numbers" from the phrase "some numbers" may perplex students

who are simultaneously learning a second language while developing their skills in math; see Patricia Gándara and Russell Rumberger, "Immigration, Language, and Education: How Does Language Policy Structure Opportunity?" *Teachers College Record* 111 (2009): 750–782.

31. Jeanne Batalova and Margie McHugh, "The Languages Spoken by English Language Learners Nationally and by State" (Washington, DC: Migration Policy Institute, 2010), http://www .migrationinformation.org/ellinfo/FactSheet_ELL3.pdf.

32. It would be negligent, at this point, not to acknowledge the fact that simple race, social class, and language status categories continue to be inadequate descriptors of socioculturally diverse individual and group identities. Skin color is much less clearly the social class indicator it once was: see Jencks and Phillips, *The Black-White Test Score Gap* and Paul Taylor et al., *Marrying Out* (Washington, DC: Pew Research Center, 2010). Pan-ethnic labels such as "Hispanic" or "Latina/o" tend to cloud important differences between, say, immigrant Mexican Americans and third-generation Cuban Americans, while bilingualism and other important language ability variations typically get overlooked when proficiency with language is reduced to a yes/no box to check off. Notwithstanding the reconfiguration and blending of what may have once been more distinctly bounded ethnoracial indicators, such categories remain powerful and sometimes divisive forces that bear mightily upon inequalities in schooling in the United States. See Samuel Bowles, Herbert Gintis, and Melissa O. Groves, *Unequal Chances: Family Background and Economic Success* (Princeton, NJ: Princeton University Press, 2005); Jonathan Kozol, *The Shame of the Nation: The Restoration of Apartheid Schooling in America* (New York: Random House, 2005); and Robert Ream and Gregory Palardy, "Re-examining Social Class Differences in the Availability and the Educational Utility of Parental Social Capital," *American Educational Research Journal* 45, no. 2 (2008): 238–273. Thus, we are persuaded to attend to the necessity of employing descriptors such as "Hispanic" or "poor" or "English learner" even as we argue the importance of questioning whether these categories faithfully mirror the increasing complexity of the social world; see Mica Pollock, "Race Wrestling: Struggling Strategically with Race in Educational Practice and Research," *American Journal of Education* 111 (2004): 25–67; Erik O. Wright, *Class Counts: Comparative Studies in Class Analysis* (Cambridge, UK: Cambridge University Press, 1997). In short, we employ common social categorizing in acknowledgement of outcome gaps as very real phenomena that have serious social, economic, and political consequences.

33. Chapman, Laird, and Ramani, "Trends in High School Dropout and Completion Rates in the United States."

34. Christopher D. Chapman, Jennifer Laird, and Angelina Kewal Ramani, "Trends in High School Dropout and Completion Rates in the United States: 1972–2008," NCES Report No. 2011-012 (Washington, DC: National Center for Education Statistics, Institute of Education Sciences, U.S. Department of Education, 2010).

35. Ibid.

36. For example, a fairly recent study based on data gathered by the U.S. Census Bureau reveals impressive advances over the course of the twentieth century in Hispanic educational attainment from generation to generation. Mexican immigrants born during 1905–1909 averaged but 4.3 years of schooling. Their American-born sons, averaging 9.3 years, doubled the years of schooling. And their grandsons were high school graduates, averaging 12.2 years of schooling. See James P. Smith, "Assimilation Across the Latino Generations," *American Economic Review* 93 (2003): 315–319.

37. Richard Fry, "Hispanic Youth Dropping Out of U.S. Schools: Measuring the Challenge" (Washington, DC: Pew Hispanic Center, 2003).

38. Chapman, Laird, and Ramani, "Trends in High School Dropout and Completion Rates in the United States."

39. Both the K–12 and postsecondary systems of education in the United States have attempted to serve multiple and competing purposes through their histories. One purpose has always been to prepare youth to enter the labor force, and the importance of this role has been consistently emphasized and reemphasized over time, particularly during periods of uncertainty about the

economic position of the U.S. globally. Over the past three decades alone, numerous influential reports have asserted the inability of the nation's education system to adequately prepare the nation's youth for "college and careers." These include, among others, National Commission on Excellence in Education, *A Nation at Risk: The Imperative for Educational Reform* (Washington, DC: U.S. Department of Education, 1983); William T. Grant Foundation, "The Forgotten Half" (New York: William T. Grant Foundation, 1988); and National Center for Education Statistics, "Dropout Rates in the United States: 2005" (Washington, DC: U.S. Department of Education, 2005). In February of 2011, *Pathways to Prosperity* was published by the Pathways to Prosperity project of the Harvard Graduate School of Education, reiterating many of the claims and warnings issued in earlier reports; see William C. Symonds, Robert B. Schwartz, and Ronald Ferguson, *Pathways to Prosperity: Meeting the Challenge of Preparing Young Americans* (Cambridge, MA: Pathways to Prosperity Project at Harvard Graduate School of Education, 2011).

40. Sigal Alon, Thurston Domina, and Marta Tienda, "Stymied Mobility or Temporary Lull? The Puzzle of Lagging Hispanic College Degree Attainment," *Social Forces* 88 (2010): 1807–1832; Fabian T. Pfeffer, "Persistent Inequality in Educational Attainment and Its Institutional Context," *European Sociological Review* 24, no. 5 (2008): 543–565.

41. Jessica Godofsky, Cliff Zukin, and Carl Van Horn, "Unfulfilled Expectations: Recent College Graduates Struggle in a Troubled Economy" (New Brunswick, NJ: John J. Heldrich Center for Workforce Development, Rutgers University, 2011); Regina Deil-Amen and Stefanie DeLuca, "The Underserved Third: How Our Educational Structures Populate an Educational Underclass," *Journal of Education for Students Placed at Risk* 15 (2010): 27–50.

42. National Research Council, *Rising Above the Gathering Storm, Revisited: Rapidly Approaching Category 5* (Washington, DC: National Academies Press, 2011).

43. According to an analysis of newly released 2010 U.S. Census data by the Pew Hispanic Center, the number of U.S. Hispanics—50.5 million—is larger and has grown more quickly and more dramatically than demographers had estimated. In fact, the U.S. Latino population, which was 35.3 million in 2000, grew 43% over the past decade. Hispanics now constitute 16.3% of the total population and 17.1 million Hispanics now make up nearly a quarter of children (23.1 percent, or 17.1 million) ages 17 and younger. See Jeffrey S. Passel and D'Vera Cohn, "Census 2010: 50 Million Latinos, Hispanics Account for More Than Half of Nation's Growth in Past Decade" (Washington DC: Pew Hispanic Center, 2011). The rates of U.S. Hispanic children living in poverty, at 33%, are close to three times the rate of poverty for non-Latino whites (12%) and Asians (13%); see U.S. Bureau of the Census, *Income, Poverty, and Health Insurance Coverage in the United States: 2009* (Washington, DC: U.S. Government Printing Office, 2009). Moreover, the incidence of poverty is much higher among English learners who are immigrants or the children of immigrants; see Daniel T. Lichter, Zhenchao Qian, and Martha Crowley, "Child Poverty Among Racial Minorities and Immigrants: Explaining Trends and Differentials," *Social Science Quarterly* 86 (2005): 1037–1059. This overlap between poverty and nativity/language status is especially significant considering that between 1979 and 2008 the number of children between 5 and 17 who spoke a language other than English at home increased from 3.8 million to 10.9 million, or from 9% to 21%; see Chapman, Laird, and Ramani, "Trends in High School Dropout and Completion Rates in the United States"; and Passel and Cohn, "Census 2010: 50 Million Latinos."

44. William J. Baumol, Sue Anne B. Blackman, and Edward N. Wolff, *Productivity and American Leadership: The Long View* (Cambridge, MA: MIT Press, 1989); L. Scott Miller, *An American Imperative: Accelerating Minority Educational Advancement* (Binghamton, NY: Vail-Ballou Press, 1995); Robert Ream, *Uprooting Children: Mobility, Social Capital and Mexican American Underachievement* (New York: LFB Scholarly Publishing, 2005).

45. Jean Anyon, *Ghetto Schooling: A Political Economy of Urban Education Reform* (New York: Teachers College Press, 1997); Linda Darling-Hammond, "What Happens to a Dream Deferred? The Continuing Quest for Equal Educational Opportunity," in *Handbook of Research on Multicultural Education*, 2nd ed., ed. James A. Banks (San Francisco: Jossey-Bass, 2003), 607–630.

46. Shelley Hymel et al., "Academic Failure and School Dropout: The Influence of Peers," in *Social Motivation: Understanding Children's School Adjustment*, eds. Jaana Juvonen and Kathryn R. Wentzel (New York: Cambridge University Press, 1996).

47. Sherry B. Ortner, *Anthropology and Social Theory: Culture, Power, and the Acting Subject* (Durham, NC: Duke University Press, 2006).

48. Bronfenbrenner, *The Ecology of Human Development*.

49. Gary Orfield and Chungmei Lee, "Why Segregation Matters: Poverty and Educational Inequality" (Los Angeles: Civil Rights Project/Proyecto Derechos Civiles at UCLA, 2005).

50. Coleman et al., *Equality of Educational Opportunity*; Ronald F. Ferguson and Jal Mehta, "The Legacy of Brown and the Narrowing of the Achievement Gap," *Phi Delta Kappan* 85 (2004): 656–669; Heather Schwartz, "Housing Policy Is School Policy: Economically Integrative Housing Promotes Academic Success in Montgomery County, Maryland" (New York: Century Foundation, 2010).

51. Ronald F. Ferguson, "Paying for Public Education: New Evidence on How and Why Money Matters," *Harvard Journal on Legislation* 28 (1991): 465–498.

52. Darling-Hammond, "The Flat Earth and Education"; James Lewis et al., "Con Cariño: Teacher Caring, Math Self-Efficacy and Math Achievement among Hispanic English Learners," *Teachers College Record* 14, no. 7 (forthcoming).

53. To test the educational benefits of economic integration in elementary schools, Heather Schwartz, who is now a researcher at the RAND Corporation, examined all the elementary-age children of mostly African American families who lived in public housing from 2001 to 2007 in Montgomery County, Maryland, where housing policies require developers to set aside housing for low-income families in more privileged neighborhoods. A critical aspect of this study is that some of the children who moved to new public housing nevertheless continued to attend higher-poverty but also *higher-spending* elementary schools, while others now attended low-poverty schools. Importantly, the difference in which type of school the students attend is random. After seven years in the district, the children in the lower-poverty schools performed 8 percentage points higher on standardized math tests than their peers attending the higher-poverty schools—even though the county had targeted them with extra resources. This lends fresh support to an idea critical to the Supreme Court's 1954 ruling in *Brown v. Board*: segregated schools are rarely as effective as integrated ones at educating low-income minority students (see Schwartz, "Housing Policy Is School Policy").

54. Harris Cooper et al., "The Effects of Summer Vacation on Achievement Test Scores: A Narrative and Meta-analytic Review," *Review of Educational Research* 66 (1996): 227–268; Barbara Heyns, "Schooling and Cognitive Development: Is There a Season for Learning?" *Child Development* 58 (1987): 1151–1160.

55. Karl L. Alexander, Doris R. Entwisle, and Linda S. Olson, "Schools, Achievement, and Inequality: A Seasonal Perspective," *Educational Evaluation and Policy Analysis* 23 (2001): 171-191.

56. Doris R. Entwisle, Karl L. Alexander, and Linda S. Olson, *Children, Schools, and Inequality* (Boulder, CO: Westview Press, 1997).

57. One recent study identified a troubling exception to the pattern whereby gaps in children's cognitive skills widen less when elementary school is in session than when it is not. Using a nationally representative sample of 17,000 kindergartners in fall 1998 who were followed through the spring of first grade in 2000, Douglas B. Downey, Paul T. von Hippel, and Beckett Broh, "Are Schools the Great Equalizer? Cognitive Inequality During the Summer Months and the School Year," *American Sociological Review* 69 (2004): 613–635 show that gaps in cognitive skills between blacks and whites grow faster than expected when school is in session. Their findings suggest that something about early schooling exacerbates black-white test-score gaps even while early schooling reduces gaps between Hispanics and non-Hispanic whites. See also Downey, von Hippel, and Broh, "Are Schools the Great Equalizer?"; Gamoran, "American Schooling and Educational Inequality."

58. Selcuk Sirin, "Socioeconomic Status and Academic Achievement: A Meta-analytic Review of Research," *Review of Educational Research* 75, no. 3 (2005): 417–453.

59. Rothstein, *Class and Schools*.

60. Gregory Duncan and Katherine Magnuson, "Can Family Socioeconomic Resources Account for Racial and Ethnic Test Score Gaps?" *Future of Children* 15 (2005): 35–54.

61. National Center for Education Statistics, *Digest of Educational Statistics: 2006* (Washington, DC: U.S. Department of Education, 2006).

62. Russell Rumberger, "Parsing the Data on Student Achievement in High-Poverty Schools," *North Carolina Law Review* 86 (2007): 1293–1314.

63. Laurence Steinberg, *Beyond the Classroom: Why School Reform Has Failed and What Parents Need to Do* (New York: Simon & Schuster, 1997).

64. Betty Hart and Todd R. Risley, *Meaningful Differences in the Everyday Experience of Young American Children* (Baltimore, MD: Brookes Publishing, 1995).

65. Larry V. Hedges and Amy Nowell, "Changes in the Black-White Gap in Achievement Test Scores," *Sociology of Education* 7 (1999): 111–135; Barton and Coley, "The Black-White Achievement Gap."

66. Jencks and Phillips, *The Black-White Test Score Gap*.

67. Cecily R. Hardaway and Vonnie C. McLoyd, "Escaping Poverty and Securing Middle Class Status: How Race and Socioeconomic Status Shape Mobility Prospects for African Americans During the Transition to Adulthood," *Journal of Youth and Adolescence* 38 (2009): 242–256; Amy J. Orr, "Black-White Differences in Achievement: The Importance of Wealth," *Sociology of Education* 76 (2003): 281–304; W. Jean Yeung and Dalton Conley, "Black-White Achievement Gap and Family Wealth," *Child Development* 79, no. 2 (2008): 303–324.

68. Estimates from the Survey of Income and Program Participation indicate that in 2002, Latino households had a net worth of about $8,000 while African American households had a net worth of only $6,000. See Rakesh Kochhar, *The Wealth of Hispanic Households: 1996 to 2002* (Washington, DC: Pew Hispanic Center, 2004). White households, on the other hand, had a median net worth of approximately $90,000. Stated in slightly different terms, 95 percent of Latino and black households have a net worth below the median level of white households. A growing consensus among scholars who study wealth is that a fundamental, and perhaps primary, source of wealth disparities is divergent access to inheritances and in vivo transfers. See Robert B. Avery and Michael S. Rendall, "Lifetime Inheritances of Three Generations of Whites and Blacks," *American Journal of Sociology* 107, no. 4 (2002): 1300–1346; and William A. Darity, "Forty Acres and a Mule in the 21st Century," *Social Science Quarterly* 89, no. 3 (2008): 656–664.

69. Yeung and Conley, "Black-White Achievement Gap and Family Wealth," 303.

70. Ibid., 322.

71. Dalton Conley, "Capital for College: Parental Assets and Postsecondary Schooling," *Sociology of Education* 74, no. 1 (2001): 59–72; Pfeffer, "Persistent Inequality in Educational Attainment and Its Institutional Context."

72. Thomas Shapiro, Tatjana Meschede, and Laura Sullivan, "Racial Wealth Gap Increases Fourfold" (Waltham, MA: Institute on Assets and Social Policy, Brandeis University, 2010).

73. Claude M. Steele, "A Threat in the Air: How Stereotypes Shape Intellectual Identity and Performance," *American Psychologist* 52 (1997): 613–629.

74. McKinsey & Company Social Sector Office, "The Economic Impact of the Achievement Gap in America's Schools," May 16, 2011, http://www.mckinsey.com/clientservice/socialsector/achievement_gap_report.pdf; Chapman, Laird, and Ramani, "Trends in High School Dropout and Completion Rates in the United States."

75. Henry M. Levin et al., "The Costs and Benefits of an Excellent Education for All of America's Children" (New York: Center for Cost Based Studies, Columbia University, 2007), www.cbsce.org.

76. National Center for Public Policy and Higher Education, "Policy Alert: Income of U.S. Workforce Projected to Decline *if* Education Doesn't Improve" (San Jose, CA: National Center for Public Policy and Higher Education, 2005).

77. Levin et al., "The Costs and Benefits of an Excellent Education for All of America's Children"; Cecilia E. Rouse, "Quantifying the Costs of Inadequate Education: Consequences of the Labor Market," in *The Price We Pay: Economic and Social Consequences of Inadequate Education*, eds. Clive R. Belfield and Henry M. Levin (Washington, DC: Brookings Institution, 2007), 99–124.

78. Symonds, Schwartz, and Ferguson, *Pathways to Prosperity*.

79. As Kirkland (2010) documents, the history of this phrase, "the achievement gap," dates at least back to the early 1960s when Chicago's Hauser Report anticipated that desegregation and expanding educational opportunities would instigate "a major closing of the achievement gap." See Phillip M. Hauser et al., *Integration of the Public Schools: Chicago* (Chicago: Chicago Board of Education, Chicago Public Schools, 1964), 20–21, emphasis added; David E. Kirkland, "'Black Skin, White Masks': Normalizing Whiteness and the Trouble with the Achievement Gap," *Teachers College Record*, advance online publication, ID Number: 16116.

80. Levin et al., "The Costs and Benefits of an Excellent Education for All of America's Children"; Elaine L. Chao, Emily DeRocco, and Maria K. Flynn, "Adult Learners in Higher Education: Barriers to Success and Strategies to Improve Results," in *Adult Education: Issues and Developments*, eds. Patricia N. Blakely and Anna H. Tomlin (New York: Nova Science Publishers, 2008), 271–354.

81. Barton and Coley, "The Black-White Achievement Gap."

82. Miller, *An American Imperative*.

83. Bronfenbrenner, *The Ecology of Human Development*; James Traub, "What No School Can Do," *New York Times*, January 16, 2000.

84. Robert L. Crowson, ed., *Community Development and School Reform* (Oxford: Elsevier Science Ltd., 2001); Ellen B. Goldring and Charles Hausman, "Civic Capacity and School Principals: The Missing Links for Community Development," in *Community Development and School Reform*, ed. Robert L. Crowson (Oxford: Elsevier Science Ltd., 2001), 193–209.

85. Lorraine McDonnell and Richard Elmore, "Getting the Job Done: Alternative Policy Instruments," *Educational Evaluation and Policy Analysis* 9 (1987): 133-152.

86. Jeffery R. Henig and S. Paul Reville, "Why Attention Will Return to Non-School Factors," *Education Week*, May 25, 2011.

87. Erik Olin Wright, *Envisioning Real Utopias* (London: Verso, 2010).

88. Leon Wieseltier, "Post-Post Imperialist," *The New Republic* 242 (2011): 36.

Chapter 3

1. See, for example, the references to Bureau of the Census reports, and the U.S. Immigration Commission in Marvin Lazerson, *Origins of the Urban School: Public Education in Massachusetts, 1870–1915* (Cambridge, MA: Harvard University Press, 1971), 262–263.

2. See, for example, National Governor's Association, "Closing the Achievement Gap," www.subnet .nga.org/educlear/achievement/, which mentioned only four options: early childhood education; improving teacher quality; early intervention for college, and after-school programs. Similarly, Russell W. Rumberger and Brenda D. Arrellano, "Examining the Achievement Gap Among English Learners in Elementary School," report for the Western Regional Laboratory (San Francisco: WestEd, 2007), mention three: reducing the gaps that children come to school with, through pre-schools or family income programs; out-of-school programs including summer and after-school programs; and improving student behavior through parent education or smaller classes.

3. The analysis of dynamic inequality is developed more fully in W. Norton Grubb, *The Money Myth: School Resources, Outcomes, and Equity* (New York: Russell Sage Foundation, 2009), in chapter 6 on conceptions of equity and in chapter 7 on the estimation of growth equations.

4. For documentation of the differences at school entrance see George Farkas, "Racial Disparities and Discrimination in Education: What Do We Know, How Do We Know It, and What Do We Need to Know?" *Teachers College Record* 105, no. 6 (2003): 1119–1146, and *The Future of Children* 15, no. 1 (2005).

5. See, for example, Rumberger and Arrellano, "Examining the Achievement Gap," Table A-5, who show that kindergartners who attended center-based preschool had higher language skills and math achievement, but that this did not eliminate the effects of language status and socio-economic status.

6. For example, Ronald G. Fryer and Steven D. Leavitt, "The Black-White Test Score Gap Through Third Grade," NBER Working Paper 11049 (Cambridge, MA: NBER, 2005), show that modest black-white differences at the beginning of kindergarten, largely explained by some simple socio-economic status variables, increase until the spring of third grade. Meredith Phillips, James Crouse, and John Ralph, "Does the Black-White Test Score Gap Widen After Children Enter School?" in *The Black-White Test Score Gap,* eds. Christopher Jencks and Meredith Phillips (Washington, DC: Brookings Institution, 1998), 229–272 estimate that initial black-white differences are roughly doubled by the end of 12th grade. Scores on the Peabody Individual Achievement Test for the middle 50% of students widen steadily over time (Charles H. Hargis, "Setting Standards: An Exercise in Futility?" *Phi Delta Kappan* 87, no. 5 (2006): 393–395). My own analysis of NELS88 data for 8th to 10th to 12th grades (W. Norton Grubb, "When Money Might Matter: Using NELS88 to Examine the Weak Effects of School Finance," *Journal of Education Finance* 31, no. 4 (2006): 360–378) shows divergence in test scores over this period, associated with race/ethnicity, measures of family background, and school resources.

7. See Karl L. Alexander, Doris R. Entwisle, and Linda S. Olson, "Schools, Achievement, and Inequality: A Seasonal Perspective," *Educational Evaluation and Policy Analysis* 23, no. 2 (2001): 171–191; Barbara Heyns, *Summer Learning and the Effects of Schooling* (New York: Academic Press, 1978), about her research on Atlanta; and Daniel M. O'Brien, "Family and School Effects on the Cognitive Growth of Minority and Disadvantaged Elementary School Students" (working paper, Green Center for the Study of Science and Society, University of Texas at Dallas, 1998) research on a Texas district. In the analysis of kindergarten and first grade by Douglas B. Downey, Paul T. von Hippel, and Beckett Broh, "Are Schools the Great Equalizer? School and Non-school Sources of Inequality in Cognitive Skills," *American Sociological Review* 69, no. 5 (2004): 613–635, schooling tends to reduce inequality (except for black-white differences), but not by enough to offset differences created over the summer.

8. W. Norton Grubb, *The Money Myth: School Resources, Outcomes, and Equity* (New York: Russell Sage Foundation, 2009), 145.

9. Some evidence of difficult transitions is anecdotal, for example as teachers complain about the transition from third to fourth grade. For quantitative evidence of "bursts" of inequality from either to tenth grade, see Grubb, *The Money Myth,* chapter 7. Phillips, Crouse, and Ralph, *The Black-White Test Score Gap,* Table 7.7, find a particularly high increase in the relative gap of reading and math scores between white and black students in 7th and 8th grades, and the variation in Peabody scores reported by Hargis, "Setting Standards," increases markedly in grades 3 and 7.

10. National Association of Elementary School Principals, *Early Childhood Education and the Elementary School Principal: Standards for Quality Programs for Young Children,* 2nd ed. (Alexandria, VA: National Principals' Resource Center, National Association of Elementary School Principals, 1998). Available as ERIC Report 450466.

11. Charles M. Payne, *So Much Reform, So Little Change: The Persistence of Failure in Urban Schools* (Cambridge, MA: Harvard Education Press, 2008).

12. Balanced approaches draw on both behaviorist and constructivist approaches to teaching, rather than following only one or the other.

13. Grubb, *The Money Myth.*

14. Grubb, "When Money Might Matter," 360–378.

15. This conception of school resources is developed more carefully in W. Norton Grubb, Luis A. Huerta, and Laura Goe, "Straw into Gold, Revenues into Results: Spinning Out the Implications of the 'Improved' School Finance," *Journal of Education Finance* 31, no. 4 (2006): 334–359, with other support in the school finance literature analyzing the limits of considering

funding only. On the limits of increasing funding as a way of enhancing compound, complex, and abstract resources, see Grubb, "When Money Might Matter."

16. Anthony Bryk, Penny Sebring, Elaine Allensworth, Stuart Leppuscu, and John Easton, *Organizing Schools for Improvement: Lessons from Chicago* (Chicago: University of Chicago Press, 2010); Anthony Bryk, "Organizing Schools for Improvement," *Phi Delta Kappan* 91, no. 7 (2010): 23–30.

17. David K. Cohen and Susan L. Moffitt, *The Ordeal of Inequality: Did Federal Regulation Fix the Schools?* (Cambridge, MA: Harvard University Press, 2009).

18. Note the evidence in Jaekyung Lee and Kenneth Wong, "The Impact of Accountability on Racial and Socioeconomic Equity: Considering Both School Resources and Achievement Outcomes," *American Educational Research Journal* 41, no. 4 (2004): 797–832, that accountability systems do not enhance school resources, and do not enhance equity. Note also Laura S. Hamilton et al., *Standards-Based Accountability Under No Child Left Behind: Experiences of Teachers and Administrators in Three States* (Santa Monica, CA: RAND Corporation, 2007), who also conclude that accountability cannot work unless teacher and administrator capacity for improvement is developed.

19. Grubb, *The Money Myth*, chapter 2.

20. David Conley, *Redefining College Readiness*. Eugene, OR: Educational Policy Improvement Center, 2007.

21. See Rebecca D. Cox, *The College Fear Factor: How Students and Professors Misunderstand One Another* (Cambridge, MA: Harvard University Press, 2009); and my forthcoming research about basic skills instruction in community colleges.

22. This section is based on reports of students in the Principal Leadership Institute and on a study of 12 schools in the Bay Area, reported in Grubb, *The Money Myth*, chapter 8.

23. I have borrowed this expression from oral presentations of John Easton, now director of the Institute for Educational "Science" and one of the co-authors of Bryk et al., *Organizing Schools for Improvement*. The systematic attention to the five "pillars" in the Chicago Consortium's work is, of course, antithetical to "programmitis."

24. Most research on Out-of-School Time (OST) programs, including before- and after-school programs, has been largely negative; see Thomas Kane, *The Impact of After-School Programs: Interpreting the Results of Four Recent Evaluations* (New York: William T. Grant Foundation, 2004); Susan Bodilly and Megan K. Beckett, *Making Out-of-School-Time Matter: Evidence for an Action Agenda* (Santa Monica, CA: RAND Corporation, 2005); and a slightly more positive meta-analysis by Patricia A. Lauer et al., *The Effectiveness of Out-of-School-Time Strategies in Assisting Low-Achieving Students in Reading and Mathematics: A Research Synthesis,* updated ed. (Aurora, CO: Mid-continent Research for Education and Learning, 2004), which concludes that the most effective programs are tutoring programs for reading. On tutoring, a rough consensus is that effective practices include a coordinator knowledgeable about reading and writing instruction; structure in tutoring sessions; training for volunteers; and coordination between classroom instruction and volunteers. See also Batya Elbaum, Sharon Vaughn, Marie Tejero Hughes, and Sally Watson Moody, "How Effective Are One-to-One Tutoring Programs in Reading for Elementary Students at Risk for Reading Failure? A Meta-analysis of the Intervention Research," *Journal of Educational Psychology* 924 (2000): 605–619; Barbara A. Wasik and Robert Slavin, "Preventing Early Reading Failure with One-to-One Tutoring: A Review of Five Programs," *Reading Research Quarterly* 28, no. 2 (1993): 178–200.

25. Grubb, *The Money Myth*, chapter 4; see also Charles T. Clotfelter, Helen F. Ladd, and Jacob L. Vigdor, "The Academic Achievement Gap in Grades 3 Through 8," NBER Working Paper 12207 (Cambridge, MA: NBER, 2006), www.nber.org/papers/w12207.

26. For a similar argument that schools need to face racial and ethnic issues squarely, see *Los Angeles Times*, "Learning in Color: Narrowing the Achievement Gap in Schools Requires Acknowledging Race, not Ignoring It," September 16, 2007. See also Jeannie Oakes, John Rogers, and Martin Lipton, *Learning Power: Organizing for Education and Justice* (New York: Teachers College

Press, 2006); Angela Valenzuela, *Subtractive Schooling: U.S.-Mexican Youth and the Politics of Caring* (Albany: State University of New York Press, 1999); Jean Anyon, "Race, Social Class, and Educational Reform in an Inner-City School," *Teachers College Record* 97 (1995): 69–95. The enormous literatures on culturally-relevant pedagogy (e.g., Geneva Gay, *Culturally Responsive Teaching: Theory, Research, and Practice* [New York: Teachers College Press, 2000]) and on multi-cultural education in its many forms (James A. Banks and Cherry A. McGee Banks, eds., *Handbook of Research on Multicultural Education* [New York: Macmillan, 2005]) are also arguments for facing racial and ethnic issues up front.

27. See, for example, Nisbett, Richard, "Race, Genetics, and IQ," in The Black-White Test Score Gap, eds. Christopher Jencks and Meredeth Phillips (Washington DC: Brookings Institution Press, 1998), 86–102, who examines an enormous amount of evidence on blackwhite differences; Roland Fryer, "Testing for Racial Differences in the Mental Ability of Young Children" (unpublished paper available at post.economics.harvard.edu/faculty/fryer/papers.html, 2006); Fryer and Leavitt, "The Black-White Test Score Gap," who show that small black-white differences at kindergarten can be completely explained by socioeconomic factors; and Geoffrey B. Saxe, Steven R. Guberman, and Maryl Gearhart, "Social Processes in Early Number Development," *Monographs of the Society for Research in Child Development* 52, no. 2 (1987): 160–163, who show that there are no black-white differences in mathematical ability at age two, though differences start to emerge by age 4 in response to the greater amount of "math talk" in middle-class families.

28. For example, see the efforts of Jennifer Morazes, "High School Students Whose Parents Did Not Attend College: Do Stressful Circumstances Impede Their Academic Success?" (unpublished dissertation, School of Social Work, University of California, Berkeley, 2011) to incorporate the effects of family stress, life event stress, and cumulative stress on school performance.

29. Grubb, *The Money Myth*, chapter 4, reviews this evidence. See also the reviews by Zirkel (Sabrina Zirkel, "Ongoing Issues of Racial and Ethnic Stigma in Education 50 Years After *Brown*," *Urban Review* 37, no. 2 (2005): 107–126; Sabrina Zirkel, "Creating More Effective Multiethnic Schools," *Social Issues and Policy Review* 2 (2008): 187–241; and Sabrina Zirkel, "The Influence of Multi-cultural Practices on Student Outcomes and Intergroup Relations," *Teachers College Record* 110, no. 6 (2008): 1147–1181). In addition, much of the literature on critical race theory is based on autobiographical and other incidents of racial/ethnic mistreatment. See also Angela Valenzuela, *Subtractive Schooling: U.S.-Mexican Youth and the Politics of Caring* (Albany: State University of New York Press, 1999); Anyon, "Race, Social Class, and Educational Reform," 69–95.

30. See, for example, Ronald F. Ferguson, "Teachers' Perceptions and Expectations and the Black-White Test Score Gap," in *The Black-White Test Score Gap,* eds. Christopher Jencks and Meredith Phillips (Washington DC: Brookings Institution, 1998), 318–374; and, more generally, Rhona S. Weinstein, *Reaching Higher: The Power of Expectations in Schooling* (Cambridge, MA: Harvard University Press, 2002).

31. William Ayers et al., eds., *Zero Tolerance: Resisting the Drive for Punishment* (New York: New Press, 2001).

32. Claude M. Steele, *Whistling Vivaldi and Other Clues to How Stereotypes Affect Us* (New York: W. W. Norton, 2010); Claude M. Steele and Joshua Aronson, "Stereotype Threat and the Intellectual Test Performance of African Americans," *Journal of Personality and Social Psychology* 69 (1995): 797–811; Lionel D. Scott, "The Relation of Racial Identity and Racial Socialization to Coping with Discrimination Against African American Adolescents," *Journal of Black Studies* 33, no. 4 (2003): 520–538; Janet E. Helms, "Racial Identity in a Social Environment," in *Multicultural Counseling in School: A Practical Handbook*, eds. Paul B. Pedersen and John C. Carey (Boston: Allyn and Bacon, 2003), 44–58; Laura A. Szalacha et al., "Perceived Discrimination and Resilience," *Resilience and Vulnerability: Adaptation in the Context of Childhood Adversities*, ed. Suniya S. Luthar (New York: Cambridge University Press, 2003); Susan Stone, "Non-academic Needs of Students: How Can Schools Intervene?" in *Raising Children: Emerging Needs, Modern Risks, and Social Responses*, eds. Jill Duerr Berrick and Neil Gilbert (New York: Oxford University Press, 2007).

33. See Rebecca Wheeler, "Code-Switching: Insights and Strategies for Teaching Standard English in Dialectically Diverse Classrooms" (unpublished paper, Christopher Newport University, Newport News, VA, 2007), www.ncte.org/profdev/onsite/consultants/wheeler on contrastive analysis and code-switching; and Kris Gutiérrez, Patricia Baquedano-Lopez, and Carlos Tejada, "Rethinking Diversity: Hybridity and Hybrid Language Practices in the Third Space," *Mind, Culture, and Activity* 6, no. 4 (1999): 286–303.

34. There appear to be many presenters and workshops intending to help schools discuss racial issues; see for example Glenn E. Singleton and Curtis W. Linton, *Courageous Conversations About Race: A Field Guide for Achieving Equity in Schools* (Thousand Oaks, CA: Corwin Press, 2006). For the awkward conversations that often take place, see Mica Pollak, *Colormute: Race Talk Dilemmas in an American School* (Princeton, NJ: Princeton University Press, 2004).

35. For an introduction see Gloria Ladson-Billings, "Toward a Theory of Culturally Relevant Pedagogy," *American Educational Research Journal* 32, no. 3 (1995): 465–491; Gay, *Culturally Responsive Teaching*, and Banks and Banks, *Handbook of Research on Multicultural Education*.

36. There have been periodic efforts in the U.S. to develop systems of school inspections, modeled on those in England. These methods can be extraordinarily helpful in clarifying and reforming classroom practices, but they can also be highly destructive if carried out in punitive ways associated with accountability systems; see W. Norton Grubb, "Opening Classrooms and Improving Teaching: Lessons from School Inspection in England," *Teachers College Record* 102, no. 4 (2000): 696–723.

37. Rumberger and Arellano, "Examining the Achievement Gap," present some of the appropriate numbers. On the magnitude of the ELL gap see Patricia Gándara, Russell W. Rumberger, Julie Maxwell-Jolly, and Rebecca Callahan, "English Learners in California Schools: Unequal Resources, Unequal Outcomes," *Educational Policy Analysis Archives* 11 (2003), http://epaa.asu.edu/epaa/v11n36/.

38. On the inequities in resources, see Gándara et al., "English Learners in California Schools." On segregation, see Russell W. Rumberger, Patricia Gándara, and Barbara Merino, "Where California's English Learners Attend School and Why It Matters," *UC LMRI Newsletter* 15 (2006): 1–2, http://lmri.ucsb.edu/publications/newsletters/v15n2.pdf.

39. Susana Dutro and Carrol Moran, "Rethinking English Language Instruction: An Architectural Approach," in *English Learners: Reaching the Highest Levels of English Literacy*, ed. G. G. García (Newark: International Reading Association, 2003), 227–258.

40. These conclusions come from Fred Genesee, Kathryn Lindholm-Leary, Bill Saunders, and Donna Christian, *Educating English Language Learners: A Synthesis of Research Evidence* (New York: Cambridge University Press, 2006), chapter 6. The conclusions are quite consistent with findings in Diane August and Timothy Shanahan, eds., *Developing Literacy in Second Language Learners: Report of the National Literacy Panel on Language Minority Children and Youth* (New York: Lawrence Erlbaum, 2006); Eugene García, *Teaching and Learning in Two Languages: Bilingualism and Schooling in the United States* (New York: Teachers College Press, 2005), especially chapter 3; John Cummins, *Negotiating Identities: Education for Empowerment in a Diverse Society* (Ontario, CA: California Association for Bilingual Education, 1996); Wayne P. *Thomas* and Virginia *Collier, A Longitudinal Analysis of Programs Serving Language Minority Students* (Washington, DC: National Clearinghouse on Bilingual Education, 1995); and Masahiko Minami and Carlos J. Ovando, "Language Issues in Multicultural Contexts," in *Handbook of Research on Multicultural Education*," 2nd ed., eds. James A. Banks and Cherry McGee Banks (San Francisco: Jossey-Bass, 2004), 567–588.

41. See Cummins, *Negotiating Identities*, chapter 5. The evaluation of Prop 227 found that fewer than 40% of ELL students could be designated as English proficient after 10 years; see Thomas Parrish et al., Effects of the Implementation of Proposition 227 on the Education of English Learners, K–12 (Sacramento, CA: American Institutes for Research and WestEd, for the California Department of Education).

42. See Valenzuela, *Subtractive Schooling*, for the idea of "subtractive schooling," which subtracts from rather than adding to knowledge.

43. See especially García, *Teaching and Learning in Two Languages*, 164, and the citations on page 41 about the negative treatment of bilingualism in most American schools.

44. On variation among countries in the inequality of income and in poverty, see the many tables of LIS, "Luxembourg Income Study," www.lisdatacenter.org; see also Richard Wilkinson and Kate Picket, *The Spirit Level: Why Greater Equality Makes Societies Stronger* (New York: Bloomsbury Press, 2009).

45. Some critics going back to George Counts, *Dare the School Build a New Social Order?* (Carbondale, IL: Southern Illinois University Press, 1932; 1978) have argued that it is impossible to reform schools without first changing our inequitable form of capitalism; others, including George W. Bush and the Education Trust, have argued that anyone using inequality as an explanation for achievement gaps is "giving up" on poor and racial minority children. I take here a Deweyan approach that both school reform and attention to non-school sources of inequality are necessary to eliminate achievement gaps. See Grubb, *The Money Myth*, 279–281 for a fuller statement of these conflicts.

46. Joy Dryfoos, *Full-Service Schools: A Revolution in Health and Social Services for Children, Youth, and Families* (San Francisco: Jossey-Bass, 1994). Comer schools (James P. Comer, *Rallying the Whole Village: The Comer Process for Reforming Education* [New York: Teachers College Press, 1996]) also rely on the community to provide a variety of services.

47. See the federal government's description of Promise Neighborhoods, U.S. Department of Education, "Promise Neighborhoods," www2.ed.gov/programs/promiseneighborhoods/index.html.

48. See Robert William Blum, Clea McNeely, and Peggy Mann Rinehart, "Improving the Odds: The Untapped Power of Schools to Improve the Health of Teens" (Minneapolis: Center for Adolescent Health and Development, University of Minnesota, 2002), http://www.allaboutkids.umn.edu. The argument about the school environment is made at much greater length in National Research Council, Committee on Increasing High School Students' Engagement and Motivation to Learn, *Engaging Schools: Fostering High School Students' Motivation to Learn* (Washington DC: National Academy Press, 2004), chapter 6.

49. W. Norton Grubb and Jean Y. Anyon, "A Trio of Changes Supporting Students: Integrating School Reforms and Support Services" (unpublished paper prepared for the Woodrow Wilson Early College High School Initiative, UC Berkeley, School of Education, October 2010).

50. Russell W. Rumberger and Katherine A. Larson, "Student Mobility and the Increased Risk of High School Dropout," *American Journal of Education Research* 107 (1998): 1–35; Grubb, *The Money Myth*.

51. Paul Krugman, *The Conscience of a Liberal* (New York: W. W. Norton, 2007), chapter 11.

52. Gosta Esping-Anderson, *Three Worlds of Welfare Capitalism* (Princeton, NJ: Princeton University Press, 1990).

53. On distributed leadership, see James P. Spillane, *Distributed Leadership* (San Francisco: Jossey-Bass, 2006); on internal accountability, see Martin Carnoy, Richard Elmore, and Leslie Siskins, *The New Accountability: High Schools and High Stakes Testing* (New York: Routledge Falmer, 2003); and Charles Abelmann and Richard Elmore, "When Accountability Knocks, Will Anyone Answer?" CPRE Research Report Series RR-42 (Philadelphia: Consortium for Policy Research in Education, University of Pennsylvania, 1999); on trust, see Anthony Bryk and Barbara Schneider, *Trust in Schools: A Core Resource for Improvement* (New York: Russell Sage Foundation, 2002); on the hostile relationships within many urban schools, see Payne, *So Much Reform, So Little Change*. See also the summary of "organic management" in Brian Rowan, "Commitment and Control: Alternative Strategies for the Organizational Design of Schools," in *Review of Research in Education*, vol. 16, ed. Courtney B. Cazden (Washington DC: American Educational Research Association, 1990), 353–389; and Robert J. Miller and Brian Rowan, "Effects of Organic Management on Student Achievement," *American Educational Research Journal* 43, no. 2 (2006): 210–253. Among the case studies highlighting these forms of

reorganization, see the example of "Railside School," where mathematics teachers worked collaboratively to shape their own teaching methods and design their own curriculum (Jo Boaler and Megan Staples, "Creating Mathematical Futures Through an Equitable Teaching Approach: The Case of Railside School," *Teachers College Record* 110, no. 3 [2008]).

54. Bryk et al., *Organizing Schools for Improvement.*

55. On district issues, see Springboard Schools, *Minding the Gap: New Roles for School Districts in the Age of Accountability* (San Francisco: Springboard Schools, 2006) on Elk Grove, Oak Grove, and Rowland; James E. Austin, Robert B. Schwartz, and Jennifer M. Suesse, "Long Beach Unified School District: Change That Leads to Improvement" (Boston: Harvard Business School Publishing, PEL-006, September 2006) on Long Beach, which has had the added advantage of stability in superintendents; and Linda Darling-Hammond et al., "Building Instructional Quality: 'Inside out' and 'Outside in' Perspectives on San Diego's School Reform" (Seattle: Center for the Study of Teaching and Policy, University of Washington, 2006) on San Diego. See also Grubb, *The Money Myth*, 231–241.

56. See especially James P. Spillane and Charles L. Thompson, "Reconstructing Conceptions of Local Capacity: The Local Education Agency's Capacity for Ambitious Instructional Reform," *Educational Evaluation and Policy Analysis* 19, no. 2 (1997); Jason Snipes, Fred Doolittle, and Corinne Herlihy, *Foundations for Success: Case Studies of How Urban School Systems Improve Student Achievement* (Washington, DC: Council of Great City Schools, 2002); Milbrey McLaughlin and Joan Talbert, *Reforming Districts: How Districts Support School Reform* (Seattle: Center for the Study of Teaching and Policy, 2003); Joseph Murphy and Phillip Hallinger, "Characteristics of Instructionally Effective School Districts," *Journal of Educational Research* 81, no. 3 (1998): 175–181.

Chapter 4

1. Organisation for Economic Co-Operation and Development, *PISA 2009 Results: Learning Trends: Changes in Student Performance Since 2000,* vol. V (Paris: OECD, 2010), http://dx.doi.org/10.1787/9789264091580-en.

2. Gary N. Marks, John Cresswell, and John Ainley, "Explaining Socioeconomic Inequalities in Student Achievement: The Role of Home and School Factors," *Educational Research and Evaluation* 12, no. 2 (2006): 105–128; Gary Orfield and Chungmei Lee, *Why Segregation Matters: Poverty and Educational Inequality* (Cambridge, MA: The Civil Rights Project, Harvard University, 2005). http://www.civilrightsproject.ucla.edu/research/deseg/Why_Segreg_Matters.pdf.

3. No Child Left Behind Act of 2001, Pub. L. No. 107–110, § 115 Stat. 1425 (2002).

4. Betty Hart and Todd R. Risley, *Meaningful Differences in the Everyday Experience of Young American Children* (Baltimore, MD: Brookes Publishing, 1995).

5. Audrey L. Amrein and David C. Berliner, "The Effects of High-Stakes Testing on Student Motivation and Learning," *Educational Leadership* 60, no. 5 (2003): 32–38; Gerald W. Bracey, "Put Out Over PISA," *Phi Delta Kappan* 86, no. 10 (2005): 797–798; Gerald W. Bracey, "The First Time 'Everything Changed,'" *Phi Delta Kappan* 89, no. 2 (2007): 119–136.

6. Organisation for Economic Co-Operation and Development, *Assessing Scientific, Reading and Mathematical Literacy: A Framework for PISA 2006* (Paris: OECD, 2006); Organisation for Economic Co-Operation and Development, *PISA 2009 Assessment Framework: Key Competencies in Reading, Mathematics and Science* (Paris: OECD, 2009); Organisation for Economic Co-Operation and Development, *PISA 2009 Results.*

7. Organisation for Economic Co-Operation and Development, *PISA 2003 Data Analysis Manual: SAS Users* (Paris: OECD, 2005), http://www.pisa.oecd.org/dataoecd/53/22/35014883.pdf.

8. Jihyun Lee, Wendy S. Grigg, and Patricia L. Donahue, *The Nation's Report Card: Mathematics 2007*, NCES, 2007-494 (Washington, DC: U.S. Department of Education, Institute of Education Sciences, National Center for Education Statistics, 2007), http://nces.ed.gov/nationsreportcard/pdf/main2007/2007494.pdf; Jihyun Lee, Wendy S. Grigg, and Patricia L. Donahue, *The Nation's Report Card: Reading 2007*, NCES, 2007-496 (Washington, DC: U.S. Department of

Education, Institute of Education Sciences, National Center for Education Statistics, 2007), http://nces.ed.gov/nationsreportcard/pdf/main2007/2007496.pdf.

9. Ibid., U.S. Department of Education, National Center for Education Statistics, "Reading Performance of Students in Grades 4, 8, and 12," *The Condition of Education 2007*, NCES 2007-064, Indicator 11, (Washington, DC: U.S. Government Printing Office, 2007b), http://nces.ed.gov/programs/coe/2007/pdf/11_2007.pdf.

10. Gary W. Phillips, *Chance Favors the Prepared Mind: Mathematics and Science Indicators for Comparing States and Nations* (Washington, DC: American Institute for Research, 2007).

11. Jack O'Connell, "Standardized Testing and Reporting (STAR) Program: Summary of 2006 Results," 2006, http://www.cde.ca.gov/nr/ne/yr06/yr06rel89.asp; D. E. (Sunny) Becker and Christa C. Watters, eds., *Independent Evaluation of the California High School Exit Examination (CAHSEE): 2007 Evaluation Report* (Alexandria, VA: Human Resources Research Organization [HumRRO], 2007).

12. Jennifer Sable and Nick Gaviola, *Numbers and Rates of Public High School Dropouts: School Year 2004–05*, NCES 2008-305 (Washington, DC: U.S. Department of Education, Institute of Education Sciences, National Center for Education Statistics, 2007), http://nces.ed.gov/pubs2008/2008305.pdf.

13. California Department of Education, DataQuest search mechanism, 2008, http://data1.cde.ca.gov/dataquest/.

14. Ibid.

15. O'Connell, "Standardized Testing and Reporting (STAR) Program."

16. Education Trust–West, *Achievement in California 2006: Small Gains, Growing Gaps* (Oakland, CA: Education Trust–West, 2006).

17. California Department of Education, DataQuest search mechanism.

18. Becker and Watters, *Independent Evaluation of the California High School Exit Examination*; California Department of Education, DataQuest search mechanism.

19. Becker and Watters, *Independent Evaluation of the California High School Exit Examination*.

20. For example, National Research Council, *How People Learn: Brain, Mind, Experience, and School* (Washington, DC: Commission on Behavioral and Social Sciences and Education, 2000).

21. Gregory Austin, T. Hanson, G. Bono, and Z. Cheng, *The Achievement Gap, School Well-Being, and Learning Supports*, CHKS Factsheet #8 (Los Alamitos, CA: WestEd, 2007); Albert Bennett et al., *All Students Reaching the Top: Strategies for Closing Academic Achievement Gaps* (Naperville, IL: Learning Point Associates, 2004); David K. Cohen and Deborah Loewenberg Ball, "Making Change: Instruction and Its Improvement," *Phi Delta Kappan* 83, no. 1 (2001): 73–77; EdSource, *Similar English Learner Students, Different Results: Why Do Some Schools Do Better? A Summary of a Research Study* (Mountain View, CA: EdSource, 2007); Education Trust, *Gaining Traction, Gaining Ground: How Some High Schools Accelerate Learning for Struggling Students* (Washington, DC: Education Trust, 2005); Anne T. Henderson and Karen L. Mapp, *A New Wave of Evidence: The Impact of School, Family, and Community Connections on Student Achievement* (Austin, TX: National Center for Family & Community Connections with Schools, 2002); Patricia J. Kannapel and Stephen. K. Clements (with Diana Taylor and Terry Hibpshman), *Inside the Black Box of High-Performing High-Poverty Schools: A Report from the Prichard Committee for Academic Excellence* (Lexington, KY: Prichard Committee for Academic Excellence, 2005); U.S. Department of Education, Office of Innovation and Improvement, *Charter High Schools: Closing the Achievement Gap, Innovations in Education* (Washington, DC: U.S. Department of Education, 2006); Trish Williams, Michael Kirst, and Edward Haertel, *Similar Students, Different Results: Why Do Some Schools Do Better? A Large-Scale Survey of California Elementary Schools Serving Low-Income Students* (Mountain View, CA: EdSource, 2005).

22. Eva L. Baker, "From Usable to Useful Assessment Knowledge: A Design Problem" (paper presented at the Keynote Session, "Usable Assessment Knowledge: A Design Problem," International Congress for School Effectiveness and Improvement, Sydney, Australia, January 2003); Eva L. Baker, "From Usable to Useful Assessment Knowledge and Evaluation," *Estudios Sobre Educación*

(special issue) 16 (2009, June): 37–54; Denise Huang et al., *Exploring the Intellectual, Social and Organizational Capitals at LA's BEST*, CSE Technical Report 714 (Los Angeles: University of California, National Center for Research on Evaluation, Standards, and Student Testing, 2007).

23. James W. Popham, *Building Tests to Support Instruction and Accountability: A Guide for Policymakers* (Washington, DC: National Education Association, 2001), http://www.nea.org/accountability/buildingtests.html.

24. *The Inquirer*, "Fixing No Child Left Behind," *The Inquirer Digital*, March 16, 2011, http://www.philly.com/philly/blogs/inq_ed_board/Fixing-No-Child-Left-Behind.html.

25. Joan L. Herman, Ellen Osmundson, and David Silver, *Capturing Quality in Formative Assessment Practice: Measurement Challenges*, CRESST Report 770 (Los Angeles: University of California, National Center for Research on Evaluation, Standards, and Student Testing, 2010).

26. Eva L. Baker, "Empirically Determining the Instructional Sensitivity of an Accountability Test" (paper presented at the annual meeting of the American Educational Research Association, New York, March 2008); Eva L. Baker, "Consideraciones de validez prioritaria para la evaluación formative y de rendición de cuentas" ("Priority Validity Considerations for Formative and Accountability Assessment"), *Revista de Educación* 348 (2009b, Enero-Abril): 91–109; Robert L. Linn, Eva L. Baker, and Stephen B. Dunbar, "Complex, Performance-Based Assessment: Expectations and Validation Criteria," *Educational Researcher* 20, no. 8 (1991): 15–21 (ERIC Document Reproduction Service No. EJ 436 999).

27. Terry P. Vendlinski et al., *Developing High-Quality Assessments That Align with Instructional Video Games*, CRESST Report 774 (Los Angeles: University of California, National Center for Research on Evaluation, Standards, and Student Testing, 2010).

28. Jon Wergin, "Higher Education: Waking Up to the Importance of Accreditation," *Change* 37 (2005): 30–33; Western Association for Schools and Colleges (WASC), *Handbook of Accreditation* (Alameda, CA: WASC, 2001).

29. Eva L. Baker, "Model-Based Assessments to Support Learning and Accountability: The Evolution of CRESST's Research on Multiple-Purpose Measures," *Educational Assessment* (special issue) 12, nos. 3&4 (2007): 179–194; Baker, "Empirically Determining the Instructional Sensitivity of an Accountability Test"; Julia Phelan, David Niemi, Kilchan Choi, and Terry Vendlinski, "Some Aspects of the Technical Quality of Formative Assessments in Middle School Mathematics" (paper presented at the annual meeting of the American Educational Research Association, New York, March 2008).

Chapter 5

1. Gloria Ladson-Billings, "2006 Presidential Address: From the Achievement Gap to the Education Debt: Understanding Achievement in U.S. Schools," *Educational Researcher 35*, no. 7 (2006): 3.

2. Committee on Scientific Principles for Education Research, Richard J. Shavelson, and Lisa Towne, eds. *Scientific Research in Education.* (Washington, DC: National Academy Press, 2002), 2.

3. Kathryn M. Anderson-Levitt, "Reading Lessons in Guinea, France, and the United States: Local Meanings or Global Culture?" *Comparative Education Review* 48 (2004): 229–252.

4. Barry J. Fraser et al. "Syntheses of Educational Productivity Research," *International Journal of Educational Research* 11, no. 2 (1987): 145–252; Jaap Scheerens and Roel Bosker, *The Foundations of Educational Effectiveness* (Oxford, UK: Pergamon, 1997); Tina Seidel and Richard J. Shavelson, "Teaching Effectiveness Research in the Past Decade: The Role of Theory and Research Design in Disentangling Meta-analysis Results," *Review of Educational Research* 77, no. 4 (2007): 454–499.

5. Y. Lee, "Koreans in Japan and the United States," in *Minority Status and Schooling: A Comparative Study of Immigrant and Involuntary Minorities*, eds. Margaret A. Gibson and John U. Ogbu (New York: Garland Publishing, 1991), 131–167.

6. Frederick Erickson, "Transformation and School Success: The Politics and Culture of Educational Achievement," *Anthropology & Education Quarterly* 18, no. 4 (1987): 335–356; R. P. McDermott, "Social Relations as Contexts for Learning in School," *Harvard Educational Review* 47, no. 2 (1977): 199–213.

7. Seidel and Shavelson, "Teaching Effectiveness Research in the Past Decade."

8. Thomas L. Good, "Teacher Expectations and Student Perception," *Educational Leadership* 38 (February 1981): 415–442.

9. Seidel and Shavelson, "Teaching Effectiveness Research in the Past Decade."

10. Lee S. Shulman, "Knowledge and Teaching: Foundations of the New Reform," *Harvard Educational Review* 57: 1–22.

11. Karen Hammerness et al. "How Teachers Learn and Develop," in *Preparing Teachers for a Changing World: What Teachers Should Learn and Be Able to Do*, eds. L. Darling-Hammond and J. Bransford (San Francisco: Jossey-Bass, 2005), 358–389.

12. Seidel and Shavelson, "Teaching Effectiveness Research in the Past Decade," 476.

13. Pauline Gibbons, "Mediating Language Learning: Teacher Interactions with ESL Students in a Content-Based Classroom," *TESOL Quarterly* 37 (2003): 247–274.

14. Lisa Delpit, *Other People's Children: Cultural Conflict in the Classroom* (New York: New Press, 1995).

15. E. S. Clemens, "From Society to School and Back Again: Questions About Learning in and for a World of Complex Organizations," in *Issues in Education Research: Problems and Possibilities*, eds. Ellen Condliffe Lagemann and Lee S. Shulman (San Francisco: Jossey-Bass/Clemens, 1999), 116.

16. Edmund T. Hamann, Victor Zúñiga, and Juan Sánchez García, "Pensando en Cynthia y su hermana: Educational Implications of U.S./Mexico Transnationalism for Children," *Journal of Latinos and Education* 5, no. 4 (2006): 253–274.

17. Margaret A. Gibson, *Accommodation Without Assimilation: Sikh Immigrants in an American High School* (Ithaca, NY: Cornell University Press, 1988).

18. Kathleen Cotton, *Effective schooling practices: A research synthesis, 1995 Update* (Portland, OR: Northwest Regional Educational Laboratory, 1995).

19. Jana J. Echevarria, MaryEllen J. Vogt, and Deborah J. Short, *Making Content Comprehensible for English Learners: The SIOP Model*, 3rd ed. (Boston: Allyn & Bacon, 2008).

20. Robert J. Marzano, Debra J. Pickering, and Jane E. Pollock, *Classroom Instruction That Works: Research-Based Strategies for Increasing Student Achievement* (Alexandria, VA: Association for Supervision and Curriculum Development, 2001).

21. Center for Research on Education, Diversity and Excellence, *The CREDE Five Standards for Effective Pedagogy and Learning* (Berkeley: CREDE, Graduate School of Education, UC Berkeley, retrieved January 15, 2011), http://crede.berkeley.edu/research/crede/standards.html; Roland G. Tharp, "Effective Teaching: How the Standards Come to Be," *Effective Teaching* 1 (2008), http://crede.berkeley.edu/research/crede/tharp_development.html.

22. James H. Mosenthal et al., *Elementary Schools Where Students Succeed at Reading* (Providence, RI: LAB at Brown University, 2001), 30.

23. John T. Guthrie, "Contexts for Engagement and Motivation in Reading," *Reading Online* 4, no. 8 (March 2001), http://www.readingonline.org/articles/handbook/guthrie/index.html; Linda Harklau, "From the 'Good Kids' to the 'Worst': Representations of English Language Learners Across Educational Settings," *TESOL Quarterly* 34, no. 1 (2000): 35–67; Robert T. Jiménez, "Strategic Reading for Language-Related Disabilities: The Case of a Bilingual Latina Student," in *The Best for Our Children: Critical Perspectives on Literacy for Latino Students*, eds. M. de la Luz Reyes and J. J. Halcón (New York: Teachers College Press, 2001), 153–167; Julie Meltzer and Edmund T. Hamann, *Meeting the Literacy Development Needs of Adolescent English Language Learners Through Content Area Learning, Part One: Focus on Motivation and Engagement* (Providence, RI: Education Alliance at Brown University, 2004); Julie Meltzer and Edmund T. Hamann, *Meeting the Needs of Adolescent English Language Learners for Literacy Development and Content*

Area Learning, Part Two: Focus on Classroom Teaching and Learning Strategies (Providence, RI: Education Alliance at Brown University, 2005); Michael W. Smith and Jeffrey D. Wilhelm, *Reading Don't Fix No Chevys: Literacy in the Lives of Young Men* (Portsmouth, NH: Heinemann, 2002); Jeffrey D. Wilhelm, *You Gotta BE the Book*, 2nd ed. (New York: Teachers College Press, 2008).

24. For example: Arnetha F. Ball, "Evaluating the Writing of Culturally and Linguistically Diverse Students: The Case of the African American Vernacular English Speaker," in *Evaluating Writing: The Role of Teachers' Knowledge About Text, Learning, and Culture*, eds. C. R. Cooper and L. Odell (Urbana, IL: National Council of Teachers of English Press, 1998), 225–248; Arnetha F. Ball and M. Farr, "Language Varieties, Culture, and Teaching the English Language Arts," in *Handbook of Research on Teaching the English Language Arts*, eds. J. Flood, D. Lapp, J. Squire, and J. Jenson (Mahwah, NJ: Lawrence Erlbaum, 2003), 435–445; Carol D. Lee, "Literacy in the Academic Disciplines," *Voices in Urban Education* 3 (Winter/Spring 2004): 14–25; Meltzer and Hamann, *Meeting the Literacy Development Needs of Adolescent English Language Learners Through Content Area Learning, Part One*.

25. Nell K. Duke and P. David Pearson, "Effective practices for developing reading comprehension," in *What Research Has to Say About Reading Instruction*, 3rd Edition, eds. Alan E. Farstrup and S. Jay Samuels (Newark, DE: International Reading Association, Inc., 2002), 205–242; National Reading Panel, *A Report of the National Reading Panel: Teaching Children to Read* (Washington, DC: National Institutes of Child Health and Development, 2000), http://www.nichd.nih.gov/publications/nrp/findings.htm; Michael Pressley, "Comprehension Instruction: What Makes Sense Now, What Might Make Sense Soon," *Reading Online* 5, no. 2 (September 2001), http://www.readingonline.org/articles/art_index.asp?HREF=/articles/handbook/pressley/index.html.

26. Anderson-Levitt, "Reading Lessons in Guinea, France, and the United States."

27. B. Zolkower and S. Shreyar, "A Teacher's Mediation of a Thinking-Aloud Discussion in a 6th Grade Mathematics Classroom," *Educational Studies in Mathematics* 65 (2007): 179.

28. Gibbons, "Mediating Language Learning."

29. Christine Chin, "Teacher Questioning in Science Classrooms: Approaches That Stimulate Productive Thinking," *Journal of Research in Science Teaching* 44 (2007): 815–843; Robyn M. Gillies, "The Effects of Communication Training on Teachers' and Students' Verbal Behaviours During Cooperative Learning," *International Journal of Educational Research* 41 (2004): 257–279; Michael B. W. Wolfe and Susan R. Goldman, "Relations Between Adolescents' Text Processing and Reasoning," *Cognition and Instruction* 23 (2005): 467–502.

30. For example: Kris Anstrom, *Academic Achievement for Secondary Language Minority Students: Standards, Measures and Promising Practices* (Washington, DC: National Clearinghouse for Bilingual Education, 1997), http://www.ncela.gwu.edu/pubs/reports/acadach.htm; Gibbons, "Mediating Language Learning"; Bernard Mohan and Gulbahar Huxur Beckett, "A Functional Approach to Research on Content-Based Language Learning: Recasts in Casual Explanations," *Modern Language Journal* 87 (2003): 421–432; Bernard Mohan and Tammy Slater, "A Functional Perspective on the Critical 'Theory/Practice' Relation in Teaching Language and Science," *Linguistics and Education: An International Research Journal* 16 (2005): 151–172; Cinthia Salinas, Maria E. Franquiz, and Steve Guberman, "Introducing Historical Thinking to Second Language Learners: Exploring What Students Know and What They Want to Know," *Social Studies* 97 (2006): 203–207; Mary J. Schleppegrell, "The Linguistic Challenges of Mathematics Teaching and Learning: A Research Review," *Reading & Writing Quarterly* 23 (2007): 139–159; Mary J. Schleppegrell, "At Last: The Meaning in Grammar," *Research in the Teaching of English* 42 (2007): 121–128; Mary J. Schleppegrell, Mariana Achugar, and Teresa Orteiza, "The Grammar of History: Enhancing Content-Based Instruction Through a Functional Focus on Language," *TESOL Quarterly* 38 (2004): 67–94; Mary J. Schleppegrell and Luciana C. de Oliveira, "An Integrated Language and Content Approach for History Teachers," *Journal of English for Academic Purposes* 5 (2006): 254–268.

31. McDermott, "Social Relations as Contexts for Learning in School."

32. Meltzer and Hamann, *Meeting the Literacy Development Needs of Adolescent English Language Learners Through Content Area Learning, Part One.*

33. For example: Judith A. Langer, *Beating the Odds: Teaching Middle and High School Students to Read and Write Well*, Research Report 12014 (Albany, NY: National Research Center on English Learning and Achievement, State University of New York at Albany, 1999); Theodore R. Sizer, *Horace's Compromise* (Boston: Houghton Mifflin, 1984); Jeffrey D. Wilhelm, Tanya N. Baker, and Julie Dube Hackett, *Strategic Reading: Guiding Students to Lifelong Literacy 6–12* (Portsmouth, NH: Boynton/Cook Heinemann, 2001).

34. For example: Gina Biancarosa and Catherine Snow, *Reading Next: A Vision for Action and Research in Middle and High School Literacy* (New York: Carnegie Corporation of New York and Alliance for Excellent Education, 2004); John T. Guthrie and Nicole M. Humenick, "Motivating Students to Read: Evidence for Classroom Practices That Increase Reading Motivation and Achievement," in *The Voices of Evidence in Reading Research*, eds. P. McCardle and V. Chhabra (Baltimore, MD: Brookes Publishing, 2004), 213–234; Linda Kucan and Isabel L. Beck, "Thinking Aloud and Reading Comprehension Research: Inquiry, Instruction, and Social Interaction," *Review of Educational Research* 67, no. 3 (1997): 271–299; Langer, *Beating the Odds*; Roland G. Tharp, "Proofs and Evidence: Effectiveness of the Five Standards for Effective Pedagogy," *Effective Teaching 2* (January 1999), http://www.crede.ucsc.edu/Standards/Effectiveness/effectiveness.html.

35. For example: Ray Reutzel, "The Importance of Reading Trade Books," Scholastic Web site, retrieved September 28, 2003, from http://teacher.scholastic.com/products/paperbacks/pdfs/ImportofReadingTradeBks.pdf; Hersh C. Waxman and Kip Tellez, "Effective Reaching Practices for English Language Learners" (Philadelphia: Laboratory for Student Success, the Mid-Atlantic Regional Educational Laboratory, 2002), http://www.temple.edu/LSS/pdf/spotlights/700/spot705.pdf.

36. M. E. Curtis, "Adolescent Reading: A Synthesis of Research (paper presented at the U.S. Department of Education and the National Institute of Child Health and Human Development Conference on Adolescent Literacy, Baltimore, MD, May 2002), 10, http://216.26.160.105/conf/nichd/synthesis.asp.

37. Robert Marzano et al., *What Works in Classroom Instruction* (Aurora, CO: Mid-Continent Research for Education and Learning [MCREL], 2000); Marzano, Pickering, & Pollock (2001).

38. Reading Recovery Council of North America, "What Works Clearinghouse (WWC) Documents Reading Recovery's Scientific Research Base," http://www.readingrecovery.org/research/what_works/index.asp; Yaoying Xu, Jeffrey Gelfer, and Peggy Perkins, "Using Peer Tutoring to Increase Social Interactions in Early Schooling," *TESOL Quarterly* 39, no. 1 (2005), 83–106.

39. Xu, Gelfer, and Perkins, "Using Peer Tutoring," 83–106.

40. Ladson-Billings, "2006 Presidential Address."

41. Eugene E. Garcia and Tom Stritikus, "Proposition 227 in California: Issues for the Preparation of Quality Teachers for Linguistically and Culturally Diverse Students," in *Preparing Quality Educators for English Language Learners: Research, Policies, and Practices*, eds. K. Tellez and H. C. Waxman (Mahwah, NJ: Lawrence Erlbaum, 2006), 99–120; Tamara Lucas, Rosemary Henze, and Ruben Donato, "Promoting the Success of Latino Language-Minority Students: An Exploratory Study of Six High Schools," *Harvard Educational Review* 60, no. 3 (1990): 315–340; Angela Valenzuela, *Subtractive Schooling: U.S.-Mexican Youth and the Politics of Caring* (Albany: State University of New York Press, 1999).

42. Leonard Valverde, *Improving Schools for Latinos: Creating Better Learning Environments* (Lanham, MD: Rowman & Littlefield Education, 2006).

43. Gloria Ladson-Billings, *The Dreamkeepers: Successful Teachers of African American Children* (San Francisco: Jossey-Bass, 1994).

44. Donald McCrary, "Represent, Representin', Representation: The Efficacy of Hybrid Text in the Writing Classroom," *Journal of Basic Writing* 24 (2005): 72–91.

45. J. Banks et al., "Teaching Diverse Learners," in *Preparing Teachers for a Changing World*, eds. L. Darling-Hammond and J. Bransford (San Francisco: Jossey-Bass, 2005), 232–274.

46. Barry A. Osborne, "Practice into Theory into Practice: Culturally Relevant Pedagogy for Students We Have Marginalized and Normalized," *Anthropology & Education Quarterly* 27, no. 3 (1996): 285–314.

47. Erickson, "Transformation and School Success."

48. Courtney Cazden and H. Mehan, "Principles from Sociology and Anthropology," in *Knowledge Base for the Beginning Teacher*, ed. M. C. Reynolds (New York: Pergamon Press, 1989), 47–57.

49. Erickson, "Transformation and School Success"; McDermott, "Social Relations as Contexts for Learning in School."

50. Mica Pollock, *Colormute: Race Talk Dilemmas in an American School* (Princeton, NJ: Princeton University Press, 2004).

51. Eric A. Hanushek, John F. Kain, Daniel O'Brien, and Steven Rivkin, *The Market for Teacher Quality* (Cambridge, MA: National Bureau of Economic Research, 2005).

52. UC/Accord and UCLA IDEA, *The 2007 California Educational Opportunity Report: The Racial Opportunity Gap* (Los Angeles: UCLA Institute for Democracy, Education, and Access; University of California All Campus Consortium on Research for Diversity, 2007), http://www.idea.gseis.ucla.edu/publications/eor07/state/pdf/StateEOR2007.pdf; M. Wechsler et al., *The Status of the Teaching Profession 2007* (Santa Cruz, CA: Center for the Future of Teaching and Learning, 2007).

53. Brian M. Stecher, Daniel F. McCaffrey, and Delia Bugliari, "The Relationship Between CSR Exposure and Achievement at the School Level," in *What We Have Learned About Class Size Reduction in California, Capstone Report*, Appendix B, eds. G. W. Bohrnstedt and B. Stecher, (Palo Alto, CA: American Institutes for Research, CSR Research Consortium, 2002), B-2, www.classize.org/techreport/index-02.htm.

54. Lawrence P. Gallagher, "Class Size Reduction and Teacher Migration, 1995–2000," in *What We Have Learned About Class Size Reduction in California, Capstone Report*, Appendix C, eds. G. W. Bohrnstedt and B. Stecher (Palo Alto, CA: American Institutes for Research, CSR Research Consortium, 2002), C-12, www.classize.org/techreport/index-02.htm.

55. For example: Jerome V. D'Agostino, "Instructional and School Effects on Students' Longitudinal Reading and Mathematics Achievements," *School Effectiveness and School Improvement* 11 (2000): 197–235; Adam Gamoran, Andrew C. Porter, John Smithson, and Paula A. White, "Upgrading High School Mathematics Instruction: Improving Learning Opportunities for Low-Achieving, Low-Income Youth," *Educational Evaluation and Policy Analysis* 19 (1997): 325–338; Patricia Gándara, "Introduction," in *The Dimensions of Time and the Challenge of School Reform*, ed. P. Gándara (Albany: State University of New York Press, 1999), 1–10; L. Kyriakides, R. J. Campbell, and A. Gagatsis, "The Significance of the Classroom Effect in Primary Schools: An Application of Creemers' Comprehensive Model of Educational Effectiveness," *School Effectiveness and School Improvement* 11 (2000): 501–529; Hans Luyten and Rob de Jong, "Parallel Classes: Differences and Similarities: Teaching Effects and School Effects in Secondary Schools," *School Effectiveness and School Improvement* 9 (1998): 437–473.

56. Jeannie Oakes, *Keeping Track: How Schools Structure Inequality* (New Haven, CT: Yale University Press, 1985).

57. Thomas L. Good, "Teacher Expectations and Student Perception," *Educational Leadership* 38 (February 1981): 415–442.

58. McDermott, "Social Relations as Contexts for Learning in School."

59. Ladson-Billings, "2006 Presidential Address."

60. Sizer, *Horace's Compromise*.

61. Edmund Hamann, *The Educational Welcome of Latinos in the New South* (Westport, CT: Praeger, 2003).

62. Seidel and Shavelson, "Teaching Effectiveness Research in the Past Decade"; John Dewey, *Experience and Education* (New York: Touchstone, 1938).

63. Marilyn Cochran-Smith and Susan Lytle, eds., *Inquiry as Stance: Practitioner Research for the Next Generation* (New York: Teachers College Press, 2009).

64. Osborne, "Practice into Theory into Practice," 304.

65. Jamal Abedi, "The No Child Left Behind Act and English Language Learners: Assessment and Accountability Issues," *Educational Researcher* 33, no. 1 (2004): 4–14; Jamal Abedi, "Issues and Consequences for English Language Learners," in *Uses and Misuses of Data for Educational Accountability and Improvement: The 104th Yearbook of the National Society for the Study of Education, Part 2*, eds. J. L. Herman and E. H. Haertel (Malden, MA: Blackwell, 2005), 175–198.

66. Jonathan Cohen, "Social, Emotional, Ethical, and Academic Education: Creating a Climate for Learning Participation in a Democracy, and Well-being," *Harvard Educational Review* 76, no. 2 (2006).

Chapter 6

1. Paul E. Barton, "Why Does the Gap Persist?" *Educational Leadership* 62, no. 3 (2004): 13.

2. Barton, "Why Does the Gap Persist?," 13.

3. Paul Tough, "What It Takes to Make a Student," *New York Times*, November 26, 2006.

4. Governor's Committee on Education Excellence, *Report of the Governor's Committee on Education Excellence* (Sacramento, CA, 2007), 8.

5. David K. Cohen and Susan L. Moffitt, "The Influence of Practice on Policy," in *Shaping Education Policy: Power and Process*, chap. 3, ed. D. E. Mitchell, R. L. Crowson, and D. Shipps (New York: Routledge Taylor & Francis Group, 2011).

6. David K. Cohen, Stephen W. Raudenbush, and Deborah Loewenberg Ball, "Resources, Instruction, and Research," *Educational Evaluation and Policy Analysis* 25 (2003): 119–142.

7. Anthony S. Bryk and Barbara L. Schneider, *Trust in Schools: A Core Resource for Improvement*, Rose Series in Sociology (New York: Russell Sage Foundation, 2002).

8. Lorraine M. McDonnell and Richard F. Elmore, "Getting the Job Done: Alternative Policy Instruments," *Educational Evaluation and Policy Analysis* 9, no. 2 (1987): 134 (emphasis added).

9. Lorraine M. McDonnell, *Politics, Persuasion, and Educational Testing* (Cambridge, MA: Harvard University Press, 2004), 23 (emphasis added).

10. Jane Hannaway and Nicole Woodroffe, "Policy Instruments in Education," *Review of Research in Education* 27, no. 1 (2003): 1–24.

11. Oliver E. Williamson, *The Economic Institutions of Capitalism* (New York: Free Press, 1985); Ernest R. House, *Schools for Sale: Why Free Market Policies Won't Improve America's Schools, and What Will*, Critical Issues in Educational Leadership Series (New York: Teachers College Press, 1998).

12. Tom Loveless, *The Great Curriculum Debate: How Should We Teach Reading and Math?* (Washington, DC: Brookings Institution, 2001).

13. Judith Haymore-Sandholtz, Rodney T. Ogawa, and Samantha Paredes Scribner, "Standards Gaps: Unintended Consequences of Local Standards-Based Reform," *Teachers College Record* 106, no. 6 (2004): 1177–1202.

14. Jay P. Heubert and Robert M. Hauser, *High Stakes Testing for Tracking, Promotion, and Graduation* (Washington, DC: National Academy Press, 1999); Russell W. Rumberger, Katherine A. Larson, Robert K. Ream, and Gregory J. Palardy, *The Educational Consequences of Mobility for California Students and Schools*, Research Series (Stanford, CA: Policy Analysis for California Education, 1999).

15. Peg Tyre, "To Catch a Cheat: The Pressure Is on for Schools to Raise Test Scores," *Newsweek* 150, no. 16 (2007): 41.

16. Andy Porter, "Doing High-Stakes Assessment Right," *School Administrator* 57, no. 11 (2000): 28–31.

17. Lauren B. Resnick and Chris Zurawsky, "Standards and Tests: Keeping Them Aligned," *Research Points* 1, no. 1 (2003): 1–4.

18. Wayne Au, "High-Stakes Testing and Curricular Control: A Qualitative Metasynthesis," *Educational Researcher* 36, no. 5 (2007): 258–267.

19. Bruce Fuller, Joseph Wright, Kathryn Gesicki, and Erin Kang, "Gauging Growth: How to Judge No Child Left Behind?" *Educational Researcher* 36, no. 5 (2007): 268–278.

20. Richard Rothstein, "Leaving 'No Child Left Behind' Behind," *American Prospect* 19, no. 1 (2008).

21. Linda Darling-Hammond et al., "Building Instructional Quality: 'Inside-Out' and 'Outside-In' Perspectives on San Diego's School Reform: A Research Report" (Seattle: Center for the Study of Teaching and Policy, 2003).

22. Donald E. Mulcahy, "The Continuing Quest for Equal Schools: An Essay Review," *Education Review* 9, no. 2 (2006): 10.

23. Governor's Committee on Education Excellence, Report of the Governor's Committee on Education Excellence.

24. Adam Gamoran and Daniel A. Long, "School Effects in Comparative Perspective: New Evidence from a Threshold Model" (paper presented at the annual meeting of the American Sociological Association, Montreal, Quebec, Canada, August 2006).

25. Jeannie Oakes and Amy S. Wells, "Detracking for High Student Achievement," *Educational Leadership* 55, no. 6 (1998): 38–41; Reba Neukom Page, *Lower-Track Classrooms: A Curricular and Cultural Perspective* (New York: Teachers College Press, 1991).

26. Linda M. McNeil, *Contradictions of School Reform: Educational Costs of Standardized Testing* (New York: Routledge, 2000).

27. Robert B. Pittman and Perri Haughwout, "Influence of High School Size on Dropout Rate," *Educational Evaluation and Policy Analysis* 9, no. 4 (1987): 337–343.

28. Joseph E. Kahne, Susan E. Sporte, and John Q. Easton, "Creating Small Schools in Chicago: An Early Look at Implementation and Impact," *Improving Schools* 8, no. 1 (2005): 7–22; Patricia A. Wasley, "Small Classes, Small Schools: The Time Is Now," *Educational Leadership* 59, no. 5 (2002): 6–10.

29. Frederick M. Hess and Martin R. West, *A Better Bargain: Overhauling Teacher Collective Bargaining for the 21st Century* (Cambridge, MA: Harvard University Program on Education Policy and Governance, 2006).

30. Lorraine M. McDonnell and Paul T. Hill, *Newcomers in American Schools: Meeting the Educational Needs of Immigrant Youth* (Santa Monica, CA: RAND Corporation, 1993).

31. Robert K. Ream and Ricardo Stanton-Salazar, "The Mobility/Social Capital Dynamic: Understanding Mexican American Families and Students," in *Narrowing the Achievement Gap: Strategies for Educating Latino, Black, and Asian Students*, eds. S. Paik and H. Walberg (New York: Springer, 2007), 67-89.

32. Richard M. Ingersoll, "Teacher Turnover and Teacher Shortages: An Organizational Analysis," *American Educational Research Journal* 38, no. 3 (2001): 499–534.

33. Rumberger et al., *Educational Consequences of Mobility*; Robert K. Ream, *Uprooting Children: Mobility, Social Capital, and Mexican American Underachievement* (New York: LFB Scholarly Publishing, 2005).

34. Rumberger et al., *Educational Consequences of Mobility*.

35. Ed Collum and Douglas E. Mitchell, "Home Schooling as a Social Movement: Identifying the Determinants of Home Schoolers' Perceptions," *Sociological Spectrum* 25 (2005): 273–305.

36. Janet M. Currie, "Health Disparities and Gaps in School Readiness," *Future of Children* 15, no. 1 (2005): 117–138.

37. Trish Williams, Kenji Hakuta, and Edward Haertel, *Similar English Learner Students, Different Results: Why Do Some Schools Do Better? A Follow-up Analysis, Based on a Large-Scale Survey of California Elementary Schools Serving Low-Income and EL Students* (Mountain View, CA: EdSource, 2007), 13.

38. Donald Boyd, Pamela Grossman, Hamilton Lankford, Susanna Loeb, and James Wyckoff, "How Changes in Entry Requirements Alter the Teacher Workforce and Affect Student Achievement,"

Education Finance and Policy 1, no. 2 (2006): 176–216; Thomas J. Kane, Jonah E. Rockoff, and Douglas O. Staiger, *What Does Certification Tell Us About Teacher Effectiveness? Evidence from New York City* (New York: Columbia University, 2006); Susanna Loeb and Luke C. Miller, *A Review of State Teacher Policies: What Are They, What Are Their Effects, and What Are Their Implications for School Finance?* (Stanford, CA: Institute for Research on Education Policy & Practice, Stanford University, 2006).

39. Dan D. Goldhaber and Dominic J. Brewer, "Does Teacher Certification Matter? High School Teacher Certification Status and Student Achievement," *Educational Evaluation and Policy Analysis* 22, no. 2 (2000): 129–145.

40. Linda Darling-Hammond, *Professional Development Schools: Schools for Developing a Profession* (New York: Teachers College Press, 2005).

41. Steven G. Rivkin, Eric A. Hanushek, and John F. Kain, "Teachers, Schools and Academic Achievement," *Econometrica* 73 (2005): 417–458.

42. Ibid.

43. Susan Moore Johnson, *Finders and Keepers: Helping New Teachers Survive and Thrive in Our Schools* (San Francisco: Jossey-Bass, 2004).

44. Ross E. Mitchell, "Why Are Low-Performing Students Concentrated in Multi-track Year-Round Schools," in *An Expert Witness Paper* (Los Angeles, CA: Mexican American Legal Defense and Education Fund, 2002).

45. Susan Rotermund, "Alternative Education Enrollment and Dropouts in California High Schools," in *California Dropout Research Project*, Research Report 3 (Santa Barbara, CA: California Linguistic Minority Research Institute, 2007): 1.

46. Gamoran and Long, 2006: 8.

47. Rumberger, R.W. and J. Connell, "Strengthening school district capacity as a strategy to raise student achievement in California," in Getting from facts to policy: An education policy convening (Sacramento, CA: EdSource, 2007).

48. Tyack, D.B. The one best system : a history of American urban education. (Cambridge, Mass.: Harvard University Press, 1974).

49. Callahan, R.E. Education and the cult of efficiency; a study of the social forces that have shaped the administration of the public schools. (Chicago: University of Chicago Press, 1962).

50. The Elementary and Secondary Education Act of 1965 (20 USC 2701 et seq.)

51. Gamoran and Long, "School Effects in Comparative Perspective," 16–17.

52. Beth C. Rubin, "Tracking and Detracking: Debates, Evidence, and Best Practices for a Heterogeneous World," *Theory into Practice* 45, no. 1 (2006): 4–14.

53. Doris Alvarez and Hugh Mehan, "Whole-School Detracking: A Strategy for Equity and Excellence," *Theory into Practice* 45, no. 1 (2006): 82–89.

54. George Ansalone and Frank Biafora, "Elementary School Teachers' Perceptions and Attitudes to the Educational Structure of Tracking," *Education* 125, no. 2 (2004): 249.

55. Eric A. Hanushek, John F. Kain, Jacob M. Markman, and Stephen G. Rivkin, "Does Peer Ability Affect Student Achievement," NBER Working Paper 28502 (Cambridge, MA: National Bureau of Economic Research, 2001).

56. Russell W. Rumberger and Gregory J. Palardy, "Does Segregation Still Matter? The Impact of Student Composition on Academic Achievement in High School," *Teachers College Record* 107, no. 9 (2005): 1999–2045.

57. Gamoran and Long, "School Effects in Comparative Perspective," 19 (citing Orfield 2001).

58. Ronald G. Ehrenberg, Dominic J. Brewer, Adam Gamoran, and J. Douglas Willms, "Class Size and Student Achievement," *Psychological Science in the Public Interest* 2, no. 1 (2001): 1–30.

59. Spyros Konstantopoulos, "Do Small Classes Reduce the Achievement Gap between Low and High Achievers? Evidence from Project STAR," *The Elementary School Journal* 108, no. 4 (2008): 275–291.

60. Valeria E. Lee, *Restructuring High Schools for Equity and Excellence: What Works* (New York: Teachers College Press, 2001), 157.

61. Anthony S. Bryk, Valeria E. Lee, and Peter B. Holland, *Catholic Schools and the Common Good* (Cambridge, MA: Harvard University Press, 1993), 299.
62. Mahna T. Schwager, Douglas E. Mitchell, Tedi K. Mitchell, and Jeffrey B. Hecht, "How School District Policy Influences Grade Level Retention in Elementary Schools," *Educational Evaluation and Policy Analysis* 14, no. 4 (1992): 421–438.
63. Rivkin, Hanushek, and Kain, "Teachers, Schools and Academic Achievement," 417–458.
64. David K. Cohen, Susan H. Fuhrman, and Fritz Mosher, *The State of Education Policy Research* (Mahwah, NJ: Lawrence Erlbaum, 2007).
65. Frederick M. Hess, *Spinning Wheels: The Politics of Urban School Reform* (Washington, DC: Brookings Institution, 1998).
66. Rumberger and Connell, "Strengthening School District Capacity."
67. Lee, *Restructuring High Schools for Equity and Excellence*, 161–162.
68. Amy Gutmann, *Democratic Education,* rev. ed. (Princeton, NJ: Princeton University Press, 1999).
69. Robert K. Ream and Gregory J. Palardy, "Re-examining Social Class Differences in the Availability and the Educational Utility of Parental Social Capital," *American Educational Research Journal* 45, no. 2 (2008): 238-273.
70. Ibid., 244.
71. Concha Delgado-Gaitan, "Involving Parents in Schools: A Process of Empowerment," *American Journal of Education* 100, no. 1 (1991): 20–46.
72. Ream and Palardy, "Re-examining Social Class Differences," 257.
73. Douglas E. Mitchell, "California Regional Occupational Centers and Programs (ROCP) 2004 Longitudinal Study, Technical Report" (Riverside, CA: University of California, School Improvement Research Group, 2004, http://www.carocp.org/2004LongitudinalStudy.pdf. Supported by the California Department of Education; Douglas E. Mitchell, "California Regional Occupational Centers and Programs (ROCP) 2006 Longitudinal Study, Technical Report" (Riverside, CA: University of California, School Improvement Research Group, 2006, http://www.carocp.org/2006LongitudinalStudy.pdf.
74. Governor's Committee on Education Excellence, Report of the Governor's Committee on Education Excellence.
75. Ream, *Uprooting Children*, 165.
76. Hugh Mehan, *Constructing School Success: The Consequences of Untracking Low-Achieving Students* (Cambridge, UK and New York: Cambridge University Press, 1996); Larry Guthrie and Grace Guthrie, *Longitudinal Research on AVID 1999–2000: Final Report* (Burlingame, CA: Center for Research Evaluation and Training in Education, 2000).
77. Ream, *Uprooting Children*.
78. Patricia Gandara, Katherina Larson, Hugh Mehan, and Russell Rumberger, "Capturing Latino Students in the Academic Pipeline," *CLPP Policy Report* 1, no. 1 (1998).
79. Justin King, *Closing the Achievement Gap Through Expanded Access to Quality Early Education in Grades PK–3*, Issue Brief 3 (Washington, DC: New America Foundation, Early Education Initiative, 2006).
80. National Commission on Excellence in Education, *A Nation at Risk: The Imperative for Educational Reform* (Washington, DC: U.S. Department of Education, 1983).
81. Gamoran and Long, "School Effects in Comparative Perspective," 15.
82. Governor's Committee on Education Excellence, *Report of the Governor's Committee on Education Excellence*.
83. Gamoran and Long, "School Effects in Comparative Perspective," 19.
84. Tough, "What It Takes to Make a Student."
85. James S. Coleman, *Equality of Educational Opportunity (COLEMAN) Study (EEOS)* (Washington, D.C.: United States Department of Health, Education, and Welfare, 1966).
86. William G. Bowen and Derek Curtis Bok, *The Shape of the River: Long-Term Consequences of Considering Race in College and University Admissions* (Princeton, NJ: Princeton University Press, 1998).

87. King, *Closing the Achievement Gap*.
88. Rothstein, 2004.
89. Susanna Loeb, Jason Grissom, and Katharine Strunk, "District Dollars: Painting a Picture of Revenues and Expenditures in California's School Districts" (paper presented at the Governor's Committee on Education Excellence, Stanford, CA, 2006).

Chapter 7

1. Christopher Jencks and Meredith Phillips, eds., *The Black-White Test Score Gap* (Washington, DC: Brookings Institution, 1998); Jaekyung Lee, "Racial and Ethnic Achievement Gap Trends: Reversing the Progress Toward Equity?" *Educational Researcher* 31 (2002): 3–12; Richard Rothstein, *Class and Schools: Using Social, Economic, and Educational Reform to Close the Black-White Achievement Gap* (Washington, DC: Economic Policy Institute, 2004); Stephan Thernstrom and Abigail Thernstrom, *No Excuses: Closing the Racial Gap in Learning* (New York: Simon & Schuster, 2003).
2. U.S. Department of Education, 2003, Title 1, Sec. 1001.
3. McKinsey & Company, "The Economic Impact of the Achievement Gap in America's Schools" (New York: McKinsey & Company, 2011), pp. 5-6, http://www.mckinsey.com/clientservice/Social_Sector/our_practices/Education/Knowledge_Highlights/Economic_impact.aspx.
4. Jack O'Connell, "State of Education Address," February 17, 2008, http://www.cde.ca.gov/eo/in/se/yr08stateofed.asp.
5. See California P-16 Council, *Closing the Achievement Gap*, report of Superintendent Jack O'Connell's California P-16 Council (Sacramento: California Department of Education, 2008), http://www.cde.ca.gov/eo/in/pc/.
6. Jencks and Phillips, *The Black-White Test Score Gap*; Rothstein, *Class and Schools*.
7. Jencks and Phillips, *The Black-White Test Score Gap*; McKinsey, "The Economic Impact of the Achievement Gap in America's Schools."
8. Elena Rouse and James J. Kemple, eds., *The Future of Children: America's High Schools*, vol. 19, no. 1 (Princeton and Washington, DC: Woodrow Wilson School of Public and International Affairs at Princeton University and the Brookings Institution, 2009).
9. Thomas D. Snyder and Sally A. Dillow, *Digest of Education Statistics 2010*, NCES 2011–015 (Washington, DC: National Center for Education Statistics, U.S. Department of Education, 2011), table 36, http://nces.ed.gov/pubsearch/pubsinfo.asp?pubid=2011015.
10. Ibid., table 43.
11. Data reported in this and following three paragraphs obtained from Dataquest; retrieved February 17, 2008, from http://data1.cde.ca.gov/dataquest/.
12. Susan Rotermund, *Which California Schools Have the Most Dropouts?* (Santa Barbara: California Dropout Research Project, University of California, Santa Barbara, 2008), http://lmri.ucsb.edu/dropouts/pubs.htm.
13. Data obtained from the California Postsecondary Commission; retrieved February 25, 2008, from http://www.cpec.ca.gov/OnLineData/CACGR_API.asp?Year=2006.
14. See, e.g., Grace Calisi Corbett and Tracy A. Huebner, "Rethinking High School: Preparing Students for Success in College, Career, and Life" (San Francisco: WestEd, 2008), http://www.wested.org/cs/we/view/rs/842.
15. Diane Friedlaender and Linda Darling-Hammond, *High Schools for Equity* (Stanford, CA: Stanford University, School Redesign Network, 2008), http://www.srnleads.org/resources/publications/hsfe.html.
16. For information about the study, see: http://nces.ed.gov/surveys/nels88/.
17. Anthony S. Bryk, Valerie E. Lee, and Peter B. Holland, *Catholic Schools and the Common Good* (Cambridge, MA: Harvard University Press, 1993); Valerie E. Lee and Julia B. Smith, "Effects of High School Restructuring and Size on Gains in Achievement and Engagement for Early Secondary School Students," *Sociology of Education* 68 (1995): 241–279; Valerie E. Lee and Julia B. Smith, "High School Size: Which Works Best for Whom?" *Educational Evaluation and Policy*

Analysis 19 (1997): 205–227; Russell W. Rumberger and Gregory J. Palardy, "Test Scores, Drop-out Rates, and Transfer Rates as Alternative Indicators of High School Performance," *American Educational Research Journal* 41 (2005): 3–42.

18. Barbara Schneider et al., "Estimating Causal Effects Using Experimental and Observations Designs," report from the Governing Board of the American Educational Research Association Grants Program (Washington, DC: American Educational Research Association, 2007).

19. Geoffrey D. Borman, Gina M. Hewes, Laura T. Overman, and Shelly Brown, "Comprehensive School Reform and Achievement: A Meta-analysis," *Review of Educational Research* 73 (2003): 125–230.

20. Jeremy D. Finn and Charles M. Achilles, "Tennessee's Class Size Study: Findings, Implications, Misconceptions," *Educational Evaluation and Policy Analysis* 21 (1999): 97–110.

21. Borman et al., "Comprehensive School Reform and Achievement: a Meta-analysis," 163.

22. Comprehensive School Reform Quality Center, "CSRQ Center Report on Middle and High School Comprehensive School Reform Models" (Washington, DC: American Institutes for Research, 2006).

23. Schneider et al., "Estimating Causal effects Using Experimental and Observations Designs."

24. Jacob Cohen, *Statistical Power Analysis for the Behavioral Sciences*, 2nd ed. (Hillsdale, NJ: Lawrence Erlbaum, 1988).

25. Jeremy D. Finn, Susan B. Gerber, and Jayne Boyd-Zaharias, "Small Classes in the Early Grades, Academic Achievement, and Graduating from High School," *Journal of Educational Psychology* 97 (2005): 214–223.

26. Borman et al., "Comprehensive School Reform and Achievement: A Meta-analysis."

27. Russell W. Rumberger and Gregory J. Palardy, "Test Scores, Dropout Rates, and Transfer Rates as Alternative Indicators of High School Performance," *American Educational Research Journal* 41 (2005): 3–42.

28. Russell W. Rumberger and Brenda Arellano, "Student and School Predictors of High School Graduation in California" (Santa Barbara, CA: University of California, California Dropout Research Project, 2007).

29. Eric A. Hanushek, "The Economics of Schooling: Production and Efficiency in Public Schools," *Journal of Economic Literature* 24 (1986): 1141–1177; Henry M. Levin, "Raising School Productivity: An X-Efficiency Approach," *Economics of Education Review* 16 (1997): 303–311.

30. Naftaly S. Glasman and Israel Biniaminov, "Input-Output Analyses of Schools," *Review of Educational Research* 51 (1981): 509–539; Hanushek, "The Economics of Schooling"; Charles Tedlie and David Reynolds, eds., *The International Handbook of School Effectiveness Research* (New York: Falmer Press, 2000).

31. Richard F. Elmore, "School Decentralization: Who Gains? Who Loses?" in *Decentralization and School Improvement*, eds. Jane Hannaway and Martha Carnoy (San Francisco: Jossey-Bass, 1993); Brian Rowan, Richard Correnti, and Robert J. Miller, "What Large-Scale, Survey Research Tells Us About Teacher Effects on Student Achievement: Insights from the Prospects Study of Elementary Schools," *Teachers College Record* 104 (2002): 1525–1567; H. Jerome Frieberg, ed., *School Climate: Measuring, Improving, and Sustaining Healthy Learning Environments* (New York: Falmer Press, 2007).

32. Bryk, Lee, and Holland, *Catholic Schools and the Common Good*; James S. Coleman, Thomas Hoffer, and Sally B. Kilgore, *High School Achievement: Public, Catholic, and Private Schools Compared* (New York: Basic Books, 1982).

33. David Card and Alan B. Krueger, "School Resources and Student Outcomes," *Annals of the American Academy of Political & Social Science* 559 (1998): 39–53; David N. Figlio, "Functional Form and the Estimated Effects of School Resources," *Economics of Education Review* 18 (1999): 241–252; Rob Greenwald, Larry V. Hedges, and Richard D. Laine, "The Effect of School Resources on Student Achievement," *Review of Educational Research* 66 (1996): 361–396; Hanushek, "The Economics of Schooling"; 1996a, 1997; Eric A. Hanushek, "The Economics of Schooling: Production and Efficiency in Public Schools," *Journal of Economic Literature* 24

(1986): 1141-1177; Eric A. Hanushek. "A More Complete Picture of School Resource Policies," *Review of Educational Research* 66 (1996a): 397-409; Eric A. Hanushek, "Assessing the Effects of School Resources on Student Performance: An Update," *Educational Evaluation and Policy Analysis* 19 (1997): 141-164; Charles Jacques and B. Wade Brorsen, "Relationship Between Types of School District Expenditures and Student Performance," *Applied Economics Letters* 9 (2002): 997–1002.

34. Hanushek, "The Economics of Schooling."

35. Larry V. Hedges, Richard D. Laine, and Rob Greenwald, "Does Money Matter? A Meta-analysis of Studies of the Effects of Differential School Inputs on Student Outcomes," *Educational Researcher* 23 (1994): 13.

36. Eric A. Hanushek, "Outcomes, Costs, and Incentives in Schools." Pp. 29-52 in *Improving America's schools: The role of Incentives,* edited by E. A. Hanushek and D. W. Jorgenson. Washington, D.C.: National Academy Press, 1996b.

37. Ibid., 30.

38. Hanushek, "The Economics of Schooling"; 1996a, 1997.

39. Snyder and Dillow, *Digest of Education Statistics 2010*, table 184.

40. Linda Darling–Hammond, Barnett Berry, and Amy Thoreson, "Does Teacher Certification Matter? Evaluating the Evidence," *Educational Evaluation and Policy Analysis* 23 (2001): 57–77; Rowan, Correnti, and Miller, "What Large-Scale, Survey Research Tells Us"; Andrew J. Wayne and Peter Youngs, "Teacher Characteristics and Student Achievement Gains: A Review," *Review of Educational Research* 73 (2003): 89–122; Harold Wenglinsky, "How Schools Matter: The Link Between Teacher Classroom Practices and Student Academic Performance," *Education Policy Analysis Archives* 10 (March 29, 2008), http://epaa.asu.edu/epaa/v10n12/.

41. Wayne and Youngs, "Teacher Characteristics and Student Achievement Gains," 107.

42. Rumberger and Arellano, "Student and School Predictors of High School Graduation in California."

43. Julian R. Betts, Kim S. Rueben, and Anne Danenberg, *Equal Resources, Equal Outcomes? The Distribution of School Resources and Student Achievement in California* (San Francisco: Public Policy Institute of California, 2008), table 5, http://www.ppic.org/main/allpubs.asp.

44. Ronald G. Ehrenberg, Dominic J. Brewer, Adam Gamoran, and J. Douglas Willms, "Class Size and Student Achievement," *Psychological Science in the Public Interest* 2, no. 1 (2001): 1–30; Alan B. Krueger, "Economic Considerations and Class Size," *Economic Journal* 113 (2003): F34–F63.

45. Betts et al., *Equal Resources, Equal Outcomes?*

46. Deborah Reed, *Educational Resources and Outcomes in California, by Race and Ethnicity* (San Francisco: Public Policy Institute of California, 2008), table 5, http://www.ppic.org/main/allpubs.asp.

47. Rumberger and Arellano, "Student and School Predictors of High School Graduation in California."

48. Ross E. Mitchell and Douglas E. Mitchell, "Student Segregation and Achievement Tracking in Year-Round Schools," *Teachers College Record* 107 (2005): 529–562; Douglas D. Ready, Valerie E. Lee, and Kevin G. Welner, "Educational Equity and School Structure: School Size, Overcrowding, and Schools-Within-Schools," *Teachers College Record* 106 (2004): 1989–2014.

49. Harris Cooper, Jeffrey C. Valentine, Kelly Charlton, and April Melson, "The Effects of Modified School Calendars on Student Achievement and on School and Community Attitudes," *Review of Educational Research* 73 (2003): 1–52.

50. David K. Cohen, Stephen W. Raudenbush, and Deborah Loewenberg Ball, "Resources, Instruction, and Research," *Educational Evaluation and Policy Analysis* 25 (2003): 132.

51. Fred M. Newmann, "Beyond Common Sense in Educational Restructuring," *Educational Researcher* 22 (1993): 4–13.

52. James J. Heckman, "Policies to Foster Human Capital," *Research in Economics* 54 (2000): 3–56.

53. Milbrey Wallin McLaughlin, "Learning from Experience: Lessons from Policy Implementation," *Educational Evaluation and Policy Analysis* 9 (1987): 172.

54. Jacqueline Ancess, *Beating the Odds: High Schools as Communities of Commitment* (New York: Teachers College Press, 2003); Carol A. Barnes, *Standards Reform in High-Poverty Schools* (New York: Teachers College Press, 2002); Anthony S. Bryk and Barbara Schneider, *Trust in Schools: A Core Resource for Improvement* (New York: Russell Sage Foundation, 2002); Richard F. Elmore, *School Reform from the Inside Out* (Cambridge, MA: Harvard Education Press, 2004); James P. Spillane, *Standards Deviation: How Schools Misunderstand Education Policy* (Cambridge, MA: Harvard University Press, 2004).

55. Bryk and Schneider, *Trust in Schools*, 144.

56. Wayne K. Hoy, C. John Tarter, and Anita Woolfolk Hoy, "Academic Optimism of Schools: A Force for Student Achievement," *American Educational Research Journal* 43 (2006): 425–446.

57. Anthony S. Bryk and Mary Erina Driscoll, *The High School as Community: Contextual Influences and Consequences for Students and Teachers* (Madison, WI: National Center on Effective Secondary Schools, 1988); Newmann, "Beyond Common Sense in Educational Restructuring"; James P. Spillane, "School Districts Matter: Local Educational Authorities and State Instructional Policy," *Educational Policy* 10 (1996): 63–87.

58. Adam Gamoran, "Social Factors in Education," in *Encyclopedia of Educational Research,* ed. Marvin C. Alkin (New York: Macmillan, 1992): 1222–1229.

59. Anthony S. Bryk and Yeow Meng Thum, "The Effects of High School Organization on Dropping Out: An Exploratory Investigation," *American Educational Research Journal* 26 (1989): 353–383; Ralph B. McNeal, "High School Dropouts: A Closer Examination of School Effects," *Social Science Quarterly* 78 (1997): 209–222; Russell W. Rumberger, "Dropping Out of Middle School: A Multilevel Analysis of Students and Schools," *American Educational Research Journal* 32 (1995): 583–625.

60. James S. Coleman et al., *Equality of Educational Opportunity* (Washington, DC: U.S. Government Printing Office, 1966); Valerie E. Lee and Anthony S. Bryk, "A Multilevel Model of the Social Distribution of High School Achievement," *Sociology of Education* 62 (1989): 172–192; Valerie E. Lee, Julia B. Smith, and Robert G. Croninger, "How High School Organization Influences the Equitable Distribution of Learning in Mathematics and Science," *Sociology of Education* 70 (1997): 128–150.

61. Pete Goldschmidt and Jia Wang, "When Can Schools Affect Dropout Behavior? A Longitudinal Multilevel Analysis," *American Educational Research Journal* 36 (1999): 715–738; Susan S. Mayer, "How Much Does a High School's Racial and Socioeconomic Mix Affect Graduation and Teenage Fertility Rates?" in *The Urban Underclass*, eds. C. Jencks and P. Peterson (Washington, DC : Brookings Institution, 1991), 321–341; Rumberger, "Dropping Out of Middle School"; Russell W. Rumberger and Gregory J. Palardy, "Test Scores, Dropout Rates, and Transfer Rates as Alternative Indicators of High School Performance," *American Educational Research Journal* 41 (2005): 3–42; Bryk and Thum, "The Effects of High School Organization on Dropping Out"; Valerie E. Lee and David T. Burkam, "Transferring High Schools: An Alternative to Dropping Out?" *American Journal of Education* 100 (1992): 420–453.

62. Betts et al., *Equal Resources, Equal Outcomes?*, 186.

63. Rumberger and Arellano, *Student and School Predictors of High School Graduation in California.*

64. Betts et al., *Equal Resources, Equal Outcomes?*, 189.

65. Rotermund, *Which California Schools Have the Most Dropouts?*

66. See http://www.cde.ca.gov/re/di/or/division.asp?id=csd.

67. Rotermund, *Which California Schools Have the Most Dropouts?*

68. Adam Gamoran, "Student Achievement in Public Magnet, Public Comprehensive, and Private City High Schools," *Educational Evaluation and Policy Analysis* 18 (1996): 1–18; Christopher Lubienski and Sarah Theule Lubienski, *Charter, Private, Public Schools and Academic Achievement: New Evidence from NAEP Mathematics Data* (New York: National Center for the Study of Privatization in Education, Teachers College, Columbia University, 2006).

69. Rumberger and Arellano, "Student and School Predictors of High School Graduation in California."

70. Valerie E. Lee and David T. Burkam, "Dropping Out of High School: The Role of School Organization and Structure," *American Educational Research Journal* 40 (2003): 353–393; Valerie E. Lee and Julia B. Smith, "High School Size: Which Works Best for Whom?" *Educational Evaluation and Policy Analysis* 19 (1997): 205–227; McNeal, "High School Dropouts"; Meredith Phillips, "What Makes Schools Effective? A Comparison of the Relationships of Communitarian Climate and Academic Climate to Mathematics Achievement and Attendance During Middle School," *American Educational Research Journal* 34 (1997): 633–662; Rumberger, "Dropping Out of Middle School."

71. Rumberger and Palardy, "Test Scores, Dropout Rates, and Transfer Rates as Alternative Indicators of High School Performance."

72. Betts et al., *Equal Resources, Equal Outcomes?*

73. Janet Quint, *Meeting Five Critical Challenges of High School Reform: Lessons from Research on Three Reform Models* (New York: MDRC, 2008).

74. Valerie E. Lee and Julia B. Smith, "Effects of School Restructuring on the Achievement and Engagement of Middle-Grade Students," *Sociology of Education* 66 (1993):164–187; Valerie E. Lee and Julia B. Smith, "Effects of High School Restructuring and Size on Gains in Achievement and Engagement for Early Secondary School Students," *Sociology of Education* 68 (1995): 241–279; Valerie E. Lee, Julia B. Smith, and Robert G. Croninger, "How High School Organization Influences the Equitable Distribution of Learning in Mathematics and Science," *Sociology of Education* 70 (1997): 128–150; Stephen L. Morgan and Aage B. Sorensen, "Parental Networks, Social Closure, and Mathematics Learning: A Test of Coleman's Social Capital Explanation of School Effects," *American Sociological Review* 64 (1999): 661–681.

75. William J. Carbonaro and Adam Gamoran, "The Production of Achievement Inequality in High School English," *American Educational Research Journal* 39 (2002): 801–827; Lee, Smith, and Croninger, "How High School Organization Influences the Equitable Distribution of Learning in Mathematics and Science"; Rumberger and Palardy, "Test Scores, Dropout Rates, and Transfer Rates as Alternative Indicators of High School Performance."

76. Bryk, Lee, and Holland, *Catholic Schools and the Common Good.*

77. James S. Coleman, "The Concept of Equality of Educational Opportunity," *Harvard Educational Review* 38 (1968): 223.

78. James S. Coleman, Ernest Q. Campbell, Carol J. Hobson, James McPartland, Alexander M. Mood, Frederic D. Weinfeld, and Robert L. York, *Equality of Educational Opportunity* (Washington, DC: U.S. Government Printing Office, 1966).

79. Betts et al., *Equal Resources, Equal Outcomes?*

80. For a discussion of the limitations of this study, see ibid., 173–174.

81. Ibid., 135.

82. University of California, Los Angeles Institute for Democracy, Education, and Access (UCLA/IDEA), "California Educational Opportunity Report," February 25, 2008, http://idea.gseis.ucla.edu/publications/eor07/index.html.

83. National Research Council, Committee on Increasing High School Students' Engagement and Motivation to Learn, *Engaging Schools: Fostering High School Students' Motivation to Learn* (Washington, DC: National Academies Press, 2004).

84. Russell W. Rumberger, "What the Federal Government Can Do to Improve High School Performance" (Washington, D.C.: Center on Education Policy, 2009).

85. National Research Council, Committee on Increasing High School Students' Engagement and Motivation to Learn, *Engaging Schools: Fostering High School Students' Motivation to Learn* (Washington, D.C.: The National Academies Press. 2004).

86. National Governors Association Center for Best Practices, National Conference of State Legislatures, National Association of State Boards of Education, and Council of Chief State School Officers, *Accelerating the Agenda: Actions to Improve America's High Schools* (Washington, DC: Author, 2009).

87. David T. Burkam and Valerie E. Lee, *Inequality at the Starting Gate: Social Background Differences in Achievement as Children Begin School* (Washington, DC: Economic Policy Institute, 2002); Russell W. Rumberger, "Parsing the Data on Student Achievement in High Poverty Schools," *North Carolina Law Review* 85 (2007):101–119.

88. Rothstein, *Class and Schools*.

89. James S. Coleman, "Toward Open Schools," *Public Interest* 9 (1967): 20–21.

Chapter 8

1. We include African American, Latino, and Native American students in the definition of "students of color" or "underrepresented " students and refer to them also throughout the paper as culturally and linguistically diverse (CLD) students. Data from Susan Aud and Gretchen Hannes, eds., *The Condition of Education* (Washington, DC: National Center for Education Statistics, 2011), 2009 Common Core of Data.

2. Linda Darling-Hammond and Joan Baratz-Snowden, eds., "A Good Teacher in Every Classroom: Preparing the Highly Qualified Teachers Our Children Deserve," *Educational Horizons* 85, no. 2 (2007): 111–132.

3. David K. Cohen, Stephen W. Raudenbush, and Deborah Loewenberg Ball, "Resources, Instruction, and Research," *Educational Evaluation and Policy Analysis* 25, no. 2 (2004): 119–142.

4. Anthony S. Bryk and Barbara Schneider, *Trust in Schools: A Core Resource for Improvement*, Rose Series in Sociology (New York: Russell Sage Foundation, 2002).

5. Charles T. Clotfelter, Helen F. Ladd, and Jacob L. Vigdor, "Teacher Credentials and Student Achievement: Longitudinal Analysis with Student Fixed Effects," *Economics of Education Review* 26, no. 6 (2007): 673–682.

6. Donald Boyd, Hamilton Lankford, Susanna Loeb, and James Wyckoff, "The Draw of Home: How Teachers' Preferences for Proximity Disadvantage Urban Schools," *Journal of Policy Analysis and Management* 24, no. 1 (2005): 113–132; Eric A. Hanushek, "The Economics of Schooling: Production and Efficiency in Public Schools," *Journal of Economic Literature* XXIV (1986): 1141–1177; Eric A. Hanushek, "The Trade-off Between Child Quantity and Quality," *Journal of Political Economy* 100 (1992): 84–117; William L. Sanders and Sandra P. Horn, "Research Findings from the Tennessee Value-Added Assessment System (TVAAS) Database: Implications for Educational Evaluation and Research," *Journal of Personnel Evaluation in Education* 12, no. 3 (1998): 247–256; William L. Sanders and June C. Rivers, *Cumulative and Residual Effects of Teachers on Future Student Academic Achievement: Research Progress Report* (Knoxville, TN: University of Tennessee Value Added-Research and Assessment Center, 1996); S. Paul Wright, Sandra P. Horn, and William L. Sanders, "Teacher and Classroom Context Effects on Student Achievement: Implications for Teacher Evaluation," *Journal of Personnel Evaluation in Education* 11, no. 1 (1997): 57–67; Steven G. Rivkin, Eric Hanushek, and John F. Kain, "Teachers, Schools, and Academic Achievement," *Econometrica* 73, no. 2 (2005): 417–458; Jonah Rockoff, "The Impact of Individual Teachers on Student Achievement: Evidence from Panel Data," *American Economic Review*, 94(2): 247–252(2004), http://econwpa.wustl.edu:8089/eps/pe/papers/0304/0304002.pdf.

7. William L. Sanders, Arnold M. Saxton, and Sandra P. Horn, "The Tennessee Value-Added Assessment System (TVAAS): A Quantitative, Outcomes-Based Approach to Educational Assessment," in *Grading Teachers, Grading School*, ed. Jason Millman (Thousand Oaks, CA: Corwin Press, 1997), 137–162; Sanders and Rivers, *Cumulative and Residual Effects of Teachers*.

8. Douglas N. Harris, *Value-Added Measures of Education Performance: Clearing Away the Smoke and Mirrors*, Policy Analysis for California Education (Palo Alto, CA: Stanford University, 2010), http://www.stanford.edu/group/pace/PUBLICATIONS/PB/PACE_BRIEF_OCT_2010.pdf; Robert L. Linn, "Measurement Issues Associated with Value Added Methods" (report to the National Research Council and National Academy of Education, 2008) , http://www7.nationalacademies.org/BOTA/VAM_Robert_Linn_Paper.pdf; Richard Murnane and Jennifer Steele, "What Is the Problem? The Challenge of Providing Effective Teachers for All Children," *Future of Children* 17 (2007): 15–44.

9. Donald Boyd, Hamilton Lankford, Susanna Loeb, Jonah Rockoff, and James Wyckoff, "The Narrowing Gap in New York City Teacher Qualifications and Its Implications for Student Achievement in High-Poverty Schools" (working paper 10, Urban Institute, Washington, DC, September 2007); Ronald H. Heck, "Examining the Relationship Between Teacher Quality as an Organizational Property of Schools and Students' Achievement and Growth Rates," *Educational Administration Quarterly* 43, no. 4 (2007): 399–432; Dan D. Goldhaber and Dominic J. Brewer, "Does Teacher Certification Matter? High School Teacher Certification Status and Student Achievement," *Educational Evaluation and Policy Analysis* 22, no. 2 (2000): 129–145; Rob Greenwald, Larry V. Hedges, and Richard D. Laine, "The Effect of School Resources on Student Achievement," *Review of Educational Research* 66, no. 3 (1996): 361–396; Rivkin, Hanushek, and Kain, "Teachers, Schools, and Academic Achievement," 417-458; Brian Rowan, Richard Correnti, and Robert Miller, "What Large-Scale, Survey Research Tells Us About Teacher Effects on Student Achievement: Insights from the 'Prospects' Study of Elementary Schools," *Teachers College Record* 104, no. 8 (2002): 1525–1567.

10. Charles T. Clotfelter, Helen F. Ladd, and Jacob L. Vigdor, "Teacher Credentials and Student Achievement: Longitudinal Analysis with Student Fixed Effects," *Economics of Education Review* 26, no. 6 (2007): 673–682; Richard Murnane and Jennifer Steele, "What Is the Problem? The Challenge of Providing Effective Teachers for All Children," *Future of Children* 17 (2007): 15–44; Jonah Rockoff, *The Impact of Individual Teachers on Student Achievement: Evidence from Panel Data* American Economic Review, 94(2): 247–252(2004), http://econwpa.wustl.edu: 8089/eps/pe/papers/0304/0304002.pdf.

11. Roland G. Ehrenberg and Dominic J. Brewer, "Do School and Teacher Characteristics Matter? Evidence from 'High School and Beyond,'" *Economics of Education Review* 13, no. 1 (1994): 1–17; Ronald F. Ferguson, "Racial Patterns in How School and Teacher Quality Affect Achievement and Earnings," *Challenge* 2, no. 1 (1991): 1–35; Ronald F. Ferguson and Helen F. Ladd, "How and Why Money Matters: An Analysis of Alabama Schools," in *Holding Schools Accountable*, ed. Helen Ladd (Washington, DC: Brookings Institution, 1996), 265–298; Eric A. Hanushek, "Outcomes, Incentives, and Beliefs: Reflections on Analysis of the Economics of Schools," *Educational Evaluation and Policy Analysis* 19, no. 4 (1997): 301–308.

12. Ferguson, "Racial Patterns," 1–35; Ferguson and Ladd, "How and Why Money Matters," 265–298.

13. Clotfelter, Ladd, and Vigdor, "Teacher Credentials and Student Achievement," 673–682.

14. Boyd et al., "Narrowing Gap"; Hamilton Lankford, Susanna Loeb, and James Wyckoff, "Teacher Sorting and the Plight of Urban Schools: A Descriptive Analysis," *Educational Evaluation and Policy Analysis* 24, no. 1 (2002): 37–62; Andrew J. Wayne and Peter Youngs, "Teacher Characteristics and Student Achievement Gains," *Review of Educational Research* 73, no.1 (2003): 89–122.

15. Dan D. Goldhaber and Dominic J. Brewer, "Evaluating the Effect of Teacher Degree Level on Educational Performance" (Rockville, MD: Westat, 1996), http://eric.ed.gov; Goldhaber and Brewer, "Does Teacher Certification Matter?," 129–145; Donald Boyd et al., "The Narrowing Gap."

16. Donald Boyd et al., "The Narrowing Gap"; Harris, *Value-Added Measures of Education Performance*; Wayne and Youngs, "Teacher Characteristics," 89–122.

17. Ferguson, "Racial Patterns," 1–35; Goldhaber and Brewer, "Does Teacher Certification Matter?," 129–145; Linda Darling-Hammond, "Teacher Quality and Student Achievement: A Review of State Policy Evidence," *Education Policy Analysis Archives* 8, no. 1 (2001), http://epaa .asu.edu/epaa/v8n1/; Linn, "Measurement Issues."

18. Brian Jacob, "The Challenges of Staffing Urban Schools with Effective Teachers," *Future of Children* 17 (2007): 129–154.

19. Linda Darling-Hammond, "Inequality and the Right to Learn: Access to Qualified Teachers in California's Public Schools," *Teachers College Record* 106, no. 10 (2004): 1936–1966; Rob Greenwald, Larry V. Hedges, and Richard D. Laine, "The Effect of School Resources on Student Achievement," *Review of Educational Research* 66, no. 3 (1996): 361–396; Hanushek, "The

Trade-off Between Child Quantity and Quality," 84–117; Hamilton Lankford, Susanna Loeb, and James Wyckoff, "Teacher Sorting and the Plight of Urban Schools: A Descriptive Analysis," *Educational Evaluation and Policy Analysis* 24, no. 1 (2002): 37–62; Richard Murnane and Jennifer Steele, "What Is the Problem? The Challenge of Providing Effective Teachers for All Children," *Future of Children* 17 (2007): 15–44.

20. Lankford, Loeb, and Wyckoff, "Teacher Sorting and the Plight of Urban Schools."

21. See for example, Roneeta Guha et al., *California's Teaching Force 2006: Key Issues and Trends* (Santa Cruz, CA: Center for the Future of Teaching and Learning, 2006).

22. James E. Bruno, "The Geographical Distribution of Teacher Absenteeism in Large Urban School District Settings: Implications for School Reform Efforts Aimed at Promoting Equity and Excellence in Education," *Education Policy Analysis Archives* 10, no. 32 (2002): 1–15.

23. Ana Maria Villegas and Danne E. Davis, "Preparing Teachers of Color to Confront Racial/Ethnic Disparities in Educational Outcomes," in *Handbook of Research in Teacher Education: Enduring Questions in Changing Contexts*, ed. Marilyn Cochran-Smith (NY: Routledge, 2008), 583–636.

24. C. T. Clotfeldter, H. F. Ladd, and J. L. Vigdor, "Teacher Credentials and Student Achievement: Longitudinal Analysis with Student Fixed Effects," *Economics of Education Review* 26, no. 6 (2007): 673–682.

25. Meier, "Latinos and Representative Bureaucracy," *Journal of Public Administration Research and Theory* 3, no. 4 (1993): 393–414.

26. Thomas S. Dee, "Teachers, Race, and Student Achievement in a Randomized Experiment," *Review of Economics and Statistics* 86 (2004): 195–210.

27. Roland G. Ehrenberg, Dan Goldhaber, and Dominic J. Brewer, "Do Teachers' Race, Gender, and Ethnicity Matter? Evidence from the National Educational Longitudinal Study of 1988," RAND reprints, *Industrial and Labor Relations Review* 48, no. 3 (1995): 547–561.

28. L. A. Buchanan, "Recruiting Minorities into the Teaching Profession. Students Address the Issue: An Analysis of Four Focus Groups in Long Beach and Sacramento," conducted for the California Teachers Association (Burlingame, CA: California Teachers Association, 1999); Michele Foster, "The Politics of Race: Through the Eyes of African-American Teachers," *Journal of Education* 172, no. 3 (1990): 123–141; Michele Foster, *Black Teachers on Teaching* (New York: New Press, 1997).

29. Gloria Ladson-Billings, *The Dreamkeepers: Successful Teachers of African American Children* (San Francisco: Jossey-Bass, 1994), 17.

30. Ibid., 17.

31. Lisa Delpit, "Skills and Other Dilemmas of a Progressive Black Educator," *American Educator* 20, no. 3 (1996): 9–11, 48.

32. Kenneth J. Meier, "Latinos and Representative Bureaucracy Testing the Thompson and Henderson Hypotheses," *Journal of Public Administration Research and Theory* 3, no. 4 (1993): 393–414.

33. Douglas B. Downey and Shana Pribesh, "When Race Matters: Teachers' Evaluations of Students' Classroom Behavior," *Sociology of Education* 77, no. 4 (2004): 267.

34. Patricia M. McDonough, *Choosing Colleges: How Social Class and Schools Structure Opportunity* (Albany, NY: SUNY Press, 1997); Harriett Romo and Toni Falbo, *Latino High School Graduation: Defying the Odds* (Austin, TX: University of Texas Press, 1996); S. A. Webb and P. V. Crosbie, "Teaching in California Public Schools: More Than Academics," *1994 Yearbook of California Education Research* (Dennis S. Tierney (ed) Caddo Gap Press, San Francisco, CA, 1994), 191–205; Sharon Tettegah, "The Racial Consciousness Attitudes of White Prospective Teachers and Their Perceptions of the Teachability of Students from Different Racial/Ethnic Backgrounds: Findings from a California Study," *Journal of Negro Education* 65, no. 2 (1997): 151–163.

35. Robert Rosenthal and Leonore Jacobson, "Pygmalion in the Classroom," *Urban Review*, 1968, no. 3: 16–20.

36. Jere E. Brophy and Thomas L. Good, *Teacher-Student Relationships: Causes and Consequences* (New York: Holt, Rinehart, 1974).

37. Rhona S. Weinstein, "Perceptions of Classroom Processes and Student Motivation: Children's Views of Self-Fulfilling Prophecies," in *Research on Motivation in Education: Goals and Cognition,* vol. III, eds. Carole Ames and Russell Ames (New York: Academic Press, 1989), 187–221.

38. Michele Foster, *Black Teachers on Teaching* (New York: New Press, 1997), ix.

39. Robert K. Ream, "Counterfeit Social Capital and Mexican American Underachievement," *Educational Evaluation and Policy Analysis* 25 (2003): 237–262.

40. Boyd et al., "The Draw of Home."

41. Linda Darling-Hammond and Barnett Berry, "Highly Qualified Teachers for All," *Educational Leadership* 64, no. 3 (2006): 14–20.

42. Barbara M. Taylor, David Pearson, Kathleen Clark, and Sharon Walpole, "Effective Schools and Accomplished Teachers: Lessons About Primary-Grade Reading Instruction in Low-Income Schools," *Elementary School Journal* 101, no. 2 (2000): 21–165.

43. Ladson-Billings, *The Dreamkeepers.*

44. Timothy Z. Keith et al., "Longitudinal Effects of Parent Involvement on High School Grades: Similarities and Differences Across Gender and Ethnic Groups," *Journal of School Psychology* 36, no. 3 (1998): 335–363; Laura Desimone, "Linking Parent Involvement with Student Achievement: Do Race and Income Matter?" *Journal of Educational Research* 93, no. 1 (1999): 11–30; Gail L. Zellman and Jill M. Waterman, "Understanding the Impact of Parent School Involvement on Children's Educational Outcomes," *Journal of Educational Research* 91(6): 370–380; Michelle Frazier Trotman, "Involving the African American Parent: Recommendations to Increase the Level of Parent Involvement Within African American Families," *Journal of Negro Education* 70, no. 4 (2001): 275–285; Chad Nye, Herb Turner, and Jamie Schwartz, "Approaches to Parental Involvement for Improving the Academic Performance of Elementary School Children in Grades K–6," (2006), http://campbellcollaboration.org/doc-pdf/Nye_PI_Review.pdf; Ladson-Billings, *The Dreamkeepers.*

45. Steven Arvizu, "Family, Community, and School Collaboration," in *Handbook of Research on Teacher Education,* ed. John Sikula (New York: Simon & Schuster/Macmillan, 1996), 814–819.

46. Metropolitan Life Insurance Company, *The American Teacher 1998: Building Family-School Partnerships: Views of Teachers and Students* (New York: Metropolitan Life Insurance Company, 1997).

47. Guadalupe Valdés, *Con Respeto. Bridging the Distances Between Culturally Diverse Families and Schools: An Ethnographic Portrait* (New York: Teachers College Press, 1996).

48. Deborah Short and Shannon Fitzsimmons, *Double the Work: Challenges and Solutions to Acquiring Language and Academic Literacy for Adolescent English Language Learners,* report to Carnegie Corporation of New York (Washington, DC: Alliance for Excellent Education, 2007).

49. Jana Echevarria and MaryEllen Vogt, *Making Content Comprehensible for English Learners: The SIOP Model,* 3rd ed. (Boston: Pearson/Allyn and Bacon, 2008); Peggy Cuevas, Okhee Lee, Juliet Hart, and Rachael Deaktor, "Improving Science Inquiry with Elementary Students of Diverse Backgrounds," *Journal of Research in Science Teaching* 42 (2005): 337–357.

50. Norma González et al., *Funds of Knowledge: Learning from Language Minority Households* (Washington, DC: Center for Applied Linguistics, 1994), http://www.cal.org/resources/Digest/ncrcds01.html; Luis C. Moll, "Some Key Issues in Teaching Latino Students," *Language Arts* 65, no. 5 (1988): 465–472.

51. Zeichner, K., "Educating Teachers for Cultural Diversity," in *Currents of Reform in Preservice Teacher Education,* eds. Ken M. Zeichner et al. (New York: Teachers College Press, 1996), 133–175.

52. Ladson-Billings, *The Dreamkeepers.*

53. Center for Research in Education, Diversity, and Excellence (CREDE), *Standards and Indicators* (Berkeley, CA: University of California, Berkeley, Graduate School of Education, CREDE, 1999), www.cal.org.crede, 1.

54. Patricia Gándara, Julie Maxwell-Jolly, and Anne Driscoll, *Listening to Teachers of English Language Learners: A Survey of California Teachers' Challenges, Experiences, and Professional Development Needs* (Berkeley, CA: Policy Analysis for California Education, 2005).

55. Megan Hopkins, "Building on Their Assets: The Unique Contributions of Bilingual Teachers" (unpublished doctoral dissertation, University of California, Los Angeles, 2011).

56. Lisa Delpit, *Other People's Children: Cultural Conflict in the Classroom* (New York: New Press, 1995); Lisa Delpit, "Skills and Other Dilemmas of a Progressive Black Educator," *American Educator* 20, no. 3 (1996): 9–11, 48.

57. CREDE, *Standards and Indicators*.

58. Eugene E. Garcia, "Preparing Instructional Professionals for Linguistically and Culturally Diverse Students," in *Handbook of Research on Teacher Education*, ed. John Sikula (New York: Simon & Schuster/Macmillan, 1996), 802–813; Barbara Merino, "Identifying Critical Competencies for Teachers of English Learners," *LMRI Newsletter* 16, no. 4 (2007), http://www.lmri.ucsb.edu/publications/newsletters/download.php?file=v16n4.pdf; Robert Milk, Carmen Mercado, and Alexander Sapiens, "Re-thinking the Education of Teachers of Language Minority Children: Developing Reflective Teachers for Changing Schools," *NCBE Focus: Occasional Papers in Bilingual Education* 6, Summer (1992), www.ncbe.gwu.edu; Patricia Gándara, *Review of the Research on Instruction of Limited English Proficient Students: A Report to the California Legislature* (Davis, CA: University of California, Davis, Language Minority Research Institute, 1997).

59. Richard A. Figueroa, "Dificultades o desabilidades de aprendizaje?" *Learning Disability Quarterly* 28, no. 2 (2004): 163.

60. Alfredo Artiles and Alba Ortiz, eds., *English Language Learners with Special Education Needs* (Washington, DC: Center for Applied Linguistics, 2002).

61. Martin Haberman, "Selecting 'Star' Teachers for Children and Youth in Urban Poverty," *Phi Delta Kappan* 76, no. 10 (1995): 777–781.

62. Zeichner, "Educating Teachers for Cultural Diversity."

63. Tamara Lucas and Rosemary Henze, "Promoting the Success of Latino Language-Minority Students: An Exploratory Study of Six High Schools," *Harvard Educational Review* 60, no. 3 (1990): 315–341.

64. Zeichner, "Educating Teachers for Cultural Diversity."

65. CREDE, *Standards and Indicators*.

66. Ladson-Billings, *The Dreamkeepers*.

67. Haberman, "Selecting 'Star' Teachers," *Phi Delta Kappan* 76, 777–781.

68. Kip Téllez and Hersh C. Waxman, "Preparing Quality Teachers for English Language Learners: An Overview of Critical Issues," in *Preparing Quality Teachers for English Language Learners: Research, Policies, and Practices*, eds. Kip Téllez and Hersholt C. Waxman (Mahwah, NJ: Lawrence Erlbaum, 2006).

69. Robert Milk, Carmen Mercado, and Alexander Sapiens, "Re-thinking the Education of Teachers of Language Minority Children: Developing Reflective Teachers for Changing Schools," *NCBE Focus: Occasional Papers in Bilingual Education* 6, Summer (1992), www.ncbe.gwu.edu.

70. Deborah Short, "Language Learning in Sheltered Social Studies Classes," *TESOL Journal* 11, no. 1 (2002): 18–24.

71. Megan Hopkins, "Building on Their Assets."

72. Diane August and Kenji Hakuta, *Improving Schooling for Language Minority Children: A Research Agenda* (Washington, DC: National Academy Press, 1997); Claude Goldenberg, "Teaching English Language Learners: What the Research Does and Does Not Say," *American Educator* (Summer 2008); William Saunders and Claude Goldenberg, "Research to Guide English Language Development Instruction," in *Improving Education for English Learners: Research-Based Approaches* (Sacramento: California Department of Education, 2010), 24–81.

73. Mary J. Schleppegrell, *The Language of Schooling: A Functional Linguistics Perspective* (Mahwah, NJ: Lawrence Erlbaum, 2004).

74. Timothy Reagan, "The Case for Applied Linguistics in Teacher Education," *Journal of Teacher Education* 48, no. 3 (1997): 185–196; Lily Wong Fillmore and Catherine E. Snow, *What Teachers Need to Know About Language*, Special Report (Washington DC: ERIC Clearinghouse on Languages and Linguistics, 2000).

75. Saunders and Goldenberg, "Research to Guide English Language Development"; Alison L. Bailey and Frances A. Butler, *An Evidentiary Framework for Operationalizing Academic Language for Broad Application to K–12 Education: A Design Document* (Los Angeles: CRESST/University of California, 2003); Fred Genesee, Kathryn Lindholm-Leary, Bill Saunders, and Donna Christian, eds., *Educating English Language Learners: A Synthesis of Research Evidence* (New York: Cambridge University Press, 2006); Diane August and Timothy Shanahan, eds., *Developing Literacy in Second Language Learners: Report of the National Literacy Panel on Language-Minority Children and Youth* (Mahwah, NJ: Lawrence Erlbaum, 2006).

76. Mary J. Schleppegrell, "Linguistic Features of the Language of Schooling," *Linguistics and Education* 12, no. 4 (2001): 431–459.

77. Ibid.

78. Jana Echevarria and Deborah Short, "Teacher Skills to Support English Language Learners," *Educational Leadership* 62, no. 4 (2005): 8–13.

79. Katherine Hayes and Jesus Jose Salazar, *Evaluation of the Structured English Immersion Program, Final Report: Year I* (Los Angeles: Los Angeles Unified School District, 2001).

80. Rebecca M. Callahan, "Academic Achievement and Course Taking Among Language Minority Youth in U.S. schools: Effects of ESL Placement," *Educational Evaluation and Policy Analysis* 32 (2010): 84–117.

81. Patricia Gándara, Dianna Gutierrez, and Susan O'Hara, "Planning for the Future in Rural and Urban High Schools," *Journal of Education for Students Placed at Risk (JESPAR)* 6, no. 1–2 (2001): 73–93; Margaret Gibson, Patricia Gándara, and Jill Peterson Koyama, eds., *School Connections: U.S. Mexican Youth, Peers, and School Achievement* (New York: Teachers College Press, 2004).

82. Julie Meltzer and Edmund T. Hamann, *Meeting the Literacy Development Needs of Adolescent English Language Learners Through Content Area Learning, Part One: Focus on Motivation and Engagement* (Providence, RI: Education Alliance at Brown University, 2004).

83. National Collaborative on Diversity in the Teaching Force, *Assessment of Diversity in America's Teaching Force* (Washington, DC: National Education Association, 2004);Sonia Nieto, *Affirming Diversity: The Sociopolitical Context of Multicultural Education* (White Plains, NY: Longman, 1996).

84. Etta Hollins and Maria Torres Guzman, "Research on Preparing Teachers for Diverse Populations," in Studying Teacher Education: The Report of the AERA Panel on Research and Teacher Education, eds. Marilyn Cochran Smith and Kenneth M. Zeichner (Mahwah, NJ: Lawrence Erlbaum Associates, 2005), p. 479.

85. National Collaborative on Diversity in the Teaching Force, *Assessment of Diversity*.

86. Hollins and Guzman, "Research on Preparing Teachers."

87. Christine E. Sleeter, "Preparing Teachers for Culturally Diverse Schools: Research and the Overwhelming Presence of Whiteness," *Journal of Teacher Education* 52, no. 2 (2001): 94–106.

88. Ibid., 96.

89. Robert F. Littleton Jr., "Educational Review Teams: Bridging Competing Theories to Ensure Successful Student Outcomes," *International Journal of Disability, Development and Education* 45, no. 4 (1998): 489–500.

90. Diane R. Becket, "Increasing the Number of Latino and Navajo teachers in Hard-to-Staff Schools," *Journal of Teacher Education* 49, no. 3 (1998): 196–205.

91. Haberman, "Selecting 'Star' Teachers"; Haberman, "Selecting and Preparing Culturally Competent Teachers," in *Handbook of Research on Teacher Education*, 747–760.

92. Haberman, "Selecting 'Star' Teachers," 777.

93. Boyd et al., "The Draw of Home."

94. Ibid, 127.

95. Sleeter, "Preparing Teachers for Culturally Diverse Schools."

96. Hollins and Guzman, "Research on Preparing Teachers," 490.

97. Zeichner, "Educating Teachers for Cultural Diversity."

98. Kenneth Zeichner, "The Adequacies and Inadequacies of Three Current Strategies to Recruit, Prepare, and Retain the Best Teachers for All Students," *Teachers College Record* 105, no. 3 (2003): 490–519.

99. Kenneth Zeichner and Susan L. Melnick, "The Role of Community Field Experiences in Preparing Teachers for Cultural Diversity," in *Currents of Reform in Preservice Teacher Education*, eds. K. M. Zeichner, S. Melnick, and M. L. Gomez (New York: Teachers College Press, 1996).

100. Etta Hollins and Maria Torres Guzman, "Research on Preparing Teachers for Diverse Populations," in *Studying Teacher Education: The Report of the AERA Panel on Research and Teacher Education*, eds. Marilyn Cochran Smith and Kenneth M. Zeichner (Mahwah, NJ: Lawrence Erlbaum, 2005), 495.

101. Edmund T. Hamann, *Advice, Cautions, and Opportunities for the Teachers of Binational Teachers: Learning from Teacher Training Experiences of Georgia and Nebraska Teachers in Mexico* (Lincoln: University of Nebraska, 2008), http://digitalcommons.unl.edu/cgi/viewcontent.cgi?article=1074&context=teachlearnfacpub.

102. G. Williamson McDiarmid, "What to Do About Differences? A Study of Multicultural Education for Teacher Trainees in the Los Angeles School District," *Journal of Teacher Education* 43, no. 2 (1992): 83–93.

103. Zeichner, "Educating Teachers for Cultural Diversity," 162.

104. Michael S. Garet et al., "What Makes Professional Development Effective? Results from a National Sample of Teachers," *American Educational Research Journal* 38, no. 4 (2001): 915–945; Susan Loucks-Horsley, Peter W. Hewson, Nancy B. Love, and Katherine E. Stiles, *Designing Professional Development for Teachers of Science and Mathematics* (Thousand Oaks, CA: Corwin Press, 1998); William R. Penuel, Barry J. Fishman, Ryoko Yamaguchi, and Lawrence P. Gallagher, "What Makes Professional Development Effective? Strategies That Foster Curriculum Implementation," *American Educational Research Journal* 44, no. 4 (2007): 921–958; Ralph T. Putnam and Hilda Borko, "What Do New Views of Knowledge and Thinking Have to Say About Research on Teacher Learning?" *Educational Researcher* 29, no. 1 (2000): 4–15.

105. Garet et al., "What Makes Professional Development Effective?"

106. Linda Darling-Hammond and Milbrey W. McLaughlin, "Policies That Support Professional Development in an Era of Reform," *Phi Delta Kappan* 76, no. 8 (1995): 597–604; Beth Kubitskey and Barry J. Fishman, "A Role for Professional Development in Sustainability: Linking the Written Curriculum to Enactment," in *Proceedings of the 7th International Conference of the Learning Sciences*, vol. 1, eds. Sasha Barab, Kenneth Hay, and Daniel Hickey (Mahwah, NJ: Lawrence Erlbaum), 363–369.

107. Gándara, Maxwell-Jolly, Driscoll, *Listening to Teachers of English Language Learners*.

108. Patricia Gándara, Russell Rumberger, Julie Maxwell-Jolly, and Rebecca Callahan, "English Learners in California Schools: Unequal Resources, Unequal Outcomes," *Education Policy Analysis Archives* 11, no. 36 (2003), http://epaa.asu.edu/epaa/v11n36/.

109. Patricia Gándara and Gary Orfield, "Moving from Failure to a New Vision of Language Policy," in *Forbidden Language: English Learners and Restrictive Language Policies*, eds. Patricia Gándara and Megan Hopkins (New York: Teachers College Press, 2010), 216–226.

110. Betty Achinstein and Steven Z. Athanases, *Focusing New Teachers on Diversity and Equity: Toward a Knowledge Base for Mentors* (Santa Cruz, CA: New Teacher Center, University of California, Santa Cruz, and University of California, Davis, 2007).

111. Georges Vernez, Richard A. Krop, and C. Peter Rydell, *Closing the Education Gap: Benefits and Costs* (Santa Monica, CA: RAND Corporation, 1999).

Chapter 9

1. See citation to Ellwood Patterson Cubberly, *School Funds and Their Apportionment* (New York: Teachers College Press, 1905), 1.

2. Eric Hanushek, "The Impact of Differential Expenditures on School Performance," *Educational Researcher* 18 (1989): 45–62; Eric Hanushek, "Assessing the Effects of School Resources on

Student Performance: An Update," *Educational Evaluation and Policy Analysis* 19, no. 2 (1997): 141–164.

3. For the evidence from a number of high-cost California programs, see W. Norton Grubb, *The Money Myth: School Resources, Outcomes, and Equity* (New York: Russell Sage Foundation, 2009), 210–212. More generally, there is a substantial random-assignment literature on the effects of discrete programs—the approach that I and others label "programmitis"—showing insignificant results, which is other evidence of costly but ineffective programs.

4. Brian Aaron Jacob, "The Challenges of Staffing Urban Schools with Effective Teachers," *Future of Children* 17, no. 1 (2007): 129–153, Table 1.

5. See Rosalind Levacic and Anna Vignoles, "Researching the Links Between School Resources and Student Outcomes in the U.K.: A Review of Issues and Evidence," *Education Economics* 10, no. 3 (2002): 313–331, for the United Kingdom.

6. For example, see the entries in Hanushek, "The Impact of Differential Expenditures," Table 3.

7. W. Norton Grubb, "When Money Might Matter: Using NELS88 to Examine the Weak Effects of School Finance," *Journal of Education Finance* 31, no. 4 (2006): 360–378; W. Norton Grubb, *The Money Myth: School Resources, Outcomes, and Equity* (New York: Russell Sage Foundation, 2009), chapter 3.

8. Brian M. Stecher and George W. Bohrnstedt, *Class Size Reduction in California: Findings from 1999–00 and 2001–02* (Palo Alto, CA: Ed Source, 2002).

9. Charles M. Payne, *So Much Reform, So Little Change* (Cambridge, MA: Harvard Education Press, 2008); Fred M. Newmann, Betsann Smith, Elaine Allensworth, and Anthony S. Bryk, "Instructional Program Coherence: What It Is and Why It Should Guide School Improvement Policy," *Educational Evaluation and Policy Analysis* 23, no. 4 (2001): 297–321; Anthony S. Bryk and Barbara Schneider, *Trust in Schools: A Core Resource for Improvement* (New York: Russell Sage Foundation, 2002).

10. Grubb, *The Money Myth*, table 2.1.

11. Martin Carnoy, Richard Elmore, and Leslie Siskin, eds., *The New Accountability: High Schools and High-Stakes Testing* (New York: Routledge, 2003).

12. Larry Cuban,"Reforming Again, Again, and Again," *Educational Researcher*, 1990, 19(1): 3–13; the quote is on p. 3.

13. Marguerite Roza and Paul Hill, "How Can Anyone Say What's Adequate if Nobody Knows How Money Is Spent Now?" in *Courting Failure: How School Finance Lawsuits Exploit Judges' Good Intentions and Harm our Children*, ed. Eric Hanushek (Palo Alto, CA: Hoover Press, 2006).

14. See the interventions in 12 schools in Grubb, *The Money Myth*, chapter 8.

15. Stecher and Bohrnstedt, *Class Size Reduction in California*.

16. Judith Warren Little, *Professional Community and Professional Development in the Learner-Centered School* (Washington DC: National Education Association, 2006).

17. Grubb, *The Money Myth*, table B-4.

18. Daniel G. Solorzano, "Critical Race Theory, Racial Micro-aggressions, and the Experience of Chicana and Chicano Scholars," *Qualitative Inquiry* 8, no. 1 (2001): 23–44; Daniel G. Solorzano, Miguel Ceja and Tara Yosso, "Critical Race Theory, Racial Micro-aggressions, and Campus Racial Climate: The Experiences of African American College Students," *Journal of Negro Education* 69, no. 1/2 (2000): 60–73.

19. See Grubb, *The Money Myth*, chapters 4 and 9, for more detailed evidence on racial mistreatment and potential solutions; Ann Arnett Ferguson, *Bad Boys: Public Schools in the Making of Black Masculinity* (Ann Arbor: University of Michigan Press, 2000).

20. Henry Levin, "Making Cuts Wisely Can Make Your District Stronger" (Schoolwise Press Brown Bag Seminar Summary, December 2008), www.schoolwisepress.com/ seminar/teleconf_past.html; Mike Schmoker, "What Money Can't Buy: Powerful Overlooked Opportunities for Learning," *Phi Delta Kappan* 90, no. 7 (2009): 524–527; Marguerite Roza, Dan Goldhaber and Paul Hill, "The Productivity Imperative: Getting More Benefits from School Costs in an Era of Tight Budgets," *Education Week* 48, no. 34 (2009); Ben Levin and Nancy Naylor, "Using Resources

Effectively in Education," in *Intelligent Leadership*, eds. John M. Burger, Patricia Klinck, and Charles F. Webber (Dordrecht, Netherlands: Springer, 2007), 143–158.

21. W. Norton Grubb and Lynda Tredway, *Leading from the Inside Out: Expanded Roles for Teachers in Equitable Schools* (Boulder CO: Paradigm Publishers, 2010), chapter 3, Tool 3-A, 102. I have used this waste audit successfully with the aspiring principals of the Principal Leadership Institute, a program to prepare urban principals of which I am the faculty coordinator.

22. I borrow this term from John Easton, currently head of the Institute for Educational Sciences, who has used it in several speeches.

23. Grubb and Tredway, *Leading from the Inside Out*, Tool 3-B, 103–107.

24. W. Norton Grubb, "Bridging the Divide Between Research and Practice: An Educational Extension Service for Michigan" (unpublished paper, prepared for the W. W. Kellogg Foundation, 2010).

25. Everett Rogers, *The Diffusion of Innovation*, 5th ed. (New York: Free Press, 2003); Trisha Greenhalgh et al., "Diffusion of Innovations in Service Organizations: Systematic Review and Recommendations," *Milbank Quarterly* 82, no. 4 (2004): 581–629.

26. Robert E. Slavin, "Disseminating Success for All: Lessons for Policy and Practice," Report No. 30 (Baltimore, MD: Center for Research on the Education of Students Placed at Risk, Johns Hopkins University, 1999).

27. On school-based budgeting, see A. Cole, "Schools Gaining Greater Control over Their Resources: Recent Budgetary Reforms in School Districts in the U.S. and Canada" (unpublished paper, University of California, Berkeley, 2005); and Karen Hawley Miles, Kathleen Ware, and Marguerite Roza, "Leveling the Playing Field: Creating Funding Equity Through Student-Based Budgeting," *Phi Delta Kappan* 85, no. 2 (2003): 114–119.

28. Dorothy Seigel and Norm Fruchter, *Final Report: Evaluation of the Performance Driven Budgeting Initiative of the New York City Board of Education, 1997–2000* (New York: Institute for Education and Social Policy, New York University, 2002).

29. Grubb, *The Money Myth*, chapter 10.

30. Ibid.; on exemplary districts in California, see Springboard Schools, *Minding the Gap: New Roles for School Districts in the Age of Accountability* (San Francisco: Springboard Schools, 2006); on practices in many states, see especially Andrew Calkins, William Guenther, Grace Belfiore, and David Lash, *The Turnaround Challenge,* Supplement to the Main Report (Boston: Insight Education and Research Institute, 2007).

Chapter 10

1. Karin Chenoweth, "Piece by Piece: How Schools Solved the Achievement Puzzle and Soared," *American Educator* (Fall 2009): 15–29; Anthony S. Bryk, Penny Bender Sebring, and Elaine Allensworth, *Organizing Schools for Improvement: Lessons from Chicago* (Chicago: University of Chicago Press, 2010); Gerardo R. Lopez, Jay D. Scribner, and Kanya Mahitivanichcha, "Redefining Parental Involvement: Lessons from High-Performing Migrant-Impacted Schools," *American Educational Research Journal* 38, no. 2 (2001): 253–288; Jay D. Scribner, Michelle D. Young, and Anna Pedroza, "Building Collaborative Relationships with Parents," in *Lessons from High-Performing Hispanic Schools: Creating Learning Communities*, eds. Pedro Reyes, Jay D. Scribner, and Alicia Paredes Scribner (New York: Teachers College Press, 1999); Trish Williams, Michael Kirst, and Edward Haertel, *Similar English Learner Students, Different Results: Why Do Some Schools Do Better? A Large-Scale Survey of California Elementary Schools Serving Low-Income and EL Students* (Mountain View: EdSource, 2005); Trish Williams, Kenji Hakuta, and Edward Haertel, *Similar English Learner Students, Different Results: Why Do Some Schools Do Better? A Follow-up Analysis, Based on a Large-Scale Survey of California Elementary Schools Serving Low-Income and EL Students* (Mountain View: EdSource, 2007).

2. For example, Michelle Renée, Kevin Welner, and Jeannie Oakes, "Social Movement Organizing and Equity-Focused Educational Change: Shifting the Zone of Mediation," in *International Handbook of Educational Change*, 2nd ed., eds. A. Hargreaves, A. Lieberman, M. Fullan, and D.

Hopkins (New York: Springer, 2010); Clarence N. Stone, Jeffrey R. Henig, Bryan D. Jones, and Carol Pierannuzi, *Building Civic Capacity: The Politics of Reforming Urban Schools* (Lawrence, KS: University Press of Kansas, 2001). Also see Kavitha Mediratta and Norm Fruchter, *Mapping the Field of Organizing for School Improvement: A Report on Education Organizing in Baltimore, Chicago, Los Angeles, the Mississippi Delta, New York City, Philadelphia, San Francisco, and Washington, D.C.* (New York: New York University, 2011).

3. A point also noted with respect to family engagement research by Martha Boethel, *Diversity: School, Family, and Community Connections* (Austin, TX: Southwest Educational Development Laboratory, 2003); Anne T. Henderson and Karen L. Mapp, *A New Wave of Evidence: The Impact of School, Family and Community Connections on Student Achievement* (Austin, TX: Southwest Educational Development Laboratory, 2002); Aaron Schutz, "Home Is a Prison in the Global City: The Tragic Failure of School-Based Community Engagement Strategies, " in *Review of Educational Research* 76, no. 4 (2006): 691–743; Beatriz Arias and Milagros Morillo-Campbell, "Promoting ELL Parental Involvement: Challenges in Contested Times" (policy brief for Education Public Interest Center, Tempe, AZ, Arizona State University, 2008).

4. Alan A. Sadovnik et al., "Conclusion: Sociological Perspectives on NCLB and Federal Involvement," in *No Child Left Behind and the Reduction of the Achievement Gap: Sociological Perspectives on Federal Education Policy*, eds. Alan A. Sadovnik, Jennifer A. O'Day, George W. Bohrnstedt, and Kathryn M. Borman (London: Routledge, 2007), 359–373. Amy J. L. Baker and Laura M. Soden, "Parent Involvement in Children's Education: A Critical Assessment of the Knowledge Base" (paper presented at the Annual Meeting of AERA, 1997) and Doreen J. Mattingly, Radmila Prislin, Thomas L. McKenzie, James L. Rodriguez, and Brenda Kayzar, "Evaluating Evaluations: The Case of Parent Involvement Programs," *Review of Educational Research* 72, no. 4 (2002): 549–576 articulate what has been a consistent concern about the lack of experimental studies exploring the links between family involvement, community supports, and student achievement.

5. See Lora Cohen-Vogel, Ellen Goldring, and Claire Smrekar, "The Influence of Local Conditions on Social Service Partnerships, Parent Involvement and Community Engagement in Neighborhood Schools," *American Journal of Education* 117, no. 1 (2010): 51–78, for new research on variation in community school partnership strategies across neighborhood types.

6. Extensive reviews of research on family engagement were released at that time (e.g., Henderson and Mapp, *A New Wave of Evidence*; Martha Boethel, *Diversity: School, Family, and Community Connections* [Austin, TX: Southwest Educational Development Laboratory, 2003]; Martha Boethel, *Readiness: School, Family, and Community Connections* [Austin, TX: Southwest Educational Development Laboratory, 2004]). Some school health related studies from as early as 1993 were also reviewed. Also see Catherine Jordan, Evangelina Orozco, and Amy Averett, *Emerging Issues in School, Family and Community Connections* (Austin, TX: Southwest Educational Development Laboratory, 2001).

7. This research defines "success" in a variety of ways: relatively low dropout rates/high graduation rates (e.g., Miguel Socias, Lenay Dunn, Thomas Parrish, Mari Muraki, and LaRena Woods, *California High Schools That Beat the Odds in High School Graduation* [Santa Barbara, CA: American Institutes for Research, 2007]), relatively high standardized test scores (e.g., Williams, Kirst, Haertel, *Large-Scale Survey of California Elementary Schools*; Scribner, Young, and Pedroza, "Building Collaborative Relationships"; Williams, Hakuta, Haertel, *A Follow-up Analysis*; Chenoweth, "Piece by Piece"), and combinations of criteria (e.g., Diane Friedlander and Linda Darling-Hammond, *High School for Equity: Policy Supports for Student Learning in Communities of Color* (Stanford, CA: School Redesign Network/Stanford University, 2007; Bryk, Sebring, and Allensworth, *Organizing Schools for Improvement*). Primary research and related literature reviews also employ a variety of approaches to defining their target population, focusing alternately on schools that mitigate the effects of poverty (e.g., Whitney C. Allgood, "The Need for Adequate Resources for At-Risk Children" (working paper, Economic Policy Institute, 2006); Williams, Kirst, Haertel, *A Large-Scale Survey of California Elementary Schools*), schools that serve racially/ethnically diverse populations well (e.g., Friedlander and Darling-Hammond, *High School for Equity*),

schools that serve English language learners well (e.g., Williams, Hakuta, Haertel, *A Follow-up Analysis*; Scribner, Young, and Pedroza, "Building Collaborative Relationships"), and schools that statistically would not be expected to succeed based on student demographics (e.g., Chenoweth, "Piece by Piece"). Most recently, Bryk, Sebring, and Allensworth, *Organizing Schools for Improvement*, have begun to differentiate between disadvantaged and "truly disadvantaged" populations by also taking into account factors such as concentration of poverty, racial isolation, and neighborhood factors such as comparatively high rates of crime and child abuse and neglect. This research generates many overlapping conclusions about key qualities of these schools, although distinct emphases and elements emerge as well.

8. Ronald F. Ferguson, "Teacher Perceptions and Expectations and the Black-White Test Score Gap," in *The Black-White Test Score Gap*, eds. Christopher Jencks and Meredith Phillips (Washington, DC: Brookings Institution Press, 1998): 273–317; Claude Steele, "Stereotype Threat and African American Student Achievement," in *Young, Gifted, and Black: Promoting High Achievement Among African American Students*, eds. T. Perry, C. Steele, and A. Hilliard (Boston: Beacon Press, 2003), 109–130.

9. Christine Enyeart, Juliet Diehl, Gillian Hampden-Thompson, and Marion Scotchmer, *School and Parent Interaction by Household Language and Poverty Status: 2002–2003* (Washington DC: IES/U.S. Department of Education, 2006).

10. For example, "Parent Involvement in Elementary School and Educational Attainment," *Children and Youth Services Review* 26, no. 1 (2004): 39–62; Sophia Catsambis and Andrew A. Beveridge, "Does Neighborhood Matter? Family, Neighborhood, and School Influences on Eighth-Grade Mathematics," *Achievement Sociological Focus* 34, no. 4 (2001): 435–457; Melissa A. Clements, Arthur J. Reynolds, and Edmund Hickey, "Site-Level Predictors of Children's School and Social Competence in the Chicago Child-Parent Centers," *Early Childhood Research Quarterly* 19, no. 2 (2004): 273–296; Michelle M. Englund, Amy E. Luckner, and Gloria J. L. Whaley, "Children's Achievement in Early Elementary School: Longitudinal Effects of Parental Involvement, Expectations, and Quality of Assistance," *Journal of Educational Psychology* 96, no. 4 (2004): 723–730; Xitao Fan and Michael Chen, "Parental Involvement and Students' Academic Achievement: A Meta-analysis," *Educational Psychology Review* 13, no. 1 (2001): 1–22; Nancy E. Hill and Diana F. Tyson, "Parental Involvement in Middle School: A Meta-analytic Assessment of the Strategies That Promote Achievement," *Developmental Psychology* 45, no. 3 (2009): 740–763; Seehee Hong and Hsiu-Zu Ho, "Direct and Indirect Longitudinal Effects of Parental Involvement on Student Achievement: Second-Order Latent Growth Modeling Across Ethnic Groups," *Journal of Educational Psychology* 97, no. 5 (2005): 32–42; Jan N. Hughes, Katie A. Gleason and Duan Zhang, "Relationship Influences on Teachers' Perceptions of Academic Competence in Academically At-Risk Minority and Majority First-Grade Students," *Journal of School Psychology* 43, no. 4 (2005): 303–320; William H. Jeynes, "A Meta-analysis: The Effects of Parental Involvement on Minority Children's Academic Achievement," *Education and Urban Society* 35, no. 2 (2003): 202–218; William H. Jeynes, "A Meta-analysis of the Relation of Parental Involvement to Urban Elementary School Student Academic Achievement," *Urban Education* 40, no. 3 (2005): 237–269; William H. Jeynes, "The Effects of Parental Involvement on the Academic Achievement of African American Youth," *Journal of Negro Education* 74, no. 3 (2005): 260–274; William H. Jeynes, "The Relationship Between Parental Involvement and Urban Secondary School Student Academic Achievement: A Meta-analysis," *Urban Education* 42, no. 1 (2007): 82–110; Shane Jimerson, Byron Egeland, L. Alan Sroufe, and Betty Carlson, "A Prospective Longitudinal Study of High School Dropouts Examining Multiple Predictors Across Development," *Journal of School Psychology* 38, no. 6 (2000): 525–549; Christopher Spera, "A Review of the Relationship Among Parenting Practices, Parenting Styles, and Adolescent School Achievement," *Educational Psychology Review* 17, no. 2 (2005): 125–146; Endya B. Stewart, "School Structural Characteristics, Student Effort, Peer Associations, and Parental Involvement: The Influence of School and Individual-Level Factors on Academic Achievement," *Education and Urban Society* 40, no. 2 (2008): 179–204; Wenfan Yan and Qiuyun Lin, "Parent Involvement and Mathematics

Achievement: Contrast Across Racial and Ethnic Groups," *Journal of Educational Research* 99, no. 2 (2005): 116–127.

11. James Comer, *Leave No Child Behind: Preparing Today's Youth for Tomorrow's World* (New Haven, CT: Yale University Press, 2004); Scribner, Young, and Pedroza, "Building Collaborative Relationships."

12. Ibid.

13. For example, Miguel Socias, Lenay Dunn, Thomas Parrish, Mari Muraki, and LaRena Woods, *California High Schools That Beat the Odds in High School Graduation* (Santa Barbara, CA: American Institutes for Research, 2007); Heather B. Weiss, M. Elena Lopez, and Deborah R. Stark, *Breaking New Ground: Data Systems Transform Family Engagement in Education* (Cambridge, MA: Harvard Family Research Project, 2011), downloaded at http://www.hfrp.org/publications-resources/browse-our-publications/breaking-new-ground-data-systems-transform-family-engagement-in-education2.

14. For example, Socias et al., *California High Schools*; Michael W. Kirst and Andrea Venezia, eds., *From High School to College: Improving Opportunities for Success in Postsecondary Education* (San Francisco: Wiley and Sons, 2004).

15. For example, The Harlem Children's Zone (Harlem Children's Zone (2008), http://www.hcz.org/index.html) has established a comprehensive network of community organizations and institutions that promote high expectations.

16. See, for example, Sean Kelly, "Race, Social Class, and Student Engagement in Middle School English Classrooms," *Social Science Research* 37 (2007): 434–448, for a review of some of these debates.

17. For example, Luis C. Moll, Cathy Amanti, Deborah Neff, and Norma Gonzalez, "Funds of Knowledge: Using a Qualitative Approach to Connect Homes and Classrooms," *Theory into Practice* 31, no. 2 (1992): 132–141; Paul E. Heckman, "The Educational and Community Change Project and Community Education," *Community Education Journal* 23, no. 3 (1996): 27–31.

18. Much of this work reflective of Jean Lave and Etienne Wenger, *Situated Learning: Legitimate Peripheral Participation* (London: Cambridge University Press, 1991).

19. Pedro Reyes and Barbara Pazey, "Creating Student-Centered Classroom Environments: The Case of Mathematics," in *Lessons from High Performing Hispanic Schools*, eds. P. Reyes, J. Scribner, and A. Paredes Scribner (New York: Teachers College Press, 1999), 94–130.

20. Williams, Hakuta, and Haertel, *A Follow-Up Analysis*; Gloria Ladson-Billings, *The Dreamkeepers: Successful Teachers of African American Children* (San Francisco: Jossey Bass, 1994); Scribner, Young, and Pedroza, "Building Collaborative Relationships"; Comer, *Leave No Child Behind*; Moll et al., "Funds of Knowledge," 132–141.

21. Socias et al., *California High Schools*; Friedlander and Darling-Hammond, *High School for Equity*.

22. Melinda Mechur Karp, Juan Carlos Calcagno, Katherine L. Hughes, Don Wook Jeong, and Thomas R. Bailey, *The Postsecondary Achievement of Participants in Dual Enrollment: An Analysis of Student Outcomes in Two States* (St. Paul, MN: National Research Center for Career and Technical Education, 2007); Friedlander and Darling-Hammond, *High School for Equity*.

23. For example, Karl L. Alexander, Doris R. Entwisle, and Linda Steffel Olsen, "Lasting Consequences of the Summer Learning Gap," *American Sociological Review* 72, no. 2 (2007): 167–180; David T. Burkam, Douglas D. Ready, Valeria E. Lee, and Laura F. LoGerfo, "Social-Class Differences in Summer Learning Between Kindergarten and First Grade: Model Specification and Estimation," *Sociology of Education* 77, no. 1 (2004): 1–31; Tiffani Chin and Meredith Phillips, "Social Reproduction and Child-Rearing Practices: Social Class, Children's Agency, and the Summer Activity Gap," *Sociology of Education* 77, no. 3 (2004): 185–210.

24. Socias et al., *California High Schools*; Scribner, Young, and Pedroza, "Building Collaborative Relationships"; Friedlander and Darling-Hammond, *High School for Equity*; Chin and Phillips, "Social Reproduction and Child-Rearing practices"; Melissa Ingram, Randi B. Wolfe, and Joyce M. Lieberman, "The Role of Parents in High-Achieving Schools Serving Low-Income, At-Risk

Populations," *Education and Urban Society* 39, no. 4 (2007): 479–497; Suh Ru Ou and Arthur J. Reynolds, "Early Childhood Intervention and Educational Attainment: Age 22 Findings from the Chicago Longitudinal Study," *Journal of Education for Students Placed at Risk* 11, no. 2 (2006): 175–198; Chenoweth "Piece by Piece"; National Research Council, Institute of Medicine, Division of Behavioral and Social Sciences and Education, Board on Children, Youth, and Families, Committee on Increasing High School Students' Engagement and Motivation to Learn, *Engaging Schools: Fostering High School Students' Motivation to Learn.* (Washington, DC: National Academies Press, 2004); Heather B. Weiss, M. Elena Lopez, and Deborah R. Stark, *Breaking New Ground: Data Systems Transform Family Engagement in Education* (Cambridge, MA: Harvard Family Research Project, 2011), downloaded at http://www.hfrp.org/publications-resources/browse-our-publications/breaking-new-ground-data-systems-transform-family-engagement-in-education2.

25. Diana Brannon, "Addressing the Decline of Parent Involvement in Middle School," *Principal* 87, no. 2 (November/December 2007): 62–63; Lionel H. Brown and Kelvin S. Beckett, "Parent Involvement in an Alternative School for Students at Risk of Educational Failure," *Education and Urban Society* 39, no. 4 (2007): 498–523; Jacquelynne Eccles and Rena Harold, "Parent-School Involvement During the Early Adolescent Years," *Teachers College Record* 94 (1993): 568–587; Joyce L. Epstein, "Attainable Goals? The Spirit and Letter of the No Child Left Behind Act on Parental Involvement," *Sociology of Education* 78, no. 2 (2005): 179–182; Joyce L. Epstein, "A Case Study of the Partnership Schools Comprehensive School Reform (CSR) Model," *Elementary School Journal* 106, no. 2 (2005): 151–170; Joyce L. Epstein, "Connections Count: Improving Family and Community Involvement in Secondary Schools," *Principal Leadership* 8, no. 2 (2007): 16–22; Pamela A. Halsey, "Parent Involvement in Junior High Schools: A Failure to Communicate," *American Secondary Education* 34, no. 1 (2005): 57–69; Eva M. Pomerantz, Elizabeth A. Moorman, and Scott D. Litwack, "The How, Whom, and Why of Parents' Involvement in Children's Academic Lives: More Is Not Always Better," *Review of Educational Research* 77, no. 3 (2007): 373–410; Arthur J. Reynolds, Katherine Magnuson, and Suh-Ruu Ou, *PK–3 Education: Programs and Practices That Work in Children's First Decade* (Minneapolis, MN: Early Childhood Research Collaborative, University of Minnesota, 2006); Edward Seidman, Laura E. Lambert, LaRue Allen, and J. Lawrence Aber, "Urban Adolescents' Transition to Junior High School and Protective Family Transactions," *Journal of Early Adolescence* 23, no. 2 (2003): 166–193.

26. Miguel Socias et al., *California High Schools*; Scribner, Young, and Pedroza, "Building Collaborative Relationships."

27. Karen L. Mapp and Soo Hong, "Debunking the Myth of the Hard to Reach Parent," in *Handbook of School-Family Partnerships*, eds. S. L. Christenson and A. L. Reichly (New York: Routledge, 2010), 345–361.

28. Centers for Disease Control and Prevention, "Coordinated School Health," http://www.cdc.gov/healthyyouth/CSHP/; Amy Joyner, "The Healthy Approach: Coordinated School Programs Show That Proper Nutrition, Exercise, and Learning Go Hand-in-Hand," *American School Board Journal* 194, no. 6 (2007): 42–45.

29. The Carnegie Council Task Force on Education of Young Adolescents, *Preparing American Youth for the 21st Century* (New York: Carnegie Council on Adolescent Development, 1989).

30. Paula K. Braverman, "Conceptualizing measures of health disparities," *Annual Review of Public Health* 27 (2005): 167–194.

31. Oscar Barbarin et al., "Children Enrolled in Public Pre-K: The Relation of Family Life, Neighborhood Quality and Socio-economic Resources to Early Competence," *American Journal of Orthopsychiatry* 76, no. 2 (2006): 265–276; Nicholas Freudenberg and Jessica Ruglis, "Reframing School Dropout as a Public Health Issue," *Preventing of Chronic Disease* 4, no. 4 (2007): 1–11; Angus Deaton, "Policy Implications of the Gradient of Health and Wealth," *Health Affairs* 21 (2002): 13–30; Catherine Ross and Chia-ling Wu, "The Links Between Education and Health," *American Sociological Review* 60 (1995): 719–745; Steven H. Woolf, "Potential Health

and Economic Consequences of Misplaced Priorities," *Journal of the American Medical Association* 297, no. 5 (2007): 523–526; California Dropout Research Project and Joshua Breslau, "Health in Childhood and Adolescence and High School Dropout," http://www.cdrp.ucsb.edu/dropouts/pubs_reports.htm.

32. Joshua Breslau, Michael Lane, Nancy Sampson, and Ronald C. Kessler, "Mental Disorders and Subsequent Educational Attainment in a U.S. National Sample," *Journal of Psychiatric Research* 42, no. 9 (2008): 708–716.

33. Victoria K. Ngo et al., "Providing Evidence-Based Practice to Ethnically Diverse Youth: Examples from the Cognitive Behavioral Intervention for Trauma in Schools (CBITS) Program," *Journal of the American Academy of Child and Adolescent Psychiatry* 47, no. 8 (2008): 858–862.

34. See Centers for Disease Control and Prevention, "Coordinated School Health," http://www.cdc.gov/healthyyouth/CSHP/. Nancy G. Murray, Barbara J. Low, Christine Hollis, Alan W. Cross, and Sally M. Davis, "Coordinated School Health Programs and Academic Achievement: A Systematic Review of the Literature," *Journal of School Health* 77, no. 9 (2007): 589–600.

35. Joyner, "The Healthy Approach," 42–45.

36. David Evans et al., "A School Health Education Program for Children with Asthma Aged 8–11 years," *Health Education Quarterly* 14, no. 3 (1987): 267–279; Noreen M. Clark et al., "Effects of a Comprehensive School-Based Asthma Program on Symptoms, Parent Management, Grades, and Absenteeism," *Chest* 125, no. 5 (2004): 1674–1679.

37. Ellen E. Kisker and Randall S. Brown, "Do School-Based health Centers Improve Adolescents' Access to Health Care, Health Status, and Risk-Taking Behavior?" *Journal of Adolescent Health* 18 (1996): 335–343; Gail Gall et al., "Utility of Psychosocial Screening at a School-Based Health Center," *Journal of School Health* 70, no. 7 (2000): 292–298; Samira Soleimanpour, Sara P. Geierstanger, Shelly Kaller, Virginia McCarter, and Claire Brindis, "The Role of School Health Centers in Health Care Access and Client Outcomes," *American Journal of Public Health* 100, no. 9 (2010): 1597–1603; Jeff J. Guo, Terrance J. Wade, Wei Pan, and Kathryn N. Keller, "School-Based Health Centers Cost Benefit Analysis and Impact on Health Care Disparities," *American Journal of Public Health* 100, no. 9 (2010): 1617–1623; Miles A. McNall, Lauren F. Lichty, and Brian Mavis, "The Impact of School-Based Health Centers on the Health Outcomes of Middle School and High School Students," *American Journal of Public Health* 100, no. 9 (2010): 1604–1610.

38. Gail Gall et al., "Utility of Psychosocial Screening," 292–298; Kisker and Brown, "School Based Health Centers," 335–343; Marcella McCord, Jonathan Klein, Jane M. Foy, and Kate Fothergill, "School-Based Clinic Use and School Performance," *Journal of Adolescent Health* 14, no. 2 (1993): 91–98; Mayris Webber et al., "Burden of Asthma in Inner-City Elementary Schoolchildren," *Archives of Pediatrics and Adolescent Medicine* 157 (2003): 125–129.

39. UCLA Center for Healthier Children, Families and Communities, "Sustainability of California's Healthy Start Initiative," 2006, http://www.healthychild.ucla.edu/sustainabilitycaliforniashealthystart.asp; Lisa R. Villarreal, "California's Healthy Start: A Solid Platform for Promoting Youth Development," *New Directions for Youth Development* 107 (2005): 89–97; Mary M. Wagner and Shari Golan, *A Healthy Start for California's Children and Families: Early Findings from a Statewide Evaluation of School-Linked Services* (Menlo Park, CA: SRI International, 1994).

40. Camilla A. Lehr, Mary F. Sinclair, and Sandra L. Christenson, "Addressing Student Engagement and Truancy Prevention During the Elementary School Years: A Replication Study of the Check & Connect Model," *Journal of Education for Students Placed at Risk* 9, no. 3 (2004): 279–301; Mary F. Sinclair, Sandra L. Christenson, and Martha L. Thurow, "Promoting School Completion of Urban Secondary Youth with Emotional or Behavioral Disabilities," *Exceptional Children* 71, no. 4 (2005): 465–482.

41. Patricia Gándara, Katherine Larson, Hugh Mehan, and Russell Rumberger, "Capturing Latino Students in the Academic Pipeline" (Berkeley: Chicano Latino Policy Project/University of California, 1998), http://escholarship.org/uc/item/84h2j4qs#page-1.

42. For example, Chenoweth, "Piece by Piece"; Bryk, Sebring, and Allensworth, *Organizing Schools for Improvement.*
43. Comer, *Leave No Child Behind*; Concha Delgado-Gaitan, *The Power of Community: Mobilizing for Family and Schooling* (Lanham, MD: Rowman & Littlefield, 2001); Scribner, Young, and Pedroza, "Building Collaborative Relationships"; Friedlander and Darling-Hammond, *High School for Equity*; Andrew Calkins, William Guenther, Grace Belfiore, and Dave Lash, *The Turnaround Challenge: Why America's Best Opportunity to Dramatically Improve Student Achievement Lies in Our Worst-Performing Schools* (Boston, MA: Mass Insight Education and Research Institute, 2007); Janice M. Hirota, *Reframing Education: The Partnership Strategy and Public Schools* (New York: Carnegie Corporation of New York, 2005); Janice Hirota and Lauren E. Jacobs, *Vital Voices: Building Constituencies for Public School Reform* (Chicago: Chapin Hall Center for Children, University of Chicago, 2003); Miguel Socias et al., *California High Schools*; Stone et al., *Building Civic Capacity.*
44. Hirota, *Reframing Education.*
45. Kelly Bathgate and Elena Silva, "Joining Forces: The Benefits of Integrating Schools and Community Providers," *New Directions for Youth Development*, no. 127 (2010): 63–72.
46. Eileen M. Foley, Allan Klinge, and Elizabeth Reisner, Evaluation of New Century High Schools: Profile of an Initiative to Create and Sustain Small, Successful High Schools (Washington, DC: Policy Studies Associates, 2007, rev. 2008), http://www.newvisions.org/node/313/10/1/49; Howard S. Bloom, Saskia L. Thompson, Rebecca Unterman, with Corinne Herlihy and Collin Payne, "Transforming the High School Experience: How New York City's New Small Schools Are Boosting Student Achievement and Graduation Rates" (New York: MDRC, June 2010), http://www.mdrc.org/project_29_96.html.
47. Eileen M. Foley, *Approaches of Bill & Melinda Gates Foundation–Funded Intermediary Organizations to Structuring and Supporting Small High Schools in New York City* (Washington DC: Policy Studies Associates, 2010), http://www.mdrc.org/project_29_96.html; Hirota, *Reframing Education.*
48. Lee Benson, Ira Harkavy, and John Puckett, "An Implementation Revolution as a Strategy for Fulfilling the Democratic Promise of University-Community Partnerships: Penn-West Philadelphia as an Experiment in Progress," *Nonprofit and Voluntary Sector Quarterly* 29, no. 1 (2000): 24–45; Ellen B. Goldring and Pearl Sims, "Modeling Creative and Courageous School Leadership Through District-Community-University Partnerships," *Educational Policy* 19, no. 1 (2005): 223–249.
49. Calkins et al., *The Turnaround Challenge*; Friedlander and Darling-Hammond, *High School for Equity*; Bloom et al., "Transforming the High School Experience."
50. For example, see Tamar Cooper and Jeffrey Vincent, *Joint Use School Partnerships in California: Strategies to Enhance Schools and Communities* (Berkeley, CA: Center for Cities and Schools, UC Berkeley, 2008).
51. Martin J. Blank, Reuben Jacobson, Atelia Melaville, and Sarah S. Pearson, "Financing Community Schools: Leveraging Resources to Support Student Success" (report for the Coalition for Community Schools, Institute for Educational Leadership, 2010) found sites that they studied leveraged approximately $3 for each $1 of district funding (p.9). Because their report does not present data and methods, we are unable to independently verify this finding.
52. For example, Odis Johnson, "Assessing Neighborhood Racial Segregation and Macroeconomic Effects in the Education of African Americans," *Review of Educational Research* 80, no. 4 (2010): 527–575.
53. For example, Robert Crosnoe, "Academic Orientation and Parental Involvement in Education During High School," *Sociology of Education* 74, no. 3 (2001): 210–230; Stone et al., *Building Civic Capacity*; Gavin Shatkin and Alec Ian Gershberg, "Empowering Parents and Building Communities: The Role of School-Based Councils in Educational Governance and Accountability," *Urban Education* 42 (2007): 582–615.
54. Mark R. Warren, "Communities and Schools: A New View of Urban Education Reform," *Harvard Educational Review* 75, no. 2 (2005): 133–173.

55. See The Harlem Children's Zone, "The HCZ Project," http://www.hcz.org/about-us/the-hcz-project.
56. Will Dobbie and Roland G. Fryer Jr., "Are High Quality Schools Enough to Close the Achievement Gap? Evidence from a Social Experiment in Harlem" (working paper 15473, National Bureau of Economic Research, Cambridge, MA, 2009), http://www.nber.org/papers/w15473.
57. Bryk, Sebring, and Allensworth, *Organizing Schools for Improvement.*
58. Ibid., 22.
59. See, for example, Minority Student Achievement Network (http://msan.wceruw.org/), a national coalition of multiracial, suburban-urban school districts that have come together to study and eliminate achievement gaps that exist in their districts; members share a history of high academic achievement, connections to major research universities, and resources that generally exceed those of neighboring districts.
60. Novella Z. Keith, "Can Urban School Reform and Community Development Be Joined? The Potential of Community Schools," *Education and Urban Society* 28, no. 2 (1996): 237–268.
61. See, for example, Jean Anyon, *Ghetto Schooling: A Political Economy of Urban Educational Reform* (New York: Teachers College Press, 1997); Amanda Datnow et al., "Comprehensive School Reform in Culturally and Linguistically Diverse Contexts: Implementation and Outcomes from a Four-Year Study," *Educational Evaluation and Policy Analysis* 25, no. 2 (2003): 143–170; John Diamond, "Still Separate and Unequal: Examining Race, Opportunity and School Achievement in 'Integrated' Suburbs," *Journal of Negro Education* 75, no. 3 (2006): 495–505; and Pedro A. Noguera and Jean Y. Wing, eds., *Unfinished Business: Closing the Racial Achievement Gap in Our Schools* (San Francisco: Jossey Bass, 2006) for further discussion of structural racism and classism and educational reform.
62. The work of this initiative is reported in From the Community to the Classroom, "A Youth-Directed Documentary of How Davis Young People Led Their Community Closer Toward Educational Equity," http://communityclassroom.wordpress.com/.
63. Institute for Educational Leadership, "Coalition for Community Schools," http://www.communityschools.org/aboutschools/what_is_a_community_school.aspx.
64. Joy Dryfoos, Jane Quinn, and Carol Barkin, *Community Schools in Action: Lessons from a Decade of Practice* (New York: Oxford University Press, 2005); Keith, "Urban School Reform and Community Development," 237–268.
65. Mark R. Warren, "Communities and Schools: A New View of Urban Education Reform," *Harvard Educational Review* 75, no. 2 (2005): 133–173; Claire Smrekar, Lora Cohen-Vogel, and J. Lee, "Mapping Family-School Relations in Comprehensive School Reform Models and Charter School Designs: A Call for a New Research Agenda," in *Handbook of School-Family Partnerships*, eds. Sandra L. Christenson and Amy L. Reschly (New York: Routledge, 2010), 380–406.
66. We draw heavily in this section from several comprehensive reviews of research, including Sandra L. Christenson and Amy L. Reschly, *Handbook of School Family Partnerships* (New York: Routledge, 2009); Henderson and Mapp, *A New Wave of Evidence*; Boethel, *Diversity: School, Family, and Community Connections*; and *Readiness: School, Family, and Community Connections.*
67. Melanie E. Trevino and Jann Murray-García, "Cultural Humility Versus Cultural Competency: A Critical Distinction in Defining Physician Training Outcomes in Multicultural Education," *Journal of Health Care for the Poor and Underserved* 9, no. 2 (1998): 117–125, coined the term "cultural humility" to describe a set of understandings and practices that enable effective engagement across cultures, as genuine cultural capacity is not always possible.
68. Martin J. Blank et al., "Financing Community Schools"; Wagner and Golan, *A Healthy Start*; Villarreal, "California's Healthy Start," 89–97.
69. Andrew L. Bundy, "Aligning Systems to Create Full-Service schools: The Boston Experience, So Far," *New Directions for Youth Development* 107 (2005): 79.
70. Meredith I. Honig and Kyle Fiore, *Working with Young People as Partners: A Guide for School-Linked Services Sites* (Davis, CA: California Healthy Start Field Office, UC Davis, 1997), http://hsfo.ucdavis.edu/hsfo.html; Jonathan K. London, Kristen Zimmerman, and Nancy Erbstein,

"Youth-Led Research and Evaluation: Tools for Youth, Organizational, and Community Development," *New Directions for Evaluation* 98 (2003): 33–45.

71. Clarence N. Stone, "Civic Capacity and Urban School Reform," 250–274; Ellen B. Goldring and Charles S. Hausman, "Civic Capacity and School Principals," in *Community Development and School Reform*, ed. Robert L. Crowson (London: Elsevier Science, 2001).

72. Joyce L. Epstein and Mavis G. Sanders, "Prospects for Change: Preparing Educators for School, Family, and Community Partnerships," *Peabody Journal of Education* 81, no. 2 (2006): 81–120.

73. According to the Harlem Children's Zone website, in 2010, their annual budget was approximately $48 million, or about $5000 per child (The Harlem Children's Zone, "The HCZ Project," http://www.hcz.org/about-us/the-hcz-project).

74. For example, Title 1 funds, NCLB tutoring provisions, Migrant Education funds, Homeless Youth program funds, Foster Youth program funds, 21st Century Community Learning Center funds, Home Visitation program funds, etc.

75. For example, see Nancy Erbstein and Joanne Bookmyer, "Afterschool Evaluation Practices in California" (Davis, CA: Center for Community School Partnerships, UC Davis School of Education, 2005), www.afterschoolresources.org/kernel/images/ccspeval.pdf for a study of California afterschool program evaluation practices.

76. Glenn E. Singleton and Curtis W. Linton, *Courageous Conversations About Race: A Field Guide for Achieving Equity in Schools* (Thousand Oaks, CA: Corwin Press, 2006).

Chapter 11

1. Julian R. Betts, "Critical Path Analysis 2: California's K–12 Sector," (Sacramento: California Council on Science and Technology, 2002).

2. EdSource, "Governor's Committee on Education Excellence," http://www.edsource.org/school-finance.html/ReformProposals/GovernorsCommitteeReport/tabid/185/Default.aspx.

3. Frederick M. Hess, *With the Best of Intentions* (Cambridge,: MA:, Harvard Education Press, 2005); Charles M. Payne, *So Much Reform, So Little Change: The Persistence of Failure in Urban Schools* (Cambridge, MA: Harvard Education Press, 2010), 4–39; Clarence N. Stone, Jeffrey R. Henig, Bryan D. Jones, and Carol Pierannunzi, *Building Civic Capacity: The Politics of Reforming Public Schools,* Studies in Government and Public Policy (Lawrence, KS: University Press of Kansas, 2001).

4. Payne, *So Much Reform,* 4.

5. Ibid., 5.

6. David K. Cohen and Susan L. Moffitt, *The Order of Equality: Did Government Regulation Fix the Schools?* (Cambridge, MA: Harvard University Press, 2009).

7. Francis Schrag, "Postsecondary Schooling/ Education for All," in *Philosophy of Education 2007*, ed. Barbara S. Stengel (Glasgow, UK: Wiley-Blackwell, 2007), 36.

8. Ibid.

9. Larry Cuban and Michael Usdan, *Powerful Reforms with Shallow Roots: Improving America's Urban Schools* (New York: Teachers College Press, 2003): 165.

10. C. D. Jerald, "Diversity in Early Childhood Intervention Leadership," *Education Week Quality Counts: The Urban Challenge* (1998).

11. National Center for Education Statistics, "The Condition of Education," http://nces.ed.gov/programs/coe/indicator_pcp.asp.

12. Charles M. Blow, "Empire at the End of Decadence," *The New York Times,* February 18, http://www.nytimes.com/2011/02/19/opinion/19blow.html?_r=1.

13. The Harlem Children's Zone, www.hcz.org.

14. Bradley D. Stein et al., "A Mental Health Intervention for Schoolchildren Exposed to Violence: A Randomized Control Trial," *Journal of the American Medical Association* 290, no. 5 (2003): 630.

15. Ibid., 603.

16. Jill Tucker, "Children Who Survive Urban Warfare Suffer from PTSD, Too," *San Francisco Chronicle,* August 26, 2007.

17. Ibid.

18. Paul E. Barton and Richard J Coley, "The Black and White Achievement Gap: When Progress Stopped," Educational Testing Service: Policy Information Report, (Princeton: Educational Testing Service, 2008).

19. Ibid.

20. The Broader, Bolder Approach to Education, http://www.boldapproach.org/index.php?id=01.

21. Norton Grubb, "Dynamic Inequality and Intervention: Lessons from a Small Country," *The Phi Delta Kappan* 89, no. 2 (2007): 105–114.

22. Some disparage the argument that out-of-school factors should be taken into account suggesting that such an argument is an excuse for failure. That is not the argument here. Schools need to be held accountable for the quality of education that they provide. But, the current grab-bag of sanctions against persistently low-performing schools is unlikely to help solve the achievement gap.

23. Thomas Timar, Manuelito Biag, and Michael Lawson, *California Dropout Research Project* (Santa Barbara, CA: Gevirtz Graduate School of Education, 2008).

24. Clarence N. Stone, *Changing Urban Education: Studies in Government and Public Policy* (Lawrence, KS: University Press of Kansas, 1998); Stone et al., *Building Civic Capacity*; Cuban and Usdan, *Powerful Reforms.*

25. Anthony S. Bryk, *Organizing Schools for Improvement: Lessons from Chicago* (Chicago, Illinois: The University of Chicago Press, 2010), 187.

26. Ibid., 194.

27. Ibid., 196.

28. National Commission on Excellence in Education, *A Nation at Risk: The Imperative for Educational Reform* (Washington, DC: U.S. Department of Education, 1983).

29. Robert D. Putnam, *Making Democracy Work* (Princeton,: NJ:, Princeton University Press, 1993); Francis Fukuyama, *Trust: The Social Virtues and the Creation of Prosperity* (New York. NY, Free Press, 1995), Anthony S. Bryk and Barbara Schneider, *Trust in Schools: A Core Resource for Improvement* (New York: Russell Sage Foundation, 2002); Anthony S. Bryk et al., *Organizing Schools for Improvement: Lessons from Chicago* (Chicago, Illinois: The University of Chicago Press, 2010): 187–196; David Kirp and Thomas Timar, *Managing Educational Excellence* (London: Falmer Press, 1988).

30. Lorraine M. McDonnell and Richard F. Elmore, "Getting the Job Done: Alternative Policy Instruments," *Educational Evaluation and Policy Analysis* 9, no. 2 (Summer 1987): 133–152.

31. Kirp and Timar, *Managing Educational Excellence.*

32. Paul Berman and Milbery Wallin McLaughlin, *Federal Programs Supporting Educational Change:* vol. VIII, (Santa Monica, CA: RAND Corporation, 1978).

33. James S. Coleman et al., *Equality of Educational Opportunity* (Washington, DC: U.S. Department of Health, Education and Welfare, 1966); Bryk and Schneider, *Trust in Schools*; Bryk, *Organizing Schools for Improvement*, 187–196; Martin Carnoy, *Cuba's Academic Advantage: Why Students in Cuba Do Better in School* (Stanford, CA: Stanford University Press, 2007); Putnam, *Making Democracy Work.*

34. Cuban and Usdan, *Powerful Reforms*; Stone, *Changing Urban Education*; Stone et al., *Building Civic Capacity*; Bryk and Schneider, *Trust in Schools*; Bryk et al., *Organizing Schools for Improvement*; Hess, *With the Best of Intentions.*

35. Payne, *So Much Reform*, 26.

36. Fukuyama (1995), Putnam (1995).

37. Penny Bender Sebring, Anthony S. Bryk, John Q. Easton et al, "Charting Reform: Chicago Teachers Take Stock," (report from the Consortium on Chicago School Research, 1995), 61.

38. Quote from Payne, *So Much Reform*, 36.

39. Ibid., 39; italics in original.

40. Thomas Timar and Kris Kim Chyu, "State Strategies to Improve Low-Performing Schools: California's High Priority Schools Grant Program," *Teachers College Record* 112, no. 7 (2010): 1897–1936.

41. Ibid.

42. Mark G. Yudof, David Kirp, Betsy Levin, and Rachel Moran, *Educational Policy and the Law* (St. Paul, MN: Wadsworth Publishing, 1992), 699.

43. Arthur E. Wise, *Legislated Learning: The Bureaucratization of the American Classroom* (Berkeley: University of California Press, 1979); David Kirp and Donald Jensen, *School Days, Rule Days*, (Philadelphia: Falmer Press, 1986).

44. Kirp and Timar, *Managing Educational Excellence*, 3.

45. Deepa Srikantaiah, "How State and Federal Accountability Policies Have Influenced Curriculum and Instruction in Three States: Common Findings from Rhode Island, Illinois, and Washington" (Washington, DC: Center on Education Policy, 2009).

46. Richard Kahlenberg, "Low Income Students and KIPP Charter Schools: A Reply to Matthew Yglesias," *A Century Foundation Group* (blog), June 3, 2011, takingnote.tcf.org.

47. Cohen and Moffitt, *The Order of Equality*; David K. Cohen, Stephen W. Raudenbush, and Deborah Loewenberg Ball, "Resources, Instruction and Research," *Educational Evaluation and Policy Analysis* 25, no. 2 (2003): 122.

48. Thomas Piketty and Emmanuel Saez, "Income Inequality in the United States: 1913—1998," *The Quarterly Journal of Economics* 117, no. 1 (2003).

49. The Gini Coefficient is used as the standard measure of income distribution. The scale is between zero and one, where one is total inequality. In 2008, the United States had a Gini of 0.48. Australia and Canada had scores of 0.305 and 0.321 respectively. See Blow, "End of Decadence."

50. Susan Aud et al., *The 2010 Condition of Education* (Washington, D.C.: Institute of Education Sciences and National Center for Education Statistics, 2010).

51. Ibid., 2.

52. Ibid., 7.

53. Wall Street Journal, adcorp.org/news/pdfs/WSJ%20DOE%20HPN%202010.pdf.

54. Jennifer Gollan, "Willie Brown Academy, Born in 1992 with High Hopes, Will Close in May, a Failure," *The New York Times*, April 16, 2011.

55. Brian Rowan, Richard Correnti, and Robert J. Miller, "What Large-Scale, Survey Research Tells Us About Teacher Effects on Student Achievement: Insights from the Prospects Study of Elementary Schools" (Princeton, NJ: Consortium for Policy Research in Education, University of Pennsylvania, 2002).

Acknowledgments

This work was a group effort and owes a great deal to a number of individuals. First of all, the editors would like to recognize the former California Superintendent of Public Instruction, Jack O'Connell, for conceiving of the P-16 Commission on Closing the Achievement Gap, which was the impetus for most of the papers in this volume, and the members of the commission who called for the research support for their work, which these papers represent. The Gates Foundation provided the funding for the original papers, many of which are included in this volume, edited to reflect a more nationwide focus. We are grateful for this initial support although the papers do not represent the position of the foundation.

Key staff members at the University of California, Davis, and the Sacramento, California, office of WestEd were extremely helpful as well. In particular, the organizational effort to commission, edit, and disseminate the original P-16 papers would not have been possible without the guiding hand of Ginger Adams Simon. We also thank Kelsey Krausen for her able assistance in formatting and copyediting the current volume and the graduate and other students who contributed to compiling and summarizing the literature for these chapters and the original papers on which they are based.

We are grateful to the authors who contributed to this volume for their professionalism and the high quality of their work. We also thank the publisher, Harvard Education Press, for deciding to publish this volume. In particular the suggestions and guidance of Doug Clayton of the Press, along with those of the reviewers, have resulted in a much stronger work.

Finally, we would like to recognize and thank the many dedicated educators for the extraordinary work they do in classrooms and schools every day to help students learn.

About the Editors

THOMAS B. TIMAR is a professor and the executive director of the Center for Applied Policy in Education in the University of California, Davis, School of Education. His research focuses on education policy, politics, governance, and finance. His most recent research is on school and district reform and the use of resources in schools.

JULIE MAXWELL-JOLLY is a senior researcher and the managing director of the Center for Applied Policy in Education at the University of California, Davis, School of Education. Her research focus is policy and practice related to the instruction of English language learners.

About the Contributors

EVA L. BAKER is a Distinguished Professor at the University of California, Los Angeles, and director of the National Center for Research on Evaluation, Standards, and Student Testing (CRESST) and the Center for Advanced Technology in Schools. Her research focus is the integration of instruction and measurement, including design and empirical validation of principles for developing instructional systems, and new measures of complex human performance.

KILCHAN CHOI is principal research analyst at the American Institutes for Research (AIR). He specializes in issues of multisite evaluations, growth models, school effectiveness, and school accountability.

NAOMI and VICTOR CHUDOWSKY are consultants with Caldera Research, LLC. For much of the past decade they have conducted research on testing and accountability for the Center on Education Policy and other clients.

NANCY ERBSTEIN is an assistant research scientist in the University of California, Davis, Department of Human and Community Development. Her research focuses on promoting equitable outcomes for youth—in particular exploring the challenges and resources of marginalized places and youth populations, the ways that schools and their communities produce and confront disparate youth opportunities, and the relationship between educational reform, public health, and community development.

JOSE A. ESPINOZA is a doctoral candidate in the Graduate School of Education at the University of California, Riverside.

PATRICIA GÁNDARA is codirector of the Civil Rights Project/Proyecto Derechos Civiles at UCLA. Gándara's research focuses on educational equity for racial and linguistic minority students, school reform, access to higher education, the education of Latino students, and language policy.

NOELLE C. GRIFFIN is assistant director for Research and Evaluation at the National Center for Research on Evaluation, Standards, and Student Testing (CRESST) at the University of California, Los Angeles. She has led numerous evaluations of national, state, and local educational initiatives, with a focus on assessment-based innovations.

W. NORTON GRUBB is a professor and the David Gardner Chair in Higher Education at the School of Education, the University of California, Berkeley. He is also the faculty coordinator for the Principal Leadership Institute, a program preparing leaders for urban schools. His interests include higher education, especially community colleges; the effects of resources in schools; the occupational roles of education, including vocational education and training (VET); secondary schools and their reforms; and equity issues.

EDMUND T. HAMANN is an associate professor at the University of Nebraska–Lincoln in the Department of Teaching, Learning, and Teacher Education. Trained as an anthropologist of education, he studies the relationships between how various student groups (e.g., ELLs, Latino newcomers in the "New Latino Diaspora," students in Mexico with previous experience in the U.S.) are conceptualized by teachers, administrators, community leaders, and others and how this conceptualizing translates into local educational policy that affects what school practices these students encounter and how they fare.

NANCY KOBER has been a consultant to the Center on Education Policy since 1995. She has written or coauthored numerous CEP publications on such topics as student achievement trends and implementation of the No Child Left Behind Act.

ELIZABETH MILLER is chief of adolescent medicine at Children's Hospital Pittsburgh, the University of Pittsburgh Medical Center. Her research has included examination of sex trafficking among adolescents in Asia, teen dating abuse, and reproductive health, with a focus on underserved youth populations, including pregnant and parenting teens and foster, homeless, and gang-affiliated youth.

DOUGLAS E. MITCHELL is a professor of education at the University of California, Riverside. His research focus is on education policy analysis, philosophy of science, and research methods.

ROBERT K. REAM is an associate professor in the Graduate School of Education at the University of California, Riverside. His areas of specialization are education policy, social capital, and Latina/o social demography.

JENELLE REEVES is an associate professor in the department of Teaching, Learning, and Teacher Education at the University of Nebraska-Lincoln. She researches teacher development and the preparation of teachers to work with English language learners in K–12 classrooms.

RUSSELL W. RUMBERGER is vice provost for education partnerships for the University of California Office of the President and professor of education in the Gevirtz Graduate School of Education at UC Santa Barbara. His research interests include: education and work; the schooling of disadvantaged students, particularly school dropouts and linguistic minority students; school effectiveness; and education policy.

SARAH M. RYAN is a doctoral candidate in the Graduate School of Education at the University of California, Riverside. Ms. Ryan is a dissertation fellow of the Association for Institutional Research (AIR).

Index

Abecedarian Project, 137
ability-group tracking, 119
"A Broader, Bolder Approach to Education," 234
abstract resources, 61–62, 75, 191, 193, 198, 200
academic achievement
  low, 45
  poverty, 50
  racial/ethnic differences in, 37
  teacher-to-home communication, 171
academic disparities, partnering to address, 205–226
academic emphasis, 153
academic expectations, 85
academic language and second-language learners, 176
academic literacy, discipline-specific, 102–103
Academic Performance Index (API), 83, 145, 148
academic readiness and ability, 111
Accelerated Schools, 238, 246
accountability systems, 62, 88–89
achievement differences, history of, 36
achievement gaps
  ability-group tracking, 119
  African American students, 82–83, 197
  American Indian students, 197
  Asian American students, 197
  average yearly change in, 26
  California, 77–94, 142–145
  causes, 91
  closing, 1–2, 79–80
  college, 2, 42–45
  college readiness, 63
  consequences, 52–53
  contextual framework, 2
  costs to society, 52–53
  curricular reforms, 114
  defining, 57, 78–80
  dropout rates, 2
  dynamic process creating, 60
  early childhood programs, 58
  ebb and flow, 37–40
  education policy outside schools, 80
  eliminating, 52–53
  English language learners (ELLs), 164
  genetic inevitability of, 38–39
  high-performing nations, 141
  high schools, 6, 42–45, 155–159
  immigrant and native-born students, 57
  inequalities, 74
  international and national, 5, 80–82
  K–12 academic, 5–6
  Latino students, 82, 197
  marker approach, 79
  measures of, 86–90
  median rates of change, 13, 27–28
  metrics, 78–79
  minority family conditions and, 37–38
  mistreatment in schools, 66–67
  multiple, 2, 57, 62–64
  NAEP, 40–42
  nonschool sources of, 8, 70–74, 80
  organizational strategies addressing, 111–139
  period of scarcity and, 198–204
  persistence, 78, 91
  policies, 57–58, 77, 135–136, 245
  progress in, 4, 13
  racial/ethnic inequality, 66, 197
  reduction research, 84–86
  reform policies, 7–8
  reframing ecology of, 35–56
  resistance to narrowing, 2, 74
  schools, 6, 8
  social justice, 109
  social systems, 112–113
  sources of, 46–52

achievement gaps, *continued*
  standards, 77–78
  state rates of change, 28–29
  state tests, 11–33, 22–26
  strategies, 63–64
  support services, 70–72
  time required to close, 26–29
  in tough times, 187–204
  United States, 141
  urban education, 232
  white students, 197
administrators and professional
    development, 222
adolescents, 71, 178
affective outcomes, 103–104
African American students
  achievement gaps, 13, 82, 83, 197
  alienation of, 67
  biology programs, 44
  California High School Exit Exam
    (CAHSEE), 84
  California high schools, 143–144
  classroom behavior, 169
  college educational attainment, 44
  cost of educating, 185
  discipline policies, 67
  dropout rates, 43, 63, 83
  educational improvements, 12, 233
  instructional strategies, 105
  median rates of change, 13, 27–28
  NAEP scores, 82
  North Carolina, 168
  parental dropouts, 50
  poverty, 232
  public schools, 187
  resegregation, 46–48
  state tests, 12–13, 18
  stereotype threat, 52
  teachers and, 104, 167
  test scores, 40–41, 144
African American teachers, 169–171
after-school programs, 65, 72, 195
Agricultural Extension Service, 202
ALAS, 212, 213
Alexander, Karl, 48
alternative certification programs, 122
alternative education, 196
alternative schools, 126
alternative structures, 154

American Educational Research Journal, 96
American Education Research Association,
    95
American Indian students, 187, 197
America's Choice, 202
Anthropology and Education Quarterly, 96
API. *See* Academic Performance Index (API)
aptitude tests, 39
artist unions, 124
Asian American students
  achievement gaps, 197
  California high schools, 143
  dropout rates, 43
  state tests, 12
  test performance (2009), 24
  test scores, 144
  trends for, 17
Asian Pacific American students, 40–41
assessment knowledge, 173
assessments, 115–117
  cognitive readiness, 89
  documenting, 93–94, 115
  formative uses of, 92
  reforms, 116
  relationship with instruction, 100
  revised and blended, 90–91
  statewide system of, 92
  student and teacher learning needs, 92,
    115
assistant principals, professional capacities
    of, 62
attendance boundaries, 127–128
AVID, 132, 238

background knowledge, 105
Bad Boys (Ferguson), 198
Baltimore City Public Schools, 48
Barton, Paul, 37
basic academic preparation, 63
basic skills instruction, 59
Beacon Schools, 212
Beginning Teacher Support and Assessment,
    122
beliefs, 216
Bell, Terrel, 37
The Bell Curve (Herrnstein and Murray),
    38–39
bilingual/bicultural education, 69

bilingual teachers, 173
English language learners (ELLs), 176, 184
Black English, 104
blacks. *See* African American students
Bronfenbrenner, Urie, 39
Brown decisions (1954 and 1955), 133
Brown v. Board, 227
bubble kids, 244
bullying, 97
business/industrial model, 126

CAHSEE. *See* California High School Exit Exam (CAHSEE)
California
academic performance, 93
Academic Performance Index (API), 83, 148
achievement gaps, 77–94
African American students, 83, 163
alternative certification program, 122
alternative schools, 126, 154
background characteristics of students, 151
Beacon Schools, 212
Beginning Teacher Support and Assessment, 122
California High School Exit Exam (CAHSEE), 83–84
California Learning Assessment System (CLAS) test, 116
California Standards Test (CST), 83–84
charter schools, 154
class size, 107, 128, 138, 151, 190
closing achievement gap, 141–142
Common Core State Standards, 82
desegregation, 134
districts and counties, 235, 247
frameworks, 90
funding, 235
Governor's Committee on Education Excellence, 227
Healthy Start, 212
high schools, 142–145, 154–156
in-service training, 183
judicial intervention, 133
Latino students, 83–84
lower ranks in NAEP scores, 82

low-performing schools, 240, 243
overcrowding schools, 159
P-16 Council, 142
preservice screening tests, 122
Proposition 13 (1978), 133, 235
Race to the Top funds, 247
reform model, 9
resources, 151, 157, 158
school by school change, 246–247
school-linked initiatives, 212
school location, 154
school lunch program, 157
special education services, 132
standards, 86–87
standards-based reforms, 117
state accountability system, 148
subgroups, 93
teacher absenteeism and school location, 167
testing concerns, 87–88
truancy, 235
well-trained teachers, 107
Williams case, 125
year-round high schools, 152
California Achievement Test (CAT), 48
California Collaborative on District Reform, 238
California Council on Science and Technology, 227
California Governor's Committee on Educational Excellence, 112, 132, 134, 227
California High School Exit Exam (CAHSEE), 83–84
California Learning Assessment System (CLAS) test, 116
California P-16 Council, 3
California Standards Test (CST), 83–84, 144, 227
California State University (CSU), 143
Canada, Geoffrey, 55, 233
capacity, 60–62, 75
Carnegie Council Task Force on Education of Young Adolescents, 210
Carnegie's Alliance for Education Excellence, 172
CAT. *See* California Achievement Test (CAT)
categorical funding, 202

Catholic schools, 149
CCSR. *See* Chicago Consortium on School Research (CCSR)
CCSS. *See* Common Core State Standards (CCSS)
CDE Web site, 83
Center for Education Policy (CEP), 243
Center for Research on Education, Diversity, and Excellence (CREDE), 101, 172–174
The Center for the Future of Teaching and Learning, 167
Center on Education Policy (CEP), 4, 11, 29
CEP. *See* Center for Education Policy (CEP)
certified teachers, 166
charity schools, 187
charter schools, 120–121, 127, 154
  dropouts, 126
  low-performing schools, 8, 243–244
  successes, 244
Check & Connect, 212
Chicago
  mayoral control of schools, 235
  relationships within schools, 239
  social resources, 153
Chicago Child-Parent Center and Expansion Program, 137
Chicago Consortium on School Research (CCSR), 61, 236
childhood mental disorders, 211
children
  impact of violence on, 233
  poverty, 232
  seasonality of learning, 48–50
  vocabulary scores and home life, 50
child welfare programs, 73
Christmas tree schools, 65, 200
Civil Rights Act (1964), 37, 46
civil rights movement, 242
classes, detracking, 119
classroom-level restructuring options, 118–121
classroom observation, 67, 70
classrooms
  community social services, 121
  compositions, 127–128, 136
  organization, 6, 111–139, 118
  performance, 136
  redistributing achievement within, 136
  segregating students, 118

  size of, 128–129, 138
  socio-historico-political realities, 105
CLDs. *See* culturally and linguistically diverse students (CLDs)
closing achievement gap, 197
  bottom-up policies, 9–10
  high schools, 6
  policies, 2
  policy makers, 1–2
  progress in, 4
  reframing policy and practice, 227–249
  schools succeeding in, 247
  top-down policy instruments, 9–10
Closing the Achievement Gap: Report of Superintendent Jack O'Connell's California P-16 Council (2008), 7
Coalition for Community Schools, 217
Coalition of Essential Schools, 238, 246
cognitive outcomes, 97–98
cognitive readiness, 89
cognitive strategies, 63
coherence, 61, 92
Coleman, James, 37, 156, 159–161, 238
Coleman Report, 37, 48, 54
Coley, Richard, 37
collaboration, 248
collaborative learning, 103
collaboratives, reorganizing, 131–132
collective efficacy, 153
college
  attainment, 42–45
  attendance and completion rates, 2, 63
college for all ideology, 44
college readiness, 63–64, 148
Comer Process, 246
Comer Schools, 238
Commager, Henry Steele, 231
Common Core State Standards (CCSS), 77, 82, 86–87, 90
communities
  collaboration, 7
  constituencies, 220
  development, 216
  including in school life, 171–175
  partnerships, 205–226
  powerful influence of, 137
  resources, 46
  social capital, 236
community schools, 217

Comparative Education Review, 96
complex resources, 61–62, 75, 190, 193, 198
  auditing, 200
  inequalities, 61
  professional development, 196
  compound resources, 61–62, 75, 193
auditing, 200
class size reduction, 190
inequalities, 61
replacing simple resources, 196
conceptual understanding, 63
Co-nect schools, 246
Conley, Dalton, 51
consistency, 74–76
consortia, 131–132
content-area literacies strategies, 177
contextualization, 101
cooperative learning, 97, 100, 104
Coordinated School Health (CSH), 211
core technology
  addressing, 117–118
  assessment, 115–117
  instruction, 114–115
  reforms, 113–114, 117–118
  restructuring options, 113–118
Council of Chief State School Officers
    (CCSSO), 77
counseling, 190
counselor/mentors, 212–213
CREDE. *See* Center for Research on
    Education, Diversity, and Excellence
    (CREDE)
CRESST. *See* National Center for Research
    on Evaluation, Standards, and Student
    Testing (CRESST)
cross-cultural communication skills, 219
CSH. *See* Coordinated School Health
    (CSH)
CSSO. *See* Council of Chief State School
    Officers (CSSO)
CST. *See* California Standards Test (CST)
CSU. *See* California State University (CSU)
Cubberly, Ellwood, 188
cultural capacity, 219
cultural humility, 219
culturally and linguistically diverse (CLD)
    students, 99, 168
  background knowledge, 105
  effective teachers, 170–171, 179–183

  instructional strategies, 104–106
  key disadvantages, 163
  knowledge, 172
  teaching, 105–106, 163, 174
  well-trained teachers, 107
  white teachers, 171
culturally relevant approaches, 70
culturally relevant classroom management,
    106
culturally relevant pedagogy, 68
curriculum, 156
  development and assessment reforms, 116
  reforms, 113–114
  standards, 114

dame schools, 194
Darling-Hammond, Linda, 117, 123
data
  analysis and organization, 135
  year-to-year comparability of, 30
David and Lucille Packard Foundation,
    132
Davis, California, 216
DEAR method. *See* Drop Everything And
    Read (DEAR) method
de-categorical funding, 139
decentralized school control, 75
Delpit, Lisa, 169
democratic participation in schools, 130–
    131
desegregating system, 120
detracking classes, 119
developmental education, 59
developmental research, 217
differentiated instruction, 64, 120
disadvantaged high schools, 159
disadvantaged students
  improving performance of, 1
  test scores, 144–145
disaggregating system, 119–120
disciplinary language, 103
discipline
  data analysis, 67
  policies, 67–68
distributed leadership, 75
districts
  aggregating data, 130
  consortia of, 131–132

districts, *continued*
  critical conditions for teaching and
    learning, 130
  external partners relationships, 130
  governance, 129–131
  hiring outsiders, 129–130
  instruction, 75–76
  leadership, 130, 223–225
  meeting benchmarks, 130
  planning, 223–225
  political activism and policy change,
    129
  reform strategies, 160
  resources, 202–203
  spending, 188
  student assessment data, 115
  technical support and assistance, 130
  tiers of schools, 203
diverse students, 7
Dream Schools program, 248
Drop Everything And Read (DEAR)
  method, 102
drop outs. *See* high school dropout rates
Duncan, Arne, 234
dynamic inequality, 58–62, 234

Early Childhood Longitudinal Study of the
    Kindergarten Class (1998-99), 50
early childhood programs, 58
ecological systems theory, 39
economic, social, and cultural status (ESCS)
    scale, 81
economically disadvantaged students, 212
economic model of schooling, 149
Economic Opportunity Act, 37
EdSource Report (2007), 121
education
  achievement differences, 36
  agenda for reforms, 4–5, 35–56
  budgets, 117
  closing achievement gap, 1–2
  inequities, 36–37, 39
  minorities, 44–45
  most important elements of, 238
  multicultural, 68
  poverty and, 241
  randomness of, 248
  social and political equality, 241

  standards and accountability reforms,
    35–36
  structural and governance issues, 93
educational attainment, 45, 211
Educational Extension Services, 202
educational market structures, 126–127
educational performance, 40
educational policy, 80, 93, 113
educational production functions, 150
Educational Researcher, 96
Educational Testing Service, 37, 234
education management organizations, 132
Education Week, 123
Education Week's Quality Counts (1998),
    232
effectiveness, 200–202
effective teachers, 165–167
  academic and language needs, 173–174
  centers of teaching research and
    excellence, 185
  characteristics, 168–171
  CLD students, 174, 185
  communicating and motivating, 171, 177
  consistency, 174
  content-area literacies strategies, 177
  coursework, 181–182
  critical competencies, 185–186
  culturally and linguistically diverse
    (CLD) students, 168–171, 179–183
  culture of students, 172
  English language learners (ELLs), 175–
    179
  families and communities, 171–175
  fieldwork, 182
  high expectations of, 170, 174–175
  language skills and knowledge, 176
  placement of, 167
  professional development, 174, 182–184
  program contexts, 176
  recommendations, 183–186
  recruitment, 180–181
  resources, 175
  role models, 168–169
  school and local approach, 184
  student backgrounds, 169
  support, 184
  teacher preparation and induction
    programs, 184
effect size (ES), 147

ELD. *See* English Language Development (ELD)
ELD programs, 121
Elementary and Secondary Education Act (ESEA) (1965), 2, 55, 125, 127, 223, 227
Elementary and Secondary Education Act (ESEA) Title I, 9, 241–242
elementary schools, 48–50
Eliezer Williams et al. vs. State of California et al., 107
eliminating waste, 199–200
ELLs. *See* English language learner (ELLs)
Elmore, Richard, 238, 246
English as a Second Language (ESL), 68–69, 176
English immersion programs, 69
English Language Development (ELD), 68, 176
English language instruction, 69
English language learners (ELLs), 153, 163
    academic literacy among, 177
    acceptance, 179
    achievement gaps, 164
    addressing issues of, 68–70
    alternative approaches for, 70
    bilingual teachers, 176
    differences among, 69
    effective teachers and, 175–179
    language barrier and parents, 173
    language proficiency, 173
    lower-track classes, 179
    monolingual teachers, 176
    motivation, 178
    native languages, 69
    peer review, 104
    peer tutoring, 104
    resources, 68–69
    response groups, 104
    safety, 179
    secondary-level, 178–179
    teachers, 167, 175
    test scores, 41–42, 144–145
English language Sheltered Instruction Observation Protocol model (SIOP), 172
English language SIOP. *See* English language Sheltered Instruction Observation Protocol model (SIOP)

English Learner Advisory Committees, 223
English-only approaches, 69
English the second language (L2), 69
environmental factors, 111
Equality of Educational Opportunity (Coleman), 37
ES. *See* effect size (ES)
ESCS scale. *See* economic, social, and cultural status (ESCS) scale
ESEA. *See* Elementary and Secondary Education Act (ESEA)
ESL. *See* English as a Second Language (ESL)
Espinoza, Jose A., 35–56
ethnic disparities, 216
ethnicity
    mistreatment of students, 197–198
    scope of challenge, 164
    student achievement based on, 11
    unequal progress through schools, 63
evaluation studies and comprehensive school reform (CSR) models, 146, 147, 148
external accountability, 74

facilities, 156
failing schools, 236
families, 85
    background, 59, 66, 70–71
    choice, 126–127
    communications with, 208
    connections with school experience, 104
    education-related disparities, 234
    including in school life, 171–175
    involvement, 7
    marginalized and normalized groups, 105
    partnering with, 205–226
    poverty, 50
    powerful influence of, 137
    resources, 62, 208
    socioeconomic status, 50
family support programs, 73
federal government
    collaboration, 248
    Institute of Education Sciences, 134
    judicial branches, 133–134
    NCLB renewal of Elementary and Secondary Education Act, 134
    professional networks, 248

federal government, *continued*
  Race to the Top, 134
  research on critical competencies, 185
  standards-based accountability systems,
    135, 235
  student achievement standards, 1
  What Works Clearinghouse, 200–201
feedback, 100
Ferguson, Ann, 198
Ferguson, Ronald, 48
First Things First, 63
fiscal resources, 150
Five Standards for Effective Pedagogy and
    Learning, 101
Florida and Latino students, 168
focus, strategy for maintaining, 75
formal induction programs, 122
formative assessment, 92
frameworks, 90
Fullan, Michael, 238
Full Service Community Schools Act, 223
full-service schools, 71
fundamentals and applied context, 91
funding
  not affecting student outcomes, 202
  teachers, 151
future aspirations, 51

GATE program, 216
genetic inevitability of achievement gaps,
    38–39
goals
  achievement gaps, 57–58
  achieving, 74–76
  consistency, 74–76
  dynamic inequality, 58–60
  English language learners, 68–70
  enhancing school capacity and resources,
    60–62
  immigrant students, 68–70
  interventions, 64–66
  multiple gaps and multiple strategies, 62–64
  nonschool sources, 70
  programmitis limits, 64–66
  racial and ethnic issues, 66–68
  reorganization, 74–76
  resources, 58, 74–76
  support services, 70–72

Goldhaber, Dan, 199
governance system, 132–134
grassroots organizations, 55
The Great Curriculum Debate (Loveless), 114
Great Society reforms (1960s), 1, 227
Great Society's War on Poverty programs,
    37, 135
Green Dot, 8
Grubb, Norton, 234
guidance, 190

habits of mind, 98–99
Hanushek, Eric, 188
Harlem Children's Zone, 8–9, 55, 71, 215,
    222, 233, 244, 247–248
Hart, Betty, 50
Harvard Business School, 245
Harvard Education Review, 38, 96
Harvard University's Achievement Gap
    Initiative director, 47
Head Start, 37, 125
health, 210–213
health services, 73
Healthy Start, 212
Herrnstein, Richard, 38–39
high-cost continuation schools, 196
high-performing nations achievement gaps,
    141
high-poverty schools, 232
high-quality instruction, 5–6, 106–108
  fixed set of policies and, 236
  school accountability, 8
  strategies, 95–110
high-quality preschools, 137–138
high-quality teachers, 181
high school dropout rates, 2, 63, 148
  African American students, 43, 83
  alternative schools and charter schools,
    126
  Asians, 43
  California high schools, 143, 145
  Early Childhood Longitudinal Study of
    the Kindergarten Class (1998-99), 50
  Hispanic students, 42–44, 83
  larger schools, 148, 154
  reducing, 53
  school characteristics impact on, 148
  whites, 43

high school graduates
  California high schools, 143
  as minimal threshold, 52
high schools
  achievement gap, 42–45
  achievement gaps, 155–159
  case studies, 145–146
  challenges and limitations, 159–161
  closing achievement gap, 6
  correlational studies, 146
  educational attainment beyond, 53
  effective, 159
  evaluation studies, 146–148
  features of effective, 149–155
  fiscal resources, 150
  human resources, 152
  improving, 141–161
  low-achieving students, 154
  lower-status tracks, 190
  material resources, 150–152
  measuring performance, 148
  overcrowded, 152
  personalizing, 194
  research on, 145–148
  resources, 149–153
  school practices, 155
  social resources, 153
  socioeconomic status of students, 159
  structural characteristics, 154–155
  student characteristics, 153–154
High/Scope Perry Preschool Project, 137
high-SES, education-related disparities, 234
high-stakes accountability, 243–244
high-stakes testing programs, 116
Hill, Paul, 199
Hispanic students. *See* Latino students
home schooling, 120, 127
Horace's Compromise (Sizer), 108
hortatory jawboning policies, 113
human capital, 136–137, 152
human resources, 152
Human Resources Research Organization, 30
hypotheses, generating and testing, 100–101

ICIC. *See* Initiative for Competitive Inner
    City (ICIC)
ICIC models, 247
identity development, 178

IEP. *See* Individual Education Plan (IEP)
immigrant students, 68–70
improving high schools, 141–161
Improving Schools for Latinos (Valverde), 104
income inequality, 11, 245–246
  United States, 232
income-support policies, 73
incompetent teachers, 195
Individual Education Plan (IEP), 64–65,
    138
individual identity, 51–52
ineffective instructional practices, 195–196,
    199
ineffective teachers, 166
inequality, 74
infant day-care programs, 125
Initiative for Competitive Inner City
    (ICIC), 245
initiatives, coherence among, 160
inner cities and violence, 73
inquiry-based learning, 103
in-school factors, 39–40
in-service professional development, 109
Institute of Education Sciences, 134
institutional partners, 220
instruction, 114–115
  assessment of learners and, 100
  choices, 92
  cognitive outcomes, 97
  dimensions of, 190
  effectiveness, 89
  high-quality, 5–6, 106–108
  improvement, 75
  learner-centered, 103
  learning processes, 97
  motivational-affective outcomes, 97
  reform strategies and, 114–115
  student-centered, 103
  trust, 96–97
Instructional Rounds Network, 238, 246
instructional strategies
  African American students, 105
  challenging activities, 101
  content-oriented, 99–103
  contextualization, 101
  cooperative learning, 100
  culturally and linguistically diverse
      students (CLDs), 104–106
  effective, 95–97

instructional strategies, *continued*
  generating and testing hypotheses, 100–101
  goals and feedback, 100
  habits of mind, 98–99
  high-quality, 95–110
  homework and practice, 100
  language development, 101
  Latino students, 105
  learning outcomes, 109
  literacy skills, 102
  motivational and affective outcomes,
      103–104
  nonlinguistic representation, 100
  pedagogical techniques and, 97–104
  policy implications, 108–110
  prior knowledge, 101
  reading, 101–102
  report methodology, 95–96
  teachers and, 109
  verbal thinking, 102
integrated services partnerships, 213
intellectual capital, 85
intelligence tests, 39
intermediate units, reorganizing, 131–132
international community educational
      policies, 80
International Monetary Fund, 232, 245
interventions, 59
  improving, 64–66
  partnerships, 213
  Response to Intervention (RTI), 65
  self-contained, 65–66
isolation, 232

Jensen, Arthur, 38
JESPAR. See Journal of Education of
      Students Placed at Risk (JESPAR)
Johns Hopkins University, 48
Johnson, Lyndon, 46
Journal of Education of Students Placed at
      Risk (JESPAR), 96
Journal of the American Medical Association,
      233
Joyce Foundation, 132

K–12 academic achievement gap, 5–6
Kennedy, Robert, 127

KIPP schools, 8, 244
knowledge base, 201–202

L1. *See* English learner's native languages (L1)
L2. *See* English the second language (L2)
Ladson-Billings, Gloria, 168–169
language development, 101
language skills and knowledge, 176
larger schools' dropout rates, 148, 154
Latino students, 169
  achievement gaps, 13, 27–28, 82, 197
  alienation of, 67
  biology programs, 44, 45
  California High School Exit Exam
      (CAHSEE), 84
  California high schools, 143–144
  college level educational attainment, 44
  cost of educating, 185
  discipline policies, 67
  dropout rates, 42–44, 63, 83
  educational gains, 43–44
  English language arts (ELA), 83–84
  Florida, 168
  instructional strategies, 105
  parental dropouts, 50
  resegregation, 46–48
  schooling and achievement, 104
  scoring below national average, 41
  state test scores, 12–13, 18
  teachers, 104, 167
  test scores, 144
Latino teachers, 169, 171
Latino-white gap, 66
leadership, 61, 219–220
learner-centered classroom, 103
learning
  after-school and summer programs, 138
  background knowledge, 105
  class size reduction, 138
  de-categorical funding, 139
  high-quality preschools, 137–138
  partnerships, 208–210
  school-community clinics, 138
  seasonality of, 48–50
  strategies for improving, 137–139
  targeted school integration, 138–139
  transfer and generalization goal, 89
  traumatic events and, 211

Learning Centers, 64
learning community, 75
learning processes, 97
learning trajectories, 59
Lee, Chungmei, 46
Levin, Ben, 199
Levin, Henry, 52, 199
linguistic groups, 164
literacy development, 103
local networks, 220
long-term policy strategies, 245–246
Los Angeles, hiring ex-governor of
    Colorado, 129
Los Angeles Unified School District, 177,
    233
Loveless, Tom, 114
low-achieving students, 79
    discouragement of, 58–59
    equal opportunities to learn (OTL), 79
    health and, 210–211
    high schools, 154
    Individual Education Plan (IEP), 64–65
    mobility, 120
    noneducational needs, 71
    rate of growth, 79
    regulations helping, 242
    resources, 60–62
    schools and, 62, 64
    support services, 71
lower-SES families and education-related
    disparities, 234
lower-status tracks, 190
lower-track classes, 107
low-income families and housing problems,
    73
low-income schools and parent involvement,
    171–172
low-income students
    achievement gains, 12–13
    low expectations, 170
    median rates of change, 13, 28
    mobility, 73
    narrowing achievement gaps, 18, 21
    small classes, 147
    state tests, 12–13, 18
    teachers, 167
low-performing schools, 62
    authorized movement, 237–238
    charter schools, 243–244

cooperation and collegiality, 240
curriculum, 243
firing teachers and administrators, 244
improvements in, 240–241
instability and incoherence, 239–241
life in, 236–241
localist dimension, 238
organizational factors, 240
policy initiatives, 236
reforms, 237–239
social capital, 238–239
stability and consistency, 241

macropolicies, 237–238
mainstream schools, 126
mandated class size, 107
Mann, Horace, 76, 187
marginalized populations interventions and
    services, 213
material resources, 150–152
math NAEP results, 17
math teachers, 209
McKinsey & Company, 141
McNeil, Linda, 119
means, 31
mean scores, 12, 21–22
measures of achievement gaps, 86–90
median percentages proficient, 24–26
medians, 31
medical research, 217
mentors, 212
Mexican American students, 132, 170
Mexico and teachers, 182
middle-class white students discipline
    policies, 67
Migrant Education Program, 223
minority schools, 171–172
minority students
    achievement gains, 12–13
    achievement gaps, 44–45
    equalization, 1
    improved family conditions, 37
    individual identities, 52
    low expectations, 170
    stereotypes, 52
mistreatment in schools, 66–67
Mitchell, R., 125
Model Cities program, 37

money and closing achievement gap, 194–
    198
Money Myth, 58, 188, 194
monolingual English-speaking teachers,
    173, 176
motivational-affective outcomes, 97–98,
    103–104
multicultural education, 68
Murray, Charles, 38–39

NAEP. *See* National Assessment of
    Educational Progress (NAEP)
narrowing achievement gaps
    diagnosing and reducing dynamic
        inequality, 58–60
    United States, 57–76
National Assessment of Educational
    Progress (NAEP), 81–82, 160, 227
    achievement gaps, 22–24, 40–42
    benchmark testing system, 116
    criticism of, 117
    math results, 17
    mean scores trends, 14–17
    nation's report card, 40–42
    state-level trends (2005-2009), 12
    states that performed well on, 90
    state test comparisons and, 32–33
    student performance, 116
    tests of statistical significance, 32–33
National Board certification, 123
National Center for Education Statistics,
    32, 42–43
National Center for Public Policy and
    Higher Education, 53
National Center for Research on Evaluation,
    Standards, and Student Testing
    (CRESST), 90
National Education Longitudinal Study of
    1988 (NELS88), 146, 168, 191, 195
National Governors Association (NGA), 77
National Labor Relations Act (NLRA)-style
    collective bargaining, 124
National Research Council, 96, 160
National School Lunch Program (NSLP),
    41
National Writing Project, 238
A Nation at Risk, 37, 39, 133, 228, 237
nation's report card, 40–42

Native American students
    median rate of narrowing for, 28
    progress in narrowing gaps, 18, 21
    state test score gaps, 12–13, 18
Naylor, Nancy, 199
NCLB. *See* No Child Left Behind (NCLB)
neighborhoods
    social and economic resources, 62
    strong social capital, 239–240
Nell Soto Parent/Teacher Involvement
    Grant, 223
NELS88. *See* National Education
    Longitudinal Study of 1988 (NELS88)
New Century Schools, 214
New York, 214–215
    New Century Schools, 214
    Performance-Driven Budgeting (PDB)
        initiative, 203
    shifted control over schools to mayors, 235
New York University, 51
NGA. *See* National Governors Association
    (NGA)
Nisbett, Richard E., 38–39
No Child Left Behind (NCLB) Act (2001),
    1, 40, 87, 141
    accountability for academic progress, 1
    achievement trends, 116
    blinkered version of school reform, 234
    bureaucratizing school improvement, 246
    congressional renewal of, 135
    educational attainment, 115–116
    Elementary and Secondary Education Act
        renewal, 134
    group-level differences in student
        achievement, 55
    performance-based accountability, 243
    reauthorization of, 234–235
    school governance, 236
    school safety policy, 120–121
    standards-based accountability, 2
    state tests, 12
    test results, 30
    undermining professionalism, 246
    waste, 200
noneducational services, 71
nonschool sources
    achievement gaps, 8, 70–74
    family support and child welfare
        programs, 73

health services, 73
income-support policies, 73
labor market policies, 73
mobility of low-income students, 73
urban development policies, 73
nonstandard English, 67
Norfolk State University, 180
North Carolina and African American
   students, 168
Northwestern University, 128
Northwest Regional Educational Laboratory
   (NWREL), 99–101
novice teachers, 107
NSLP. *See* National School Lunch Program
   (NSLP)
NWREL. *See* Northwest Regional
   Educational Laboratory (NWREL)

Obama, Barack, 44, 234
O'Connell, Jack, 3, 141–142
OECD. *See* Organisation for Economic
   Co-Operation and Development
   (OECD)
Office of Educational Research and
   Improvement, 134
opportunities to learn (OTL), 79
Orfield, Gary, 46
Organisation for Economic Co-Operation
   and Development (OECD), 80–81
organizational capital, 85
organizational practices, 155
organizational strategies
   achievement gap, 111–139
   classroom level restructuring options, 118–121
   core technology restructuring options,
      113–118
   federal policy and research directions,
      134–135
   options, not prescriptions, 112–113
   reorganizing intermediate units and
      collaboratives, 131–132
   reshaping state policy and governance
      system, 132–134
   restructuring school and district
      governance, 129–131
   restructuring school organizations, 125–129
   restructuring teaching profession, 121–125
OTL. *See* opportunities to learn (OTL)

outcomes
   holding schools and teachers responsible
      for, 115
   when money does matter, 194–195
   worse, 195–198
out-of-school factors, 39–40

parent-community-school ties, 62, 75
Parent Information Resource Centers
   (PIRCs), 222
parents, 50–51
   academic learning, 209
   child rearing, 46
   high school dropouts, 50
   involvement, 105, 130–131
   postsecondary requirements and
      resources, 208
   school norms, 208
   support of, 119
   trust, 165
partners are prepared, 219–220
partnerships
   academic teaching and learning, 208–210
   achievement gaps, 212–213
   assessing student and family resources
      and needs, 212–213
   conditions for successful, 222–225
   contributions, 207–208
   coordination, 221
   diversity of students, 218
   enacting, 220
   evaluation, 221
   Fresno Unified School District and Long
      Beach Unified School District, 247
   funding, 220, 222–223
   integrating strategies, 217
   knowledge, resources, and opportunities,
      214
   leadership, 214–215, 223–225
   locally responsive programs and services,
      212–213
   multiplicity of practices, 206
   normative, 218–219
   parents and communities, 205–226
   partners are prepared, 219–220
   physical space, 220
   postsecondary institutions and systems,
      208

partnerships, *continued*
  practices and strategies, 220
  professional development, 222
  relationships, 220
  resources, 212–215, 220–221
  schools, 215–218
  social support, 210–214
  strategic, 221
  successful, 218–221
  transiency of efforts, 221
partnership strategies
  integrating, 217
  public and private funding, 223
Payne, Charles, 230, 238
P-16 Council, 60, 142
pedagogical techniques and instructional
    strategies, 97–104
pedagogy
  course contributions, 166
  culturally relevant, 68
peer review, 104
peer tutoring, 104
performance
  gaps, 24
  measuring for high schools, 148
  tests, 89
Performance-Driven Budgeting (PDB)
    initiative, 203
period of scarcity and achievement gaps
  allocating resources, 202–203
  effectiveness, 200–202
  eliminating waste, 199–200
  instituting planning mechanisms, 203
  resource audits, 200
  state policies, 203
personalizing high schools, 194
personal relationships, 191
The Pew Charitable Trusts, 132
philanthropic foundations, 132
PIRCs. *See* Parent Information Resource C
    enters (PIRCs)
PISA. *See* Programme for International
    Student Assessment (PISA)
planning mechanisms, 203
policies
  agenda, 37
  The Bell Curve, 38–39
  closing achievement gap, 233
  collaborative and cooperative networks, 246

economic development initiatives, 245
Elementary and Secondary Education Act
    (ESEA) Title I, 241–242
  failure to produce improvements, 113
  federal and state programs, 242–243
  influence over performance study, 113
  instabilities, 133
  instructional strategies implications,
      108–110
  long-term strategies, 245–246
  new paradigm creation, 244–247
  professional communities development,
      246
  Promise Neighborhoods initiative, 247
  versus reality, 236–241
  reframing relationship with practices,
      247–249
  rethinking, 241–244
  school officials, 242
  short-term strategies, 246–247
  standards and accountability movement,
      39–40
  standards-based reform, 243
  systemic reform, 243
policy makers, 53, 237
Porter, Michael, 245
positive learning environment, 210–214
posttraumatic stress disorder (PTSD), 233
poverty, 232
practices
  reframing, 227–249
  relationship with policies, 247–249
  rethinking, 241–244
preservice education, 109
primary education and reform, 35–56
principals, 75, 184
prior knowledge, 101
private schools, 123, 127
professional communities, 246
professional development, 85, 122–123, 222
  complex resources, 196
  effective teachers, 182–183, 184
  English language learners (ELLs), 183
  in-service, 109
  reform-oriented, 183
  school-based budgeting, 202–203
  self-guiding, 109
  simple forms of, 196
  traditional, 182–183

professional networks, 248
professional organizations, 248
Programme for International Student
  Assessment (PISA), 79–81
programmitis, 64–66, 199–201, 201
programs
  combining with social services, 121
  high-quality teaching and learning, 248
  reasons for adopting, 65–66
  school-centered, 213
Progressive Era, 74
Project STAR experiment, 138, 168
Promise Neighborhoods, 55, 71–72, 223, 247
Proposition 13 (1978), 133, 235
prospective teachers and stereotypes, 182
PTSD. *See* posttraumatic stress disorder
  (PTSD)
public schools
  African Americans, 187
  American Indians, 187
  changes needed in, 112
  effectiveness, 149
  as failure factories, 8
  teacher compensation, 123
Puente Project, 132

race and ethnicity
  achievement gaps, 66
  addressing issues head-on, 66–68
  closing achievement gaps, 11
  differences defined in terms of, 66–68
  discussions of, 67–68, 70
  inequality, 63, 66, 197
  state test scores, 12–13
  stereotypes, 67
  students mistreated, 197–198
Race to the Top, 134
racism, 106
RAND Corporation, 185
random interventions, 65
reading trends in achievement on NAEP, 17
reading wars, 114
Ream, Robert K., 35–56
reform fatigue, 195
reform-oriented professional development,
  183
reforms, 230
  agendas, 4–5, 231–232

authorized movement, 237–238
closing achievement gap, 1–2
compound rather than simple resources
  needed, 196
consistency, 74
instruction, 63
localist dimension, 238
low-performing schools, 237–239
macropolicies, 237–238
persistence, 74
policies, 245
principals and, 75
progress in, 56
scope and pace of change, 244
slack, 74
social capital, 238–239
stability, 74
standards-based, 243
student achievement impact, 245
systemic, 243
regional networks, 220
regulative, 98–99
relational trust, 153
relevant policy arenas, 220
remedial track, 195
remediation, crisis of, 59
remedies and race-neutral terms, 66
reorganization, 74–76
research
  achievement gap reduction, 84–86
  directions, 134–135
  high schools, 145–148
resegregation, 46–48
resource audits, 200
resources, 74–76, 189, 220
  abstract, 61–62, 75, 191, 193, 198
  achievement gap reduction, 85
  additional spending, 194
  affecting outcomes, 60–61, 63, 191
  cannot be bought, 74, 192, 196–197
  communities, 46
  complex, 61–62, 75, 190, 193, 198
  compound, 61–62, 75, 190, 193
  cultivating, 214–215
  differential, 63
  enhancing, 60–62
  fiscal, 150
  high-quality teaching and learning, 248
  high schools, 149–153

resources, *continued*
  human, 152
  increasing allocation, 202–203
  inequality, 68–69, 192–193
  low-performing students, 60–62
  material, 150–152
  money can buy, 189
  planning mechanisms, 203
  recognizing, 191
  school-community partnership, 225–226
  shifting from money to, 189–193
  simple, 189–190, 193–194
  social, 153
  stability, 192
  state policies, 203
  sufficient and sustained, 220–221
  teachers, 151
  test scores, 191
response groups, 104
Response to Intervention (RTI), 65
restructuring
  classrooms, 118–121
  school and district governance, 129–131
  teaching profession, 121–125
Review of Educational Research, 96
Risley, Todd, 50
role models, 168–169
Rosenthal, Robert, 170
Roza, Marguerite, 199
RTI. *See* Response to Intervention (RTI)
Ryan, Sarah M., 35–56

Safe Streets Act, 37
SAHMSA, 223
sanctions against federally and state-defined
  failing schools, 236
San Diego, hiring federal prosecutor as
  school superintendent, 129
San Francisco Unified School District, 247–
  248
SBHCs. *See* school-based health centers
  (SBHCs)
Schmoker, Mike, 199
school-based budgeting and professional
  development, 202–203
school-based health centers (SBHCs), 71–
  72, 211–212
school-centered programs, 213

school-community clinics, 138
school-community partnerships, 223–226
  academic teaching and learning, 208–210
  health promotion models, 213–214
  sense of connection to school, 210
  trusting and trustworthy relationships,
    210
school completion rates, 213
school districts. *See* districts
school facilities, 152
school leadership, 214–215
school-linked services, 212
school organization
  achievement gap and, 6
  alternative schools, 126
  attendance boundaries, 127–128
  class size, 128–129
  educational market structures, 126–127
  family choice, 126–127
  grade configurations, 125
  school and classroom composition, 127–
    128
  school size, 128–129
  year-round educational calendars, 125–
    126
schools
  academic achievement, 50
  academic expectations, 85
  achievement gaps, 8, 39, 230
  achievement progress for students, 54
  acquisition of knowledge, 91
  adequate progress strategies, 244
  after-school programs, 65
  assessment data, 85, 115
  attitudes toward, 63
  barriers to students' learning, 221
  business/industrial model, 126
  capacity, 60–62
  charter schools, 127
  classroom structures, 118
  climate, 191
  closing achievement gaps, 36
  collaborative professional and civic
    networks, 248
  communities, 171–175, 219
  community partnerships, 7, 85
  composition, 127–128
  conceptual model, 149
  consortia of, 131–132

cultures, 249
curriculum, 156
declining performance, 61
democratic participation, 130–131
desegregation, 37
disadvantaged communities, 216
distributed leadership, 74–75
educational outcomes, 36, 62
engagement, 215–217
expenditures per pupil, 188–189
external accountability, 74
facilities, 156, 224
families, 7, 171–175
feelings of connectedness, 72
fiscal constraints, 139
full-service, 71
funding, 222–223
governance, 129–131
high-quality instruction, 8
home connections with, 104
improvement, reform, and Money Myth, 188
improvement efforts and capacity building in, 160
inequality, 60, 62–63, 216, 230
inputs, 149
instruction, 76
instructional guidance, 61, 75
instructional materials, 85
instructional systems, 244
integrating services into, 72
integration and, 9, 138–139
intermediate-level organizations, 131
internal accountability, 75
knowledge/competency resources, 85
leadership, 61, 223–225
learning community, 75
limited strategies, 65
location, 154
low-performing students, 62, 71, 236–241
mistreatment in, 66–67
monopolistic control, 126
neighborhoods and resources, 62
open enrollment requirements, 127
organizational and operational characteristics of, 6, 111–139
organizational practices, 155
parental involvement, 130–131

parent-community-school ties, 62, 75
partnerships, 231–235
performance, 61, 155–156
personal relationships, 191
planning, 223–225
policies and social dynamics outside, 216
policy initiatives, 125
poverty, 50
practices, 149, 155
professionalism, 61–62
Progressive Era, 74
quality of, 37, 244
racial and ethnic groups, 231
racism, 106
random interventions, 65
reforms, 64, 72, 160, 230
relationships within, 74, 239
reorganization, 74
resegregation, 46–48
resources, 37, 58–62, 151, 202–203
risk for failing, 89
safety in, 120–121
school vouchers, 127
segregation, 120, 127–128
shared beliefs and expectations, 85
size of, 119–120, 128–129, 154–155
social composition, 153
spending and outcomes, 7
student achievement, 37
student-centered learning climates, 75
student outcomes, 243
support services, 71
tax support, 188
testing, 89
test scores, 65
Title I sanctions, 242
transportation, 224
trust, 239
tutoring efforts, 65
as unit of change, 246
unrealistic expectations of, 36
wraparound instructional support, 85
School Site Councils, 223
school-specific knowledge, 48–49
school vouchers, 127
science performance and economic, social, and cultural status (ESCS) scale, 81
SDAIE. *See* Specifically Designed Academic Instruction in English (SDAIE)

seasonality of learning, 48–50
Seattle, hiring retired general for
    superintendent, 129
secondary education and reform, 35–56
secondary-level ELLs, 178–179
secondary schools, 91, 191
second-chance programs, 196
second-language instruction, 70
second-language learners, 176
segregation, 231
self-contained interventions, 65–66
self-guiding professional improvement, 109
SELPA agencies. *See* Special Education
    Local Planning Area (SELPA) agencies
Serrano v. Priest (1974), 134
Service Learning grants, 223
Sheltered Instruction Observation Protocol
    (SIOP), 100
short-term policy strategies, 246–247
simple resources, 189–190, 193–194
    auditing, 200
    compound resources needed instead of, 196
    emphasis on allocating, 197
small classes and student achievement, 151
social capital, 85, 215, 236, 238–239
    communities, 215
    development of, 130
    formation, 136–137
    neighborhoods with strong, 239–240
    teaching and learning, 238
social inequality, 1, 53–54
social justice, 80, 109
socially disadvantaged students, 212
social resources, 153
social services, 121
social skills and wealthier students, 209
social supports for positive learning
    environment, 210–214
social systems, 112–113
socioeconomic disparities, 216
socioeconomic status, 50–51
"Solving the Funding-Achievement Puzzle,"
    199
sources of achievement gap
    future aspirations, 51
    individual identity, 51–52
    parenting, 50–51
    quality teacher distribution, 46–48
    resegregation, 46–48

seasonality of children's learning, 48–50
    socioeconomic status, 50–51
    stereotype threat, 52
    wealth, 51–52
Special Education Local Planning Area
    (SELPA) agencies, 132
special education services, 132
special education students, 138, 196
special language instruction, 69–70
Specifically Designed Academic Instruction
    in English (SDAIE), 69
spending and schools, 188–189
stability, 191–192
stabilizing system, 120
staff
    development, 190
    preparation of, 219
staff-pupil ratio, 194
standards, 86–87
    accessing and interpreting, 78
    achievement gaps, 77–78
    Center for Research on Education,
        Diversity and Excellence's (CREDE's),
        101
    Common Core State Standards, 86–87
    transitions from older standards and tests,
        78
standards and accountability movement,
    39–40
standards-based accountability, 2
    defensive teaching, 119
    federal government, 135
standards-based assessments, 246
standards-based reform, 243
standards movement, 114
states
    accountability, 76
    achievement gaps, 28–29
    alternative certification programs, 122
    assessment reforms, 116
    collaboration, 248
    collective bargaining provisions, 124
    critical competencies research, 185
    departments of education, 115
    education budgets and expenditures, 223
    education policy initiators, 133
    fiscal stability, 134
    formal induction programs, 122
    funding, 74, 133, 139

high-stakes tests, 116
judicial branches, 133–134
policy coherence, 134
professional networks, 248
reshaping policy, 132–134
setting policies, 133, 203
standards, 114
waste, 200
state tests
achievement gaps, 11–33
average annual changes, 31
differences in, 13–14, 18–21
disaggregating data requirements, 29
high-quality instruction, 88
indicators of achievement, 11–12
means, 31
mean scores, 12, 14–17, 21–22
medians, 31
NAEP comparisons and, 32–33
percentages proficient, 11–12, 21–22
state curriculum standards, 116
states and, 14, 30–31
statistical significance, 33
subgroups and, 13–17
subgroups and achievement indicator,
18–24
validity evidences, 88
Steele, Claude, 51–52
Steinberg, Laurence, 50
stereotypes, 52, 67, 106, 182
"Strengthening School District Capacity as
a Strategy to Raise Student
Achievement in California"
(Rumberger and Connell), 130
structural features, 154–155
structural racism, 216
student body characteristics, 156
student-centered instruction, 103
student-centered learning climates, 75
students
academic and language needs, 173–174
academic expectations, 85
achievement, 151, 153, 159
African American students, 163
aspirations of, 63–64
counselor/mentors, 212–213
engagement, 209
English language learners (ELLs), 153
factors outside of schools, 48

free or reduced-price lunch, 153
habits of mind, 98–99
health, 210–212
high expectations for, 174–175
high schools, 153–154
in-school factors, 39–40
language of schooling, 101
learning assessments, 115
linguistic match, 169
low performance, 58–59
mobility, 120
motivation, 119
objects of special services, 243
out-of-school factors, 39–40
performance patterns, 93
poverty, 232
racial, social class, and linguistic groups,
36
school outcomes, 57
sense of connection to school, 210
small classes, 128
smaller schools, 119–120
social support system, 137
socioeconomic status, 159
support for different, 92
teachers and, 170
tracking, 127
trust, 165
urban schools, 237
students with disabilities test scores, 144–145
subgroups
achievement gains, 12–13
achievement gaps, 24, 36
college participation rates, 44
differences among, 78
mean percentage proficient, 21–22
means, 31
median percentage proficient, 24–26
medians, 31
percentages proficient, 24
performance, 14
state-level trends (2005-2009), 12
state tests, 12–17, 18–24
Success for All, 202
successful schools
academic achievement, 208
supporting student learning, 214–215
summer effects, 59
support services, 71–72

systemic functional linguistic (SFL)
    approach, 103
systemic policies, 230
systemic reform, 243
systems of accountability, 64

teacher candidates, 181, 185
teacher education programs, 108–109
teacher-guided reporting, 98
teacher-leaders, 62
teachers
    absenteeism, 120, 167
    advanced certification, 125
    advanced training, 123
    African American, 171
    alternative certification programs, 122
    assessment knowledge, 173
    assessment system and, 88
    backgrounds, 151, 169
    behaviors, 67
    best-prepared, 48, 163
    bilingual, 173, 176
    certification, 121–122, 166
    characteristics, 151, 156
    collective bargaining, 124–125
    compensation, 123–124
    credentials, 123
    distribution of, 46–48
    diversity and, 181–182
    effectiveness, 165–167
    efficiency, 97
    emergency credentials, 123
    English language learners (ELLs), 167
    English-only approaches, 69
    expenditures, 151
    formal induction programs, 122
    highly qualified, 167
    high school level, 122
    incentives, 185
    ineffective, 166
    innovation, 97
    instructional strategies, 109
    interactions with students, 107–108
    Latino, 171
    linguistic match, 169
    low-income students, 167
    Mexican American students, 170
    middle-class suburban communities, 185

    migrating back to their own
        communities, 171, 185
    monolingual English-speaking, 173, 176
    National Board certification, 123
    organizations, 124–125
    personal resources, 152, 165
    preservice testing of, 121
    professional capacities, 61
    professional development, 85, 120, 122–
        123, 222
    professionalism, 115, 136
    quality of, 190
    resources, 151, 157–158
    responsibilities, 248
    restricting autonomy, 119
    school improvement, 240
    subject-matter knowledge, 85
    teaching learners how to learn, 98
    test scores and evaluation, 87
    training, 121–123
    trust, 165
    turnover, 120
    uncertified, 166
    unions, 124–125, 134
    white, 171
    working outside their certified field, 123
teachers aides, 195
Teachers College, 96
teaching
    alternative certification programs, 122
    culturally relevant practices, 105–106
    partnerships strengthening, 208–210
    quality of, 63
    restructuring, 121–125
teams working with CLD students, 184
Temple University, 50
Tennessee
    class size reduction study, 147
    Project STAR experiment, 128, 138, 168
TESOL Quarterly, 96
tests, 87–90, 115
test scores, 144–145, 166, 243
test-to-curriculum correspondence, 116
Texas
    African American students, 163
    quality of schools, 129
TIMSS. *See* Trends in International
    Mathematics and Science Study
    (TIMSS)

Title I, 125, 223, 241–243
  advisory councils, 127
  funding, 37
  School Site Plans, 223
Title IX, 245
tracking, 127
traditional professional development, 182–
  183
traditional vocational education, 195
training programs, 122–123
transaction costs, 113
traumatic events, 211
Trends in International Mathematics and
  Science Study (TIMSS), 82
trust, 96–97, 153, 165, 239
Tucker, Jill, 233
tutoring efforts, 65
twenty 21st Century Community Learning
  Centers, 223
two-way immersion programs, 69
Tyack, David, 126

UC. *See* University of California (UC)
UC Davis Center for Applied Policy in
  Education, 3
UCLA Civil Rights Project, 46
uncertified teachers, 166
undergraduate education and teacher
  effectiveness, 166
underrepresented minorities, 50
United States
  achievement gaps, 141
  cognitive readiness, 89
  college graduates, 44
  dynamic inequality, 58–60
  educational policies, 80
  educational reform, 35–56
  ethnic, linguistic, and socioeconomic
    groups, 141
  income inequality, 232, 245–246
  life expectancy, 233
  literacy, 81
  low student achievement, 93
  math and science, 233
  mathematics, 81
  narrowing achievement gaps, 57–76
  National Assessment of Educational
    Progress (NAEP), 81–82

performance, 81
PISA scores, 80–81
poverty, 232
prison population, 233
science performance, 81
separation of powers, 235
unemployment rate, 233
urban middle class, 245
universities, standards for training
    programs, 122
University of California (UC), 143, 145
School of Education, 246
University of Kansas, 50
University of Southern California Latino
    Teacher Project, 180
urban centers, 249
urban development
  policies, 73
  strategies, 245
urban schools
  achievement gaps, 232
  eliminating waste, 199–200
  less qualified teachers, 167
  personal and professional relationships,
    238
  racial isolation, 9
  second-chance efforts, 196
  students, 237
  teacher absenteeism, 167
urban students and high-poverty schools,
    232
U.S. Department of Education, 40
"Using Resources Effectively in Education,"
    199

validity, 88, 93
value-added methodology (VAM), 166
VAM. *See* value-added methodology (VAM)
veteran teachers, 107

Waiting for Superman, 8
Wall Street Journal, 247
Warren, Earl, 134
Washington, D.C. control over schools, 235
waste audit, 199–200
wealthier students, 209
welfare state, 73

well-trained teachers, 107
"What Money Can't Buy," 199
What Works Institutes, 201
when money does matter, 194–195
white middle-class prospective teachers,
    181–182
white students
    achievement gaps, 13, 197
    California high schools, 143
    college level educational attainment, 44
    dropout rates, 43
    mathematics and reading, 12, 40–41

state test score gaps, 12–13
test performance (2009), 24
test scores, 144
white teachers, 171
Willie L. Brown Jr. College Preparatory
    Academy, 248

year-round educational calendars, 125–126
year-round schools, 59
year-to-year comparability of data, 30
Yeung, Wei-Jun Jean, 51